The Dot-Com Debacle
and the Return to Reason

The Dot-Com Debacle and the Return to Reason

LOUIS E.V. NEVAER

QUORUM BOOKS
Westport, Connecticut • London

Library of Congress Cataloging-in-Publication Data

Nevaer, Louis E. V.
    The dot-com debacle and the return to reason / Louis E.V. Nevaer.
      p. cm.
    Includes bibliographical references and index.
    ISBN 1–56720–415–5 (alk. paper)
    1. Electronic commerce. 2. High technology industries. I. Title.
  HF5548.32.N48 2002
  330.9—dc21   2001048117

British Library Cataloguing in Publication Data is available.

Library of Congress Catalog Card Number: 2001048117
ISBN: 1–56720–415–5

First published in 2002

Quorum Books, 88 Post Road West, Westport, CT 06881
An imprint of Greenwood Publishing Group, Inc.
www.quorumbooks.com

Printed in the United States of America

The paper used in this book complies with the
Permanent Paper Standard issued by the National
Information Standards Organization (Z39.48–1984).

10 9 8 7 6 5 4 3 2 1

Copyright Acknowledgments

Excerpts from Robert H. Frank and Philip J. Cook, *The Winner-Take-All Society*
reprinted with the permission of the Free Press, a Division of Simon & Schuster, Inc.,
from *The Winner-Take-All Society* by Robert H. Frank and Philip J. Cook. Copyright ©
1995 by Robert H. Frank and Philip J. Cook.

Excerpts from "Semi-Charmed Life," words and music by Stephan Jenkins. ©1997 EMI
Blackwood Music Inc. and 3EB Publishing. All Rights Controlled and Administered by
EMI Blackwood Music Inc. All Rights Reserved. International Copyright Secured. Used
by Permission.

Excerpts from Alfred Kahn, "The Tyranny of Small Decisions," *Kyklos* (1966), reprinted
with author's permission.

Dedico este libro a Vicente Fox,
Quien nos ha librado del mal

CONTENTS

ACKNOWLEDGMENTS

This book would not have been possible without the inspiration and instruction from Robert Frank, William Lambert, Alfred Kahn, Milton Friedman, John Kenneth Galbraith, and the late Rose Goldsen. These individuals taught me to think not only about economics but also how human beings think about their world and interact with each other. Kevin Lombardi at Alias|WaveFront generously allowed me to enter into the world of high technology and extended his friendship along the way. Eric Valentine, my publisher, was steadfast in his support through this entire process, including his frustration at his inability to keep track of me while I traveled between Silicon Valley, Silicon Alley, and Silicon Beach in the United States, and as I wandered through Canada, England, France, Spain, Mexico, and Japan. Sandy Close generously allowed me to use Pacific News Service as an impromptu headquarters during the researching of this book. Robert Brenner first suggested the idea for this book over drinks at the Top of the Mark in San Francisco. Finally, I am grateful to the late Carlos Castillo Peraza, whose example teaches the importance of remaining faithful to one's principles and working diligently toward and in defense of those principles.

INTRODUCTION

"Progress, far from consisting of change, depends on retentiveness.
Those who cannot remember the past are condemned to repeat it."
George Santayana

This book sets out to distinguish the differences between the New and Old Economies. For a time in the 1990s it was fashionable to believe that, somehow, the laws of economics had been suspended. The New Economy promised to defy the laws of economics in the same way that two scientists claimed in 1989 that cold fusion defied the laws of physics. The result was a spectacular rush of venture capitalists hoping to strike it rich in the Silicon Gold Rush. Inexplicable companies, with neither rhyme nor reason, mushroomed overnight, and throughout the 1990s, eager multitudes arrived in San Francisco, San Jose, and the communities that together constitute "Silicon Valley."

The NASDAQ correction, however, burst the delusional schemes of fortune seekers. Once their stock options began to be rendered worthless after their dot-coms began to be unplugged by venture capitalists, the San Francisco Ninety-Niners—the *parvenu* who began to return to the East Coast at the end of 1999—retreated in defeat, not unlike many of the gold digging Forty-Niners who never struck it rich. "After a while, I woke up and said, 'What am I doing? I'm investing in this company that's not going to be around much longer and is run by a bunch of freaks,'" a Ninety-Niner is quoted as saying upon returning to New York City after failing to strike it rich in San Francisco's Internet boom.[1] She was not alone. Four out of five dot-coms in the San Francisco Bay Area went out of business in 2000 and 2001, resulting in the loss of 30,000 direct Internet jobs. The thousands of Forty-Niners who returned back East penniless, were joined 150 years later by the thousands of Ninety-Niners whose bubbles were burst by the cold realities of economics.[2]

It is with confidence that one can report that the laws of economics have not been suspended. If the lines were blurred in the 1990s, then the discussion presented in this book strives to put things into clear focus. The problem with proponents of the New Economy, after all, was a matter of substance. Bill Gates' bestseller, *Business @ the Speed of Thought,* begs the obvious question: What's the rush to do business at the speed of thought if one doesn't have an idea?

The New Economy offers tremendous opportunities, but by its very nature, the online world remains a fraction of the off-line world. Precisely how the New Economy's opportunities can be seized upon, however, requires reflection and the willingness to seek out antidotes to the hype. The online economy will always be dependent on the real world, because human beings are not metaphysical: we are real beings in three dimensions. The euphoria over the promise of the Internet, like water, has a way of blurring our vision. Fascination with how light reflects, bends, and distorts reality in a pool of water is child's play. Business, on the other hand, is not child's play. This is why it is imperative to distinguish between both economies and to understand how they interact, and how one can see through the distortions. One doesn't have to go *on*line to avoid becoming a *flat*-line. By remembering the mistakes of the California Forty-Niners past, savy Old Economy companies have avoided repeating them.

This book is divided into two parts. Part I presents a series of discussions that explain precisely how the fundamental laws of economics apply to e-commerce. It functions not unlike a foreign language dictionary; but instead of taking, say, a word in French and providing the corresponding one in English, it takes ideas from the Old Economy (classical economics) and translates them to the New Economy (Internet technologies). By taking an English-French dictionary approach, moreover, what we end up with is more than an Old Economy-New Economy dictionary. We have, in fact, keys that allow us to understand the underlying economic principles that govern the New Economy.

These economic principles, happily, are familiar. The fundamental rules of supply and demand prevail in cyberspace as the NASDAQ "correction" throughout 2000 made clear to stunned investors around the world. But it is also true that the online economy is characterized by distortions for the simple reason that, by its nature, it exaggerates the effects of certain market phenomena. The proliferation of winner-take-all contests, the impact of tyrannies of small decisions and Prisoner's Dilemmas, for instance, work to distort, blur, and disguise the underlying principles of economics at work. Each of these phenomena is individually explained in a thorough manner. Once these distortions are discussed properly, the reader will be able to understand why the online economy works the way it does.

To this end, Chapter 1 begins with a discussion of how, contrary to what Internet enthusiasts would have the world believe, e-commerce is not a revolution. It is an *evolution*. It is the next step in the development of human knowledge, a way of expanding trade and commerce. That by its nature it is technology-intensive does not detract from the fact that it is an instrument for greater efficacy in how human beings communicate, learn, and work. It thus becomes a tool for the real-world development of business and nations.

The online economy, on the other hand, has certain characteristics that make it prone to distort markets in unsettling ways. Chapter 2 examines how the winner-take-all contests that are found throughout the online economy exacerbate market imperfections and contribute to the proliferation of market failures. That the marketplace is not perfect is not a surprise; human societies are not perfect either. What is a legitimate concern, for us as individuals, for companies doing business in a free market, and for policymakers who are charged with making sure that the playing field is fair, however, is in deciding for ourselves how we believe these issues are to be addressed. What are the remedies for the distortions created by market imperfections and market failures? How is society to share in a fair and equitable manner the enormous investment costs that incremental technological innovations require? How are the unintended social effects of the online economy to be corrected?

To understand these issues better, it is necessary to examine how individual decisions over time can lead to inferior collective outcomes. Adam Smith argued in his invisible hand theory that society does best when each individual is free to pursue his or her own interests in the marketplace. In other words, Adam Smith's invisible hand fails when individual choices impact others negatively. In Chapter 3 we examine how phenomena referred to as "the tyranny of small decisions" and the "Prisoner's Dilemma" describe circumstances where individuals, by refusing to cooperate beforehand with each other, make choices that, while individually beneficial to each one on a case-by-case basis, result in a societal collective outcome that is inferior. Driving to work may be the best option for each of us individually given the places to go and things to do in our busy schedules, but when we all get in our cars, we end up in bumper-to-bumper traffic jams going everywhere slowly.

These are true paradoxes, but understanding their dynamics is important in order to make sense of how the online economy is developing. Paradoxes lead to differences of opinion, and in the twentieth century welfare economists argued over how to best address the problems that arise from them. Chapter 4 examines how John Kenneth Galbraith and Milton Friedman offered different opinions about the proper role of policymakers in correcting the distortions that emerge over time. The collapse of socialism presumed that the argument had been settled. However, the online economy has reopened it. Indeed, this debate is far from settled for the reason that technological innovations are ever changing, in legal terms, fundamental ideas about the nature of privacy, the definition of intellectual property rights, and the rules of fair play in a market economy. In the 1990s critics and advocates rallied to decry and praise the Internet—and the entrepreneurs, nerds, and financiers who made it all possible. This chapter allows the reader to understand the pros and cons offered in this growing public debate.

Against this background, the final discussion in the first part is presented. Chapter 5 defines the differences between the "Old" and "New" Economies. The disorientation that characterized Bechtel Group's initial foray into cyberspace is one shared by many companies throughout corporate America. What, precisely, constitutes the "New" Economy? And, as important, who does business there? This is an interesting question, if for no other reason than it has been debated by social scientists since the 1950s. Human beings interact with human beings; human beings interface with machines. The personality traits that are well-suited for interacting are not always the same that are ideal for interfacing.

Furthermore, the psychological profile of those who are *creating*— and those who are *using*—the online economy offers its own set of distinct challenges. It isn't a question of awkward geeks with few social graces, but rather, it is about an economy that is emerging in which emotional detachment and social alienation are two of the underlying characteristics. This is the darker side of the online economy, one that must be examined honestly and objectively.

With this background, it is now possible to discuss the true "New Economy." Part II assumes the reader has a clear understanding of the ideas discussed in the first part, which are subsequently refreshed and reinforced in how the discussion proceeds. Each chapter applies these economic keys to the New Economy in a manner that rises above the contemporary fray of the dot-com world by placing economic theories in the center of cyberspace. To accomplish this, the definition for the New Economy presented in Part I is the basis for discussing each of the six sectors that comprise the New Economy. With the laws of classical economics at the center of cyberspace, it is then possible to see how the gravitational forces of its logic pull things into their proper orbits. An intrinsic appeal of the New Economy technologies concerns itself with the power of entertainment. What has been hailed as the inevitability of interactivity manifests itself primarily through entertainment. Publications and syndication, digital music, video gaming, gambling, adult entertainment, and privacy concerns are six components that together constitute the New Economy. To put these industries of the online entertainment economy in a familiar perspective, we shall avail ourselves to the inevitable logic of proper economics—making a profit is more important than adopting a hipster marketing pose.

Chapter 6 examines the online publishing industry. This is not about Amazon.com taking orders for books to be delivered physically—that's Old Economy. Stephen King publishing his novels online and the *Wall Street Journal* selling subscriptions, on the other hand, constitutes a different industry altogether. The use of syndication by newspapers, magazines, and wire services offers a model of a tried-and-true method of compensating writers and publishers. How this is being applied in the emerging "e-publishing" is discussed.

Chapter 7 takes on the more contentious issue concerning the distribution of music and film online. The court injunction against Napster, for instance, has set the stage for a series of court decisions that will determine how musicians and filmmakers are compensated for their intellectual property. The issues concerning both the distribution of music and film, as well as the compensation mechanism for the downloading video-on-demand or in some cases, "Web casts" over the Internet, offers insights into how copyright and intellectual property rights are to be interpreted with the advent of technological innovations that stand to redefine them. This chapter also examines how the issues were resolved before, when radio and television offered a mechanism for playing music and showing films to wide audiences for free.

The fact that video games and software programs are more technologically sophisticated than files with music or films results in the use of encryption technology to ensure proper compensation, or at least make piracy more difficult. Chapter 8 discusses how the sale of videos and software programs are facilitated by the online economy, making features, such as the possibility of continuous upgrades to both games and software programs a powerful incentive for rendering this industry viable. How games are distributed is a splendid model for other industries' emerging online economy.

A different kind of game, the game of chance, is discussed in Chapter 9. The casino industry has united to lobby Congress concerning online gambling, which is evidence of the growing popularity of gambling on the Internet. This chapter examines this industry, particularly because it is growing so rapidly. How online casinos, usually hosted on servers located in the Caribbean, are emerging as a viable industry speaks directly to the niche that exists by the simple fact that Las Vegas cannot be everywhere by virtue of being somewhere.

The final and, by far, largest portion of the online entertainment economy are adult sites. Pornography is the most profitable business on the Internet. Chapter 10 examines the history, the players, and the development of pornography as an industry, which using the technological innovations of the Internet Age, is developing into an industry that knows no borders and is subject to no jurisdiction. The nature of this form of entertainment has significant social repercussions. How societies around the world strike a balance in which the rights of all parties are accommodated will determine how privacy and child welfare protection develops in the new century. Finally, Chapter 11 addresses the social and political repercussions of the loss of privacy through technological innovations. In thinking about the public policy issues involved, corporate America is destined to play a major role.

NOTES

1. Steven Bodow, "The '99ers," *New York,* April 2, 2001.

2. Cushman & Wakefield, Inc. and Rosen Consulting Group analyzed the commercial real estate market in the San Francisco Bay Area to determine these figures. See Sheila Muto, "San Francisco's Dot-Com Meltdown May Worsen," *Wall Street Journal,* March 28, 2001.

Part I

Everything Old is New Again

Chapter 1

Reports of the Birth of the "New Economy" are Greatly Exaggerated

In the decades ahead, when one looks back at the time when the twentieth century gave way to the twenty-first, there will be nostalgia. There will be smiles of knowing amusement and incredulous awe at the naiveté that suffused discussions surrounding the gestation of the Internet Age. The 1990s will be remembered as a period in time when few recognized, in proper perspective, how technological innovations changed the world. The ability to apply sound business principles when incorporating technological innovations has been lost among the current generation of entrepreneurs who in the 1990s made San Francisco the self-styled center of the Internet universe. The evidence for this is in witnessing the "dot-com" debacle on the NASDAQ, which begs an answer to the fundamental question: How did so many intelligent people take leave of their senses and squander so much time and money on fantasies?

Was this a seismic shift in the ability of seasoned investors and young entrepreneurs to be rational? It was not always so, of course. There were other times when Americans, living in less self-absorbed and vain times, recognized events of historic consequence for their true gravitas. Consider the year 1869, when the Empire Express railroad united, for the first time, the continental United States with the transcontinental railroad. That the nation was linked by a system of rails that brought New York and California together for the first time was properly recognized as an achievement that would catapult the United States onto the world stage, both economically and politically. This is

how the driving of the final spike, with Western Union employees sending telegraphs to both coasts, was orchestrated:

> Up between the two locomotives, with all the ties but one in place, the
> two final rails were brought down—one by a Union Pacific gang of
> Irishmen, who placed it on the west side of the ties, and one by a Central
> Pacific gang of Chinese, who set theirs down on the east side. . . . Now
> it was time to connect them to the rest of the nation. . . . With the first
> hammer-tap the connection would be made—and the driving of the last
> spike would be "heard" all around the country. In every city equipped
> with fire-alarm telegraphs, the alarm would sound. Moreover, in San
> Francisco and New York, the telegraph was also attached to cannons
> on the shores of both oceans—at the signal they would fire, warning
> shots out over the Pacific and Atlantic to the rest of the world: the Empire
> Express was won.[1]

From sea to shining sea, the nation celebrated this momentous occasion. In New York, the Reverend John Adams Dix led the nation in
prayer with these words:

> O God, the Creator of the ends of the earth, Who upholdest all things
> by the Word of Thy power, without Whom nothing is strong, nothing is
> holy; we bless and magnify Thy glorious name that by Thy goodness
> the great work which we commemorate this day has been accomplished,
> so that the extreme borders of our land have been joined and brought
> nigh together, and a pathway opened between remote parts of the earth,
> both for the commerce of the nation and for a highway and a way
> whereby Thy Gospel may have free course, and Thy holy name may
> be glorified. We thank Thee that the wilderness and the solitary place
> are made glad, and that the desert may rejoice and blossom as the rose.[2]

When notified by telegraph at the precise moment that the Empire
Express had united the nation, Ulysses S. Grant, then president, toasted
in celebration with assembled political leaders and foreign dignitaries.
Firework celebrations in New York and San Francisco marked the historic achievement. Cities and towns around the country joined in joy-
ous celebration of this remarkable and unprecedented achievement
that fundamentally altered the nature of the American economy.

Make no mistake about the significance of the Empire Express railroad. The fact that a system of rails now crossed America changed
America. To be sure, railroads had been around for decades prior to
this national celebration, but it was not until there was one national
railway system that the unfettered contributions of the railroads, per
se, to the nation's economic, social and political life would be known.
American visions of empire and the conceit of Manifest Destiny now
had the infrastructure to expand and grow as never before. The Victo-

rians had a remarkable sense of history and of national purpose. They had the vision to see how their efforts would affect not only their lives but also Americans for generations to come. Railroads, the Victorians knew, were a new way of doing an old thing—expanding commerce.

Sixty years later, means of motorized private travel—automobiles—were an intriguing curiosity that drew crowds. One could drive around the major cities, New York, Boston, Chicago, Washington, D.C., Atlanta, and on the West Coast, of course, but it was another matter altogether to drive *between* cities. In the 1920s, however, long distance roads themselves were a greater novelty than private automobiles had been a decade earlier. Motorized vehicles gave Americans their freedom, bringing private ground transportation in the form of motorcycles, cars, buses, and trucks into the lives of Americans. This would require a different kind of nationwide network—one of roads and interstate highways.

However popular automobiles had become in the 1920s, it would take another 30 years before Congress passed the National Defense and Interstate Highway Act in 1956 that authorized the building of 42,000 miles of four-lane highways to link the nation in a network of roads. Speaking before Congress in 1956, President Eisenhower, with a sense of the need to establish a national network of interstate highways to promote transportation, commerce, and the movement of goods and people across the American landscape, argued that:

> Our unity as a nation is sustained by free communication and by easy transportation of people and goods. The ceaseless flow of information throughout the republic, matched by individual and commercial movement over a vast system of interconnected highways crisscrossing the country, joined our national borders to the north and south.
>
> Together, the united forces of our communication and transportation systems are dynamic elements in the very name we bear—United States. Without them, we would be a mere alliance of many separate parts.[3]

In other words, before automobiles could play their rightful role in the development of the nation's economy, highways that united the nation in a cost-effective grid were required. To achieve this goal, Eisenhower urged "adequate funding there must be, but contention over the method should not be permitted to deny our people these critically needed roads." In the course of this national undertaking, more than $50 billion was invested in creating the concrete arteries required to transport the lifeblood of the American economy across the North American landscape, linking the whole of the United States internally and to the international border crossings with Canada and Mexico.

Now known as the Eisenhower Interstate Highway, this project began with the Dixie Highway that linked Ontario to Miami and I-75,
which united Michigan to Atlanta (and then was extended into Florida).
That one could leave the street in front of one's home in New York and
travel to any street in Los Angeles changed forevermore how the
nation's economy worked.

There were no festivities to mark the opening of a national highway
system, but each new Interstate highway strengthened the national
network—and was duly celebrated by the communities that benefited
by now being included.[4] The Interstate highway system allowed for
commerce within the United States, and then linked the American
economy to the Canadian and Mexican ones by roads. There were no
national fireworks to commemorate this single achievement, but in the
course of the two decades that were required to link the entire nation
by highways, the surging postwar economy of the 1950s and 1960s
was celebration enough. The Interstate highway system, quite simply,
was a new way to do old things—expanding commerce and international trade and fostering the nation's development.[5]

If the railroads, then, were an achievement of the American desire
and ambition for empire, succinctly expressed in the doctrine of Manifest Destiny, then the highways were the result of the nation's political
resolve and economic wherewithal to privatize further transportation,
commerce, and communication along democratic principles. After the
Eisenhower Interstate Highway linked the nation, one no longer needed
to stop where the railroads stopped: one could go on one's merry way
behind the wheel of a car.

Forty years later, the Eisenhower Interstate Highway gave way to
the Information Highway with daunting speed. Indeed, in the mid-1990s
words unknown a few years before overtook the nation's business vocabulary and consumed the imagination of Americans. "Internet,"
"World Wide Web," "online," "e-mail," and "e-commerce" entered the
nation's vernacular and captivated our collective consciousness, as the
frenzied speculation in the NASDAQ market demonstrated. There was
another revolutionary transformation underway.

What appears odd, however, is how completely lacking in historical context the establishment of the digital network has been. Although
superlatives overflow, there is a scarcity of appropriate analogies.
"There's never been anything like the Internet because it will change
the world," Bill Gates is quoted as saying in 1995, eagerly parroting
how other communication and telecommunication revolutions before
the Internet had equally transformed the world as it communicated in
previous eras. It took less than five years for Bill Gates to understand
this. "I mean, do people have a clear view of what it means to live on

$1 a day?" he asked at the "Creating Digital Dividends" Conference held in Redmond, Washington, in November 2000. He said,

> There's no electricity in that house. None. . . . The mothers are going to walk right up to that computer and say, "My children are dying, what can you do?" They're not going to sit there and like, browse eBay or something. What they want is for their children to live. They don't want their children's growth to be stunted. Do you really have to put in computers to figure that out?[6]

As much from vanity as, perhaps, from the undisputed advances of technology that the Internet represents, there is, to paraphrase Alan Greenspan's observation of the stock market—a certain irrationality to the exuberance that lacks in proper perspective. Of the many books written about the Internet in the 1990s, few had an appropriate perspective to place the digital network into context. This was because of the simple reason that there had not been enough time—or development—of the Internet to understand more precisely the nature of the Internet, how it would impact the economy, and how the lives of ordinary consumers would be affected. The Internet in the 1990s was in gestation, its rapid growth unfolding in a chaotic and unpredictable way. It is now in the early part of the first decade of the twenty-first century that sufficient growth and evolution have taken place to understand, in more concrete terms, how the emergence of a digital network that spans the globe will transform the American economy.

The establishment of networks—first rail, then road, and now digital—has as its primary objective, to give momentum to commercial and economic growth to strengthen national development. In the nineteenth century, Reverend Dix praised the Empire Express as a "pathway opened . . . for the commerce of the nation," underscoring the almost religious fervor for economic expansion. In the twentieth century, Dwight Eisenhower reflected that the interstate highways "made possible sustainable and robust American economic growth in the 1950s."[7] The advent of the Internet, likewise, has been a harbinger of economic growth, explosive growth at that.

The exuberance over the possibilities, however, has given rise to hyperboles and misunderstandings. Nowhere is this more in evidence than in the muddled discussions of the so-called "new" economy vis-à-vis the "old" economy. These kinds of exaggerations are not uncommon to other times. Leaders in the nineteenth and twentieth centuries, however, saw themselves acting on a larger stage. These were men and women of action. There was an admirable and undeniable clearheaded and purposeful sense of direction in the construction of the transcontinental railroad first and the interstate highway system second, for instance. The assessment of generations past and the ability to put these tasks in their proper perspective are now, inexplicably, lacking.

Consider in our own more selfish, foolish, and diminished times Thomas Siebel, the CEO of Siebel Systems, writing that:

> [t]he advent of the Web was an unprecedented event that has already begun to set us on a path that will radically alter how we interact not only with computers, but with one another, with institutions both private and public, and with business associates and customers around the globe. . . . There have been other watersheds of this magnitude, but not many . . . The first, perhaps, was the invention of writing, which enabled grain merchants in Mesopotamia to rationalize their inventory. A second was the appearance of metal currency—the dramatic attack on the barter system that occurred in Lydia, on the eastern Mediterranean, several thousand years ago.[8]

Did he say the invention of *writing?*

Although Ulysses S. Grant and Dwight Eisenhower had a sense of history, neither one was audaciously arrogant enough to compare the achievements of their respective generations with the invention of writing. These are precisely the kinds of exaggerations, however, that characterize the establishment of the digital network. Po Bronson, a feature writer for *Wired* magazine and an industry observer in Silicon Valley, is bemused by the hyperboles he calls "vapor." Indeed, he rhetorically ponders:

> Doesn't the fact that the business is running on vapor—without revenues, without offices, without physical products—mean that at a certain point it will lose its ability to float? Do the principles of economics work in space, beyond the reach of gravity? Is there any oxygen up there?[9]

There is oxygen, of course—and gravity as well.

It has not always been easy to tell. "The Palm [Pilot] saga involves ridiculous stock market valuations and vanishing profits," Floyd Norris opined in the *New York Times.* "It also provides a textbook example of just how transitory success can be in the world of high technology, where there is always a possibility that some competitor may be about to introduce a product that will destroy the market for your cash cow."[10] To be sure, there are times when a healthy perspective is lost amid the relentless propaganda celebrating the unfortunate and irresponsible hype of Silicon Valley and its enthusiasts.

Consider the bombastic declarations made by Gary Hamel writing, inexplicably, in the *Harvard Business Review.* In an essay that maintains that the imperative of each and every company in corporate America is "[t]o capture [Silicon] Valley's entrepreneurial magic, your company needs to move from resource allocation to resource attraction," Hamel then proceeds to describe a world moving at warp speed. In his vision, Silicon Valley becomes Valley-of-the-Hyperboles, where the reader is informed, in no uncertain terms to:

> Face it: Out there in some garage, an entrepreneur is forging a bullet with your company's name on it. Once that bullet leaves the barrel, you won't be able to dodge it. You've got one option: you have to shoot first. You have to out-innovate the innovators, out-entrepreneur the entrepreneurs.[11]

This line of reasoning, presumably, requires executives throughout corporate America to meet the challenges of the "New Economy" by donning bulletproof vests, relocating their offices to their garages, and never forgetting that:

> The Valley is the distilled essence of entrepreneurial energy. Its ethos is simple: If it's not new, it's not cool; if it's not cool, it's not worth doing. If you don't own shares, you're getting screwed. If you've been in the same job for more than two years, your career is over. If you haven't been through an IPO, you're a virgin. This is where a $2 million house is a teardown.[12]

"Coolness," one read in the pages of the *Harvard Business Review*, had replaced sound business judgment. Never mind that within a year all those options would instantly become as "uncool" as they were worthless. As Gary Hamel argued with tremendous enthusiasm, the net result of this testosterone-laced energy was:

> Like the Florentines and Venetians [during the Italian Renaissance], they're building a new age—an age of virtual presence, of globally interconnected communities, of frictionless commerce, of instantly accessible knowledge and stunningly seductive media.[13]

And what kinds of human beings reportedly populate this Brave New World? Hamel knows, for he has been there, and he reports back to us mere mortals:

> Let's pop in for breakfast at Buck's—a popular diner in Woodside that attracts cyber-CEOs, venture capitalists, and an unending stream of entrepreneurs on the make. In the parking lot you'll find some of the world's most exotic cars, and maybe a horse or two tied up at a well-used hitching rail. . . . Now look around. . . . There's a buzz that goes beyond the caffeine.[14]

There is a laconic bewilderment at this idea that contributors in the *Harvard Business Review* imply that executives throughout corporate America, in order to pursue the future and succeed in the Internet Age, will need to have hitching rails installed outside their office doors. It is this kind of irrationality that has clouded discussions of the Internet, of its potential implications for business and of its role in our lives. *Let's pop in for breakfast at Buck's?* Let's not.

Now consider the reasoned voice of Robert Frank, an economist at Cornell University, who offers this vision:

> As in the past, new technologies will continue to generate a burst of new profits for companies that are relatively quick to adopt them. But the historical pattern has been that competition will award the long-run savings from these technologies to consumers in the form of lower prices.
>
> Thus dairy farmers who were quick to adopt bovine sematotropin, the hormone that increases milk yields by as much as 20 percent, reaped a short-term windfall, but as use of the hormone spread, increased production pushed milk prices steadily downward, eroding profit margins.
>
> A similar profit trajectory will characterize most NASDAQ purveyors of new technologies.[15]

What has been heralded as a new economy, then, is the familiar phenomenon of a short-term windfall that accompanies technological innovation. Parking attendants at parking garages in office buildings around the country, in essence, can breathe a sigh of relief for they do not need to brush up on their equestrian skills.

There was a time in the late 1990s when corporate America was asked to suspend disbelief and accept the proposition that the laws of economics no longer applied. The euphoria, however irrational, itself had basis in reality: $100,000 invested in 1992 in the NASDAQ was worth, in 2000, $850,000. This was offered as irrefutable proof of a seismic shift in the American economy: old economy firms like General Motors languished, and new economy companies such as Microsoft promised a future in which the pronouncements of Thomas Siebel and Gary Hamel seem real, or real enough.

Faced with the relentless nature of the bullish market, the calm voices of economists betrayed a certain nervousness. Federal Reserve Chairman Alan Greenspan was not the only one looking on with apprehension as the markets rose steadily, relentlessly, and inexplicably. Gurus *du jour* throughout Silicon Valley argued that the business cycle had been defeated, and a Utopian economic world had been created by the Internet. Uncomfortable economists around the world answered that what we were witnessing was a "classic case of a speculative bubble," while privately thinking, "We hope."

John Kenneth Galbraith warned of the need for government to be mindful of the speculative nature of the market as far back as October 1998.[16] Edward Chancellor wrote about the familiar history of financial speculations in the modern world, with dire predictions about the NASDAQ in the 1990s.[17] It was Robert Shiller's *Irrational Exuberance,* however, that drew the most attention, for this book examined the unprecedented public fascination with and participation in the stock market. Lamenting the decline of prudence and the ill-advised disregard for risk, Shiller expressed concern that the markets were characterized by "[e]motions and heightened attention to the market [creating] a desire to get into the game. Such is the irrational exuberance today in the United States."[18]

Paul Krugman, an MIT economist, reviewing the book in the *New York Times,* wrote, "Given the title of Mr. Shiller's book, you can guess the punch line. He makes a powerful case that the soaring stock market of recent years in a huge, accidental Ponzi scheme in progress, one that will come to a very bad end."[19]

If the market behavior at the end of the 1990s resembled a huge Ponzi scheme, it was not long before this world full of strange equations was brought back to reality as much by the forces of gravity as by the fundamental laws of the market economy. The giddy nature of Internet enthusiasts reached such sublime levels at the end of the 1990s that it became the stuff of insider jokes among bemused economists.

"The Internet bubble is rational in a certain sense," Franco Modigliani, winner of the Nobel Memorial Prize in Economics for 1985, said. "Expectations of growth produces the growth experienced. This confirms the expectation; more people will buy the stocks because their price went up. But once you are convinced it is not growing anymore, nobody wants to hold a stock because it is overvalued. Everybody wants out and it collapses, far beyond the fundamentals. The only people who did well in 1929 were those who sold too soon."[20]

It also confounded public officials. When Brazil faced a currency crisis in January 1999 that culminated in the devaluation of its currency, for example, U.S. Deputy Secretary Lawrence Summers, in an ironic observation, jested that all Brazil had to do was rename its currency from *real* to *real.*com, and there would be a flood of investment money flowing into Brazil from reckless investors willing to speculate on anything, provided it had "dot-com" at the end of it, even if it was vapor.[21]

In little over a year after this comment was made to amused colleagues, Paul Krugman gave a more complete—and less ironic—voice to the emerging consensus among economists in an editorial titled,

"Going for Broke." There was something troubling about burning through tens of millions of dollars on pure adrenaline and speculation. The collapse of boo.com, a European Internet company that spent almost $188 million in a mere six months before it was forced to liquidate its meager assets, was seen not so much as a cautionary tale as a stark reminder that the advocates of "New Economy" were mistaken to believe that the historical rules about speculative crazes had been suspended.[22] Indeed, reflecting on the business model pursued by Amazon.com, he noted that:

> Amazon's business strategy—to lose money for an extended period while building a market position—is not all that unusual. In fact, it's exactly what Japanese companies did in their export markets during the 70's and 80's, when Japan's economy seemed an unstoppable juggernaut. . . . What *is* new is the sight of Amazon and other companies pursuing a full-scale go-for-broke strategy right from the start, losing hundreds of millions before anyone is even sure that there is money to be made in their businesses.[23]

As we shall see later in this discussion, there are significant public policy issues raised when one company's decision to expand market share results in the decimation of competitors. The observations made by Robert Frank and Paul Krugman found resonance in the realities of the marketplace in short order.

In the mid-1990s, e-commerce was seen as an alien form of business, one that challenged how companies offered their goods and services to others. That new technology had created a metaphysical realm. Where *is* cyberspace? was a menacing idea. The staccato of geek-speak, where the vocabulary of nerds invaded conference rooms and managerial meetings, was overwhelming. This raised philosophical questions that challenged our understanding of the world. "The big difference between the new economy and the old is the changed nature of investment," Paul Krugman wrote, attempting to put an economist's spin on the controversy. "In the past, businesses primarily invested in tangible means of production, things like buildings and machines. . . . But now businesses increasingly invest in intangibles."[24] If it wasn't bad enough to be told that the future resided in cyberspace, suddenly, consultants pressed to elaborate simply told one that things depended not on bandwidth, but on broadband.

Was the Internet analogous to geometry, where a point indicates a position but has no length, width, or depth?

The response to this Land-of-Confusion was to classify the Internet as a creature apart and separate from the concerns and activities of traditional business. Furthermore, the fact that discussions about the Internet and e-commerce were centered around incomprehensible doublespeak, made executives throughout corporate America uncomfortable and apprehensive. The real world was difficult enough; the virtual world was the business Twilight Zone of the unknown.

After the initial euphoria surrounding the advent of the Internet, moreover, what is emerging is the consensus that technological advances offer tremendous opportunities to expand trade and commerce. In much the same way that the railroads and the interstate highways ushered in new eras of rapid economic expansion, the Internet is offering business throughout the economy another tremendous opportunity to grow. Rather than ignoring the Internet—or keeping these activities as separate initiatives—the more successful companies are implementing "click-and-mortar" strategies.

A real-world example is in order. Because Amazon.com was the first online bookseller to enjoy tremendous investor confidence and enthusiasm, let us consider how the Internet has, in fact, challenged traditional book retailing. Three of the top companies in the business of selling books have each pursued a different strategy. This affords us the ability to examine these competitive strategies comparatively.[25]

Amazon.com, which exists as an online retailer exclusively, has become the leading distributor of books and information about books. Through an aggressive set of strategies pursued by founder Jeff Bezos, Amazon.com has repositioned itself constantly. First, by introducing programs that gathered information about visitors to its site, known as cookies, it has been able to gather precise information about the consumer profile of its visitors.[26] Second, through the introduction of its affiliate program called Amazon.com Associates, it has been able to enlist approximately half a million other sites to channel sales to its site. Third, the launching of zShops program now makes it possible for Amazon.com to host thousands of small e-commerce providers on its own site, creating a fluid and flexible way of helping develop niche markets. For participating Web sites, the synergies available through this kind of program relieves them of the burden of e-commerce billing and fulfilling orders generated online.

These strategies have allowed Amazon.com to leverage its brand through a process of syndicating its state-of-the-art e-commerce capabilities, facilitating distribution and fulfillment, and, finally, packaging digital informational content for consumers. Amazon.com's explosive growth, however, has been an expensive undertaking. Investors, individual and institutional alike, have expressed reservations about the manner in which money was spent during its first years as a publicly traded company. Amazon.com has registered losses each quarter of its existence, and most analysts believe that this unproven, although tantalizing, business model may not break even until the middle part of the first decade this century, if it does so at all.

Barnes & Noble, on the other hand, fearful that it would alienate traditional customers or weaken its position by cannibalizing its sales, pursued a different strategy. This venerable bookseller decided to establish an Internet division as an entirely different entity. Bn.com, formerly known as barnesandnoble.com, was set up as a completely stand-alone company, one whose online operations had nothing to do with a traditional store. Whereas the online division attempted to compete with Amazon.com (and other online booksellers), its physical stores went about business as if the Internet did not exist.

To be sure, there were competitive advantages to Barnes & Noble's decision to create an enterprise independent of the parent company in its pursuit of opportunities on the Internet. Foremost was the ability to create an entrepreneurial culture that was unencumbered by the bureaucracy that is inherent in any established business enterprise. The online firm could also establish its presence in keeping with the emerging business ethos of the Internet culture, which includes attracting venture capital—of both a human and financial nature—without risking upsetting the existing hierarchical structure at the parent company. For Barnes & Noble, after all, it would have been unthinkable to bring people aboard who commuted to work on skateboards, attended rave concerts on weekends, and spoke in vernacular that only they could understand among each other. The independent online venture, finally, had to be nimble; the culture of Internet start-ups and the fluid nature of technological changes lent themselves splendidly to a complete separation from the existing company.

What astounds, however, is to witness how dismally bn.com performed when compared with Amazon.com. Both lost money with abandon, of course. But bn.com was seen as a *failing* business venture because some Wall Street analysts thought it wasn't losing enough money fast enough.[27] However irrational these conclusions may have been, perceptions matter almost as much as performance when it comes to instilling investor confidence. Such is the nature of the human mind. Barnes & Noble, the real world store, drifted further from bn.com the online enterprise, as if one had nothing to do with the other. There was much turmoil. Bn.com's stock price continued to fall. Investor confidence was shaken further. Jonathan Bulkeley resigned in early 2000, fueling the speculation that the "clicks" alone strategy was inappropriate for a company that had a "mortar" presence in the real world.

Although Amazon.com and bn.com captured the headlines (and investor interest), Borders, Inc., on the other hand, quietly implemented a strategy to harness the benefits of integration. Compared with the abrupt about-face in the attitudes of many "clicks and mortar" retailers who were forced to modify their virtual world strategies by the real world needs of their clients, Borders sought from the beginning to benefit from channel synchronization that the new technologies made possible.

"Channel synchronization" refers to the ability to keep individualized records, purchase history, and client profile on any specific client. Whereas a Barnes & Noble bookstore has no way of knowing what a client who walks in off the street has purchased online, Borders does. And although Amazon.com is unable to develop a relationship with a customer that is only possible by having, for instance, a book signing and reading at the in-store coffee shop (as there are no physical stores), Borders can use the Internet to publicize these kinds of events.

The absence of "mortars" has proved to be an obstacle to Amazon.com. High-tech enthusiasts who believed that the Internet would offer a mechanism for providing customer service that was (virtually) free were terribly mistaken. In the same way that in the 1960s some commentators predicted that we would no longer eat food but simply consume pills, the social nature that people require is often ignored by technology enthusiasts. Human beings require human attention. Customers want to ask questions, make inquiries, change their minds, meander into real stores, browse, and have service representatives "know" who they are without having to answer the same questions about who they are every time. It is because of these real-world realities that Borders has been able to implement the kinds of "clicks and mortar" strategy that combines the overwhelming benefits of integration.

"I am confident that within a decade every major retail company will have an Internet-enabled device in the store. This will provide a quantum leap in how we can provide customer service and how we can help customers find what they are looking for," said Rick Vanzura, president of Borders, Inc., when the firm began to install Internet kiosks in each of the their superstores.[28] "Borders will enjoy a competitive advantage by combining both everything about our products with the specific individual needs of every single customer. It will be like having your own personalized bookstore."[29]

What economists long argued—that the Internet was another step in the evolution of commerce—was clearly coming to pass. The reassuring manner in which Borders has moved ahead by doing something neither Amazon.com nor bn.com have done bolstered their position. Borders set up terminals inside their stores. By bringing the Internet into their physical stores, Borders facilitated the integration of their retail, catalog, and online information into a single database.

When a customer calls the toll-free number, goes online to make a purchase, or walks up to the information desk at any store, Borders can pull up their consolidated purchase history and customer profile at once. The synergies denied bn.com are accessible to Borders. The choice of allowing an online customer to pick up an order at a nearby store is denied to Amazon.com. This is the vision of Gordon Eiland, who directed Borders' efforts to create one central database for retail, catalog, and online sales. "We realize that we have to offer outstanding customer service," he said. "It's what is going to differentiate us from the competition. To do that, we need to make sure that we have our entire records in one place."[30]

Another advantage in channel synchronization is that once it becomes part of the business architecture at a company, it is easier to fine-tune marketing. Armed with a comprehensive profile of a customer, for instance, it becomes easier to make recommendations and offer suggestions through e-mail. There is, undeniably, some degree of cannibalization in the short term, but this allows for a more sophisticated way of selling. It allows for a more refined segmentation of the market: Although most online customers know what they want and are single-minded, shoppers who walk in off the street may just want to take their time, browse, see what they stumble upon, and make an impulse purchase. A company that accommodates these differences has a long-term competitive advantage: both customers may be the same individual at different times and in different moods.

Over time there are significant savings if there is a transition among customers from requesting catalogs to using the company's Web sites. The cost of updating an online catalog and sending e-mail are drastically lower than printing and mailing catalogs—and then processing the orders that arrive in the mail. With greater information on products made available online, moreover, returns and exchanges are significantly lower. Profit margins vanish when customer service expenses skyrocket. Fattening up profits is an appealing part of getting the right mix between "clicks" and "mortars."

The strategy implemented by Borders validates what the reassuring voices of economists have been recommending: the Internet *complements* traditional business strategies but does not *replace* them. Thus reality and virtuality are accommodated, and what emerges is a coherent business model. The same kind of impetus that shook up how the economy can work is unveiling a familiar landscape as the dust settles. What is clear, then, is that although the Internet is the means through which revolutionary technology innovates, it is necessary to keep in mind one undeniable perspective: the laws of economics, happily, have not been suspended.

On the contrary, the convulsions within the companies that deal with the Internet instead of defying the economics are conforming to models developed and refined throughout the twentieth century. The emerging body of case studies, in fact, constitutes further evidence that the basic ideas about how markets work are correct. In the next two chapters, we discuss how fundamental observations and tenets about how the market economy works are validated by the turmoil seen in both the NASDAQ exchange and the Internet companies. What has sent shivers through the collective spines of investors and what has baffled analysts is, in fact, the natural process of evolution inherent in the development of new markets and technologies. The ideas—if not *ideals*—of allocative efficiency, market imperfections, and market failures form the basic phenomena that characterize the Internet in the first decade of the twenty-first century.

In addition, there are three other fundamentals at work. Two deal with the nature of how humans behave in economic arenas, specifically, the tyranny of small decisions and the end-game strategies found in a theory of games known simply as the prisoner's dilemma.[31] The other factor centers on the nature of the Internet itself, which is strikingly similar to how the print media and entertainment industries operate in the real world. The more successful Internet ventures, indeed, are those that are incorporating the business of syndication—the backbone of the print and broadcast media alike—into their approach to developing opportunities online.

It is in these similarities that the world in which we live is evolving. The two overriding concerns about the impact of the new technologies in our personal lives—rights to privacy and intellectual property rights—have been addressed adequately in the past. As we shall see in discussions later in this book, the emergence of a self-contained online entertainment economy is one over which concerns over both privacy and intellectual rights loom large. What will be argued is that, in the same way that modern syndication developed in the twentieth century to compensate and protect the intellectual property rights of owners and individuals alike, similar mechanisms can be applied to the Internet economy.

These concerns, I maintain, are simply the old economy heard through the distorted sounds of the newfangled terminology of the Internet vernacular. The principles, legal and economic, remain the same. In the same way that railroads and highways brought forth new opportunities, without tearing asunder the existing world, so, too, has the Internet brought about new opportunities for familiar ways of expanding trade and commerce. Reports of the birth of the New Economy may be greatly exaggerated, but the opportunities the new century promises are not.

Key #1

The Internet is the next technological advance that has created a network that will enable the expansion of trade and commerce. The fundamental laws of economics apply in the virtual world as they do in the real world. Indeed, the Internet, far from defying the laws of economics, is conforming to classic theories about how market economies work. Corporate America can participate in the Internet economy through an online presence exclusively, or creating a stand-alone division, or by developing a "clicks and mortar" strategy confident that corporate strategies can be designed to maximize opportunities.

NOTES

1. David Haward Bain, *Empire Express: Building the First Transcontinental Railroad*, pp. 662–663.

2. Ibid., pp. 663–664.

3. In his State of the Union address in 1956, Eisenhower stated his commitment to a national highway system by noting that

> Legislation to provide a modern, interstate highway system is even more urgent this year than last, for 12 months have now passed in which we have fallen further behind in road construction needed for the personal safety, the general prosperity, the national security of the American people. During the year, the number of motor vehicles has increased from 58 to 61 million. During the past year over 38,000 persons lost their lives in highway accidents, while the fearful toll of injuries and property damage has gone on unabated. In my message of February 22, 1955, I urged that measures be taken to complete the vital 40,000-mile interstate system over a period of 10 years at an estimated Federal cost of approximately 25 billion dollars. No program was adopted. If we are ever to solve our mounting traffic problem, the whole interstate system must be authorized as one project, to be completed approximately within the specified time. Only in this way can industry efficiently gear itself to the job ahead. Only in this way can the required planning and engineering be accomplished without the confusion and waste unavoidable in a piecemeal approach. Furthermore, as I pointed out last year, the pressing nature of this problem must not lead us to solutions outside the bounds of sound fiscal management. As in the case of other pressing problems, there must be an adequate plan of financing. To continue the drastically needed improvement in other national highway systems, I recommend the continuation of the Federal Aid Highway Program.

4. A curious analogy to the emergence of the Internet, of course, is that the Eisenhower Interstate Highway gave rise to the industry of billboards, which are reminiscent of the ubiquity of banner-ads that litter the Internet Information Highway.

5. It is difficult to imagine any municipality orchestrating fireworks and picnics to celebrate the opening of a new on-ramp.

6. The *New York Times* applauded Mr. Gates' change of heart. "Philanthropy is not just the act of giving away money. It is the hard task of learning what money will do, and how it can work most usefully when applied in the

real world," the *New York Times* opined in an editorial on November 5, 2000. "Judging by comments Mr. Gates has made recently, the man who created the world's richest foundation may have learned more about the real world by trying to give away his wealth than he did while making it."

7. The four-lane highways, by the way, were also created to establish a mechanism by which entire cities could be evacuated in the event of nuclear conflict, thereby serving a defensive military purpose during the Cold War.

8. Thomas M. Siebel and Pat House, *Cyber Rules*, pp. 1–2.

9. Po Bronson, *The Nudist on the Late Shift*, p. xxix.

10. Floyd Norris, "Palm's Saga: A Tale of Vanishing Profits and Absurd Prices," *New York Times*, April 14, 2000.

11. Gary Hamel, "Bringing Silicon Valley Inside," *Harvard Business Review*, September-October 1999, p. 72.

12. Ibid.

13. Ibid.

14. Ibid., p. 75.

15. Robert Frank, "The Rules NASDAQ Forgot," *New York Times*, March 17, 2000.

16. John Kenneth Galbraith, "Evading the Obvious," *New York Times*, October 12, 1998.

17. Edward Chancellor, *Devil Take the Hindmost: A History of Financial Speculation*.

18. Robert J. Shiller, *Irrational Exuberance*.

19. Paul Krugman, "Dow Wow, Dow Ow," *New York Times*, February 27, 2000.

20. Personal communication, April 2000.

21. This comment was widely reported in the media at the time, including the London *Economist* and Sylvia Nasar, "Turmoil in Brazil: The Economics— One Choice Made, More to Come; Why Brazil Did It and What Options Are Left," *New York Times*, January 16, 1999.

22. In June 2000, Benjamin Nasarin of Fashionmall.com purchased the assets of boo.com, including the Web address, the boo.com brand, and the online content materials. Boo.com's back-end technology was sold to Bright Station of the United Kingdom. Analysts questioned whether the brand name had been tarnished by the scandal beyond repair.

23. Paul Krugman, "Going for Broke," *New York Times*, July 2, 2000.

24. Paul Krugman, "Unsound Bytes?," *New York Times*, October 22, 2000.

25. Although Amazon.com maintains that it is not in the "business" of selling books, but of building market shares and collecting information on consumer preferences and habits, it nonetheless pursues these goals by, in fact, primarily selling books.

26. A discussion on what cookies are and the role they play in e-commerce is found in Chapter 3.

27. An analyst from Merrill Lynch explained that if an Internet company did not lose enough money fast enough it meant it would not build sufficient market share. The implication, of course, being that the "winner" would ultimately be the one that lost the most money.

28. Borders was not the only retailer to integrate their virtual and physical

retail environments. Recreational Equipment, Inc., the outdoor goods merchant known as REI, placed Internet kiosks in each of its stores in 1999. "This allows us to give detailed information on every product," said Matt Hyde, vice president of online sales.

29. Bn.com, of course, realized that it was falling behind, to the detriment of its future. "Internet service counters represent a $25 million investment," Leonard Riggio, chairman of Barnes & Noble and bn.com, stated on October 27, 2000, when he announced that 550 Barnes & Noble superstores would install bn.com terminals. "These Internet service counters are a massive undertaking," he explained, as Barnes & Noble attempted to play catch-up to Borders.

30. Bob Tedeschi, "E-Commerce Report: Retailers are Letting Their Right Hand Know What the Left Hand is Up to For Better Customer Service," *New York Times*, July 24, 2000.

31. Although critics have argued that the Internet's unstructured nature resembles chaos theory, it is, in fact, closer to game theory. It was the work of John Harsanyi at the University of California, Berkeley that illuminated how game theory works in economics. In situations where one's decisions depend on the decisions of others, it is possible to think systematically about possible outcomes by assigning probabilities. In circumstances where players have access to different information, assigning probabilities to possible moves and outcomes establishes a framework for determining the likely outcomes. Even Solitaire, where one's opponent is one's self, constitutes a situation in which one player has to concern himself with the responses of another player. The game theory developed by John Harsanyi is useful in determining outcomes in everything, whether it is a game of chess between two friends or a trade war among several competing rival nations. John Harsanyi was awarded the Nobel Prize in Economics in 1994 for this work.

CHAPTER 2

WHY THE LAWS OF ECONOMICS APPLY IN CYBERSPACE

As incremental innovations in technology change how humans are able to live, human societies change. Not too long ago, for instance, the idea of trekking through the tropical rain forests in search of ancient Maya ruins was a romantic notion. It was Charles Lindbergh who in the 1930s flew over the Yucatan peninsula and identified pyramids jutting just above the forest canopy. As late as the 1980s, archaeologists on digs incurred danger in carrying out their work; it was not impossible to become disoriented and lost wandering beneath the canopy, with mortal consequences. With the advent of technological advances that made it possible for individuals to carry a receiver on their persons, Global Positioning System (GPS), everything changed. What was once romantic was instantly rendered mundane. Henceforth, anyone who becomes lost in the jungle will not be seen as a victim of tragedy, but rather, irresponsible.

"Invention is the mother of necessity," Thornstein Veblen wryly observed in the nineteenth century as the Industrial Revolution made abundance, that is, materialism, a reality for the first time in human existence. Once a technology, product, or custom becomes widely available, which is to say it ceases to be *scarce,* it becomes a *necessity.*

The relentless pace of innovation, moreover, has created a business culture in America in which change is constant, change is faster, and change is highly valued. In a market economy, this altered value system becomes an arena for competition: the one who introduces innovation first oftentimes enjoys a competitive advantage and is more likely to secure significant market share in the short and medium terms. "It's like what happened with Yahoo!, the first guy out in the market gets a disproportionate market share," Jim McDermott, of Stamps.com, said by way of explaining his company's business plan.[1] Paulina Borsook, a contributing writer for *Wired* magazine, who witnessed the revolutions and evolutions in Silicon Valley throughout the 1990s, argues that:

[I]t's a dirty little secret in high tech that superior marketing and inferior technology will beat out superior technology and inferior marketing every time and that other factors, aside from Darwinian fitness, determine which technologies, and which companies, thrive or perish.[2]

She attributes this deplorable state of affairs to:

[T]he winner-take-all/Casino Society that forms the backdrop to Silicon Valley, everyone also knows, or knows of, lots of other folks, just as talented and hardworking (or spacey or sneaky) whose startup tanked (as do nine out of ten startups) or never went public, or got bought out under terms where the value of their stock options would not even amount to compensation for overtime.[3]

This is all undoubtedly true. However, Borsook's criticism of this particular aspect of the market system is not entirely valid. When she decries the "winner-take-all" society as undesirable, what she, in fact, does is show a fundamental lack of understanding about the nature and role of contests in which rewards are hugely disproportionate for the participants engaged in competition.

Consider the argument put forth by economists Robert Frank and Philip Cook:

Now that most of the music we listen to is recorded, the world's best soprano can literally be everywhere at once. And since it costs no more to stamp out compact discs from Kathleen Battle's master recording of Mozart arias than from her understudy's, most of us listen to Battle. Millions of us are each willing to pay a few cents extra to hear her rather than another singer who is only marginally less able; and this enables Battle to write her own ticket.[4]

Understanding how winner-take-all contests apply to competition in the Internet economy is instrumental if one is to make sense of why Silicon Valley continues to behave the way it does. Consider how technological revolutions in communication, transportation, and information technologies have each transformed all kinds of competitive races in the free market into winner-take-all contests. Robert Frank and Philip Cook explain that:

When only barely perceptible quality margins spell the difference between success and failure, the buying public may have little at stake in
the battles that decide which products win. But to the manufacturers the
stakes are often enormous—the difference between liquidation and the
continuation of multibillion-dollar annual revenues.[5]

The result of this has been the proliferation of winner-take-all contests to spill over from traditional arenas, such as sports and entertainment, to markets where mundane competitions produced few
celebrities. The impact of these changes is felt in the culture of Silicon
Valley for the simple reason that the entrepreneurs who thrive in the
high-tech world are, for the most part, mindful of preserving their individualism. It takes a healthy dose of vanity and bravura to believe
one can change the world by changing how office workers type business correspondence, how accountants keep track of the pennies, and
how business executives make golf dates electronically with each other.
There, in essence, is the impact of Microsoft Windows on the non-geek
business world. High technology, through the sheer economic power
it wields and unglamorous as it may be, has engendered a demimonde
of "celebrities" who are largely unknown to the public at large.[6]

Robert Frank and Philip Cook argue further that the proliferation of
winner-take-all contests throughout the economy has had a sweeping
impact on society. They maintain "[w]inner-take-all markets have already wrought profound changes in economic and social life. And because many of the forces that create these markets are intensifying,
even more dramatic changes loom ahead."[7]

The advent of these technological changes makes it difficult for an
economy in which *whiners-take-some* to be accommodated of its own
volition. To impose this kind of an accommodation requires regulatory
intervention. This is the nature of imperfect markets. It is also intrinsic to the human condition by virtue of our being social creatures.
Certain industries capture our collective imagination.[8] That winner-
takes-all contests are inherently unfair is certainly true. That there is
a corresponding loss in the economic efficiencies because of the outcomes of such contests is par for the course. Whether we, as a society, decide that a greater good is served by such intervention is another
matter altogether, however.[9] Specific circumstances under which antitrust considerations may be applicable to the cyberspace companies
is discussed later. The arguments presented are based on the concern
that because a disproportionate number of contests among online
companies are of a winner-take-all nature, the aggregate result is
the limiting of healthy competition and the proliferation of online
oligopolies.

What Borsook alludes to correctly are the challenges in achieving
allocative efficiencies in any society and adequately managing the

market imperfections and market failures that are prevalent through-out the high-tech economy. That allocative efficiencies are lacking in the winner-take-all model of competition is not lost on most econo-mists. Robert Frank and Philip Cook are alarmed at the misallocation of resources that has resulted from the proliferation of winner-take-all contests throughout the economy. Among the more troubling social repercussions they identify are the growing income disparity between rich and poor, a proliferation of wasteful investment and consumption, the misleading incentives that lure talented individuals into unproduc-tive tasks, and the limited opportunities for the vast majority of people who do not have certain educational credentials.

Consider how winner-take-all markets offend our innate sense of fairness—to speak nothing of undermining the economist's theory of wages—when incomes are distorted grossly by these kinds of competitions. This is how Robert Frank and Philip Cook describe the phenomenon:

> In winner-take-all markets, however, pay distributions will be more spread out—often dramatically so—than the underlying distributions of effort and ability. It is one thing to say that people who work 10 per-cent harder or have 10 percent more talent should receive 10 percent more pay. But it is quite another to say that such small differences should cause pay to differ by 10,000 percent or more. Olympic gold medalists go on to receive millions in endorsements while the runners-up are quickly forgotten—even when the performance gap is almost too small to measure.[10]

Now imagine not Olympic gold medalists, but a community of highly-but-narrowly-educated, socially—awkward, high-tech entrepre-neurs whose value system is at odds with those espoused by modern democratic societies.

Within Silicon Valley, Borsook identifies those individuals whose values embody characteristics alien to American society's sense of both egalitarianism and justice as "cypherpunks." She describes these mostly young adult men as perverse and immature creatures who "seem to take gleeful pleasure in imagining this [Brave New World-style subjugation of humanity by technology] hell, just as teenage boys love the dark, ghoulish, and apocalyptic and revel in a world of heavy metal music."[11]

She notes that the fact that cypherpunks are exalted in the high-tech subculture has a chilling effect on society, for it further intensifies the cynical commodification of outcomes in winner-take-all contests. Borsook further argues that there is, in fact, a dysfunctional aspect to Silicon Valley where money is managed childishly.

One reason why small children have no money of their own is because they lack the maturity to make responsible decisions for themselves. Were children free to make economic decisions on their own—what they would eat, when they would sleep, and what they would do during their waking hours—their aggregate decisions would in short order result in an economy that would be unrecognizable. One reason parents are in charge is that society recognizes that for minors to grow up to be educated, healthy, and responsible adults, significant economic and emotional resources have to be allocated in enlightened ways. It is only when children become fully rational that they are allowed to make economic decisions on their own.[12]

This is not to say all societies in all times have been successful in achieving communal objectives. In Judeo-Christian societies, for instance, traditions encourage the use of alcohol in custom and celebration. These cultural practices contribute to certain dilemmas when substance abuse arises. Misguided attempts at outright prohibition have failed spectacularly, which is why legal and social resources are instead directed at controlling the negative impact of excessive or irresponsible alcohol consumption on both individuals and society alike. Unlike Muslim societies, which have enjoyed greater, though not absolute, success through legislative bans, or Jewish communities that inculcate discipline among their members, liberal democracies struggle to balance individual freedoms and social responsibilities.

Alcohol is an appropriate example of the kinds of challenges with which economists concern themselves when they discuss allocative efficiencies. In a free society, one is entitled to celebrate by having drinks with friends and family. At the same time, one has the right to live without having to worry about motorists driving recklessly. The individual choices made by each member of society—when to drink, how much to drink, and being vigilant around someone who drinks—contribute to an aggregate outcome for society: so many celebratory toasts equals so many vehicular homicides in any given year.

As we shall see in the next chapter, these are the small decisions that result in a larger outcome that impacts the whole of society. Concern for individual freedom and a sense of fairness prohibit the targeting of certain segments of the population. Although it is younger men who are responsible for the overwhelming majority of problems associated with alcohol abuse, there is a reluctance to single them out, if for no other reason than it is this segment of the population upon which society depends for protecting all of us in military confrontations.

Critics of the Internet argue that, by virtue of placing a disproportionate value on technology for the sake of technology, resources are thus misdirected. One has to look at the fate of Iridium to see the ensuing folly.[13] At the time of its bankruptcy, Iridium had 66 satellites in its constellation, at a cost of $6 billion, orbiting the earth. To think that billions of dollars were squandered on a venture of unimaginable, but misguided, ambition is a tremendous loss not only to the investors who lost fortunes, but also to the society that has to absorb the misallocation of resources on a monumental level.

The sense of allowing the unfettered allocation of society's resources without restriction is often questioned. It is true that society has a valid interest in safeguarding its resources—both human and material. Thomas Payne first championed this idea in America as political discourse in *Common Sense.* The acceptability of using resources in ways that are superfluous or ill advised has greater currency with the advent of the Internet. What encourages this kind of criticism and debate is precisely the winner-take-all outcomes that offend our ideas about fairness. That the outcomes of these contests result in an exaggerated allocation of society's resources raises questions about the ability of the marketplace to reconcile demand and supply.

The argument that society needs to reconcile the inherent conflict between the private and the public as a matter of social policy was nicely addressed in *Private Wants and Public Needs,* a series of essays compiled and edited by Edmund Phelps.[14] The consequences of the outcomes for these contests determine how society's resources are allocated precisely because the players are involved in an industry that affects virtually everyone. The conflict between the private and the public is at the heart of Borsook's criticism of the Silicon Valley. When young men, who are immature but blessed with extraordinary talents, are allowed to act selfishly in winner-take-all contests, then society has a legitimate stake in addressing the negative impacts that are the by-products of the outcomes in these contests.

This is different from claiming moral outrage that Americans are walking around with cell phones while children in Bangladesh are starving. The question of allocative efficiencies, rather, addresses the wasteful investments made (recall Iridium) and the distorted rewards at stake in these contests (consider stock options worth hundreds of millions of dollars paid by firms that have never made a profit). Robert Frank and Philip Cook make a point that "rewards tend to be concentrated in the hands of a few top performers, with small differences in talent or effort often giving rise to enormous differences in incomes."[15]

Frank and Cook examined the explosion in income inequalities in the United States by researching incomes in all kinds of labor markets. Intrigued by the inability of classic economic theory to explain this phenomenon, they concluded that "[t]raditional economic theories focus on differences in the education, training, experience, and other attributes that people bring to their jobs—important factors, to be sure.

Yet growing inequality has not resulted from significant changes in these factors."[16] They also conclude that the distorted distribution of human capital—people who work—can be best explained by the absence of allocative efficiencies that exist. "At a minimum," Frank and Cook wrote, "we can say that the data are largely consistent with the winner-take-all explanation, but largely inconsistent with competing explanations."[17]

What emerges, then, is the proliferation of winner-take-all contests throughout the economy in general, and in the high-tech industry in particular. The unprecedented wealth created by Internet companies has fueled further speculation in the high-tech market. Alan Greenspan's concern that the market surge in the 1990s was characterized by an "irrational exuberance" was another way of voicing concern that traditional theories about how the world works were not consistent with the predicted or anticipated data.

Once upon a time in Holland a tulip bulb cost more than a house.[18] That was not the product of rational market forces; it was the result of human folly. When Gary Hamel boasts in the *Harvard Business Review* that in Silicon Valley a $2 million house is a teardown, this isn't an achievement: it *is* an affront to our very sense of decency.

The winner-take-all contests that characterize the Internet economy create distortions that undermine allocative efficiencies of society's resources. This is to say that traditional market forces are interrupted by how competition is structured. It is the unsustainable valuations of companies built on the vapor of dreams, the naked greed exacerbating the speculative frenzies when IPOs (Initial Public Offerings) are launched, and incomes based not on absolute performance but on speculation that make market valuations impossible to sustain. Furthermore, distortions are created when resources are allocated in an inefficient and irresponsible manner. When $6 billion is spent to have 66 satellites orbiting the earth (to no one's benefit) and then ends in the loss of this investment capital, then everyone is worse off.

That winner-take-all contests have proliferated at such a breathtaking pace is partly a result of imperfect markets and traditional market failures. That's the bad news. The good news, of course, is that rather than defying the laws of economics, by virtue of the behavior of Silicon Valley and the Internet as an industry conforms to theories about how world works, these theories are validated. If there is any unease, after all, in realizing that the labor market of Silicon Valley runs counter to classic theories about wages in a traditional market economy, then it is reassuring to see that the winner-take-all theory of rewards steps in to offer a satisfactory explanation.

That the explanation for the observed phenomenon *makes sense* is one thing. That it is *desirable* is quite another. The rapid-fire pace of the Internet, in both a relentless pace of innovation and how completely it is penetrating all aspects of our economic and social lives, is in fact daunting. That these markets resemble those for celebrities—movie and rock stars, entertainment personalities and champion athletes—raises the fundamental question: Should business be a form of celebrity entertainment or non-contact professional sports or something else?

There is no right or wrong answer to this question, of course. Throughout the second half of the twentieth century, economists commented on the consistent—but puzzling—fact that in many instances, individual decisions lead to less than optimal outcomes. This is true whether we look at an individual consumer or an individual company. Economists have long noted the fact that markets often fail to conform to the "invisible hand" that Adam Smith praised. What is puzzling is the idea that individual self-interest could, somehow, undermine the Darwinian impulse to move things along the continuum known as progress. Then again, sedimentary rocks are littered with the fossils of mutants and the extinct. In the competition to preserve a species' protoplasm, the dinosaurs are big-time losers, after all. They aren't around; we are. Economists refer to such doomed experiments as market imperfections and market failures.

In the brief history of the Internet, the diversity of technology and the competition for resources has been fierce. The forces of competition in a market economy have been exaggerated by the winner-take-all outcome inherent in technological innovations. This is to say that changes in technology at times alter fundamentally the terms of competition, changing the playing field altogether. It is like playing a football game in which not only do the goal posts keep moving, but so do the lines on the field. A firm may be engaged in competition for a market that may be rendered obsolete by new technology (Iridium was doomed by cheaper telephony technologies), or its market may cease to exist (real-time market quotes rendered obsolete satellite services of the market ticker). To a considerable degree, the volatility throughout Silicon Valley reflects the unforgiving impact of classic market forces on emerging companies, developing markets and rapidly evolving technological advances. To understand how Silicon Valley is not exempt from the market forces of the "old economy," let us consider the role of market imperfections and market failures.

MARKET IMPERFECTIONS AND MARKET FAILURES

If a given market consists of products that are not completely developed, or that are in conflict on some level, then the market is imperfect. The most vivid example was the competition within the video format technology. The two competing formats—VHS and Beta—

existed simultaneously, which created an imperfect market. The VHS format won meaning that for the duration of the competition for market share (survival), the disadvantage falls on the consumers still using the Beta format.[19] Markets in which technological innovations change the terms of competition in this manner contribute to a tumultuous business environment. Markets for products and services throughout the high-tech industry are characterized by these kinds of market imperfections and market failures. It is not surprising that the aggregate outcomes in these contests are far from optimal, for individual companies, any given market, or the economy as a whole.

In market imperfections and market failures alike, externalities play a significant role. An externality, sometimes called a "neighborhood effect," is something that distorts the true costs or profits of a business. Consider a youngster who starts a business out of his parents' home with mom and dad helping out for free. If the business is slightly profitable, but only because it does not reflect the rent, salaries, taxes, and other costs associated with running a business properly, then there are serious questions about the viability of the venture. Absent the direct subsidy provided by the parental home, it is not clear whether a youngster's entrepreneurial effort would be profitable.

What is true for a youngster who launches a business from his parents' garage is also true for society as a whole. Consider high tech where technologies developed under government contract (think of vast investments in research and development carried out for national defense and space exploration technologies) subsequently benefit the private sector. Critics point out that the so-called New Economy depends to a considerable degree on the appropriation of publicly funded technological advances and innovations realized through considerable taxpayer-funded outlays in physical and educational infrastructure. This can be persuasively argued, and constitutes the transfer of public intellectual property and innovation to the private sector. In other words, when know-how and technologies developed with public funds are transferred to the private sector, which then benefits handsomely, what we have is an externality that enriches private investors while depriving taxpayers of a reasonable return on their (public) investment.[20]

To understand how the transfer of public goods to private individuals has worked historically, let us now turn to a brief discussion of one externality, specifically, the real estate market in Greater Miami. In south Florida, where there are significant numbers of retired people, there are certain opinions voiced that reflect a lack of generosity. It is not uncommon for older Americans to want to live in communities that exclude young children. There are a few communities that prohibit residence by minors, simply because the like-minded residents wish to live free from the noise and ruckus that is inevitable when children are at play. Courts have upheld that this is their right, and there is nothing inherently objectionable with a community that wishes to exclude a certain segment of the population on the basis of their age. The wish to live out one's retirement without children in one's life may appear to be peculiar, but it is neither incomprehensible nor offensive.[21]

It could be argued that these impulses reflect a kind of self-interest that borders on the selfish. Perhaps, but it certainly does not come as a surprise that many of these people also object to government intervention in the economy. Scattered within the high-rise condominiums that run up and down Brickell Avenue in Miami and flank Collins Avenue in Miami Beach, many older Americans look out upon sweeping views of south Florida, while they sit back and decry the costs of carrying out public works and projects. Generalized opinions oftentimes reflect familiar arguments: the lifestyle they enjoyed is the product of their work over many decades; the intervention of government in economic matters only weakens the market system; and the ambitious government programs squander resources because they are invariably ill-conceived and poorly executed.

The transformation of south Florida from swamps into swank high-rise condominiums, however, is in fact the product of direct government intervention. It is the U.S. Army Corps of Engineers that changed the landscape by creating the intercoastal waterway that made it possible for private developers to come in and profit handsomely from the bonanza handed them for the taking. Where swamps, mangroves, and marshes once were, Miami Beach and the ports of Miami and Everglades now stand. Interstate 95 now runs up and down the coast of Florida, uniting beach communities to the rest of the country. It was an ambitious government program that transformed the landscape and made urban real estate development possible. All it takes is one look at old photographs of Miami and Miami Beach to see what an inhospitable place Miami-Dade County used to be before the U.S. Army Corps of Engineers embarked on their programs to build infrastructure.

That real estate prices never reflected the actual cost of transforming a series of mosquito-infested tropical ponds into a sun-filled tropical paradise is a perfect example of an externality. The "market value" of these transactions among private sellers does not compensate all parties adequately for the true costs for the simple reason that one party is the taxpayers—through the institution of the U.S. Army Corps of Engineers, which provided its services for free. This is to say that the costs for the services provided by the U.S. Army Corps of Engineers was paid for by taxpayers and that the value added by this government agency was transferred free of charge to the private sector. Real estate in south Florida is an example of privately inappropriable social benefits transferred from government to a few private parties. That these private parties are able to enjoy privately the benefits the intra-coastal work projects have achieved is a classic example of how an externality contributes to an unfair competitive advantage.

In Silicon Valley and its surrounding communities, the U.S. Army Corps of Engineers plays an active role in transforming the physical landscape that allows for the creation of new real estate for the voracious appetite of expanding high-tech companies. If a $2 million house is nothing but a teardown, then it is clear that real estate is very scarce—and therefore highly coveted. In such a marketplace, when the U.S. Army Corps of Engineers dredges the San Francisco south bay, allows the destruction of marshes, and participates in safeguarding surrounding habitats so that business can expand, society has the right to request that taxpayers be compensated adequately for the wealth they have engendered. The difference between Biscayne Bay in Miami and the whole of San Francisco Bay is that in the former, the wealth created has benefited one segment of the population; while the wealth of the latter benefits an industry that has no need to be subsidized by society at large, apart from the job creation associated with the work of the Army Corps of Engineers.

Now consider the idea economists refer to as Intergenerational Equity. This concept refers to the idea that societies are oftentimes required to incur short-term debt in order to make investments deemed necessary and that rightfully will be paid off over time. Consider the construction of the interstate highways. If the United States incurred national debt in order to build the Eisenhower Highway System, it is only fair that this debt be paid by the various generations of taxpayers who use and benefit from these highways. The same argument is made for other social investments, whether these are to provide public universities, build hospitals, or construct hydroelectric plants that will generate electricity for decades to come.

It is here that economists make a distinction between spending and investing. In the United States, proponents for a "balanced budget" amendment to the Constitution fail to consider that there may be times when one generation incurs debt (fiscal deficit) to pay for something (a national highway system) that will be paid for over several generations (through taxes or tolls, or both). Consider someone who incurs debt in order to get a college education. This debt, in the form of "student loans," is, in fact, "deficit spending." This kind of expenditure is far different from a person who takes the same money and then takes a cruise around the world. Although deficit spending to secure an education is seen as an investment, incurring debt to take a self-indulgent vacation is imprudent spending. When an individual graduates and is then able to work at a professional level, the higher income over the course of that person's career will allow not only the payoff of the student loans, but also will allow the person to live a more satisfying life, both personally and materially. This cannot be said of someone who returns from an around-the-world cruise, which was paid for by incurring debt.

What holds true for an individual is also true for society. The problem with requiring that the government never incurs deficit spending is that it limits society's choices. Instead of constructing, for instance, a national highway system all at once, such an endeavor would have to be undertaken in piecemeal fashion. Of greater consequence for all concerned would be the difficulty in waging a successful military campaign if debt could not be incurred. That the United States was able to win the Second World War was due to a considerable degree to the sales or war bonds and the economic sacrifices made by an entire generation of Americans. Government bonds are one way the federal government sells its debt to the private sector. Deficits incurred by society are also justified if the ends are to make long-term investments that will benefit all members of society. Highways increase commerce, facilitate travel, and bring the nation closer together. Hospitals ensure that everyone's health and lives are safeguarded. Electric power makes everyone's life better.

Since the conclusion of the Second World War, significant investment in education and scientific and academic research has expanded dramatically the wealth of human knowledge. These advances are the products of investments made by two generations of taxpayers that build on human knowledge accumulated throughout history. That the Internet stands to increase exponentially the kinds of information, business opportunities, and options from which people will benefit will contribute to the diversification and growth of the economy for decades to come. It is clear that future technological and commercial innovations will require significant investments.

There are institutional mechanisms in place to direct private capital and investment into these endeavors. But the private sector cannot provide the long-term capital investments of the magnitude required exclusively on its own. It is not often clear how capital investments in infrastructure will benefit certain industries or markets specifically. The question of how these kinds of "deficit spending" investments will be paid can be more effectively addressed as they have in the past, which is through Intergenerational Equity. Recent advances in biotechnology, as breathtaking as the revolutions unleashed by microprocessors, are the result of joint research between the public and private sectors. The benefits of these discoveries, to individuals and to markets alike, are unknown, but definitely lucrative.[22] There is no guarantee that any specific research will be fruitful. But the costs of such research, however, can be determined, and they are staggering. That the Internet has begun to make tangible to individuals and business recent technological advances raises the question of how intergenerational equity can be more effectively and fairly determined. Recall that during the Gilded Age, Robber Baron Collis Huntington made a fortune for the Central Pacific Railroad by securing significant government loans on very lucrative terms, something that critics pointed out constituted an unfair competitive advantage. Questions about the obligation of private parties to compensate society adequately for the knowledge developed at taxpayer expense are valid ones.

What is clear, however, is that Silicon Valley has entered a consolidation phase, one in which the initial euphoria has subsided. The technology is better understood. The role the Internet is playing in the nation's economy is better defined. As Silicon Valley's economy conforms to the models about how the economy works, the basis is being laid for considering ways to ameliorate both market imperfections and market failures. That technological advances occur only after significant investments over a period of years, if not decades, requires careful consideration of how Intergenerational Equity will play a role in the continuing evolution of the market. These are dilemmas for individual investors, businesspersons, and public officials alike.

In the next chapter, we discuss how these dilemmas are more effectively addressed. In the quest of reaching rational decisions that allow us, individually and as a society, to reach optimal levels of efficiencies, certain ways of thinking about the Internet illuminate the challenges more clearly than others. Too many discussions about the Internet are filled with references to the "old economy" and the "new economy" in a careless manner that confuses the debate. If the consequences and opportunities new technologies offer are to be appraised properly, the level of discourse needs to examine intelligently the nature of these dilemmas and choices in broader terms.

Key #2

The Internet as an industry is characterized by the proliferation of winner-take-all contests and are subject to distorting natural market imperfections. The distortions that have emerged in e-commerce are further heightened by the role market imperfections and market failures play in the high-tech economy. Market imperfections refer to competition within evolving technology markets that are neither completely interchangeable nor mature. Market failures arise from the appropriation of technologies and innovations developed through public capital investments that are subsequently transferred to the private sector without fully compensating taxpayers. Public policy questions emerge if society is to be compensated by the diseconomies of externalities and how intergenerational equity will be addressed as advances in technologies require greater investment of societal resources.

NOTES

1. Mark Kellner, "Making Mailing Easy," *Silicon Alley Reporter*, Issue 26, Vol. 3, No. 6.

2. Paulina Borsook, *Cyberselfish: A Critical Romp through the Terribly Libertarian Culture of High-Tech*, p. 54.

3. Ibid., p. 205.

4. Robert Frank and Philip Cook, *The Winner-Take-All Society*, p. 2.

5. Ibid., p. 3.

6. When such a celebrity becomes widely known, the nature of his celebrity changes; when Carl Sagan, the Cornell University astronomer, became "famous" after making several appearances on the *Tonight Show* with Johnny Carson, his standing among his peers fell, for he upset the hierarchy within academia.

7. Robert Frank and Philip Cook, *The Winner-Take-All Society*, p. 4.

8. Glamorous companies such as airlines are always in the news whereas nonglamorous ones, such as waste management, are seldom mentioned. That an airline may lose money year after year while a waste management company may enjoy higher revenue and tremendous profits makes no difference to the amount of coverage either one receives; the public craves information about companies that fly airplanes and is indifferent to those that take care of society's refuse.

9. We routinely intervene in the economy to protect competition or alter the playing field in many areas of economic life, whether it is to prevent banking oligopolies or to ensure that firms historically subjected to racist discrimination are not disadvantaged in securing public projects.

10. Robert Frank and Philip Cook, *The Winner-Take-All Society*, p. 17.

11. Paulina Borsook, *Cyberselfish: A Critical Romp through the Terribly Libertarian Culture of High-Tech*, p. 18.

12. Guardianships are granted on behalf of adult individuals who are not capable of making decisions that consider their own well being, as well as the well being of others in society at large, in responsible ways.

13. The idea that engineers were required to spend thousands of hours—and the company's last cash reserves—to lower Iridium's 66 satellites to safe orbits in order to make sure that when they entered the Earth's atmosphere and burned, their debris did not fall on populated areas is a moral outrage, for it is such a waste.

14. Edmund S. Phelps, ed., *Private Wants and Public Needs*.

15. Robert Frank and Philip Cook, *The Winner-Take-All Society*, p. 24.

16. Ibid., p. 85.

17. Ibid.

18. A comprehensive survey of this speculative bubble is found in Mike Dash's book, *Tulipomania: The Story of the World's Most Coveted Flower*.

19. Consider in the 1970s the eight-track tape format for music.

20. Economists note that where externalities, such as unpaid social costs, exist, markets often fail to achieve Pareto-optimal results.

21. When communities of retirees want to exempt themselves from paying taxes to support public schools, however, a certain threshold is crossed.

It is in the interest of everyone in society to educate children, regardless of how many (if any) children one has. This is discussed in greater detail in Part II.

22. Consider the market reaction to patented gene therapy that cures cancer, or prevents the common cold. If such biomedical advances are made by government-sponsored research, how will the intellectual property rights be patented and marketed by the private sector in a way that compensates society fairly for having made this long-term investment?

CHAPTER 3

THE TYRANNIES AND DILEMMAS OF E-COMMERCE

In the 1980s, I recall participating in brainstorming sessions with Joann Andrews, a neighbor in Mexico, who was heading efforts to help the Mexican government protect wetlands that were vital breeding grounds for five species of endangered sea turtles. Her efforts were rewarded after years of work when Celestun, on the Gulf of Mexico, became a protected park. A sanctuary for endangered sea turtles, it is presently managed in partnership between the Mexican Government; Pronatura, a nonprofit organization working to safeguard Mexico's environment; and the Nature Conservancy because this park is one of that organization's "Last Great Places." During occasional visits to witness leatherback turtle hatchlings dash to the water, the mothers of which had been previously tagged, I would often engage conservationists who had spent weeks protecting these nests.

Once I noticed that someone had driven an old Volkswagen Beetle all the way from Berkeley, California. There was a sticker on the bumper that read, "Extinction is forever." True enough. But extinction is often the result of incremental steps, small decisions, and developments that unfold over the course of life, both of an individual and of a species. Over a longer period of time, some choices result in disappearance altogether.[1]

Where humans are concerned, the cumulative impact of a series of small individual decisions results in collective outcomes for a community and an economy. In some instances, we are held hostage to the unexpected (or undesired) outcomes of these small decisions. This is different from ordinary observations about supply and demand. If not enough people want nonstop service between New York City and Darwin, Australia, then that service will not be offered. One can always get from either of these cities to the other via connections. This is a straightforward proposition: absent sufficient demand, a product or service is not supplied.

Analyzing the unintended cumulative outcome of individual small decisions over an extended period of time is something altogether different. Economists have pondered this phenomenon since the 1960s when Alfred Kahn discerned the nature of "extinction" in the economic arena, which is simply the elimination of choices. What happens, in other words, when an individual's choice, over the medium- or long-term, results in unexpected consequences in the marketplace? What happens when choosing "x" over "y" is done so precisely because one assumes there will always be a choice between "x" and "y"? What if enough people choosing "x" results, at some point in time, in "y" no longer being offered? And what happens when, by virtue of "x" being the only option left, people feel deprived by the simple fact that they no longer have a choice?[2]

This phenomenon is referred to as the "tyranny of small decisions." Kahn, who first theorized about this curious example of a market failure, writes how this contradiction occurred to him:

> The event that first suggested the phenomenon to this writer was the disappearance of passenger railroad service from Ithaca, a small and comparatively isolated . . . community in upstate New York. It may be assumed the service was withdrawn because over a long enough period of time the individual decisions travellers made, for each of their projected trips into and out of Ithaca and other cities served, did not provide the railroads enough total revenue to cover incremental costs (defined over the same period). Considering the comparative comforts and speeds of competing media, those individual decisions were by no means irrational: the railroad was slow and uncomfortable.
>
> What reason, then, was there to question the aggregate effect of those individual choices—withdrawal of the service? The fact is the railroad provided the one reliable means of getting into and out of Ithaca in all kinds of weather; and this insufficiently-exerted option, this inadequately-used alternative was something I for one would have been willing to pay something to have kept alive.[3]

That passenger railroad service was discontinued resulted in a permanent reduction in the options consumers in Ithaca had available to them. However infrequently they may have exercised that choice is immaterial. The fact remains that the options the each individual consumer had were permanently reduced. This is how Kahn explains the impact:

When each traveller or potential traveller chose between the local airline, his own automobile, and the railroad, his individual choice had an
only negligible effect on the continued availability of the latter; it would
therefore have been irrational for him to consider this possible implication [discontinuation of passenger railroad service] of his decision. The
fact remains that [because] each selection of x over y constitutes also
a vote for eliminating y, each time necessarily on the assumption that
y will continue, y may in fact disappear. And its disappearance may constitute a genuine deprivation . . . [for] the total effect of individual opti-
mizing decisions may fall short of a collective optimum.[4]

It is clear that people in Ithaca, when planning a trip, considered
whether to take the train, plane, or their cars without thinking their
choice would become a referendum on whether passenger railroad
service should be permanently eliminated. Everyone thought they
would always have the railroad as an option. On cloudy or snowy days,
as Kahn points out, when the narrow country roads were impassable
and the airport was snowed in, the only reliable transportation in and
out of Ithaca was the railroad. On snowy days when the airport had
been shut down and the roads were impassable, travelers flocked to
the station and happily boarded the trains, however slow and uncomfortable they may have been.

There were not enough days of such inclement weather over the
course of the year to provide enough passengers to pay for the
railroad's operating costs to service Ithaca, however. Over time, the
railroad was unable to cover the marginal costs of providing passenger service to Ithaca. In due course passenger railroad service was
discontinued, thereby making it very difficult for people to travel to or
from Ithaca in winter during and after heavy snowfalls. On such days
people cancelled or postponed their travel plans. Leisure travelers were
stranded, and businesspersons had to reschedule their meetings. That
they had once decided not to ride the train on sunny days when they
could have done so now came back to haunt them.

Kahn was not the only Ithaca resident who would have been willing
to pay for the continuation of passenger railroad service, even if there
weren't so many snowy days throughout the winter. The problem, however, was that the cumulative effect of each individual consumer deciding on his mode of transportation over enough time resulted in the
entire community being subjected to the tyranny of small decisions.
In essence, the cumulative effect of each individual's decision to fly
or drive became, unbeknown to him, a free market referendum for
discontinuing passenger railroad service altogether.

Kahn observed and wrote about this phenomenon almost 40 years
ago. The problems associated with the tyranny of small decisions have
been eliminated over the past quarter century in many arenas of

economic life through the popularization of subscription sales. Consider for a moment what would happen if symphonies or major league baseball teams had to cover their costs simply on the number of tickets sold to each individual performance or game. There would most likely be insufficient attendance over the course of a season to cover their costs. To avoid empty seats in concert halls or bleachers in ballparks from becoming referendums on discontinuing concerts or ball games as options for people in any community, a solution was necessary.

It is this: by selling one subscription of tickets covering the entire season, enough revenue is raised to cover almost all of the marginal operating costs. Regardless of attendance to any individual performance or game, both symphonies and baseball teams are able to cover their minimum costs in any given year. This allows fans of classical music and professional baseball alike to guarantee that their patronage ensures the economic viability of their cultural and entertainment options for cultural and sporting events, regardless of whether aficionados and fans will be able to attend every single performance or game. Local symphonies and hometown teams, for their part, are delighted that the sale of season's tickets constitutes an economic vote of confidence that supports both musicians and baseball players.

Of course communities avail themselves to financial support from government and the private sector. Local governments use their budgets to support and strengthen both the arts and sports. Whether it is through tax breaks to build concert halls or stadiums, or by providing funding for a cultural and sports programs, public funds play an important role. So does support from the private sector, whether it takes the form of corporate sponsorship of a team or facility, or philanthropic organizations that provide underwriting. In recent years, stadiums themselves have become "branded," such as 3Comm Park in San Francisco or the American Airlines Arena in Miami, which is not too different from the way public television has "branded" the televised broadcasts of the Boston Pops.

Had the railroad in Ithaca been able to sell blocks of tickets to passengers (and potential passengers) to use during inclement weather each winter season, it may very well have been able to cover the marginal costs of continuing to provide passenger railroad service to that community.

That natural market forces eliminate choices we want is a market imperfection. There are, however, strategies for preventing market failures that occur when the marginal costs of an economic option are not covered by the market. Consider train service in Ithaca. The train service company, for example, could have sold "inclement season passes" for one price that would have been good for a given number

of rides when the airport was snowed in and the roads were impassable. Individuals such as Kahn would have purchased the pass just to
know that they were guaranteed seats on the train in the event they
had to travel somewhere during the winter months without having to
worry about snowstorms.

The knowledge that by purchasing an inclement weather pass ensures the continuation of passenger railroad services gives consumers peace of mind. In the event that they did not use all the rides for
which their pass was good, they could have given them away to others
that could have used them. They could have also traded them in for
passage on sunny days, which was one way the railroad could make
potential passengers into actual passengers during the long sunny days
of summer. Or they could simply be resigned to the fact that the purchase of the inclement weather pass was the price paid to make sure
train service remained a viable option for the community. This is what
season ticket holders for the symphony and baseball games presently
do to justify their investment when the season's over and they have
unused tickets on hand.

The feeling of deprivation is not relegated to a university professor
who likes to take train rides, or a sole music lover who delights in concerts, or an individual baseball fanatic. The deprivation of choices can
affect an entire community's sense of identity. A vivid example of how
the residents of an entire city can feel genuinely deprived when a cultural resource is taken away from it unexpectedly is found in Barcelona.
In January 1994, welders working on the stage of the Gran Teatre del
Liceu, the world-famous opera house that was the centerpiece of the
city's cultural life, accidentally set fire to stage curtains. The entire
structure was destroyed in a tremendous conflagration. Built in 1847,
the Liceu had been an integral part of the cultural lives of the people
of Barcelona. It would take $120 million and five years to rebuild. For
those five years, however, a shadow fell over the cultural life of
Barcelona in ways that people had not anticipated. The deprivation was
genuine.[5]

It is clear, then, that having remedies to ameliorate the deprivation
of economic choices that result from the tyrannies of small decisions
is necessary to prevent market failures. The integrity of market economies, in fact, is maintained when the negative impact of distortions and
imperfections is ameliorated both through intervention on a policy level
and corrective measures. The disappearance of choices, whether for
an individual or a community, is best prevented by safeguarding against
the tyranny of small decisions that impoverishes our lives.

Let us fast-forward two decades out of Ithaca and land squarely in
San Francisco, another city with inclement weather, to see how technological innovations associated with the Internet have given rise to

other tyrannies of small decisions. In the second half of the 1980s, the clever young nerds who would evolve into the "cypherpunks" decried by Paulina Borsook, were impressed with themselves. It was much ado about vanities and status. One geek tried to score one up on the others, proving his worthiness as a killer programmer, whatever that might mean at any given time. In the computer programming subculture of Silicon Valley, these contests were of one-upmanship, and the rewards were renown and respect of other truculent nerds. For most of humanity (which was out of the loop on the importance of these rivalries and contests in pursuit of status and ranking within the high-tech community) these young men's cleverness would have gone unnoticed save for the fact that they impacted the rest of us in dramatic ways.

One of the more intriguing ad hoc competitions centered on programs that would surreptitiously invade someone's computer, gather information on the user's hard drive, and report back to the originating computer. The invention of programs that could be downloaded into the hard drives for the expressed purpose of collecting information about individuals innocently surfing the World Wide Web threatened the very idea of privacy.

Imagine if information on such things as which software programs were on the hard drive, the history of Web sites the user had visited on the World Wide Web, where in each site he visited, what he downloaded or copied, and any other data the originator specified were reported back to the originating computer. This information could subsequently be stored, analyzed, and sold to anyone for any purpose. It was very difficult for someone who was not computer literate to understand the implications of such software programs. It was even more difficult for programmers to explain themselves and their achievements to non-nerds. Being able to explain themselves was important, after all, for this was a prerequisite to their being able to boast and show off.

It was serendipity that many of these meetings and interviews with outsiders were held often enough at all-night Chinese take-out restaurants in San Francisco and San Jose—and in the adjacent communities in between that are connected by Highway 101, the concrete artery that runs through the heart of Silicon Valley. "Think of these programs as if they were Trojan Horses," one programmer explained to me in the summer of 1988, explaining himself by way of an analogy. "But instead of invading like the Greeks did, the program launches itself, collects tons of data, then seals itself up and returns to the originator."

I looked puzzled. In subsequent interviews with these young men, a metaphor emerged over these late-night encounters over and over again that was inspired by the Chinese food. "Think of it this way," another programmer said, as would others over the following months. "It's like a Chinese fortune cookie. If you can read a person's habits, then you can tell what he's likely to like, likely to go, and likely to buy." One programmer went so far as to crack open a fortune cookie, unfurl the piece of paper, and hold it up for me to see, when we once met for a late-night dinner at a small restaurant in San Francisco's Chinatown near my residence. "Imagine doing this backward. The fortune is everything on your hard drive. It curls itself back up. It inserts itself into the cookie. And the cookie comes back to me. I open it, read it and then I know everything about you that I want to know. And you have no idea that I've done this!"

Instead of predicting the future, in other words, this programmer's electronic version of a Chinese fortune cookie would anticipate the future consumption behavior of an individual. Over time and because of widespread usage throughout Silicon Valley, "Chinese fortune cookie" became, simply, "cookie," a shorthand version that replaced the more cumbersome three-word phrase.

Cookies have given rise to an entire industry. The collection, analysis, and selling of personal data secured by billions of cookies gathering information on hundreds of millions of computers linked to the World Wide Web allows data brokers to generate phenomenal amounts of personal information as never before. The most exact consumer profiles can be generated, resulting in razor-sharp targeting of consumers.

DoubleClick, Inc., which is the Internet's largest advertising company, entered the information-gathering business with tremendous enthusiasm. The legal and ethical implications of the invasive nature of this emerging high-tech information industry, however, have made many people anxious, privacy advocates and investors alike. When DoubleClick purchased Abacus Direct, a database consisting of millions of names, addresses, and information about the purchasing habits of millions of consumers compiled from the largest direct-marketing mail order catalogs, the idea of combining information about the online and real-world consumer information on millions of Americans raised serious concerns. DoubleClick's announcement that it intended to combine all these data into comprehensive dossiers on millions of consumers, which would also include their browsing habits and actual identities, horrified many. Its stock plunged. The company was then forced to shelve its plans to reassure investors—and the public—that it was not engaged in a corporate effort to destroy the privacy of millions of consumers. In a few short years, the benign bravura of the first cookies now stood to become a monstrous invasion in the lives of the American people.

This is different from analyzing information gathered voluntarily from consumers. When the Federal Trade Commission (FTC) ordered the

1998 Children's Online Privacy Protection Act, which took effect in April 2000, for instance, the government was concerned that youngsters would be easily manipulated into giving out personal information about themselves and their families. These fears were well founded because almost half of children surveyed by the Annenberg Public Policy Center stated that they would provide personal information, including their names and addresses, to online companies in exchange for a $100 gift.[6] This information would provide data brokers with a more complete profile of individual consumers, thereby making it easier to target specific segments of Americans by their specific demographics. Adults are free to provide personal information in exchange for compensation, of course, but what cookies do is not this kind of private market transaction.

Even when information is given voluntarily, there are privacy issues raised. Consider the bankruptcy filing of Toysmart.com. The sale of the customer database, compiled from the public with the promise of confidentiality, was one of the assets the company sought to liquidate. The FTC issued a plan designed to limit the ability of the online retailer to sell private information as part of its assets. As lawyers and the courts struggled to hammer out the legal guidelines that will govern rules of commerce regarding the online economy, it raised important questions. Indeed, IBM announced on November 29, 2000, that it had appointed Harriet Pearson as its chief privacy officer, moving ahead of both the White House and Congress. "I want to work with industry to make privacy statements simpler, easier to understand, and much easier to communicate what they're doing with the information," she said.[7] For policymakers, nevertheless, unresolved issues lingered. Is the online surrender of privacy based on the promise of confidentiality, an asset that can be sold to a third party? Isn't Congress the proper body to resolve the disputes that arise from these issues?

Regardless of what DoubleClick's true intentions may be in seeking to combine so much information on so many consumers, however, what matters is the emerging tyranny individual decisions on the Internet represent. Instead of providing for greater options, the growing use of cookies is generating conflicts in many other areas of economic life. If people in Ithaca were unknowingly thrust into a referendum on having passenger railroad service as an option, then consumers are now subjected to the proliferation of similar market failures that not only invade their privacy, but also are fast reducing the choices they have. To understand this phenomenon, consider the impact Amazon.com has, not in cyberspace, but in the real space.

Every time someone purchases a book on Amazon.com, that is a sale a real bookstore somewhere did not make. To be sure, Amazon.com has contributed to expanding the market for books in general. There are many other people who are buying more and more books precisely because Amazon.com makes it convenient to do so. There are a significant number of consumers who live overseas and are grateful to have access to an online retailer that can sell virtually anything published in the English language (provided it is not out of print). The market for books is, in fact, larger and more diverse because of the comprehensive databases that consumers can access from the convenience of any computer linked to the World Wide Web. These databases include not only information about books, but also professional reviews, commentary from readers, suggestions on other titles that may be of interest, and rankings on popularity. An added feature, of course, is that Amazon.com entices browsers to become shoppers by offering generous discounts.

Furthermore, Amazon.com counts on billions of dollars to use in its quest to build market share. Recall Paul Krugman's puzzled observation about Internet companies that were pursuing "a full-scale go-for-broke strategy right from the start," indifferent to losing millions upon millions year after year. If Amazon.com was prepared to offer a discount for its books and, in fact, lose money on every transaction, what was the purpose of this strategy?

Amazon.com's founder, Jeff Bezos, was frank in explaining that they weren't in the book retailing business, but in the consumer information business. If losing money on every book they sold meant that they were building a market position consisting of millions of consumers whose browsing patterns they could analyze and whose online shopping habits they could track, they could compile an enormous database from which to generate marketing profiles. Amazon.com was pretending to be a bookseller when it was fast becoming an information broker. Amazon.com was fast appropriating for itself the market DoubleClick wanted to develop.

This is where two trends merge. For one, Amazon.com could only gather information through the aggressive use of cookies. In the process, however, consumers were falling into another predicament of the tyranny of small decisions. Whenever a consumer chooses between a local bookstore and Amazon.com, this has the implication that the local bookstore may disappear altogether. What Kahn observed of passenger railroad service in Ithaca, the fact remains that each selection of x over y constitutes also a vote for eliminating y, each time necessarily on the assumption that y will continue, y may in fact disappear, holds true for bookstores.

That Amazon.com had the economic wherewithal to spend hundreds of millions of dollars to create a complicated distribution and fulfillment network gave it a tremendous competitive advantage. In the time it took for an independent bookstore to place a special order,

Amazon.com could have it delivered to a customer. That Amazon.com had the discretion to pursue a strategy of building market position by losing money on every transaction proved a windfall to consumers. Although in principle most people voice support for local businesses, after all, it is in their rational self-interest to take advantage of the discount Amazon.com was able to offer that their local bookstore could not.

Consider what happened when the fourth installment in the Harry Potter series of books by J.K. Rowling was released in July 2000. Hundreds of thousands of readers took advantage of the fact the two largest online booksellers, Amazon.com and bn.com, offered the book at a 40 percent discount. Within a matter of days more than half a million copies had been sold just by Amazon.com, creating a publishing sensation. National chains were forced to offer discounts, simply to remain competitive and hoping that customers would make an additional purchase while in the stores. Independent booksellers were in a difficult position. If they matched the discounts, they would make no profit on the book. If they didn't, they lost customers to both off-line and online discounters.

Readers, of course, were making individual choices that were rational, just like people in Ithaca independently chose one by one whether to take the train, plane, or their cars on each trip. The cumulative effect, however, was that, by taking advantage of an online discount, the viability of independent bookstores was on referendum.

There are readers who are cognizant of this fact. In Coral Gables, Florida, for instance, Books & Books is an independent bookstore that has long been active in the city's cultural and literary life. The owner, Mitch Kaplan, has been facing more vigorous competition now that a large Barnes & Noble has opened up a couple of blocks away. When the Harry Potter book came out, Barnes & Noble held a party for children on the evening of July 7 just so it could start selling the books one minute past the stroke of midnight. Barnes & Noble offered cookies and coffee, costumes, and prices—a 40 percent discount on the eagerly anticipated book. To the relief of many parents who were stunned at the cost of this children's book, the discount was as tempting as it was welcome. Many readers in Coral Gables, however, purposefully chose as a matter of principle to forgo a discount simply to support Mitch Kaplan and his store. Books & Books sold about 175 copies of the Harry Potter book on the first day it went on sale, a vote of confidence for this exemplary south Florida concern.

The semblance of a backlash against discounts that threaten the existence of bookstores is recognition of the tyranny of small decisions. Between 1994 and 2000, which is the time frame in which Amazon.com embarked on an aggressive program to secure market position, the American Booksellers Association (ABA) reports that almost half the independent bookstores in the United States went out of business. In what has been described as a "guerrilla war" waged by the independent bookstores, they have continued to lose ground. As an industry, it might become extinct. Even in communities where citizens are concerned about their quality of life, the tyranny of small decisions has unintended consequences. The Corner Bookstore, which opened for business in Ithaca in 1833 and survived both the Civil War and the Great Depression, was forced to close in the aftermath of Amazon.com's aggressive discounting policy.

The disappearance of independent bookstores is not unlike the disappearance of passenger railroad service. That online booksellers are prepared to sell books at a loss continues to have the unintended effect of resulting in a referendum on whether consumers want neighborhood bookstores. When an individual goes online to buy a book, however, what that individual's decision results in is a vote for the extinction of the independent bookstore. The cumulative effect of these small decisions—book by book, sale by sale—has had, in half a decade, the cumulative effect of decimating the ranks of independent bookstores.

There are two questions that arise from these observations. The first one considers the unintended impact online book sales have on the communities in which people live. The familiar pastime of spending a rainy afternoon browsing in a bookstore, to stumble upon books by chance, is disappearing along with the bookstores. The role bookstores, like coffee shops and neighborhood cafés, have played has been to strengthen a sense of community. As places where people meet one another, run into each other, and just spend time participating in the pedestrian life of their community, local stores serve a social purpose. It is the recognition of this simple fact that has contributed to what people mean when they speak about a community's "quality of life." Concerned citizens often object to developments that weaken the quality of their community's life.

Robert Frank reflects upon this noting that:

> [W]e often hear angry complaints from the left of yet another instance of the market's failure to reward small-scale enterprises that provide personal service and show a true sense of involvement with, and commitment to, their patrons. "Rich" national chains are accused of using their superior financial resources to drive out the smaller firms that everyone really prefers.
>
> The economist has never been able to make sense of such arguments. . . . The economist argues, with the facts on his side, that the large chains' ability to outbid the smaller firm results from its superior efficiency. Faced with a choice between locally provided service at one

price and chain-outlet service at a lower price, ... consumers seem overwhelmingly to choose the latter.[8]

But if this is the case, then why the constant outcry? Isn't it possible that people instinctively realize that the small decisions they make everyday end up in a cumulative outcome that is less than optimal?

Rushing into a McDonald's is done because it is convenient, not because one wants no other options in the future. Picking up a copy of Harry Potter at a 40 percent discount is done not to drive the independent bookseller out of business, but because saving the money is too tempting to pass up. One advantage that "national" chains enjoy, too, is that by virtue of having recognizable brand names, they can attract customers that make it possible for them to put locations to better use. A New Yorker visiting south Florida, for instance, may seek out Barnes & Noble to buy a guidebook or newspaper if for no other reason than that individual recognizes the name. If Barnes & Noble weren't there, then he or she would walk an additional block into Books & Books.

In a time when national chains have an international presence, consider a tourist strolling the streets of Paris or Tokyo and the relief he feels when he sees the Golden Arches. That local French cafés and Japanese noodle shops lose business to McDonald's has more to do with brand recognition, and not the quality or price of the fare offered. The cumulative effect in each of these instances, however, is that the familiarity of the brand name generates more sales. In the same way that Amazon.com sells books, to a large part, because it offers discounts, fast-food companies offer a known product that is standardized across the country. The nation's highways, in fact, are dotted with billboards and neon signs flashing brands for motorists who are seeking only convenience and do not have time to discover hometown cooking. For many, a fast and inexpensive mediocrity is a better alternative than a chance discovery. When consumers are short on time, the familiar wins over adventure and the unknown. The overall effect is that national chains can make better use of a location simply because they can attract customers who patronize them for no other reason than the convenience of a known brand name. It can be argued that this is why "efficiencies" are self-fulfilling expectations.

The second issue raised is one of the societal effects of the tyranny of small decisions. If Amazon.com is prepared to lose millions of dollars by selling books at cost, is this an unfair business practice? If online booksellers are prepared to use millions of dollars secured from investors to build a market position by incurring losses, does this constitute a predatory behavior? If one decides on a go-for-broke strategy, does one have a moral or social obligation to repair anything that is

broken along the way, such as America's literary tradition of independent booksellers that has played an integral part in the lives of communities across the nation's landscape since the mid-nineteenth
century?

The rapid disappearance of independent booksellers is the result of
an externality. One of the more notorious examples of predatory pricing occurred when British Airways incurred substantial losses on its
New York to London route for the expressed purpose of driving Laker
Airways out of business. Laker Airways filed suit in U.S. federal court
where it alleged that British Airways, among other airlines, had engaged in predatory pricing to drive it out of business.[9] Its vindication
came long after Laker Airways had been driven out of the lucrative New
York-London route.

Independent booksellers, by virtue of being small, and often specialized, businesses, have found it similarly difficult to present a united
front to defend their market position. Through the ABA, independent
booksellers have launched Booksense.com, an Internet site that works
like a hub to host and showcase hundreds of Web sites for their
members. The Web sites are created and maintained by each independent bookstore, thereby working to preserve the character of the
independents. Another experimental approach was conceived in
Contentville.com, a site that solicits editorial content, such as recommendations, reviews, and articles about books, which is envisioned to
help develop the market for books. Independent booksellers receive
equity in the Web site, with the hopes of generating sufficient investor
interest to become a viable enterprise.

Both Booksense.com and Contentville.com were launched in mid-
2000 and speak to the sense of urgency independent bookstores felt
about their uncertain futures.[10] The continuing loss of members is nowhere more in evidence than in seeing how their sales have fallen. In
1995, for example, independent bookstores sold about $1.91 billion.
Four years later their sales had fallen to $1.58 billion. During the same
time, the retail book market grew by $600 million. The prospects that
this decline can be arrested and reversed are not promising. That online
booksellers are prepared to incur losses constitutes an externality that
is leading a market failure in the book retailing market.

There are public policy issues involved. In the same way that one
day people in Ithaca woke up to read the news that passenger railroad
service would be discontinued, Americans are finding that neighborhood bookstores are shutting their doors for good. How the disappearance of independent books changes the character and quality of life
of communities around the country is a serious matter because it affects everyone. That these changes are precipitated by what amounts

to predatory pricing is of equal concern.[11] That this strategy is being carried out for an ulterior motive—to establish dominance in the information brokering business through the widespread use of cookies—raises the specter that, once Amazon.com has secured its market position, should it withdraw from selling books, the damage done to the industry will take years, if not decades, to correct.

The realization that the tyranny of small decisions made online was affecting the off-line world has been of growing concern to activists. In 2000, several nonprofit organizations joined together to create the Turning Point Project to raise public awareness and galvanize support on behalf of besieged local establishments. "As an individual, you can do the following," their call to arms proclaimed. "First, shop local; if you can find what you need in your neighborhood, but it. Don't buy online unless absolutely necessary. The momentary convenience is not worth killing your local bookstore, specialty market, wineshop, drugstore."[12] The concern behind this plea is the sense that as individuals, and as a society, the quality of our own lives, and that of our community, diminishes when our options are reduced.

If Amazon.com is not really in the business of selling books, does it have any business in ruining merchants who are?[13]

I make these observations from the perspective of an economist. Others, however, have been equally vocal in voicing their concerns. Andre Schiffrin, who was the managing director of Pantheon, before founding the New Press, expresses his same concern from the viewpoint of an insider and publisher:

> C. Wright Mills originally organized the inquiry that showed how national brands such as Tip Top and Wonder had replaced the small bakeries that used to be in every town. The large industrial outfits initially offered bread at prices that greatly undercut local bakeries. They also encouraged local grocery stores to give more shelf space to their bread by hiking up discounts. Price differentials were at first sufficiently attractive to drive the smaller producers into bankruptcy. Having eliminated the competition, the companies raised their prices in predictable monopolistic succession and Americans were left with plastic-wrapped and plastic-tasting bread that was more expensive than the locally produced loaves it replaced. Only many decades later did specialist bakeries begin to flourish again in the large cities, selling excellent but very expensive loaves to the small numbers that can afford them.[14]

In an ideal world, options, for individuals and society alike, would be expanded. That the Internet was contributing to the erosion in the options meant that as individuals and as a society we are confronting dilemmas. The troubles of independent bookstores are a harbinger for what awaits other industries in every sector of the economy. Over a period of time, barring corrective measures, the economy would be impoverished by the unintended impact wrought by these technological innovations. What is happening to independent booksellers is not an anomaly; it is the future as it is being shaped and defined by e-commerce. One need only to examine the parallel decimation in the ranks of independent travel agents to see the tyranny of small decisions reduce our options.[15] Indeed, every time someone purchases an airline ticket online that person is unwillingly participating in a referendum on whether travel agents should go the way of passenger railroad service in Ithaca. It is clear that the impact of market failures on local communities and economies centers on the search for a mechanism that can ensure individuals are able to enjoy more options, not fewer.

Cultural and sporting events that have devised subscription sales as a way of covering their marginal operating costs and ensuring that individuals have choices offer clues to how the tyranny of small decisions can be held at bay. If the promise their advent heralded is to be realized, then, we need to have a thorough understanding of the nature of these dilemmas. If the difficulties of independent booksellers are to be ameliorated, then it is necessary to address the challenges the Internet has thrust upon us.

To understand dilemmas confronting consumers and society now that e-commerce is fast becoming an integral part of our economy, it is first necessary to consider why hockey players wear helmets. Robert Frank notes that:

> Hockey players, given a choice, will seldom wear helmets; yet, when questioned privately, they will usually insist that they favor rules requiring them to do so. Why this apparent contradiction? Hockey players care about both their safety and winning hockey games. Ever so slightly, the wearing of hockey helmets reduces the effectiveness of individual hockey players, perhaps by restricting vision or hearing. Or, where the wearing of helmets is left optional, the decision to wear one may also make it more difficult for a player to intimidate opponents psychologically.[16]

Harvard economist Thomas Schelling first discussed the dilemma confronting hockey players. He noted that where individuals have to consider the actions of others, their own decisions are affected by these considerations. Schelling argued these dilemmas are an integral part of:

> [A]ctivities in which people's behavior is influenced by the behavior of others, or people care about the behavior of others, or they both care and are influenced. Most of these activities are substantially free of

centralized management in many societies, including our own, or subject to sanctions and proscriptions that work indirectly. . . . And though
people may care how it all comes out in the aggregate, their own decisions and their own behavior are typically motivated by their own interests, and often impinged on by only a local fragment of the overall
pattern.[17]

It might make sense for me to fly to Ithaca, instead of taking the
train. It might make sense for me to save a few dollars on the new
Harry Potter book by taking advantage of a discount offered by an
online retailer. It might also make sense for an individual hockey player
to forgo wearing a helmet, because the risk of injury is less of a consideration for him than is the advantage he would enjoy by not having his periphery vision or hearing reduced, not to mention he might
intimidate his opponent besides. But in the first two cases, my personal
interests ensure that a market failure will occur in which my subsequent
options will be permanently reduced in the future. In the latter, I am
engaged in a contest in which the best possible solution, that all hockey
players are required to wear helmets, thereby protecting each player
from serious injury while giving no individual player a competitive
advantage, is undermined by the natural outcome inherent in these
dilemmas.

Taking other people's actions into account when deciding what one
does is an externality. The only reason why a five-year-old boy in my
care was adamant about wanting a Razor scooter in the summer of
2000 was because his cousin had one, and he naturally had to have
one, too. If one's brother-in-law takes a holiday to Australia, then one
suddenly finds a similarly exotic journey is in order. When one's neighbor gets a new car, other residents in the neighborhood soon follow.
These are examples of demonstration effects, of course.

Externalities, by comparison, are different. Schelling notes that,
"[t]hese are either-or situations . . . [in which] you care about my choice
or my choice affects yours. You may not care but need to know:
whether to pass on left or right when we meet. Or you may not need
to know but care: you will drive whether or not I drive, but prefer that
I keep off the road."[18]

The solution is simply to join a self-restraining coalition. This is
what hockey players do. Schelling quotes an interview with Chicago
Blackhawks star Bobby Hull in October 1969 in which he confirmed
that, "[i]t's foolish not to wear a helmet. But I don't—because the other
guys don't. I know that's silly, but most of the players feel the same
way. If the league made us do it, though, we'd all wear them and nobody would mind."[19]

As Schelling observed, however, as we don't live on desert islands, our individual decisions are affected by the individual decisions of others. Not that no man is an island, but that no man lives in isolation. The choice hockey players face in deciding whether to wear helmets, then, is a "prisoner's dilemma." The classic illustration of a prisoner's dilemma concerns two prisoners, A and B, who have committed a crime.[20] Each is taken to a separate interrogation cell. Each faces two choices: confess or remain silent. Each prisoner is then informed of the consequences of his decision. If one confesses and the other doesn't, the one who confesses will testify for the prosecution and receive no jail time, whereas the one who doesn't confess will receive the maximum sentence, say, 30 years. If both confess, they will each incriminate the other, and accordingly each will receive an intermediate sentence of, say, five years. If neither one confesses, the prosecution only has enough hard evidence to convict each of minor offenses, and each will receive one year of jail time. The prisoners are not permitted to communicate with each other. Thus the set of choices each prisoner faces is represented in Figure 3.1.

What will each prisoner do? For prisoner A, if he confesses he will either go free (if prisoner B does not confess), or he will receive a five-year sentence (if prisoner B confesses). On the other hand, if prisoner A does not confess, he will either go free (should prisoner B also refrain from confessing), or he will receive a 30-year sentence (if prisoner B confesses and testifies against him). Prisoner A, of course, does not know what prisoner B will decide to do. Therefore, acting in his own best interest, prisoner A will confess, for he will either walk out a free man or, at worst, face a reduced sentence. Prisoner B faces the

B

		Confess	Remain Silent
A	Confess	5 years for A 5 years for B	0 years for A 30 years for B
	Remain Silent	30 years for A 0 years for B	1 year for A 1 year for B

Figure 3.1 The Prisoner's Dilemma

same choices. This dilemma is resolved when each prisoner choosing to confess to the police after each rationally evaluates his options.

The paradox, of course, is that if the prisoners had been able to communicate with each other, they would have come to an agreement in which they would have refused to confess. A collectively superior outcome would have been to spend one year in jail by refusing to confess than the five years they received by snitching. Of course for an agreement to refrain from confessing to work requires an enforcement mechanism. Let us say that prisoners A and B agreed beforehand that, if caught, neither would confess. What is to prevent either of them from breaking his word, cooperating with the authorities, and walking away a free man while his accomplice languishes in jail for 30 years? Absent an ethical code of honor, the threat of retaliation, or an enforcement mechanism, even if both prisoners agreed to refrain from confessing, once they are being interrogated by the police, each will find compelling incentive to break his word and in fact confess.

Hockey players face the prisoner's dilemma insofar as, barring an enforcement mechanism, while the players may agree to wear helmets, once the game is about to begin, any number of players can go back on their word, take off their helmets, and gain a competitive advantage. Schelling points out that in such cases of binary choices with externalities, individuals are better served by voluntarily joining self-restraining coalition. In other words, the league requires all players to wear helmets, and therefore no player can participate in a game without wearing one.

The best possible outcome for everyone, then, is one in which individuals voluntarily agreed to have their behavior restricted. This is a curious realization. This is why we are faced with a paradox. That we live in a democratic society in which the economy is shaped and defined, for the most part, by market forces makes it counterintuitive that in many contests, the best outcome is reached by not competing.[21] In many contests, in fact, a superior outcome is achieved by voluntarily agreeing to have one's rights restricted. In order to achieve an optimal outcome for society as a whole, individuals oftentimes choose to have restrictions imposed on their behavior. One reason the mob is able to function, after all, is that it has the threat of certain death in order to enforce silence among its members. Hockey leagues, on the other hand, enforce the rules that, back in 1969 when Bobby Hull was interviewed, were not part of the regulations. In the course of our daily lives, we, as members of society, encounter many situations in which we recognize that our actions are restricted in order to achieve a better outcome for society. That we all agree to stop when a traffic light turns red restricts the behavior of motorists, but obeying a set of rules that indicate when we must surrender the right of way to pedestrians and other motorists ensures an orderly flow of traffic.

Robert Frank, in fact, points out that:

> Hockey players, as a group, would not freely choose to live in a society that prevented them from imposing helmet rules. The libertarian who insists that the right not to be restricted cannot, as a matter of principle, ever be negotiated away, shows contempt for the rights of people to resolve such issues for themselves.
>
> Once the issue of collective restriction of individual behavior is recognized as no more a moral than a practical one, policymakers are led to focus on the task of assessing their constituents' preferences concerning the available choices.[22]

Bobby Hull knew that there are times when having a choice is really no choice at all.

Key #3

The Internet's impact on the economy is enormous. Two unintended effects, however, are the proliferation of the tyrannies of small decisions and prisoner's dilemmas for the whole of society. Where tyrannies of small decisions exist, there is a radical transformation in the kinds of options consumers and businesses each face. The decimation in the ranks of independent booksellers and travel agents, for instance, is contributing to the deprivation and impoverishment of communities throughout the United States. In instances where prisoner's dilemmas exist, on the other hand, the use of self-restraining coalitions are required in order to achieve, as individuals and a society, superior collective outcomes which would otherwise elude us. The Internet, then, challenges us as a society to prevent the negative effects of natural market imperfections and market failures. It is in ameliorating market imperfections and preventing market failures that policymakers have a legitimate role to play.

NOTES

1. Individual choices over the many days of one's life to smoke, for instance, may result in premature death after decades of smoking. An entire species may become extinct if it is no longer able to compete effectively in its environment, which is what occurred to the dinosaurs.

2. What would happen if, by virtue that enough people wanted to fly nonstop from New York to Darwin, Australia, airline service itself would no longer be offered at all to Sydney from Darwin? Would people in Sydney, for instance, be forced to travel to Darwin by first flying to New York?

3. Alfred Kahn, "The Tyranny of Small Decisions: Market Failures, Imperfections, and the Limits of Economics," *Kyklos* 19 (1966), pp. 25–26.

4. Ibid., pp. 26–27.

5. The importance of these resources in the lives of individuals and communities can be measured in how lives are affected. Joseph Hnilo boasted that one of his sons was preparing to go off to college on a full athletic scholarship. When the Gran Teatre del Liceu reopened in October 1999, Montserrat Cabelle and Jose Carreras performed. The return of the opera house, in fact, caused such giddy anticipation and genuine excitement that King Juan Carlos and Queen Sofia traveled from Madrid to attend the opening night, a royal validation for the people of Barcelona that this absence in their lives had not gone unnoticed.

6. Annenberg Public Policy Center, "The Internet and the Family 2000."

7. Joe Wilcox, "IBM Appoints Chief Privacy Officer," CNET News.com, November 28, 2000. Available online at http://news.cnet.com/news/0-1003-200-3898890.html.

8. Robert Frank, *Choosing the Right Pond*, pp. 170–171.

9. Interestingly, British Airways retaliated by filing suit in British High Court, seeking an injunction to prevent Laker from suing in U.S. court, the end result of which became a leading case on the "comity" standard in law. (See *Laker Airways v. Sabena Belgian World Airlines*, 731 F.2d 909, 926-927 [D.C. Cir. 1994].)

10. Steven Brill announced in October 2001 that Contentville.com would be folded.

11. The counterintuitive nature of e-commerce is both unsettling and confusing. Paul Krugman himself errs when he characterizes the online sale of books as an example of price discrimination. "Dynamic pricing is a new version of an old practice: price discrimination," the MIT economist wrote in the *New York Times*, October 4, 2000. "It uses a potential buyer's electronic fingerprint—his record of previous purchases, his address, maybe the other sites he has visited—to size up how likely he is to balk if the price is high." This is simply wrong. What online booksellers have engaged in is predatory pricing, a strategy that has decimated the ranks of independent bookstores in the United States. Since the mid-1980s, independent bookstores have had to compete with national chains, such as Waldenbooks and Barnes & Noble, which implemented the practice of discounting hardcover books. In the 1990s competition intensified with an avalanche of online discounters prepared to lose money on every transaction for the sake of establishing market share. The net result of this two-part campaign was the systematic elimination of competition. In the fall of 2000, when the number of booksellers in the nation had been reduced significantly, discounts came to an end. The *New York Times* reported that "the discount era in the bookstore business has virtually come to an end," in October 9, 2000, noting that the "price increases are a notable reversal for Amazon.com." That Waldenbooks and Barnes & Noble followed suit suggests that the policy of discounting, which resulted in stores selling inventory essentially at cost, was hurting retailers. Nevertheless, the behavior of national chains and online booksellers is consistent not with dynamic pricing but with predatory pricing intended to limit competition.

Thoughtful publishers were aware of what was going on. Andre Schiffrin in *The Business of Books*, notes that "[i]t was the decision to discount books—particularly best-sellers—that made the chains the phenomenon they are to-day. In many cities, the chains were the first to establish major bookstores, and there is no question that these stores now offer Americans greater choice than existed before. On the other hand, their progressive expansion has been harmful to the remaining independent stores. In a statement made to the *Financial Times* at the time of last years Frankfurt Book Fair, the German minister of culture (and former publisher) Michael Naumann predicted that if discounting was allowed in Europe, 80 percent of Germany's four thousand bookstores would close" (p. 124). The demise of independent bookstores in the United States is clearly a stunning example of one of the negative consequences of the Internet's ability to undermine the market economy.

12. Turning Point Project, "E-Commerce and the Demise of the Community," *New York Times*, July 24, 2000.

13. This ceased to be a rhetorical question when Amazon.com announced on August 31, 2000, that "[a]s we continue to develop our business, we might sell or buy stores or assets. In such transactions, customer information generally is one of the transferred business assets." This was announced as a press release, a mass e-mail to all customers, and flagged at the bottom of the site's main Web page. Amazon.com further announced that information secured with the understanding of confidentiality would be treated as proprietary asset of the company, not customers. Thus, consumers were advised, that "in the unlikely event that Amazon.com Inc., or substantially all of its assets are acquired, customer information will of course be one of the transferred assets." Andrew Shen, of the Electronic Privacy Information Center in Washington, D.C., when asked to comment on the change in policy by Amazon.com, replied, "We think some baseline standard for privacy protection is necessary. Amazon.com's privacy policy—and the recent revisions—is just an example of why. Internet consumers should not be forced to continuously go back and check a Web site's privacy policy. Internet companies should not be able to change how they protect your personal data—and at their whim."

14. Andre Schiffron, *The Business of Books*, pp. 121–123.

15. Whereas online retailers are prepared to sell books at discounts that independent bookstores cannot match, independent travel agents are confronting online airline ticket sales and the draconian reductions in the commissions paid to them by the airlines. The question then arises: if an airline slashes commissions while offering "online fare specials" that drive travel agencies out of business, are these "specials" in fact predatory pricing that, collectively, constitute an unfair business practice? Consider that Delta Air Lines relaunched its Web site in 2000 after its online sales approached $1 billion that year. The branding campaign, designed by Leo Burnett USA in Chicago, sought to enable the airline to secure a greater market position in the booming online travel category sales—to the detriment of independent travel agents around the country.

16. Robert Frank, *Choosing the Right Pond*, p. 122.

17. Thomas Schelling, *Micromotives and Macrobehavior*, p. 24.

18. Ibid., p. 213.

19. "The Stick That Sickens," *Newsweek*, October 6, 1969, p. 95.

20. A complete discussion of game theoretics is found in *Games and Decisions* by R. Duncan Luce and Howard Raiffa.

21. In some competitions, such as tic-tac-toe, the only way to win is by not playing at all.

22. Robert Frank, *Choosing the Right Pond*, p. 225.

CHAPTER 4

PRIVATE WANTS, PUBLIC NEEDS, AND THE SEISMIC SHIFT IN THE ECONOMIC LANDSCAPE

There are times when it is difficult to know what to think. "The Pulitzer Prize Photographs: Capture the Moment," was on exhibit at the Newseum/NY in New York throughout the summer of 2000. This was the first exhibition that included all the photographs that had been awarded the Pulitzer Prize since 1941. The photographs (some accompanied by supplementary images) had a statement that described the circumstances under which each was shot. A photograph taken by Steven Starr on April 20, 1969, was awarded the prize for 1970. The image, titled "Racial Protest at Cornell University," shows armed black students leaving Willard Straight Hall, the student union, after their demands have been met by the university and their armed occupation of the building ends. The body of the text that accompanied the photograph read:

> It's Parents' Weekend at Cornell University: 2,000 visitors crowd the campus. Thirty of them are asleep in the student union early April 19, when black students seize the building. Within minutes, militants have evicted parents.
>
> Their demands: A college at Cornell run by African-Americans, amnesty for three students threatened with suspension, and a protest against a cross-burning in front of the black women's dorm. A.P. photographer Steven Starr arrives, sees a student with a rifle at the window, but doesn't have his camera ready. "I was sick that I had missed that one shot. I got out a long lens, trained it on the window and waited."

Thirty-four hours pass. The university president grants the militants'
demands for amnesty. Starr is still there. "The door opened and I felt a
cold chill. I made my picture by instinct."[1]

It seemed odd that a photographer could remain in position for 34
hours, especially because there was no guarantee that the incident
would not drag on for days, and there were neither dining nor restroom
facilities close at hand.[2] The assertions made by the Pulitzer Prize committee were also at odds with what I had been told by others who were
witnesses to these events. This suspicious disbelief on my part compelled me to drop by and visit Stephen Poleskie, a member of the faculty present during the turmoil that engulfed the campus, at his home
subsequent to his retirement. As an instructor at the art department
with a reputation for integrity, Professor Poleskie was held in high re-
gard by the students. (As one of the few faculty members who sported
long hair, rode his Harley Davidson motorcycle to class, and flew the
biplane he had built himself over Cayuga Lake on the weekends,
Stephen Poleskie was one cool cat the students could dig.) "The takeover of Willard Straight Hall ended quickly. Once the university administration agreed to the students' demands, it was over. Everyone was
surprised. It was so sudden that everyone was caught off guard."
Stephen Poleskie continued, confirming that,

Steven Starr rushed back, but when he arrived, the occupation was over.
The students, faculty and bystanders were milling around outside. He
wanted to get a photograph, so he asked [student radical leader] Thomas
Jones if he would re-enact their leaving the student union. He agreed,
since without a photograph, it wouldn't be front-page news. And everything was re-enacted for the benefit of the press. That's the photograph
that was sent over the wires. It's a photograph of the re-enactment.[3]

The Associated Press stands by Starr's account. Kelly Smith Tunney
stated for the record "the AP pictures were taken as the radical students evacuated Willard [Straight] Hall. This has never been in dispute,
nor is it now. Not only did Steve Starr, the photographer, witness the
evacuation, but so did an experienced AP reporter, other newspaper
reporters and photographers and representatives from the university.
The student leaders paraded through the campus to a Black fraternity
house, all of this well documented on camera and covered extensively
by the national press."[4] Other witnesses, however, stand by their assertion that Steven Starr asked radical student leader Thomas Jones
to step back and walk out again to afford Starr the opportunity to take
photographs. This, then, is where we stand: the Associated Press says
one thing, eyewitnesses say another. Thomas Jones, now an officer

of Citigroup in New York, declined to say one way or the other whether he reenacted the surrender of Willard Straight Hall on April 20, 1969, after his exercise in terrorism ended peacefully. It is curious to see how historical integrity is at the mercy of the frailties and failings, the ambiguities and memories of human beings. Who is one to believe, the Official Story or eyewitness accounts? This, however, is instructive in the sense that it illuminates the nature of debate that surrounds ideas about how various actors should conduct themselves in the economic arena.

Armed with the same facts, different conclusions have been reached concerning how best to strike the balance between the freedoms and rights of the individual with the needs that arise from the fact that we live in communities. Of the various actors in the drama of student protest, there were many private wants and public needs at play. Thomas Jones wanted redress for his grievances. University officials wanted a peaceful resolution a situation that could result in violence at any moment. Members of the media wanted to report accurately the stunning events—students equipped with firearms—then unfolding on the campus of an American university.[5]

This complex nature of human interactions has given rise to an entire body of study among economists that ponder how human behavior in the economic arena affects and is affected by society at large. These externalities contribute to a symbiotic relationship, one in which it is almost impossible to divorce one's decisions from the cultural, political, and social environment in which we live. People want croissants for breakfast in Paris because that's what those around them eat for breakfast and that's what is readily available. People have miso soup for lunch in Tokyo, because that is a familiar comfort food that is a part of Japanese life. In a matter of weeks in the summer of 2000, youngsters in the English-speaking world fell under the spell of Harry Potter's adventures at Hogwarts School of Witchcraft and Wizardry because that is the thing to read at the moment and those unfamiliar with these adventures become social outcasts.

What to have for breakfast, what to have for lunch, what to read are everyday decisions. The specific economic choices that individuals make in all these aspects of their lives give rise to macroeconomic consumption patterns. Since the end of the 1950s, economists have theorized about the nature of these complex interactions between private and public sectors. There is often a conflict between what we would like to happen in society and what in fact happens, if for no other reason than the individual choices made by consumers result in aggregate outcomes that are deemed undesirable. We have seen this in the previous chapter when we saw how imperfect markets and market failures affect our economy. Political economist Alvin Hansen, cognizant of these deficiencies, is concerned about their social ramifications and thus champions the right of economists to address the social implications of economics in the lives of citizenry by noting:

> No one can dispute that we have become a rich society. We have made great advances on the purely economic plane. Unfortunately the progress we have made in many of the noneconomic aspects of life is limited, and in some areas we have, I fear, definitely retrogressed. . . . How do [we in society feel when we] observe the increase in mental disorders, crime and juvenile delinquency, or, on another plane, the current predominance of neurotic art?[6]

The question of the proper role in the economy has become more urgent with the advent of the Internet technologies. In the same way that officials at Cornell University woke up one morning in the spring of 1969 to find themselves in the predicament that they had to drop everything and attend to a crisis, the music industry woke up one day in 2000 to find it had to drop everything and address how Napster challenged not only the nature of copyrights and intellectual property rights but also how it threatened their business model. Indeed, the very nature of the technological innovations developed and introduced challenge our ideas about property rights, copyrights, the nature of property itself, privacy, and legal jurisdictions. In order to gain a more thorough perspective on the online economy, it is important to understand also ideas about the proper role of government in the marketplace.

John Kenneth Galbraith and Milton Friedman have long pondered the proper role of the government in the economic life of society. Friedman maintains that the "social consensus" regarding the "rules" that govern the marketplace prevail only when "most participants most of the time conform to them without external sanctions; unless that is, there is a broad underlying social consensus."[7] In his argument, the proper role of the government is "to provide a means whereby we can modify the rules, to mediate differences among us on the meaning of the rules, and to enforce compliance with the rules on the part of those few who would otherwise not play the game."[8]

Galbraith, on the other hand, is concerned with more than the rules of the game. He argues that what we're playing *for* is just as important as are the rules by which we play. Is a game worth playing if the prize is false? Galbraith says no. The danger in living in a society filled with abundance is that there are many things that tempt us but few that fulfill us. In consumer societies, he argues, there are many misguided wants. He makes his case by first recognizing the contrived nature of our wants in a society as affluent as ours. He then questions the role persuasion plays in how demand is determined. He believes that there is an:

Even more direct link between production and wants [which is] provided by the institutions of modern advertising and salesmanship. These cannot be reconciled with the notion of independently determined desires, for their central function is to create desires—to bring into being wants that previously did not exist. . . . [Indeed, a]s a society becomes increasingly affluent, wants are increasingly created by the process by which they are satisfied. Wants thus come to depend on output.[9]

Will we be duped into wanting junk just because companies produce junk?

In Barcelona, La Rambla is a broad, tree-lined boulevard that begins at the Plaça de Catalunya and ends at the waterfront monument to Christopher Columbus. Not far from the statue of Columbus is the Placa Reial, one of the finest squares in the entire city, which is graced by tall palms and amusing lamp stands by Antonio Gaudi. Once run down, it was revitalized for the 1992 Summer Olympics and now boasts fashionable restaurants and bars. It was here that the enduring power of demonstration effects on consumer behavior became evident over lunch with a certain five-year-old boy.

His desire for a Razor scooter was shaped by an externality: His older cousin had gotten one for his birthday, and now this boy felt deprived because he did not have one. The youngster tried to persuade me that he didn't know how he had managed to get along in the world this long without one. What he wanted was to have one of his own so he could scoot about the plaza like other kids. It was not entirely an unreasonable argument altogether. A few weeks later, after I stepped out of the Newseum/NY exhibition, I strolled up Madison Avenue to the Sharper Image store just before 73rd Street precisely to buy him a Razor scooter.

Galbraith takes an interest in these kinds of consumer decisions. He prefaces his interest first with the disclaimer that:

The economist does not enter into the dubious moral arguments about the importance or virtue of the wants to be satisfied. He doesn't pretend to compare mental states of the same or different people at different times and to suggest that one is less urgent than the other.[10]

Well, the economist, as an abstraction, may not, but Galbraith certainly does, for he just admonished us for being dupes of the advertising industry, salesmen with persuasive pitches that insult our intelligence—

and the supplications of five-year-olds. Not content with this reprimand of us as dim-witted consumers, Galbraith in his writings alludes to Plato's allegory of the cave, in which he, as an enlightened one who has journeyed to the world outside, can report to us fools living in darkness and ignorance. We are, in fact, further admonished in no uncertain terms when he argues that:

> The final problem of the productive society is what it produces. This manifests itself in an implacable tendency to provide an opulent supply of some things and a niggardly yield of others. This disparity carries to the point where it is a cause of social discomfort and social unhealth.[11]

Galbraith maintains that an economy shaped by irrational consumer decisions manipulated by advertising and salesmen (even in the guise of five-year-olds) is not a healthy one.

The Sharper Image store on Madison Avenue is, in effect, a public museum of superfluous consumer goods. There is nothing in that store that can be considered necessary to human life. And yet, it does splendidly well. The nature of desire (as translated into consumer demand that is met by a corresponding supply), arguably leads to something about which Galbraith has surprisingly little to say: joy. My purchase of a Razor scooter is made because of neither coercion nor persuasion, but because of the conscious decision that this will bring joy to a young boy and that I will derive pleasure by the act of giving.

Other economists are indifferent to the small decisions individuals make. Friedman is not prepared to pass a value judgment on the merits of what any individual consumer *wants* to buy—or actually *does* buy. The overall fairness of the economic playing fields is the foremost concern on his mind. The advent of e-commerce is worrisome if for no other reason than technology has changed the rules of the economic game, as we shall see later in this chapter. As Milton Friedman observes, "[t]he major problem in deciding the appropriate activities of government is how to resolve such conflicts among the freedom of different individuals."[12]

Consider the conflict between Netscape and Microsoft, one that emerged when computer manufacturers were installing, free of charge, Microsoft's Internet browser, thereby putting Netscape at a competitive disadvantage. Netscape founder Marc Andreessen clearly believed that Bill Gates' Microsoft did not play by the rules and that he used his company's market power to compete unfairly by coercing computer manufacturers to install Microsoft's Internet Explorer on the operating system for free. The idea of giving away one's product for free to consumers until one's competitors are driven out of business is neither fair nor acceptable in a market economy.[13]

The Clinton Administration's Department of Justice, in its interpretation of the Sherman Antitrust Act, found grounds to file suit. The government argued that Microsoft stifled competition, harmed consumers, and undermined the ability of competitors to market their own software programs and other technological innovations. Judge Thomas P. Jackson agreed almost entirely with the government's argument and declared Microsoft a monopoly.[14]

Legal intervention by the government in filing an antitrust suit against Microsoft is in keeping with the mandate articulated by Milton Friedman, provided the purpose is to ensure that healthy competition takes place under the same set of rules for everyone. Galbraith, on the other hand, would also raise his concerns and make a demand for a more detailed analysis of what is taking shape—that is, the amount of the social costs of the alienation the Internet inflicts on those who use it—throughout society as a whole.

Nonsense to that, Friedman would argue back, confident that the marketplace would take care of these things on its own. Indeed, in the same way that the economy is invigorated when competition is enhanced, Friedman's arguments urge policymakers to consider that there are sufficient self-regulating mechanisms within a market structure to ensure that any negative impact on society from e-commerce will be satisfactorily addressed by the market itself. There is no need for meddlesome intervention on the part of regulators or the government (thank you very much). Friedman, in fact, writes that:

> the organization of economic activity through voluntary exchange presumes that we have provided, through government, for the maintenance of law and order to prevent coercion of one individual by another, the enforcement of contracts voluntarily entered into, the definition of the meaning of property rights, the interpretation and enforcement of such rights, and the provision of a monetary framework.[15]

In the question of how much vigilance society should play in the economy, then, are the two opposing views concerning how to think about the role of government in our economic lives. Whereas Friedman sees a consumer's credit card statement at the end of the month as a record of his whims, Galbraith sees it as evidence of his coercion and manipulation by corporations.

As I walked out the Sharper Image store, unsure of what to think about my purchase, the pros and cons of each argument were in the back of my mind. It is true that some desires are the product of suggestion; had it not been for his older cousin, whom he wants to emulate, the idea of "needing" a Razor scooter would not have entered his head at all. It is also undeniable, however, that demonstration effects are older than capitalism itself. Adam saw Eve take a bite of a certain apple, and he then allowed himself to be persuaded into taking a bite himself.

Records of whims versus *evidence of manipulation,* then, are the different lenses through which one can understand the world of what we buy and why we buy it. These competing interpretations of our economic life hold greater currency now that they stand in fierce conflict and now that consumer profiles can be compiled with ruthless precision from the analysis generated from the data collected by cookies. The indiscriminate targeting of consumers from the 1950s well into the 1980s now appears rather rudimentary, much the same way that nation-states crudely went about the business of inventing, refining, and imposing national identities in the eighteenth and nineteenth centuries.

The imposition of geographic boundaries, official languages, and national institutions were the clay from which nationalities were formed. To create national unity, after all, people needed a common language, defined borders, and a shared cultural experience. At times this involved coercion, as was the case when the French language was imposed on the geography that today is France. But as a consequence there is a very well-defined sense of identity, nationhood, and purpose among the French. The American transcontinental railroad was what connected the United States into one nation. In the process, settlers dealt harshly with any Native American nation that resisted the march of American industry, commerce, and nation building.

In the twentieth century, private enterprise adopted these strategies, albeit refining the art of persuasion (for the most part, only when the interests of nations were at stake could coercion and force be used to expand trade and commerce).[16] The techniques marketers and salesmen developed were necessary in order to create widely recognized and accepted brands. They often enough met with stunning success. For example, Coca-Cola is recognized as *the* cola soft drink of choice by billions around the world. With the technological innovations unleashed by the Internet, it now becomes possible to accumulate greater knowledge about consumers in order to define how to best reach consumers through advertising.

Although Galbraith sees a sinister manipulation at work, one in which desire (demand) is artificially created by business (supply); his protest holds less resonance in a time when amorphous targeting of entire populations is losing favor. Is it possible that I *need* what I *want?* Furthermore, his arguments suggest an economic determinism that is reminiscent of Karl Marx: Production *determines* consumption. If this is so, then the company with the bigger advertising budget would always prevail. Tell that to the stunned folks at the Coca-Cola Company who thought up New Coke.

That technology makes it possible to target endless clusters of consumers not only in terms of demographics but also by their attitudes and dispositions offers marketing opportunities as never before.[17] An adult is made aware of the existence of both Harry Potter and the Razor scooter only when a youngster makes the introduction. Is a five-year-old's desire for a Razor scooter a legitimate want? Is a 20-year-old's insistence on a windbreaker by Mark Ecko an "independently determined" need? Is a 45-year-old's fanaticism about tickets to the Super Bowl the product of corporate manipulation?

Galbraith, for his part, if he were to accompany me on a shopping expedition, would admonish me by saying, "Should we *want* a Razor scooter in the first place? Where's the sense in such an acquisition? Is there, really, *anything* in the Sharper Image store on Madison Avenue in New York that *anyone* should be *allowed* to want?"

Well, *of course* I realize that everything in the Sharper Image store is superfluous to my existence, and there is nothing that anyone cannot live a happy, productive, and fulfilling life without, but so what? I'm not ignorant of how impulse purchases affect consumer spending. I'm aware that this is discretionary spending. I understand fully well that human beings face the conflict between what they want to do and what they should do.[18] That doesn't mean that I still don't find myself saying, "Yes," to the saleswoman who asks if she can help me. And then I ask for the Razor scooter with the bright red wheels.

Friedman, on the other hand, is not inclined to care about why I want what I want. He would shrug his shoulders, and reply that it isn't anyone's right to say what a consumer should want, and, besides, the marketplace will decide what people want and what they don't want anyway. Whereas Friedman is content to have the rules of the game be fair, be explained to the players, and have referees on hand (the proper role of government), Galbraith wants the players to demonstrate common sense, good sportsmanship, and a social responsibility.

Good sportsmanship, like good manners, cannot be legislated Friedman replies. It's an impossibility to think the government can, somehow, ensure that people are pleasant and kind and fair. In a democracy, after all, one has the right to be a jerk. For Friedman, government has no business setting itself up in a no-win situation. Insofar as government has a role to play in the individual lives of people, it is in safeguarding each individual's liberty. Friedman maintains that the proper role of government is not to *micro*manage the individual's life, but to *macro*manage the conditions under which individuals are able to live their lives. This is how he explains his position:

A government which maintained law and order, defined property rights, served as a means whereby we could modify property rights and other rules of the economic game, adjudicated disputes about the interpretation of the rules, enforced contracts, promoted competition, provided a monetary framework, engaged in activities to counter technical monopolies and to overcome neighborhood effects [externalities] widely regarded as sufficiently important to justify government intervention, and which supplemented private charity and private family in protecting the irresponsible, whether madman or child—such a government would clearly have important functions to perform. The consistent liberal is not an anarchist.[19]

The only exception is when one is not capable of taking care of one's self. In such cases, Milton Friedman argues that the government, clearly, has an interest to ensure that:

Freedom is a tenable objective only for responsible individuals. We do not believe in freedom for madmen or children. The necessity of drawing a line between responsible individuals and others is inescapable, yet it means that there is an essential ambiguity in our ultimate objective of freedom. Paternalism is inescapable for those whom we designate as not responsible.

The clearest case, perhaps, is that of madmen. We are willing neither to permit them freedom nor to shoot them. . . . [Therefore] we may be willing to arrange for their care through government.[20]

Friedman would like to believe that the consistent liberal is not an anarchist. But he wrote these words four decades before he or anyone had heard of "anarcho-capitalists" and "technolibertarians," creatures engendered and empowered by the Internet. These are different beings from traditional libertarians who believe the best government is the one that governs least. The specter of madness gives us pause to reflect upon the world ushered in by the Internet. There is now, in fact, another matter for policymakers to consider: the assaultive rhythms of the Internet's primal invasion in our lives and our expanding notion of *social insanity*.[21] As Paulina Borsook reports:

[Consider] the group [of individuals] that consists of anarcho-capitalists and cypherpunks. . . . These guys believe that Real Soon Now, in an era of digital, untraceable, anonymous cash, capitalism will have triumphed in its purest global form. "Borders ain't nothing but speedbumps along the information highway," as Tim May, perhaps one of the most famous, brilliant, cranky, and vociferous of the original cypherpunks, puts it. The members of this group indulge in a wicked excitement about the withering away of states and the possibility of a Hobbesian war of all against all that would result.[22]

The revolution in technological innovation is changing in fundamental ways our private wants precisely at a time when these same new technologies threaten our public needs.

If that place known as "cyberspace" has no physical presence, then who has jurisdiction? Germany would like to know in order to enforce its laws against spreading fascist literature within its borders.[23] Americans would like to know that their right to privacy has been obliterated by a software program written by nerds in California who simply wanted to be venerated as programming gods by their fellow geeks. Corporations around the world would like to know that their communications networks won't come crashing down because teenage hackers somewhere were bored on Saturday night and couldn't think of anything better to do.

Concerns about technological anarchy are light-years ahead of the issues first raised by either Galbraith or Friedman in the 1950s and 1960s. With the advent of technology that can tear asunder our very idea of intellectual property, Galbraith's worry that too many unnecessary Razor scooters are being marketed to children by unscrupulous advertisers is rendered silly. Friedman's neat-and-tidy argument that the proper role of government is to maintain law and order, define property rights, modify the rules of the economic game, and adjudicate disputes falls apart when *every* definition is under contention. The music industry, for instance, struggles to defend its rights when technology has rendered obsolete the heretofore definitions of copyright and residuals which no longer apply.

Of equal concern is the changing nature of people's thinking. Views that to most people living in 1962, when Friedman wrote *Capitalism and Freedom,* were considered of a madman are now the *mantras* of Internet executives. Contemporary madmen are Internet enthusiasts who call for a Hobbesian sangfroid political system, a Darwinian survival-of-the-fittest economy, and a technology-fueled libertarianism that replaces human relations with a system of networks.[24] No one knows precisely what this means—it is Hobbes' political philosophy under Darwinian evolution at Internet speed even as you read this sentence—but it certainly doesn't sound charitable at all.

Internet enthusiasts are quick to counter that the world has been forevermore changed by these new technologies entering our lives at warp speed, which itself created labor issues all their own.[25] Get *with* the program or get *out* of the way, they say. We find ourselves, however, at a loss for words to describe *how* things have changed, or how these changes alter our understanding of how the world works. This lack of clarity and understanding creates a void, which is oftentimes filled with tired platitudes.

"The Internet is, and is likely to remain for a long time, a work in progress," Scott Rosenberg pontificates in Salon.com.[26] Well, human civilization, dictionaries, the *NFL Today,* and life itself are also works in progress because *everything* is a work in progress, even decay. We may lack the words for it, but the uneasiness we feel, however, is real.

It is undeniable that the economic world today is far different from the world of the 1950s and 1960s when Galbraith and Friedman articulated their ideas about how the world works.

It is peculiar, however, to witness the speed with which a debate we thought had been *settled* is now so *unsettled*. With the formal dissolution of the Soviet Union when the communist flag was lowered for the last time from the Kremlin on December 31, 1991, it appeared that Friedman had won the argument that had consumed the world for much of the twentieth century. Nations around the globe were adopting free-market policies, trading blocs emerged in both the Old and New Worlds, and international bodies pursued policies to encourage the liberalization of trade and globalization.[27]

Only the most contrarious of nations—North Korea, Cuba, or Iraq, for instance—resisted the liberal democratic capitalist model. When a country, after all, takes the official position that the Internet is a national security matter and access to it is best controlled by the state, the world community is right in asking, *What nonsense are you talking about?*[28]

Of course Galbraith was not entirely silenced by these turns of world events. As the protesters who demonstrated against the International Monetary Fund, the World Bank, and the World Trade Organization showed, the debate on the virtues of market economies raged on. Officials are not unsympathetic to the views expressed by critics. They are, however, perplexed about how best to reign in the distortions of the online economy, the negative impact of market imperfections, and the problems of market failures. No one on a policy-making level has thus far offered viable solutions to remedy the negative impact from the online economy that affects the real world. The result is that serious confusion is being strewn about how market imperfections and market failures accelerated by the online economy are creating widespread distortions throughout capitalist societies. "I contend that an open society may also be threatened from . . . excessive individualism," billionaire financier George Soros wrote with alarm at the realization that individually rational choices can, under certain circumstances, lead to outcomes that are communally less than optimal. "Unless it is tempered by the recognition of a common interest that ought to take precedence over particular interests, our present system—which, however imperfect, qualifies as an open society—is liable to break down."[29]

Is an individual's rational decision to take advantage of an online discount on *Harry Potter and the Goblet of Fire* a betrayal of the common good? Is the concern that one of the impacts of the success of "virtual" booksellers and travel agents in the "real" world is the decimation of independent booksellers and travel agents a valid one for society to address? Should the systematic destruction of an industry—

and the way of life it nurtures—be allowed to proceed with impunity, or is intervention in the marketplace an appropriate response?

Federal Reserve Chairman Alan Greenspan seems to think so, and he discussed this in his roundabout way. "While recognizing the efficacy of capitalism to produce wealth," Alan Greenspan said at the annual meeting of central bankers and economists at Jackson Hole, Wyoming, held August 25, 2000, "there remains considerable unease among some segments about the way markets distribute that wealth and about the effects of raw competition on society," he continued. "Thus, should recent positive trends in economic growth falter, it is quite imaginable that support for market-oriented resource allocation will wane and the latent forces of protectionism and state intervention will begin to reassert themselves in many countries, including the United States."

Translating from Greenspanese into plain English, the Federal Reserve chairman said that we had better figure something out, or there will more demonstrators throwing more bottles in the streets, especially when the economic expansion of the 1990s slows down or ends—and there will certainly be more voices calling for regulatory remedies.[30]

This message was repeated again and again, most notably at a conference to commemorate the 75th anniversary of the Bank of Mexico. "The arguments against the global trading system that emerged first in Seattle and then spread over the past year arguably touched a chord in many people, in part by raising the fear that they would lose local political control of their destinies," Greenspan warned.[31]

His major concerns remain that distortions were not only interfering with the success of capitalist economies, but also these market imperfections and market failures were *discrediting* the market economy in the eyes of many around the world, particularly the impoverished. Is the ability of Amazon.com to drive booksellers out of business by its willful decision to exercise its ability to lose money for years a distortion that must be addressed at once? Do these distortions, in turn, create *false* incentives for investors to make decisions that result in *greater* distortions?

Greenspan suggested at that meeting that the answers were undeniably yes, thus siding, in principle, with the protesters that had taken to the streets to protest the "excesses" of the consequences of "globalization" which were "misguided." This was of consequence for the world turned its attention to the challenges of poverty and inequitable distribution of wealth when over 170 world leaders gathered in New York for the United Nations Millennium Summit two weeks after the central bankers and economists had met.[32] Greenspan, furthermore, took note of the observation that astounding greed was playing an important and troubling role in exacerbating the inequitable distribution of wealth around the world.[33] Officials were aware that, as the online economy grew and these distortions impacted the economy, their handling of the economic prosperity was under greater scrutiny from critics concerned about the underlying principles at work. One consequence, not surprisingly, was an increase in the number of critics pointing out, among other things, the problems of too *little* regulation by government to prevent market failures.[34]

"It is clearly pragmatism, not ideology, that is the main driving force in these evolving views," Greenspan concluded, pointing to the greed and moral misconduct of the many investors who were pursuing the false incentives presented by the distortions of the online economy. "The structural policy adjustments in Western Europe and Japan, not to mention the efforts in China and Russia to move toward market capitalism, are being motivated, for the most part, by the evident ability of market competition to elevate living standards."[35]

A brief explanatory digression is in order at this juncture. To have a clear perspective of the context in which Galbraith and Friedman discuss their ideas, it is first necessary to understand how our expectations about the world are shaped by our context. Deborah Tannen has written about human expectations in what cognitive theorists call "frames."[36] This is a very simple idea that can be easily illustrated with an example.

Let us say one is walking down the street and enters a small establishment. A person employed there addresses one by way of greeting. Whether whatever is spoken by this individual makes sense, Deborah Tannen writes, depends on one's contextual expectations. In other words, we create a "frame," or context, for this social situation, and we have certain ideas about what should take place within the parameters of this "frame." For instance, one has different expectations about the content of a conversation that one expects in a restaurant as opposed to a clothing store. If one walked into a clothing store and an employee, carrying menus, asked one if one would like to be seated, one would be confused or disoriented. "Where am I?" is the natural response to a situation that is inconsistent with one's expectations. The same would occur if, having walked into a restaurant, an employee there proceeded to take out a tape measure from his pocket and asked permission to measure one's neck.

A "frame," Tannen argues, creates a "structure of expectation" that gives a context to our understanding of the world. "Frames, then, are essential parts of our cognitive repertoire," linguist Robin Lakoff writes in agreement with her colleague. "They allow us to make predictions and generalizations: I have been in a store before, I know how to operate, I know what's expected, I'm OK. . . . Within the frame, things are unmarked: normal, predictable, neutral, orderly, natural, and simple. They do not require explanation."[37]

Once frames change abruptly, however, we become unsure of ourselves and our surroundings. We need explanations. Thrust in a foreign land where the language, customs, and habits are unfamiliar to us, we become guarded and cautious. We neither want to offend, nor be conspicuous. We observe discreetly and try to understand what is expected of us, how we should conduct ourselves, and how to get along with those around us. A restaurant that takes a diner's shirt measurements is a disorienting "frame" for most of us.

Our ideas about what makes sense—and therefore what constitutes "common sense"—are defined by both the society and time in which we live. The popular television show, *Candid Camera* showcased the comedy of what happens when society's frames are turned topsy-turvy and people don't know what to think or how to react. The importance of how facts are interpreted on a social level, it turns out, is instrumental in our understanding of things that challenge or change our common sense assumptions about how the world works. Lakoff discusses this by noting:

> Common sense is one of America's favorite populist virtues, one we see as the difference between those we trust . . . and the untrustworthy types without it, who are to be scorned, pitied, and ignored: egghead professors, fuzzy-haired impractical mathematicians, starry-eyed romantics. . . .
>
> What seems common sense at one moment, or in one society, is anything but in another. Five hundred years ago, it was common sense that the sun revolved around the earth. . . . That the blood was pumped through the body by the heart would have been dismissed as nonsense: if it were true, we would continually feel and hear our hearts beating. . . . Today the frames have changed, and anyone who espouses views like these would be considered ignorant or crazy—that is, devoid of common sense. . . .
>
> So the common sense of an idea is determined by its fit within a frame currently accepted by a majority of influential people. And once an idea becomes common sense, included in a generally accepted frame, it becomes very resistant to change. Other ideas accrete around it, lending it credibility and making its abandonment even more disturbing. We need our frames and conventional assumptions.[38]

The daunting speed of the Internet has upset many of the frames we use to make sense of our world and contributes to our individual and communal sense of bewilderment. Peruse the business section of any bookstore, and there's the proof of how businesspeople are struggling to make sense of the changes transforming the landscape of corporate America. The establishment of vast digital networks, known colloquially as the Information Highway, creates radically different contexts and frames, ones in which familiar economics is still finding its bearings as it adjust to the new ways of doing familiar things.

In the first three chapters, I made a case that, contrary to the misguided rhetoric of Internet enthusiasts, the familiar laws of economics *do* apply in cyberspace. Although viewed through a new vocabulary, the phenomenon observed throughout Silicon Valley and the Internet technologies conforms nicely to the models developed in the twentieth century about how economies work. Challenges arise, however, concerning the intellectual and sociopolitical frameworks within which these new technologies will be incorporated into our society and our lives. In the same way that the "role of government" was of tantamount importance to welfare economists in the twentieth century, the Internet creates new legal and political challenges to policymakers and political leaders.

Technological innovations, in other words, have revived the debate that we thought had been pretty much settled. What is the proper role of government in maintaining law and order, defining property rights, serving as a means whereby we can modify property rights and other rules of the economic game, adjudicating disputes about the interpretation of the rules, enforcing contracts, and promoting competition in the Internet Age? Are anarcho-capitalists and cypherpunks a new kind of madmen whose freedom should not be unconditional but subject to reconsideration?[39] Then again, this is like asking, is blue more beautiful than red? There is no objective or definitive answer. But there are arguments to be made, particularly at a time when so many century-old ideas—*frames*—about how the world works—*common sense*—are being redefined.

Bronson and Borsook are two reporters who, in the tradition of Tom Wolfe, have turned to social criticism in an effort to understand more precisely the cultural impact of the ascendance of high tech and the so-called New Economy. Both worked for *Wired* magazine in the early 1990s, and both chronicled the exploits, adventures, triumphs, failures, attitudes, and approaches of the movers and shakers in Silicon Valley. Bronson wrote *The First $20 Million Is Always the Hardest,* a novel that chronicles the exploits of a high-tech start-up in a manner reminiscent of the shenanigans found in *One Flew Over the Cuckoo's Nest.* His follow-up, *The Nudist on the Late Shift,* offers compelling narratives as it chronicles in superb journalism the true adventures of the men and women who are seeking their careers—and fortunes—in Silicon Valley.

Bronson's detachment is in stark contrast to Borsook's passion. Borsook, in fact, is alarmed by the culture of selfishness that suffuses the community of anarcho-capitalists who long for a Hobbesian world where technology triumphs completely over the lives of human beings. In reporting of events in her book, *Cyberselfish: A Critical Romp through the Terribly Libertarian Culture of High Tech,* she offers a vision of monumental terror. In her assessment of things, the sci-fi fantasies of a community of socially-awkward, immature young men have taken over and set the agenda. Borsook, in essence, reports that adults have been replaced by juvenile delinquents—the anarcho-capitalists and cypherpunks she decries—who are running Silicon Valley.

I disagree with this dim assessment of the men and women working throughout the high-tech industry that makes the Internet possible. In the course of meeting with people throughout Silicon Valley (California), Silicon Alley (New York), and Silicon Beach (Miami), however, I have been struck by how many individuals have in their offices and cubicles copies of the Ayn Rand's books. Rand (1905–1982), the Russian-born American writer who founded the philosophy of Objectivism, placed the individual squarely in the center of society and capitalism as the fairest economic system of all. Although her novels met with commercial success, her intellectual legacy is found in her embrace of Aristotelian rationalism. Rand is the single-most important influential philosopher to the men and women shaping the high-tech revolution. To see copies of *Atlas Shrugged, The Fountainhead, Capitalism: The Unknown Ideal,* and *The Virtue of Selfishness* lying about in so many offices is intriguing.[40]

On a subliminal level, Rand's influence is seen in how the online economy is evolving off-line. This is how Bronson, writing about the successful CitySearch Web sites that profile municipalities, for example, evaluates the social impact of the "anarcho-capitalist" culture on society at large:

Getting rooted in the community used to be like making fine wine: it took a certain period of fermentation, followed by years of aging. But CitySearch has distilled the process down to a few fast months in what they describe as a SWAT-team approach. It aggressively hires local people to ring the doorbells of local merchants, convincing them to pay for a Web site in CitySearch's megalopolis. It can manufacture a grassroots presence according to well-honed timetables and sales quotas. When the site in Salt Lake City had success testing out radio spots featuring satisfied merchants, that type of advertising went national. . . . I don't want to give a cynical impression of what CitySearch does—it isn't faking a "community" pose in the slightest, it's just that it has applied McDonald's franchise science to the high-tech garage start-up amazingly well. . . .

> So that's Silicon Valley today. We don't need no stinking revolution-aries—we've got hordes of Generation Xers hooked on options churn-ing out a revolution-type thing. We don't need you to stay up at night worrying about your business. We've convened a panel of experts to handle that for you.[41]

What alarms, however, is how dialogue and debate are undermined by the insidious nature of the havoc wrought by both technology and the impact of Hobbesian values on society at large. If Friedman argued that the proper role of government is to referee the economic game (intervening as seldom as possible), then the Internet makes that all the more difficult because not only are the rules of the economic game changing, but also they are changing in ways that challenge our very ideas about what constitutes common sense.

Consider how Internet apologist Scott Rosenberg dismisses the out-rage many executives at the affected companies expressed when their Internet sites operations were interrupted by hackers who circumvented security protocols. "A more sober response might be to see the attacks—malicious though they may be, and however responsible for real financial losses at targeted companies—as essentially large-scale nuisances," he argued in Salon.com, without any concern for ethical considerations whatsoever. "No one's credit numbers were stolen; no one's data was compromised; no one's privacy was violated."[42]

That neither theft nor fraud was involved presumably made these actions, on moral grounds, nothing more than acceptable social "nui-sances." That these attacks, which are now euphemistically called by the value-neutral phrase "distributed denial of service attacks," are seen as an acceptable form of entertainment challenges the idea of law and order, especially because the intention is malicious and the losses are real. This is a far different ethical world than the genteel one of a bygone era to which both Galbraith and Friedman belong.

If a hacker were to enter someone's house, take a look around, pre-vent the rightful owners from having access to their home, and then leave without taking anything, would this presumably not constitute breaking and entering, provided nothing was stolen? If a hacker were to enter a business and shred all its financial records (the restoration of which subsequently cost a considerable amount of time and money), would this be acceptable, if it was done to point out a firm's inadequate security, free of charge, and nothing more? Are we to believe that, with the advent of the Internet, criminal mischief ceases to be criminal mis-chief, provided it is entertaining?[43]

These arguments run contrary to our ideas about common sense, and undermine the traditional role of government to ensure that we can live our lives without feeling violated. In the 1980s programming geniuses delighted in creating the software programs that brought us cookies, thus ushering in the technology that threatens our ideas about privacy. In the 1990s anarcho-capitalism, which is a mixture of the beliefs of Thomas Hobbes, Charles Darwin, Ayn Rand, and the libertarianism of the Cato Institute began to define the philosophical views of Internet enthusiasts.[44] In the 2000s a blind, if not naïve, belief in the ability of technological innovations to satisfy mankind's needs, physical, emotional, and spiritual, is spilling onto other areas of life.

If notions that defied common sense were relegated to small clusters, such as Silicon Valley, for instance, they could be more adequately handled. That they are not means that the conflicts that emerge are more difficult to address.

Where I agree with Borsook that there has been a negative impact of anarcho-capitalist thinking is in the sociopolitical climate among civic leaders. In San Francisco city government, a brisk stroll from the offices of Salon.com in that city's high-tech SoMa district, for example, a kind of social anarchy is beginning to unfold. In a civic embrace of a "Hobbesian war of all against all," the administration of Mayor Willie Brown actually funds agencies of extremists who, in pursuit of their own political agenda, commit perjury and testify falsely in court against those they target as their enemies.[45] That city government aligns itself and funds an agency accused by human rights organizations of being a hate group represents a fundamental breakdown in our ideas about the proper role of how municipal governments should conduct a community's civic affairs. Despite protests to cease this funding of what amounts to government-sponsorship of a hate group, Mayor Brown is so beholden to the powerful interests that their demand to continue funding to agencies of radicals proceeds without hesitation.

Brown, who has been described by Borsook as "a corrupt, out of touch, master-of-machine-politics mayor," operates in the worst tradition of unprincipled excesses of big city politics barren of integrity.[46] The wretched excesses of the Internet entrepreneurs have been described as vacuous "hipster poses" and the "voracious senses of entitlement" by social commentators. That this same arrogance characterizes how city officials in San Francisco conduct civic affairs is evidence of the "anarcho-capitalism" decried by Borsook. The nonchalant Hobbesian attitude of the Brown administration, where political expediency results in the wholesale violation of the civil rights of segments of his constituency, is a threat to our tradition about the proper role of government and the importance of character and decency in public life. Consider, for instance, that when Hispanics filed complaints with the San Francisco Human Rights Commission (SFHRC) alleging that by filing a lawsuit to silence critics, Community United Against Violence (CUAV) and its allies had conspired to deprive

Hispanics of their First Amendment rights, Mayor Brown's office contacted SFHRC Commissioner Virginia Harmon and ordered her not to proceed with the investigations of those complaints because it would prove embarrassing to City Hall.

Thus, Mayor Brown chose to remove himself from the accountability demanded by the kind of social anarchy his Hobbesian approach to city government is unleashing. Seemingly more interested in his cameo appearances in films such as Disney's *George of the Jungle* or the *Nash Bridges* television series, he's at other times nowhere to be located.[47] Kandace Bender, his putative press secretary, is unable to offer satisfactory answers to serious queries about the mayor's resolve to address this issue.[48] That conflicts within a community are exacerbated in this manner sets alarming precedents. When one group asserts its right to advance its interests by violating the rights of others—and to do so with public monies—this is where the social contract breaks down and anarchy begins.

This philosophical approach to anarcho-capitalism extends beyond one imperial mayor and his inexplicably racist City Hall, however. The belief that the evolution of jurisprudence in American society can be turned inside out threatens the courts in San Francisco. Judge Donna Hitchens, for instance, has defended her right to administer courts in which perjured statements are not challenged, the unsworn testimony of false witnesses is allowed, and defendants are denied the right to respond.[49] Cristina Llop at Superior Court expressed her own frustration that in the courts administered by Donna Hitchens false testimony against Hispanics is routinely allowed into evidence.[50] Jeff Sheehy from the district attorney's office expressed his outrage. "Everyone is entitled to an impartial court hearing. Everyone is entitled to respond to the false testimony of false witnesses," he said. There's no point in telling that to this judge. Indeed, insofar as the denial of due process advances the agenda of groups advocating her special interests, constitutional protections afforded to every American citizen are threatened.

The realization, in fact, that there are courts in California that exist not to administer justice, but rather to ratify political agendas, is a disturbing one. That the judicial process is being undermined by renegades sets an alarming precedent at a time when the frames within which common sense is understood are being redefined. Constitutional protections are tossed aside in Randian fashion by off-line hackers. The rights of others are but speed bumps in pursuit of Mayor Brown's and Judge Hitchens' personal political agendas.[51]

SWAT-team approaches to business, city government, and a community's justice system are the social off-line fallout from "anarcho-capitalism" in San Francisco. What we are left to ponder is an updated version of the differences between Galbraith and Friedman, grotesquely distorted as the pace of technological innovations continues to accelerate and change the frames within which we live. In Silicon Valley, in essence, there are those who believe the proper role of government is to get out of the way and let technological SWAT teams rule the day. At the same time, there are others who believe that the Internet is stretching the definitions of what intellectual property is and how such assets can be fairly commercialized via new technologies, which is why it is imperative that new definitions and new rules be established.

Thrown into this debate is the concern that Internet technologies are rapidly giving rise to political beliefs that combine the excesses of Darwin and Hobbes to create a civic climate of hostility and anarchy. Where civil discourse becomes hostile, civility is threatened, and society comes under assault. Friedman has expressed his opinion about the proper role of government in protecting society from madmen.

To characterize San Francisco city government under Willie Brown as such may, of course, be a hyperbole, but it is consistent with the manner in which the interests of one constituency are advanced at the expense of the civil rights of others. During the last decades of the twentieth century, however, not entirely unsympathetic social commentators became disturbed by the turmoil engulfing the lives of Americans. Tom Wolfe, for one, argued that life in America has become *absurd*. Chroniclers of the high-tech revolution look at the communities in Silicon Valley and struggle to make sense of what they see unfolding before their eyes. If Borsook's postlinear prose is any indication of the civil, political, and social disequilibrium engulfing Silicon Valley, it is understandable why policymakers don't know what to make of these challenges to the fundamental tenets of the social contract. Sometimes it's difficult to know what to think.

Key #4

In the twentieth century, welfare economists debated the proper limits of government in striking the appropriate balance between private wants and public needs. The Internet technologies threaten to unravel the consensus that emerged as a consequence of the arguments advanced primarily by John Kenneth Galbraith and Milton Friedman. These technological innovations challenge traditional definitions and understanding of how governments can maintain law and order, define property rights, and serve as a means whereby private parties modify property rights, and disputes concerning the rules of the economic game creates turmoil. One consequence is the emerging politics in which "anarcho-capitalism" asserts its own rights over those of others, in the process challenging our ideas about fairness and common sense. Technological innovations, in a fundamental way, have resulted in the undeniable fact that the social contract is up for rene-gotiation. Internet technologies, in essence, ask, Are the public's needs mere speed bumps on the road to satisfying private wants?

NOTES

1. Spot News, "Racial Protest at Cornell University," April 20, 1969. From the exhibition, "The Pulitzer Photographs: Capture the Moment," May 23–September 23, 2000, Newseum/NY, 580 Madison Avenue, New York, N.Y.

2. Such facilities were housed within Willard Straight Hall, which was under occupation. The closest rest rooms were at Uris Library and Barnes Hall; the closest dining facility was at Anabel Taylor Hall.

3. Personal communication, August 2000.

4. Letter from Kelly Smith Tunney dated May 18, 2001.

5. Neither the Pulitzer Prize Committee nor Thomas Jones responded to written requests asking for comments on the eyewitness report that the photograph taken by Associated Press photographer Steven Starr on April 20, 1969, of Thomas Jones and other militant students leaving Willard Straight Hall on the Cornell University campus was reenacted for the benefit of reporters. The Associated Press maintains Steven Starr's photographs were not re-enacted, but were instead taken as events unfolded.

6. Alvin Hansen, "Standards and Values in a Rich Society," in *Private Wants and Public Needs,* ed. Edmund Phelps, p. 11. First published in Alvin Hansen, *The American Economy.* (New York: McGraw-Hill, 1957).

7. Milton Friedman, "The Role of Government in a Free Society," in *Private Wants and Public Needs,* ed. Edmund Phelps, p. 107. First published in Milton Friedman, *Capitalism and Freedom* (Chicago: University of Chicago Press, 1962).

8. Ibid.

9. John Kenneth Galbraith, "The Dependence Effect and Social Balance," in *Private Wants and Public Needs,* ed. Edmund Phelps, pp. 25–28. First published in John Kenneth Galbraith, *The Affluent Society* (Boston, MA: Houghton Mifflin, 1958).

10. Ibid., p. 28.

11. Ibid., p. 29.

12. Milton Friedman, "The Role of Government in a Free Society," p. 107.

13. Recall British Airways' guilt in driving Laker Airways out of the New York–London route through its predatory pricing.

14. The role of government in regulating industries has had a mixed record. At times it strengthens and protects one sector, whereas at other times its intervention creates a bureaucratic and bloated industry that is unable to compete efficiently in world markets. Consider the history of government regulation in the trucking, airline, and banking industries. The one lesson that emerges, however, is that competition is healthy, provided it is encouraged through a systematic way of striving to achieve fairness to all the parties involved in competing.

15. Milton Friedman, "The Role of Government in a Free Society," in *Private Wants and Public Needs,* p. 108.

16. There are many examples of nations engaging in warfare to establish, defend, and expand trade. When Commodore Matthew Perry returned to Edo (Tokyo) Bay on February 13, 1854, with seven warships, in a matter of weeks the Japanese capitulated to his demands that Japanese ports be opened to American vessels. They also agreed to the establishment of diplomatic and trade relations between both nations; that the Japanese would guarantee the safe repatriation of American seaman; and that commercial relations between the United States and Japan would be under the most-favored-nation status. This was known as the Treaty of Kanagawa, and it essentially opened Japan to the West. Instances where companies manipulated a government into action are fewer, however. A notorious example is ITT, which, through a disinformation campaign orchestrated with the Central Intelligence Agency, engineered American support for a coup against the democratically elected government of Chile.

17. As the consumer market continues to become fragmented, many marketers are identifying consumers not by traditional demographics, such as age and race, but by attitudes and interests. Instead of targeting white males between the ages of 18 and 25, for instance, companies are beginning to target individuals who have a passion for seeing exhibitions of Pulitzer Prize photographs and have purchased Razor scooters. Technology has further defined the mass market collective into new categories, such as Positivists, New Enthusiasts, Relativists, Old Liners, and so forth.

18. I remember several times a great-granduncle commenting dryly that if I, somehow, had managed to find the time to *learn* Japanese, then it shouldn't be a problem for me to find the time to *improve* my Catalan.

19. Milton Friedman, "The Role of Government in a Free Society," in *Private Wants and Public Needs*, ed. Edmund Phelps (New York: W.W. Norton & Company, 1965), p. 115.

20. Ibid., pp. 113–114.

21. The phenomenon of youngsters opening fire on their classmates and the escalation of violence against women at rock concerts, for instance, are symptoms of social ill health.

22. Paulina Borsook, *Cyberselfish: A Critical Romp Through the Terribly Libertarian Culture of High-Tech*, pp. 17–18.

23. The government of Germany's attempt to crack down on the right-wing National Democratic Party in 2000 was thwarted by the fact that, of the more than 360 hate-speech sites identified by the domestic security agency in Lower Saxony, more than one hundred of these Web sites transferred their Web sites to servers in the United States. They were thus outside the reach of German authorities.

24. The political views of English philosopher Thomas Hobbes (1588–1679) are summed up in his landmark treatise, *Leviathan*.

25. In *White-Collar Sweatshop: The Deterioration of Work and Its Rewards in Corporate America*, Jill Andresky Fraser, an editor for *Inc.* magazine and Bloomberg Financial Services, wrote that the 24/7 work ethic in which people are on call all the time gives employees little control over their work lives and that the pace is so demanding it is similar to sweatshop conditions. "Although we thought technology would make our work lives easier and more creative,

the real impact of our laptops, our Palm Pilots, our e-mail and our cellphones is that we can't ever *not* work," she said. "There's no justification to stop working for one moment." This argument is one reason why the Washington Alliance of Technology Workers (WashTech) and the United Food & Commercial Workers (UFCW), both unions, attempted to organize Amazon.com employees in order to win better wages and conditions for workers.

26. Scott Rosenberg, "The Net Scare," Salon.com, February 20, 2000.

27. The European Union on the old continent went so far as to adopt a common currency, something other trading blocks, such as NAFTA in North America and Mercosur in South America, have yet to implement.

28. Thinking one can prevent people from demanding the right to use the Internet is like saying that only certain classes of individuals have the right to know how to read and write. In fact, Larry Ellison, founder of Oracle, goes as far as to claim that the personal computer is the modern-day equivalent of the pencil, by which he means it should be as inexpensive and widely available as pencils have become. Cheap pencils, it bears noting, are the economic and technical achievement that made widespread literacy possible in the Western world in the first place. To argue that the Internet is a "national security" issue is as absurd as arguing that so are pencils.

29. George Soros, "The Capitalist Threat," *The Atlantic Monthly,* February 1997. Soros, incorrectly, blames the capitalist system itself for the proliferation of market failures and market imperfections exacerbated by the nature of technological revolutions.

30. From Seattle to Prague and Paris to Washington, D.C., demonstrators have wrecked civil disturbance in their protests against globalization. Alan Greenspan, furthermore, is displeased with his effigy being torn to shreds by youths, particularly when he believes he is doing all he can to reign in the excesses and greed of unchecked capitalism; he called it "irrational exuberance."

31. Address given on November 14, 2000, at the Bank of Mexico in Mexico City.

32. As protestors gathered at the United Nations to protest globalization, income inequalities exacerbated by the market imperfections and market failures of the online economy emerged as a serious concern for all of humanity, which warranted the attention of world leaders who had gathered together to participate in this rather pointless summit.

33. "Excess" was evident at this conference itself. The meeting, held in the American West, afforded many participants the opportunity to relax by riding horses, attending Western rodeos, and taking "lessons" in being a cowboy in the spirit of the "Wild, Wild West." Splendid little junket, bankrolled by taxpayers from around the world, no doubt. (The meeting of world officials immediately following this one to discuss globalization issues was held in Sydney, Australia, coincidentally the same week that the Summer Olympics began. It was therefore poetic justice that the opening ceremonies were sublime; the opening number was titled "Eternity," which was reminiscent of the set of the science fiction film "Mad Max," starring Mel Gibson and Tina Turner.)

34. Writing in the *New York Times* in the summer of 2000, for instance, Robert Frank pointed out that the Firestone tire recall was, in part, a result of

deregulation instituted during the Reagan administration. "The National Highway Traffic Safety Administration once maintained an extensive network of automobile repair shops through which it gathered data that provided an early warning of potentially serious safety defects. This network would have sounded an alarm about the unusually high failure rate of one model of Firestone tires, tires whose defects, we now learn, may have resulted in scores of deaths," he wrote. "Unfortunately, the agency was forced to abandon its early warning network in the 1980's when the Reagan administration cut its budget in half, citing excessive regulatory zeal." There are times when market imperfections, such as the marketplace not "correcting" the sale of unsafe tires until there was an unprecedented crisis, result in people dying.

35. Despite the harsh criticism of many on the left, the overwhelming majority of the men and women in positions of authority are good and sincere people. The gathering at Jackson Hole, Wyoming, was one in which the ideas of Galbraith and Friedman were salient. The question, in essence, that is present at these summits remains: How can the world's international financial institutions, central bank authorities, economists, and policymakers work together to tackle the monumental challenge of making sure that humanity can live their lives with dignity and without material want?

36. Deborah Tannen, "What's in a Frame? Surface Evidence of Underlying Expectations," in *New Directions in Discourse Processing,* ed. R. O. Freedle, pp. 137–181.

37. Robin Tolmach Lakoff, *The Language War,* p. 48.

38. Ibid., page 49.

39. Juveniles found guilty of engaging in criminal mischief via the Internet are routinely ordered by the courts to refrain from using any computer, except as necessary for completing their homework, for the duration of their probation. They are, in essence, not free to go online.

40. An intriguing fact is that *Capitalism: The Unknown Ideal* is a collection of essays, several of which were written by Alan Greenspan.

41. Po Bronson, *The Nudist on the Late Shift,* pp. 234–235

42. Scott Rosenberg, "The Net Scare," Salon.com, February 20, 2000.

43. Law enforcement officials take a more serious view of these activities. "Canadian law enforcement officials said yesterday that they had arrested a Montreal high school student in one of the computer attacks that crippled some of the Internet's biggest sites in February, exposing deep vulnerabilities in the fledging world of electronic commerce," Matt Richtel wrote in the *New York Times* on April 20, 2000. The young man arrested, a 15-year-old, participated in attacks that interfered with the Web sites of CNN, Yahoo, eBay, and E*Trade, among others. The youth was charged with two counts of criminal mischief for the attack he launched against CNN.com on February 8, 2000. A few months later, Jonathan James, a 16-year-old Miami youth, became the first juvenile hacker sentenced to serve time on September 22, 2000, when he was sent to juvenile detention for six months after he pleaded guilty to penetrating the computer systems of the Defense Department and the space agency. "Breaking into someone else's property, whether it is a robbery or a computer intrusion, is a serious crime," Attorney General Janet Reno said after sentencing.

44. The Cato Institute was founded by Edward Crane and Charles Koch in San Francisco in 1977. It is now headquartered in Washington, D.C., and continues to publish policy pieces and hold symposiums dedicated to advancing the debate about the nature of the individual's liberty in society. Its embrace of individualism is the moral compass with which entrepreneurs in Silicon Valley find their political and ideological bearings.

45. See annual budgets for the City of San Francisco for Community United Against Violence (CUAV), an organization that, in pursuit of its political agenda, organized what can be accurately described as a "hate speech" rally against Edgard Mora. Jennifer Rakowski, a radical activist for that agency, spoke at that "hate-speech" rally to vilify Mr. Mora and create a climate of hostility against Latinos in June 1999, which was attended by Mayor Willie Brown.

46. Mexican activists have characterized CUAV as an "anti-Hispanic hate group" and demanded that San Francisco city government cease all funding in order to protect the civil and human rights of Hispanics. For Paulina Borsook's characterization of Mayor Willie Brown, see "How the Internet Ruined San Francisco," Paulina Boorsok, www.salon.com, October 27, 1999.

47. Vocal critics of Mayor Willie Brown, such as Chinese-American leader Edward Liu, characterize the mayor as an "over-dressed court jester." More interested in attending swank cocktail parties hosted by the Gettys about town or Oscar night bashes thrown by Vanity Fair magazine, detractors have long criticized the mayor for his inattention to the civic business of the people of San Francisco.

48. When asked to call me back should Mayor Brown decided to make a "cameo" appearance at City Hall, Ms. Bender is neither amused, nor does she ever call back.

49. In a personal communication, Donna Hitchens defended the conduct of Commissioner Marjorie Slabach, who has been accused of outright racism, to deny defendants the right to respond to the false testimony submitted by radical activists. In due course, with the assistance of the district attorney's office, the sanctions imposed by this biased court were reversed, but only after a concerted campaign.

50. Cristina Llop speculated that Donna Hitchens, who sees herself as an activist judge, allows perjured testimony prepared and submitted by officials at CUAV in order to advance her political ideology.

51. Willie Brown, Donna Hitchens, Virginia Harmon, and Marjorie Slabach were granted the right to reply but declined to comment on the criticism that their actions together constitute malfeasance, which, in effect, deprives Hispanics of their civil rights.

CHAPTER 5

DOING OLD THINGS IN A NEW WAY

As long as a good has to be moved physically from point A to point B, an online transaction is not complete.[1] The sale of a book purchased on Amazon.com is not concluded until the book is physically delivered to the recipient. This is as true for individual consumers as it is for companies, governments, and other organizations and agencies. The efficiencies and benefits derived from participating in business-to-business hubs are not realized until the goods and services secured are delivered or provided.[2] That the Internet can enable, facilitate, and generate business, for the private and public sectors alike, strengthens the characterization that the Internet represents a tremendous opportunity to expand trade and commerce. The integral role the establishment of networks—of railroads, highways, and now Internet technologies—plays in fomenting economic development is now accelerated by the exponential effects high-tech innovations provide.

If a transaction is not complete until a product or service is delivered or performed in the real world, it is part of the Old Economy. This observation offers an instructive guideline for differentiating between the Old and New Economies. If the New Economy baffles many people, this guideline on how to distinguish one from the other should end the confusion. Indeed, most of what has been called "New Economy" properly belongs to the "Old Economy."

A transaction, by comparison, that is *completed in its entirety* online belongs to the New Economy. Amazon.com is therefore a new company operating in the Old Economy. Travelocity.com is likewise a new company operating in the Old Economy. Delivering books, securing passage on airplanes and cruise ships, and thousands of other things are new ways of doing old things. As exciting as these innovations are, however, they are not the subject matter addressed in the discussion about the entertainment economy online presented in this book.

The true New Economy, on the other hand, is intrinsically confined to the ephemeral nature of cyberspace. Consider, for instance, the ability to log onto a Web site, select a song, download it onto one's account on a server, and then listen to it. Consider then visiting another Web site to do the same to a news story one wants to file away for future reference. Nothing is *physically* delivered in either of these examples, for in both cases the product is made available electronically in its entirety. The same holds true for other activities, such as transferring funds to open an online account into which proceeds from the sales of stocks or other securities can be deposited or from which the purchase of these instruments can be debited.

Any other online transaction that requires off-line completion, regardless of the technology involved, remains a new way of doing an old thing. This includes files that are downloaded (encrypted, or not) onto one's hard drive. Whether it is a film being downloaded for one's personal viewing, or the winnings from online gambling, or the latest Stephen King novel, if it occupies space on one's hard drive, it properly belongs to the New Economy.

When one considers that for most of the so-called New Economy activities goods and services have to be delivered (books or CDs) or performed (gift certificates for massages), it properly belongs to the Old Economy. Indeed, insofar as it is an Old Economy company, Amazon.com may be the world's largest online retailer, but it has built the largest off-line distribution network of any online company.[3] In fact, the construction of a nationwide distribution network of physical warehouses by Amazon.com underscores how confusing it is to distinguish between the "Old" and "New" Economies. That *virtual* orders have to become *real* packages before the sale can be completed is evidence that the Internet is an evolutionary leap—but not a revolutionary one—in the development and expansion of trade and commerce in the Old Economy.

"We have the chance to be the first company that actually marries the physical and the virtual worlds," Jeffrey Wilke, Amazon.com's president and general manager of operations, explained when the Ferney (Nevada) warehouse opened for business at the end of 1999. "Amazon.com is committed to owning and operating our distribution centers because we are committed to customer satisfaction. If a package doesn't arrive on time, you can't blame it on someone else [to whom fulfillment was outsourced]. The customer doesn't care about any of the logistics involved. While the distribution centers are the less glamorous side of the whole e-commerce world, they are definitely the most important."[4]

Amazon.com's distribution center in Ferney, Nevada, is indeed enormous. Located 35 miles east of Reno in the middle of the proverbial nowhere that resembles the surface of the moon, this mammoth facility is as "real" world as it can possibly get. Completely computerized with cutting edge inventory control software systems, there are over 10 miles of conveyor belts throughout the facility. Each item is scanned 17 times from the moment it arrives to when it is shipped to the customer. There are over one million different items housed in this warehouse, and when the holiday season is in full swing, over 70 percent of Amazon.com's employees are working at the distribution centers around the country shipping away. Amazon.com officials boast that this distribution network has the capacity to move $10 billion of merchandise in any given year. On my visit to the distribution center in Nevada desert, it was incredible to witness firsthand how dependent Amazon.com's future is to the good old-fashioned science of logistics, shipping, and transportation.

Amazon.com founder Jeff Bezos is aware for the need to have a warehouse in the Nevada desert to ship one million packages a day. "This is the fastest expansion of distribution capacity in peacetime history," he told the *New York Times*. "We were woefully unprepared when we started in 1995. We were so dumb we didn't have any packing tables and wrapped packages on the concrete floor."[5]

The image of employees on their hands and knees filling boxes to be shipped to customers is a quaint way of engendering the "virtual" future. In the real world of distribution centers and transportation logistics, the Internet means little. When Amazon.com embarked on the construction of its distribution network, it enlisted two authorities in the field. Brian Gibson of Auburn University and Christopher Norek of the University of Tennessee analyzed where best to locate each distribution facility. They also selected the Supply Chain Strategist software from i2 Technologies in Dallas to automate the on-site operations. With several billion dollars invested in warehouses across the country and service contracts with United Parcel Service and the U.S. Postal Service for actual delivery to customers, Amazon.com's distribution network brings the so-called "New" Economy to its true perspective: it is the Old Economy *disguised* as the New Economy as far as many analysts, investors, and the media are concerned.[6]

Jeff Bezos' insistence on Amazon.com operating its own distribution network is sound. It is intended to secure a competitive advantage by introducing innovations that allow it to serve customers in a more efficient manner and with greater customer service. Buy.com, whose sales in 1999 approached $400 million, is the second-largest online retailer after Amazon.com. But unlike Amazon.com, Buy.com, along with Yahoo! and eBay, decided to outsource its fulfillment operations to specialists. The advantage for these firms is that they free their companies from having to maintain an inventory and do not have to contend with shipping products to their customers. The downside to this approach is that these companies lose control over the delivery process, the crucial aspect in ensuring customer satisfaction and loyalty. The fact that these companies generate orders through their Web sites does not propel them into the New Economy, of course.

To see this more clearly, consider other companies that have never generated sales *neither* through a "real-world" store *nor* online: SkyMall and Lands' End. SkyMall and Lands' End have generated sales through their direct market catalogs and toll-free numbers. SkyMall is a decade-old catalog distributed in the backs of seats of airlines around the world. Customers can send in their orders by mail, or they can call toll-free numbers while in flight or once on the ground. Lands' End has relied almost exclusively on its direct mail to generate sales, which is why it calls itself "direct merchants." Orders can also be placed by mail or made by calling their toll-free numbers. With the advent of the Internet, SkyMall created a separate division, SkyMall.com. Whereas the print catalog showcases 2,000 items, the online catalog has over 20,000 products for sale. Lands' End's online catalog similarly has a greater selection than its printed catalog. But not unlike Amazon.com and Buy.com, SkyMall and Lands' End have each pursued different fulfillment strategies.

SkyMall.com has little of the inventory found on its Web site in stock. SkyMall.com relies on fulfillment outsourcers to take care of maintaining inventory and shipping the products to customers. For domestic clients, Sykes Enterprises ships from Fremont, California. International orders are fulfilled by Sykes distribution centers located in the Philippines or Scotland. This strategy is exactly the one pursued by online retailers such as Buy.com, Yahoo!, and eBay.

Lands' End, on the other hand, manufactures what it sells in its catalog and Web site. It maintains its own inventory and ships orders to customers directly. Its online presence evolved gradually, gently adjusting the norms of its corporate culture as it has incorporated technological innovations into its operations. Not unlike Amazon.com, Lands' End pursues a strategy of controlling each step of its operations in order to ensure the highest customer satisfaction every step of the way. That these companies have operated outside the confines of physical retail stores has made them more comfortable with the operational challenges the new technologies offered.

It is not therefore surprising that both SkyMall and Lands' End have been extremely successful in their Web sites. Their smooth back-end order-fulfillment operations have given both companies an advantage in how to establish viable online presences. For both firms, orders generated by their Web sites represent a robust percentage of each company's overall sales.

Of equal importance is taking note that no one refers to either SkyMall or Lands' End as New Economy companies, simply because they lack real-world store locations and have successful Web sites. The use of catalogs, direct mail, and toll-free numbers to build their business incorporates e-commerce in innovative ways. Claims of "marrying" the virtual and real worlds are euphemisms for admitting that, in the case of Amazon.com, pretentious declarations to the contrary, it is definitely an Old Economy company. It is undoubtedly an Old Economy company using e-commerce to sell products, as its mammoth warehouses demonstrate.

The success of any online company that has to deliver products or perform services in the off-line world will therefore be measured in the old-fashioned way: customer satisfaction, regardless of how orders are generated. This is what SkyMall and Lands' End have known for a long time. Their e-commerce business models are built on what they have learned from direct mail marketing and toll-free telephone customer service. Thus, it is only logical to classify Amazon.com, eBay, Yahoo!, and thousands of other online retailers as being part of the Old Economy, notwithstanding the fact that these generate sales through clicks, not bricks.

To be sure, there are tremendous opportunities for "Old Economy" companies to take advantage of the online economy. The nature of these opportunities, however, is consistent with those presented by other technological developments. Consider how the economy of the San Francisco Bay Area changed in the mid-nineteenth century. When word reached the East Coast that gold had been found in the hills near Sacramento in 1849, there was a human stampede westward to California. Reports trickled into the maritime ports up and down the Eastern seaboard that James Marshall had discovered gold at Sutter's Mill in California, news that captivated the American public's imagination, giving rise to wild expectations and frenzied schemes. These unsubstantiated tales—not hard facts—had spread like a low but throbbing fever because news traveled slowly back then as sailors docked in the harbors along the Atlantic. No doubt the discovery of gold was the stuff of speculation. It took almost four months for word of the discovery of gold in California to arrive on the East Coast because ships had to journey from California to New York by circumnavigating the tip of South America.

In his 1849 State of the Union address, President James Polk confirmed the rumors as true. No sooner had the discovery of gold been
verified as a fact by the U.S. government, however, that tens upon
thousands of men sought to make their fortunes in what would then
be called the Golden State. These men, a generation that went down
in the history books as the Forty-Niners, changed the economy of
California, sped up the integration of the American West into the
nation's life, and were part of the Gold Rush that is the stuff of legends.

At the Big Four Restaurant at the Huntington Hotel on Nob Hill in
San Francisco, the "Big Four" refers to the robber barons who transformed San Francisco into a modern, vibrant, and cosmopolitan city.
Charles Crocker, Mark Hopkins, Collis Huntington, and Leland Stanford
made incredible fortunes in their lifetimes, leaving a tremendous legacy
in terms of the material wealth they created and how they put northern
California on the political map of the world. None of these men, curiously enough, made their money mining gold.

Crocker, Hopkins, Huntington, and Stanford were Easterners who
went out West precisely to make their fortunes in the opportunities that
California gold promised to make real. It wasn't exactly clear where
the greatest opportunities were to be found, but few doubted they were
there and that they were real. Crocker, like thousands before him,
thought his fortune was in gold. He gave up on mining altogether,
however, when he quickly realized there was more money to be made
in *selling* supplies to other miners. Hopkins surmised as much from
the onset. He took the money he had made in iron ore in the Midwest
and set up shop in Sacramento as a merchant, selling groceries, hardware, and mining supplies to the Forty-Niners. Stanford also became
a successful merchant in the Sacramento Valley. An ambitious man,
he parlayed his skills as a businessman into building an empire. Later
on in life he became a politician and philanthropist. Huntington was
as successful a businessman as he was crafty in dealing with bureaucrats and politicians back in the nation's capital. He would shrewdly
use government loans to build up his railroad business—and a personal
fortune.

Three of these men were born in New York State, and one man in
Connecticut. In 1860, they became the founders of the Central Pacific
Railroad. As the railroads expanded throughout California and the West,
so did trade and commerce. The establishment of a railroad network
made it possible to link the East and West Coasts of the United States,
and it facilitated the movement of goods and people across the country.
There were opportunities for everyone who was willing to work and was
smart about sizing up and seizing the opportunities.[7]

These men competed fiercely with one another, but in a good-old-
boy manner, of course. They wanted to see who could build the most

extravagant mansion on San Francisco's Nob Hill. They competed to see who could mastermind the most profitable industrial empire. They schemed to see who could exercise a greater control of politicians, both in California and in Washington, D.C. Newspaper magnate William Randolph Hearst accused them in his editorials of outrageous corruption and monopolistic arrogance.[8] They were reviled by some and praised by others. Although they were not above the petty jealousies of mere mortals, these men were a breed apart. They established the Pacific Union, a private club modeled after the swank and exclusive clubs of New York and London, just to show the world that their good fortune could make San Francisco a city that was second to none. Their personal exploits and excesses filled the pages of the yellow press on both coasts.

Their political ambitions, in fact, shaped the development of the entire country. The New York–San Francisco corridor became the lifeline during the nation's era of industrialization and expansion, a time of growth, prosperity, and excess that came be to known as the "Gilded Age."[9] Often financing their ambitious plans with government funds, their prosperity was, to a significant measure, based on the willingness of government to grant rights and underwrite public works projects that proved profitable to these men's private interests. As they prospered and diversified their business interests, those Sacramento merchants became San Francisco industrialists who ran the railroads and controlled real estate, banking, and city politics.

Of the tens of thousands of men who came in search of gold, few are remembered now. There were too many men and too little gold. The average find for the average miner provided an average living, but not a fortune. For most miners, in fact, it was a subsistence existence. But if gold was the "New Economy" in the mid-nineteenth century, then it was the business of the "Old Economy"—trade, commerce, and industrialization—that was the engine that transformed California, and with it the United States. This is a historical pattern that was repeated in California as the twentieth century became the twenty-first.

When I first arrived in San Francisco, I stayed at the Park Lane Apartments on Sacramento Street on Nob Hill. The Big Four Restaurant was diagonally across the street, and it fast became a favorite place to meet friends and associates for dinner and drinks. I would cut through Cushman Place, the narrow alley that separates the Pacific Union Club from a small park and children's playground that face Grace Cathedral. Over leisurely meals in that restaurant, comparisons between the Gold Rush of 1849 and the current Silicon Gold Rush, then unfolding, were made and debated. These discussions offered a deeper understanding in the fallacy of believing that the Internet has created a "New Economy" out of nothing.

Whether there was a fortune to be made in the nineteenth century's "New Economy" of gold mining was beside the point, as the Big Four proved to the world. There were better opportunities in traditional areas of commerce, trade, and finance. The great lesson that the California Gold Rush imparted was that George Santayana was right all along: progress does consist of knowing how to *retain* things that can be used to take advantage of the business opportunities that emerge as human knowledge evolves and opportunities present themselves.

This lesson can be applied to us today by looking back at the arrival of Warren Bechtel in San Francisco. Since 1898 he and his family had been moving out West, step by step. Born in Illinois, Bechtel moved his family first to Kansas and then Nevada before making it to California. With extensive experience grading railroad rights-of-ways, the Bechtel family established their permanent base in San Francisco. Their construction business grew beyond railroad contracts. In short order the W. A. Bechtel Co. was building highways and constructing dams. In the 1930s, the construction of the Hoover Dam, for instance, established the San Francisco company as a leader in its industry.

Throughout the twentieth century, Bechtel prospered, and it successfully established itself as a force in the construction industry on an international level. Its expertise ranged from building international airports in half the countries throughout the world, to the design of NASA's Apollo Space Simulation Center, to the construction of the Channel Tunnel linking England and France, to spearheading the efforts to rebuild Kuwait's devastated oil infrastructure after the Iraqi invasion. The difficulties the firm experienced when the nuclear power–generating facilities were abruptly shelved throughout the United States in the 1980s had, by the end of the 1990s, been successfully overcome.

The Internet frenzy that engulfed much of Silicon Valley in the 1990s also affected Bechtel. It is in this San Francisco story that lessons for all in corporate America in the Internet age can be found. Not unlike the Forty-Niners who were mistaken to believe in the promise of gold in the hills, Bechtel, at first, rushed into the Silicon Gold Rush blindly. In 1996, Bechtel Enterprises purchased the Los Angeles-based ISP (Internet service provider) Genuity as a way of establishing a formidable presence in the ISP/hosting market. Within a year, however, Bechtel realized there this foray into the "New Economy" was misguided. It was an unproven business model that required significant investments in telecommunications and technology. There was also something hollow about its promise of quick riches. The losses at Genuity were "real world," that is to say, they were significant and enormous. Bechtel quickly sold off Genuity to GTE Internetworking for an undisclosed sum. Manufacturing technologist Alan Hall debunks the myth that the "New Economy" has transformed the fundamental nature of the industrial economy without apology. "A computer is a powerful tool, but a computer never made anything—it's simply an enabler that has to translate to a manufacturing process. Nothing happens until that information reaches the factory. The Old Economy is the New Economy."[10]

In the same way that Crocker, Hopkins, Huntington, and Stanford realized there were greater opportunities in selling to miners, Riley Bechtel, the great-grandson of Warren Bechtel, realized that, however successful these adventurers into the "New Economy" would ultimately be, was not the point. The opportunity did not reside in figuring out if bricks could be downloaded via fiber optics, after all. That's science fiction. For a company such as the Bechtel Group, the real-world business opportunities were in *constructing* the real-world *facilities* the "New Economy" companies needed.

In the nineteenth century, Leland Stanford would provide passage on his railroad from New York to California. What the passengers did when they got to the hills of Sacramento was none of his business, but if they went broke and needed to go home again, he was only too happy to sell a return train ticket and provide passage back East. Bechtel, likewise, concluded that instead of getting caught up in the Internet vapor and "New Economy" dreams, it would rather build the warehouses, office facilities, and infrastructure projects Internet start-ups required. Whether these dot-com ventures fail and their state-of-the-art mortar facilities would someday sit empty and idle would be none of Bechtel's business—literally.

"For Bechtel, the fulfillment side of the Internet business is interesting to us because it meshes perfectly with what we've traditionally done," Tom McKinney, Bechtel vice president, said. "Let's face it, e-commerce is largely industrial to us. Over the last year or so, the dot-com reality has become a part of our everyday life. We started to look at the build-out, back-end program for these companies and realized there was an opportunity to make money in building their real-world facilities, and even gain an equity take in some Internet ventures."[11]

In 1999, Bechtel signed its first billion-dollar deal to build 26 warehouses for Webvan Group, the online grocer based in Foster City, California. Later that year it signed a $1.2 billion contract with Equinix, of Redwood, California, to construct 32 state-of-the-art fortified "Internet Business Exchanges"—or IBX—facilities. The imperative for many *online* companies is to ensure that their facilities never go *off-line*. Equinix is in the business of renting facilities for hosting servers, housing switches and routers, and providing secured premises for telecommunications equipment. Bechtel is uniquely qualified to build facilities that can guarantee Equinix the most secure facilities, guarantee an uninterrupted power supply, and provide installations that are able to withstand earthquakes and other disasters, natural or man-made. What sets Bechtel apart from many firms in corporate America, moreover, is its ability to recognize that opportunities that are hailed as belonging properly to the New Economy are in reality part of the Old Economy.

The San Francisco Forty-Niners were ill prepared for the realities of the Gold Rush. So were those who, one would think, were positioned to benefit from them uniquely. John Sutter, who went bankrupt in his native Switzerland, was granted a 50,000-acre tract of land by the Mexican government in northern California in 1839. As his holdings expanded, so did his wealth. The discovery at his mill by John Marshall, an employee, doomed John Sutter. As thousands of fortune seekers swarmed over his land, the squatters took over his property, a fact that was rendered legal by the federal government invalidating his land grant after the conclusion of the Mexican-American War. Although few miners ever made anything that could be considered a fortune, John Sutter became destitute. He spent the last years of his life in Washington, D.C., where the questions of overlapping jurisdictions, property rights, and the interests of a growing economy were debated endlessly.

The Big Four were thoughtful men. They were also prescient in not being misled into thinking that gold itself was the future of California; it is equally important to understand how the technological innovations emerging from Silicon Valley are the instruments through which the Old Economy can be invigorated and prosper. Fire has already been discovered. The wheel has already been invented. Many of the challenges the New Economy poses, as we have seen, are not unlike other innovations and developments that humanity has confronted in the past, particularly since the Industrial Revolution.

Bechtel has it right. Bricks and mortar are, for most businesses, more substantial than clicks through cyberspace will ever be. Internet enthusiasts point to Bechtel as a company that has successfully reinvented itself for the New Economy. But simply because a company has a Web site—or uses an Intranet—does not make it part of the Internet economy. Bechtel executives and engineers who are frequent fliers may contribute to the earnings of the airlines per se, but that doesn't mean that they are part of the *transportation industry*.[12] Bechtel is in the construction business in the real world. It has, however, begun to market its construction and engineering services to online companies that are demonstrating how the Old Economy companies can best take advantage of New Economy opportunities, and in the process creating gold out of vapor.[13]

If one removes all the Web sites that require goods and services to be delivered or performed in the off-line world from the New Economy, then the New Economy shrinks to a small fraction of what it is purported to be. This is neither good nor bad, for the Old Economy grows by an equivalent and corresponding amount. The New Economy that has emerged, in other words, reflects the distinctive traits of those who design it and those who use it with greater frequency. When like-minded individuals are given access to any incipient technological industry, there is the tendency for the development of that industry to reflect the eccentric personalities of its creators and users. Recall how winner-take-all contests arise when only barely perceptible quality margins determine who will succeed or fail in a given competition.

What one also finds is that it is a small group of (mostly) men and women who are at the forefront of developing the software programs and developing the technological infrastructure that is changing how the Old Economy does business and how the New Economy is evolving. A curious phenomenon has emerged within the ranks of these individuals. Whereas as recently as the mid-1990s these men where dismissed as nerds—the perennially disheveled Bill Gates epitomized the vision of "Geek Chic"—by the beginning of the 2000s, perceptions had changed. The otherwise benign world of software engineers and high-tech workers *polarized* social commentators.

George Gilder looked upon the men and women of Silicon Valley and proclaimed them as "angels" who would deliver humanity to Utopia. Paulina Borsook, by contrast, saw an unruly brotherhood of immature young men with the worldview of adolescent boys and proclaimed them dangerous "cypherpunks" (software programmers) who were empowering "anarcho-capitalists" (start-up venture capitalists). Few were the reasoned voices, such as that of *Wired* magazine's Bronson, who took a detached and bemused approach to chronicling the history of the Silicon Valley. That reasonable people recognize instantly that the men and women who comprise the community of "techies" are, foremost, human beings like all of us, however, does not detract from trying to understand why techies inspire such impassioned defenders and detractors.

Indeed, there is something of a cult of celebrity surrounding techies. Not unlike the entertainment industry where the personality of a film star or a rock star has tremendous influence in the kinds of movies or albums that become popular, in the high-tech world the personalities of research scientists and computer programmers have a larger-than-life impact on the industry. Consider how entertainers like Elizabeth Taylor or Frank Sinatra were able to influence entire genres of films and music for much of the second half of the twentieth century. Although few techies, such as Bill Gates and Steven Jobs, are household names, it is necessary to examine how television—the precursor to the personal computer—affected American society in the 1950s and, more importantly, how social commentators assessed the impact of television technology on the lives of Americans.

To do this it is useful to examine how American society placed in perspective the men who brought into being a series of technological innovations—television, radio, telephony, and airline flight—in a previous generation in the 1950s. In their landmark book published in 1950, *The Lonely Crowd,* David Riesman, Nathan Glazer, and Reuel Denney chronicled the decline in the family life of Americans at a time when the mass media became entrenched in society. The authors believed the media culture, in turn, gave rise to the alienation that became commonplace in the second half of the twentieth century. The result was a nation in which individuals walked, as lonely strangers, in the midst of crowds of their fellow citizens with whom they had diminished relations and weakened ties to the civic life of their community.

They documented how American society was beginning to become fragmented as bonds to one's neighbors and friends weakened and television viewing replaced human interactions. In their concern for the psychological impact of this alienation, they offered a comprehensive analysis of the "inner-directed" personality. These alienated individuals they described as introspective, socially retarded, or loners. These people were at higher "risk" for becoming isolated and depressed. It is not surprising that the profile they developed in the 1950s resembles the characteristics of the kind of individual most likely to be attracted to computers and the Internet in the 2000s.

Religious leaders, sociologists, policymakers, mental health professionals, and social commentators have noted with alarm in the intervening decades how the rise in divorce, alcoholism, drug abuse, and scores of other social ills accompanied the rise of a mass market and mass media consumer economy. Fifty years after the publication of *The Lonely Crowd,* Stanford University released the results of a study that depicts habitual users of the Internet as turning away from family and friends, suffering more frequently from depression than the general population, and reducing their involvement in civic and community affairs.[14] The authors of this report feared that the ascendance of the Internet technologies was accelerating the parallel alienation Americans experienced in the 1950s and 1960s, but in a more chronic and widespread manner.

Sociologists who study the Internet report that those who are connected online for more than a few hours a week agree with this assessment. They find that Internet users experience more frequent bouts of depression, anxiety, and loneliness than the nonusers, which is consistent with the patterns first documented in the 1950s concerning the alienation habitual television watchers felt.

"If when I go home I spend the entire evening online sending emails, and wake up the next morning, I still haven't talked to my wife or kids or friends," Norman Nie, a political scientist at Stanford University who coauthored the survey with Lutz Erbring of the Free University in Berlin, said. "When you spend your time on the Internet, you don't hear a human voice and never get a hug."

Although critics refuted the study's portrayal of the Internet as contributing to a heightened form of social isolation, certain behavioral observations about the culture and lifestyle of people in Silicon Valley are consistent with this conclusion. "There's always a give-and-take with this," researcher Jose Martinez said. "It is undeniable that marginal personalities are removing themselves from society, but at the same time, the Internet has made it possible for individuals who were previously homebound to reach out to the world. The Internet is destined to have negative social consequences, of course. But it also stands to have positive ones as well. That's where the challenge for us as a society lies. We have to provide a mechanism by which alienation and social isolation among Internet users can be prevented. But we also have to ensure that people who have remained on the margins of society up to now are able to use the Internet to integrate themselves into the civic life of their communities and participate more fully in the life of humanity."[15]

Alienation among Internet users is not alarming in and of itself for two reasons. Foremost, the understanding that has emerged from studying the phenomenon of increased personal isolation and loss of human contact among people also offers insights on how to ameliorate this phenomenon. Indeed, during the second half of the twentieth century, the loss of interpersonal contact contributed to an increase in the social isolation of certain groups, such as the elderly who did not live with their families. In the past 50 years, mental health professionals and social workers have learned much about the causes of alienation and how the lonely elderly can be integrated once again into society.

Second, armed with a more precise profile of the psychological and emotional characteristics of the individuals who are more likely to become habitual users of the Internet, it is possible to incorporate features that are sensitive to the kinds of problems that may emerge. In the same way that, say, bartenders are trained to identify certain patrons as problem drinkers, Internet companies can incorporate mechanisms that can detect behavior that is symptomatic of problems.[16]

As the New Economy becomes a part of our lives, it is necessary to understand the thoughts of the people who create the technologies that shape the various environments in which we live and work. At this point I should point out that I admire techies as brilliant men and women who are generous of spirit. They are neither the angels Gilder would have us believe, nor are they monsters who threaten civilization as Borsook writes. In fact, what Borsook decries is the stereotype that the (mostly) men developing the Internet technologies are eccentric characters because they are emotionally immature and socially retarded, but economically powerful. The implication is that, because of the enormous potential these technologies represent, it isn't that these young men are *mavericks,* but that they are *irresponsible*—and therefore *dangerous.* The title of her book encapsulates the theme in her argument: technology, selfishness, capitalism, and anarchy. This disconcerting assessment is not unique in the annals of recent history to be sure. And hers is not the first warning about the threat of anarchy posed by a selfish, technology-fueled capitalism.

Twenty years before Borsook offered this dim view of techies, others reached a radically different conclusion about the high-tech entrepreneurs of the Reagan years. Gilder saw humanity's salvation in the techies. A self-styled "techno-prophet," Gilder first came to prominence during the Reagan administration when he wrote *Wealth and Poverty* in 1981. His views on what the Internet offers are different from the apocalyptic warnings from Borsook. With the fire of a convert, Gilder argued that capitalism itself was nothing less than the fulfillment of the Christian mission in the world.

Gilder's pronouncements raised eyebrows, for it portrayed capitalists and entrepreneurs as zealots, something that struck economists and policymakers alike as bizarre. His frantic prose made businessmen uncomfortable, particularly in a time when "supply-side" economics was trying to overcome its stigma as "voodoo economics." Consider the article of faith in Gilder's tortured prose protesting the doomsayers, such as the members of the pessimistic Club of Rome, who in the 1970s warned of cataclysm and global collapse from the exhaustion of the world's natural resources:

> All plans based on the calculated present, on the existing statistics, necessarily presume a declined field of choice, a contraction of possibilities, an exhaustion of resources, a diminishing of return—entropy and decay. . . . [In this scenario, t]he rates of taxation climb and the levels of capital decline, until the only remaining wealth beyond the reach of the regime is the very protein of human flesh, and that too is finally taxed, bound, and gagged, and brought to the colossal temple of the state—a final sacrifice of carnal revenue to feed the declining elite.[17]

What's wrong with writing simply, "Taxes are too high?"

What's more offensive than his prose is the undue influence Gilder wielded in the 1980s and 1990s.[18] In *Microcosm,* a subsequent book,

Gilder praised technology for the sake of praising technology. In an interview at the time, consider the rambling and conflicted way he invokes articles of faith and mystery (religion) when attempting to describe, of all things, a rational high tech economy:

> [I]n the microcosm [of quantum theory] everything is invisible and governed by quantum laws which are very mysterious and contrary to our usual beliefs and expectations. And it's quantum theory that governs the microchip. And it's quantum theory that explains the prodigal effectiveness of microelectronic technology. . . . I find that people I know with no scientific background at all . . . [gain] a new appreciation for the technologies that mystify us but also greatly dominate our lives. And so I think it gives a glimpse into the microcosm. And by understanding that it's a completely different domain from the macrocosm of our usual lives you can understand it better. I mean it's the effort to try to treat it as if it's just another mechanical technology. . . . It is a radically new technology governed by completely different rules. . . . The microchip is the most important denominate in the world today.[19]

It is peculiar that in rebutting the dire predictions of the naysayers, Gilder indulges the other extreme, describing the "macrocosm" as if it were holy and the microchip as if it were the human soul. He becomes impossibly optimistic about the ability of technology to improve the lives of humanity.

His exuberant embrace of the Internet has detractors, to be sure. "[George] Gilder's bordering-on-homophilic hero worship of high tech coffee achievers (whether entrepreneurs or technologists)," Borsook wrote with undisguised contempt, "embodies to the point of self-parody the caricature-male quality of technolibertarianism."[20] Where George Gilder worships the technological innovations of the "anarcho-capitalists" of Silicon Valley, Borsook considers these same people as antisocial and dangerous.

This debate began half a century ago, of course. In the 1950s, individuals who were a little weird or eccentric, but harmless, were known as "characters." To make sense of how techies think and how their intelligence impacts society at large, we are fortunate that we have the work of more reasonable people than either Gilder or Borsook on which to rely. In fact, 50 years before Borsook and 39 years before Gilder, of course, Riesman, Glazer, and Denney reported on the nature of "inner-directed" individuals. Their description of these loners (adults who as children played with chemistry sets, wrote fan letters to Albert Einstein, and spent Saturday afternoons watching sci-fi horror movies) stands up well in describing the high-tech nerds and entrepreneurs that populate Silicon Valley. In 1950 they wrote:

> We do not . . . explain how the inner-directed social character came about, though we follow Max Weber's lead in seeing the Protestant Ethic as linking Greek type of rationality to a Judeo-Christian type of this-worldly morality. Family structure also seemed to us of decisive importance since the nuclear family makes possible the bringing up of children with very intense identifications with parental mores although this alone is insufficient to account for that definiteness of set and conviction, that endoskeletal quality and hardness which makes many inner-directed individuals into "characters" in the colloquial sense.[21]

It is on the work of these men that we can begin to think about techies, for what is this excerpt if not a succinct description of the high-tech scientists and engineers at work in Silicon Valley?

For a more precise profile, one that offers insights into a more profound understanding of the edifying stories that abound in the high-tech world, considers that fundamental human nature has not changed, regardless of whether one is writing in the 1950s, or 1980s, or 2000s. Indeed, consider the following description of the psychological makeup of the youngsters most likely to pursue a career in Silicon Valley by virtue of the fact that:

> the inner-directed person frequently divides his life into sectors, in each of which he can test his psychic defenses against it. Within himself he remains the child, committed early to goals and ideals that may transcend his powers. If these drives are demanding, no amount of contemporary acclaim can drown the feeling of inadequacy: the acclaim of others may in fact be the by-product of efforts to satisfy the self. Within himself he must find justification not only in what he does but also in what he is; not by works but by faith is he saved. And while clever bookkeeping can transmute works into faith, self-criticism is seldom completely silenced. *Mere behavioral conformity cannot meet the characterological ideal.*
>
> These internalized standards of the inner-directed man allow him, on the other hand, a certain freedom to fail in the eyes of others without being convinced by them of his own inadequacy. Like Edison, he will try and try again, sustained by his internal judgment of his worth. For while the others cannot protect him against self-criticism, self-criticism can protect him against the others. The inner-directed man can justify his existence not only by what he has done but what he will do.[22]

This is a fine description of the creative genius that drives and motivates the techies of the Internet technologies.

Not everyone sees this dedication, discipline, talent, and sense of purpose as a good thing. Borsook warns that the cliquish male-centered world of high tech has a dangerous side. She warns, in almost unintelligible prose, that:

At their most wacko, cypherpunks have some commonality with the paranoia, self-importance, and displaced anger of militia people. With their love of what they imagine anarchy to be, cypherpunks are ravers more likely than not, though some have quaintly Heinleinesque, "Starship Troopers" notions of women betraying a streak of social conservatism. . . . It's a mind-set less well articulated but still palpably present in more moderate geek subcultures.[23]

She is not alone, of course. Consider the caustic writing of Thomas Frank in *One Market under God,* a book in which he denounces the "hipster" Internet capitalism and cyberlibertarianism of the 1990s. He echoes Borsook's warnings in a less manic tone. But the concerns of both Borsook and Frank have been raised by other, reasonable voices. Consider *The Lonely Crowd* offered a considerably more kind—and balanced—description of nerds. Riesman pointed to the fad in the 1950s for hot-rods as an example of the pursuits undertaken by inner-directed youngsters. That the stakes are higher because the technologies are more powerful is of concern. Not to all commentators, however. This is the assessment Gilder offers in *Telecosm.*[24]

Futurists falter because they belittle the power of religious paradigms, deeming them either too literal or too fantastic. Yet futures are apprehended only in the prophetic mode of the inspired historian. The ability to communicate—readily, at great distances, in robes of light—is so crucial and coveted that in the Bible it is embodied only in angels.[25]

Robes of light are fiber optics? Biblical angels are satisfied Internet users? What is this foolish man talking about?

"Whenever the computer industry has a panel about the digital divide and I'm on the panel, I always think, 'O.K., you want to send computers to Africa, what about food and electricity—those computers aren't going to be that valuable,'" Bill Gates said in an address before the Global Foundation in Melbourne (Australia) held one month after the publication of Gilder's ridiculous *Telecosm.* "They want to sit on the panel and talk about how the computers will solve all the world's problems. They're amazing in what they can do, but they have to be put into the perspective of human values. And certainly as a father of two children, thinking about the medicines I take for granted that are not available elsewhere, that sort of rises to the top of the list."

Gilder's self-indulgent prose (like that of Paulina Borsook) is indicative of the lower standards of public discourse in the last half of the twentieth century. It is not surprising that the absurd pronouncements of techno-prophet futurists ring false, whether they are to praise or to condemn technology. These rants disguised as sermons lack common sense, prudence, and moderation. It is reassuring to realize, therefore, that other, reasonable voices take a dim view of this proliferation of techno-babble—and condemn it.

"A whole industry of cybergurus has enthralled audiences (and made a fine living) with exuberant claims that the Internet will prevent wars, reduce pollution, and combat various forms of inequality," the London *Economist,* where adults still have run of the place, observed, unamused. "Even when everyone on the planet has been connected to the Internet, there will still be wars, and pollution, and inequality. As new gizmos come and go, human nature seems to remain stubbornly unchanged; despite the claims of the techno-prophets, humanity cannot simply invent away its failings. The Internet is not the first technology to have been hailed as a panacea—and it will certainly not be the last."[26]

In order to reject both Gilder and Borsook, it is necessary to update how the insights offered in *The Lonely Crowd* apply to the New Economy. The growth of the Internet is the result of high-tech scientists and researchers without a doubt. But so much misinformation is written about them that it is necessary to look at them more closely in order to understand them. If there is reticence from techies to speak about themselves, it is due in part to the punctilious manner in which they are approached by outsiders with chips on their shoulders.

Consider the condescending mockery of Dennis Cass writing in *Harper's*. This is how Cass belittles the techies of Silicon Valley:

I cross the cafeteria in search of a pair of engineers I noticed standing on the fringe. One is younger, with long red hair and surfer shorts; the other is in his forties and is wearing linen pants and a broad Panama hat, an outfit that seems to say: Iconoclast. I introduce myself and ask if I can talk to them about life in Silicon Valley. "No," says Panama Hat. It's a harsh, drawn-out sound, two syllables that start high and slide low, getting louder along the way. It's so theatrical I assume he's joking. "I don't want to talk about products or anything, just life at Apple [Computer]," I say. Another no, with even more emphasis. "How about just life in Silicon Valley?" Blank stare. "How about you?" I say to Surfer. "I won't use your names." Reluctantly he tells me he's a software engineer from Indiana. When I ask him why people come to Silicon Valley, he cites the readily available "microclimates": the sunny valley, the surf along the coast, and the snow in the mountains. "That's it?" I say. "The weather?" He nods. I ask him about the work, about what it's like to be part of the Revolution, the Future, but he pretends it's nothing, like taking pictures at the DMV.[27]

Cass' tone is disturbing for the simple reason that it is characterized by an arrogance that undermines sound reporting. In a statement that could only have been a deliberate attempt to defame techies as a group, in fact, Cass reports that entering the office of David Hecht, a computer scientist working at PARC, he makes a discovery. "I see something I realize," he ridicules, "I haven't seen anywhere else in the valley: books."

It is a generosity of spirit that high-tech companies continue to indulge journalists when one considers that Dennis Cass' diatribe is what commonly finds itself into print.[28] Not unlike other writers who indulge a self-indulgent, self-congratulatory misanthropy, Cass, when it comes across in Silicon Valley, is simply another Man-Who-Knew-Too-Little. It is not difficult, then, to sympathize with techies who are surrounded by either cult followers (Gilders) or hostile critics (Borsook) or clueless members of the media (Cass).

In the course of conducting research about the Internet technologies for more than a decade, I have sought out many of the maligned geeks and nerds who are responsible for the technological innovations that are changing the way the world does business and how people live their lives. From the late 1980s through the present, I have been fortunate to befriend many brilliant, hardworking, and dedicated people working at some of the pioneering high-tech companies that are changing the world. Everywhere they have been kind and generous—stacks of books cluttering their offices and homes—and always willing to engage in conversation about the nature of their work and its impact on society.

If the nerdy geek of yesterday looms large over our future as technological innovations take center stage, the image of techies has changed. Whether it is Gilder or Borsook, their vocabulary evokes a different image from the creature with ink stains in his breast pocket. Their image of the techie is darker, somewhat more villainous, and certainly more threatening.[29] In the popular media, black leather and latex are the uniform of techies who, more often than not, are engaged in some conspiracy to hack into computer systems, appropriate credit card numbers, and empty bank accounts through online wire transfers. With the dubious reporting from journalists and business reporters who do not understand high tech, it is understandable that a certain air of malice surrounds Silicon Valley. It is human nature to project sinister motives on what one doesn't understand, one powerful reason why ignorance rather than being blissful is too often the source of injustice. The image of techies is tarnished further by the actions of renegade programmers who unleash destructive viruses. Immature adolescents who break into corporate, government, and military computer systems for sport contribute to the public's confusion. Rogue hackers unjustly paint an unflattering portrait of the entire techie community. The public responds by conjuring up images of sinister men capable of bringing civilization as we know it to its knees.

In order to appreciate the achievements of the men and women working on the technical side of the New Economy, a brief portrait of one techie is offered. Alias|WaveFront is a wholly owned subsidiary of Silicon Graphics. Alias|WaveFront provides artists with advanced computer graphics software. It is the world's leading innovator of 2D and 3D graphics technology used in film, video, games, interactive media, and visualization markets. Alias|WaveFront touches all of our lives because we are exposed to the creative results of their software everyday. Alias|WaveFront's software known as Maya, for instance, was used in the animation of the children's film, *Stuart Little*. It is used by the designers at General Motors in the conceptual modeling, rendering, animation, visualization, and surface development of new vehicles. It is seen on thousands of interactive Web sites all over the Internet. It is used to create the animation in hundreds of the television commercials and music videos broadcast everyday. As animated music videos take strides to interactivity, the three-dimensional graphics require the sophisticated software developed by companies such as Alias|WaveFront.[30]

Kevin Lombardi is one of the senior animators at Alias|WaveFront who presented the Pentium® II Xeon™ Processor for the first time. Alias|WaveFront's Maya program was demonstrated as one of the end-user applications that benefit from Intel's new processor. Before I offer a brief profile of him, what follows is from a presentation product launch given on June 29, 1998. Because so few members of the public are able to attend these functions, it is instructive to put human faces to the technological innovations being developed throughout Silicon Valley. As you read this, form your own opinion about what kind of men these are. These are the architects of the New Economy. These are the men changing our world. Are they, in fact, eccentric and dangerous "characters"?

This is an abbreviated portion of that morning's presentation that encapsulates the humanity of techies:

ANNOUNCER: Ladies and gentlemen, please welcome vice president and general manager of Intel's Enterprise Server Group, Mr. John Miner.

JOHN MINER: Good morning. Welcome to Intel's launch of our exciting new product, the Pentium® II Xeon™ processor for servers and workstations. This morning, Pat Gelsinger and I will step you through a brief presentation, talking about this exciting new product, what it's made up of and how the industry and customers will benefit from applying this product. . . . I'd like to turn it over to Pat Gelsinger who will come up and tell us about how the other technology that makes the Pentium II Xeon processor so great, and how it works in workstations. Thanks, Pat.

PAT GELSINGER: Thank you, John. . . . Before I get into a detailed discussion of the Pentium II Xeon processor technology, I'd like to start by giving you the first taste of what the Pentium II Xeon processor can do in workstation applications. To do that I'm pleased to have Kevin Lombardi from Alias|WaveFront here and he'll give us a demonstration of the Pentium II Xeon processor in action in a demonstration. So Kevin, you have Alias|WaveFront, and I believe you've just introduced an exciting new product, Maya.

KEVIN LOMBARDI: We have. Alias|Wavefront and Maya software are being used in the software industry for creating high-end creative animation visual effects for film, television and interactive media. In fact, a lot of our customers are doing commercial production with Maya.

PAT GELSINGER: Commercials. . . .

KEVIN LOMBARDI: Think about what commercials you see on television every day. Almost every commercial incorporates some character or computer animation. . . .

PAT GELSINGER: To do something like that requires a lot of performance.

KEVIN LOMBARDI: It does, and our customers are demanding on performance. . . . We have a technique called digital puppet, which has a skeleton inside of a character. So here I can select different parts of the character and move it and have a display file in the timeline and sync that audio up at 30 frames a second. . . . Key frames are basically just a major position in the animation that you want to save different parts and positions of the character. . . . So this is really just a way of being able to move a character around very quickly so you can create animation very quickly and easily.

PAT GELSINGER: That's great. . . .

This presentation is one of thousands held throughout the 1990s up and down Silicon Valley. It is clear that the individuals are neither the angels Gilder romanticizes about, nor are they the deranged anarchists Borsook implores us to stop. Rather, what we have, in fact, are remarkable people with remarkable achievements, caught in the process of presenting an unexceptional presentation.[31] In subsequent presentations given by Steve Jobs of Apple Computer, for instance, Lombardi was hailed as a "guru" of the Maya software he helped develop.

Alias|WaveFront is based in Toronto, Canada, but it has offices in Santa Barbara, California, where the development of their software programs take place. It is here that the creative genius transforms hard work into the kinds of tangible products that are changing how the world plays and works. To understand who these people are, it is useful to take a closer look at one of them. This isn't a brief excursion into the *inner life of nerds,* however, for the realities are far different from the expectations.

I have spent time with him and his colleagues over several years in Toronto, Chicago, San Francisco, Santa Barbara, and Los Angeles. What one learns is that these men are hardworking, dedicated, and brilliant. Whatever ideas continue to be propagated by the media, it is clear that the eccentricities of a few oddballs have been distorted as attributes that describe the entire community of Internet researchers, scientists, and entrepreneurs. It is undeniable, however, that these are people who have focused interests, oftentimes with the unbridled enthusiasm that gives rise to passions.

The enthusiasm that an individual techie like Lombardi brings to his job is that of optimism, curiosity, and discipline. Why is the world the way it is? How can we develop a software program that will do what we want it to do? How are the technical obstacles to be overcome?

This requires the kind of concentration and time commitment that in most industries constitutes a workaholic. It is the nature of this commitment that makes it possible for techies not to be restricted by the standard workdays. This flexibility is one reason why the lights are on at all hours of the day and night in many office parks in Silicon Valley. What detractors consider to be "vampire" hours are, in fact, individual creative rhythms; night shift workers in hospitals and law enforcement, for instance, are not viewed suspiciously as, somehow, not being "right." Inspiration wakes some people up in the middle of the night— quite a few can't wait until morning to get working.

Techies are not angels who will save humanity through technology as Gilder would like to believe. They are not the technolibertarians who plan to bring an end to the nation-state. These are not even the ardent libertarians who, as Robert Frank said, "[insist] that the right not to be restricted cannot, as a matter of principle, ever be negotiated away, [and show] contempt for the rights of people to resolve such issues for themselves."[32]

The rush becomes an adrenaline high tinged with the sense of discovery. The high that comes from flying one's own plane, of going through the checklist, of gaining speed as one taxis down the runway, of the anticipation that builds as one lifts off the ground and takes flight is one of accomplishment. This is a different chemistry from the quiet euphoria of discovery. It is the satisfaction that comes from succeeding because of dedication, concentration and perseverance. "The electric light has caused me the greatest amount of study and has required the most elaborate experiments," Thomas Edison wrote. "I was never myself discouraged, or inclined to be hopeless of success. I cannot say the same for all my associates."

This is the realistic belief in discovering how to solve the puzzle of the possible. It creates the need for a rush, a rush that occurs when the brain is bathed in chemicals that are released when one is delighted with success. The second observation, then, is the need for the high that comes from this kind of achievement. When the workday is over, not unlike highly driven professionals in other industries, techies seek out adventure. High-risk activities, such as skydiving, bungee jumping, white water rafting, flying, and mountain climbing are normal recreational pursuits. Others seek the same rush through the challenging intellectual endeavors: creating software programs others say can't be done, pushing an application to its technological limits, reconfiguring a network to carry out improbable tasks. I have accompanied techies on "leisure" activities that have included trekking through the Australian Outback, working intensely around-the-clock to crack a software code in their offices in Silicon Valley, and participating in the Burning Man festival in the Nevada desert, where I have had the chance to meet an extraordinary number of techies from Silicon Valley and Seattle.[33]

Techies work and play hard. They are relentless in their singular pursuit of questioning the world around them. In contrast to the image painted of them by the liberal establishment along the Eastern seaboard, they read all kinds of books, from the most arcane technical manuals, to fantasy novels that take place in a futuristic medieval world, to the philosophical tomes by everyone from John Locke, Aldous Huxley, and the works of Ayn Rand.[34] They are always thinking and trying to figure out things, even when a commercial featuring animated amphibians and reptiles comes on the screen. "Before I got through," Thomas Edison was fond of recalling, "I tested no fewer than 6,000 vegetable growths, and ransacked the world for the most suitable filament material."

Thomas Edison was an inner-directed person, almost a century before the term was first popularized. The brilliant genius of the techies at the forefront of the Internet revolution taking shape was foretold half a century ago: "The inner-directed child was supposed to be jobminded even if the job itself was not clear in his mind."[35]

The "job" may not be clear in the minds of most people outside the high-tech world. Little boys and girls want to grow up to be doctors and pilots. But what six-year-old wants to grow up and become a Maya software guru?

But these are the kinds of professions—and professional achievements—being invented everyday in Silicon Valley. This is because in Silicon Valley, technology is not seen as either a panacea or the imposition of a New Economy. It is a way of finding the answers to specific technical questions, one at a time. Thomas Edison went through more than 6,000 "What ifs?" in his search for the one filament that solved the technical problem he had to resolve. This is the same process repeated everyday in Silicon Valley.

It is, quite simply, the challenge in creating something new, something better, something fun. The creative genius is not revenge of the nerds, but the creative invention of solutions. For every lunatic pontificating about creating world peace with just the right kind of software interface, there are thousands of high-tech researchers, programmers, and scientists working to solve specific problems, issues, or applications.

Technolibertarians like Tim May, whom Borsook holds as an example of an unrepentant anarcho-capitalist, are few and far between. It becomes clear that if Gilder is a Utopian, describing a perfect society where technology delivers mankind to a state of grace, then Borsook warns of a dystopia, where technology unleashes the means through which our lives are impoverished and will enslaved. Individuals such as Lombardi, who are pursuing the technical knowledge that makes the possible *possible,* are the ones responsible for creating the New Economy and transforming the old one. They are neither to be worshiped nor feared, but simply appreciated for how their talents make our lives, as individuals and a society, better. In the first decade of the twenty-first century, this means creating the technical know-how upon which an online economy is being built.

Key #5

The difference between the Old Economy and the New Economy is that in the New Economy no good or service has to be delivered or provided in the real world. As a result, many companies that are presumed to be part of the New Economy are, in fact, part of the Old Economy. In order to understand the New Economy, it is first necessary to understand the kinds of individuals who are creating the New Economy and those more inclined to participate in it. Since the 1950s, observations about the alienation that results from the mass media have shaped our ideas about the impact of technology in the lives of human beings. Internet technologies exacerbate the alienation that pervades modern civilization. As a result society must be cognizant of this and take the necessary safeguards to ameliorate the resulting unintended consequences these technological innovations produce.

Furthermore, with the advent of the New Economy, there is renewed fascination with the inner-directed nature of the people who constitute the high-tech subculture. Extremely divergent views have emerged about nerds and geeks, however. One set of critics praises them as the embodiment of the ideal of entrepreneur. Another set of critics denounces them as dangerous individuals who seek to replace human relationships with technological ones. Although certain personality traits are in common among techies, what is clear, however, is that they are as intelligent, educated, hardworking, and responsible people as they are diverse.

NOTES

1. Services, by their nature, cannot be provided online. One can make an appointment for a haircut online, but the actual haircut cannot be provided online. One can also secure an airline or hotel reservation online, be given a confirmation number, but the transaction is not completed until the service—the flight itself is taken, or one checks into the hotel—is delivered.

2. Governments and nongovernmental organizations (NGOs) can participate in "business-to-business" hubs.

3. Amazon.com operates distribution warehouses in Campbellsville, Kentucky; Coffeyville, Kansas; Ferney, Nevada; Grand Forks, North Dakota; Lexington, Kentucky; McDonough, Georgia; New Castle, Delaware; and Seattle, Washington in the United States and two additional ones in Europe.

4. Joelle Tessler, "Where the Web Gets Real: Amazon.com's Huge Nevada Warehouse Turns Virtual Orders into Cardboard Boxes Filled with Merchandise," [San Jose] *Mercury News*, November 20, 1999; personal communication, December 1999.

5. Saul Hansell, "For Amazon, a Holiday Risk: Can It Sell Acres of Everything?" *New York Times,* November 28, 1999.

6. This is true the world over. In Latin America where delivery of goods has traditionally been associated with national postal services—and the service has been poor—e-commerce companies are relying on delivery companies such as United Parcel Service, DHL, and FedEx. DHL, for instance, invested more than $30 million in 1999–2000 to upgrade the facilities in Latin America and now counts on two major hubs, one in Panama City and Buenos Aires. FedEx, for its part, now operates a major distribution center in Toluca, near Mexico City, and is expanding facilities in Miami, Florida. With over 500 million people in Latin America, the market has tremendous potential where the Old Economy nature of e-commerce is evident: the challenge is in getting access to the Internet to people as much as getting the real-world infrastructure to make actual deliveries. "The potential for e-commerce in Latin America is still a number of years away," said Gregory Rossiter, a FedEx spokesperson. "We need to have the infrastructure to move packages, expedite Customs and have delivery vans on the streets."

7. Levi Strauss, a German Jew, became successful when he began to manufacture sturdy dungarees that were ideally suited for prospecting. Levi's denim jeans have survived long after many mining towns became forgotten ghost towns.

8. Collis Huntington, the man who headed the Central Pacific Railroad during the time it expanded greatly on the largesse of government loans, was particularly targeted by William Randolph Hearst's newspapers for criticism.

He was, in fact, accused of using public money to create a private monopoly. When Leland Stanford became governor of California (1861-1863), his business dealings were scrutinized as well.

9. The excess was deemed "wretched," and two of the more vocal social critics were the writers, who were also journalists for newspapers, Mark Twain and Ambrose Bierce.

10. Alan Hall, "The Old Economy Is the New Economy," *Business Week Online*, November 13, 2000.

11. Alan Saracevic, "Bricks For the Clicks: Bechtel Understood Long Ago That the Net Would Need Real-World Facilities," *Business 2.0*, June 2000.

12. However frequent a flier one is, that person remains a "passenger." (In the industry, in fact, passengers are reduced to "revenue miles." That is, of course, unless one flies on a free ticket. Then the "passenger" is simply an inconvenience that has must be accommodated.)

13. Bechtel was proved right in short order. "Webvan, the online grocer that epitomized the buoyant optimism that the Internet could revolutionize even the most entrenched industries, closed yesterday and said it would seek bankruptcy protection," Saul Hansell reported in the *New York Times* on July 10, 2001. "After spending almost all of the $1.2 billion," he wrote, Webvan was history—and Bechtel was not.

14. Stanford Institute for the Quantitative Study of Society, February 2000. This survey is based on a nationwide random sample of 4,113 individuals over the age of 18. Of the respondents, 13 percent indicated they were spending less time with friends and family; 8 percent reported attending fewer social events; and 25 percent are working more at home (without a corresponding decline in their work at the office).

15. Personal communication, Center for Ethical Studies, Havana, Cuba, December 2, 2000.

16. Paternalistic laws require bartenders to refuse to sell drinks to patrons who appear intoxicated and securities firms to verify the net worth of clients engaged in high-risk investments. Companies limit their own liability, such as when bars that provide free coffee or cab rides to patrons, or when investment companies limit the amount of an investor's capital that is placed in high risk instruments. These are models for similar safeguards for Internet companies dealing directly with the public.

17. George Gilder, *Wealth and Poverty,* p. 258.

18. That upon his father's untimely death George Gilder was watched over by his father's school friend, David Rockefeller, allowed him to present his ideas to America's elite.

19. George Gilder, C-SPAN *Booknotes*, broadcast on September 24, 1989.

20. Paulina Borsook, *Cyberselfish: A Critical Romp through the Terribly Libertarian Culture of High-Tech,* p. 143.

21. David Riesman, Nathan Glazer, and Reuel Denney, *The Lonely Crowd*, pp. xxv–xxvi.

22. Ibid., pp. 124–125. Italics appear in the original.

23. Paulina Borsook, *Cyberselfish: A Critical Romp through the Terribly Libertarian Culture of High-Tech,* pp. 18–19. "Ravers" refers to entertainment pursuits enjoyed by members of Generations X and Y.

24. *Telecosm* should have been titled Tele*nonsense*. Gilder argues that the mere existence of technology will foster revolution. It is as naïve a claim as stating that the mere existence of enough food on the planet renders hunger a thing of the past. The existence of food does not eliminate hunger when transportation logistics, political boundaries, and purchasing power stand in the way of feeding the hungry. Les Vadasz made the same point in his review of the book in the *Wall Street Journal*: "If we are to reap the benefits of all the wonderful technological advances in communications, technology alone will not be enough," he wrote in his review published October 12, 2000. "The service has to be deployed in comparable numbers, in the hundreds of millions and more. And we are very, very far from that." If we are unable to make sure everyone on the planet has a piece of bread to eat everyday, how are we going to make sure everyone is online with infinite bandwidth?

25. George Gilder, *Telecosm: How Infinite Bandwidth Will Revolutionize Our World*, pp. 3–4.

26. The London *Economist* takes Americans in particular to task for irrational optimism. "Grandest of all the claims are those made by some of the *savants* at the Massachusetts Institute of Technology about the Internet's potential as a force for peace. One guru, Nicholas Negroponte, has declared that, thanks to the Internet, the children of the future 'are not going to know what nationalism is.'" His colleague, Michael Dertouzos, has written that digital communications will bring "computer-aided peace" which "may help stave off future flare-ups of ethnic hatred and national break-ups." From The London *Economist*, August 19, 2000, pp. 11–12.

27. Dennis Cass, "Let's Go: Silicon Valley!: Wherein the Author Stalks the Flighty Webhead in His Habitat," *Harper's*, July 2000, p. 62.

28. When Dennis Cass was given a tour of Oracle, for instance, he was required to sign a standard non-disclosure agreement: "'There are customers who are meeting here today, and we can't have you writing who is here,' [Anna del Rosario, his host at Oracle] says. Over on the wall is a list of the day's visitors, and I can't imagine why a famous Australian brewery that sells beer in big blue cans would care if people found out it was here, but I agree not to name names and sign."

29. It is also more sexual. Consider that in the mainstream media, films such as *The Matrix* with Keanu Reeves and *Mission: Impossible* with Tom Cruise have sexually charged leading characters who dress fashionably as they hack.

30. Digital Hip Hop, for instance, was one of the first companies that used interactivity to bring music fans to computers, where music and videos were brought together in a singular entertainment experience.

31. There is nothing in this presentation that is out of the ordinary. In the same way that hearing physicians make a presentation on an experimental treatment, or listening to art historians discuss newfound works by early Venetian Renaissance painters, this conference is characterized by vernacular known to professionals in the same fields.

32. Robert Frank, *Choosing the Right Pond*, p. 225.

33. "Burning Man" can be best described as an empty-headed neon surrealist encampment of radical inclusiveness in which many Silicon Valley

techies participate. It began, of course, in San Francisco and lasts an entire week out in the Nevada desert. On one occasion when I attended, I was delighted by the chance to meet an engineer about whom I had heard many good things. Because of the circumstances upon which we met, however, I agreed to divulge neither his name nor the company for which he works. A description of that meeting should be enough to convey the eccentric and singular nature of genius. When he was ready to meet me, he walked over our encampment. He was wearing a Viking-style helmet, with upturned horns. He was wearing body paint on his face and chest, evoking the male-affirming and neo-pagan rituals popularized by Robert Bly. He was wearing rubber galoshes, a leather jock strap—and nothing else. He volunteers that he is somewhat "stoned" but eager to speak; the present excess is a mechanism for relieving the stress of his work. In the course of our hour-long chat, two-thirds through it, he announces he has to urinate. He falls silent for a moment, and then I notice he is relieving himself as he resumes speaking, the urine splashing on the desert sand, and running down the insides of his thighs into his galoshes. This man is a brilliant engineer, one whose pioneering work continues to affect the development of the high-tech industry. I would run into him on two more occasions in the course of Burning Man, each time under similarly peculiar circumstances. After this initial encounter with him, as he wanders off into the afternoon sun, I was struck by the randomness of brilliance—and I notice how the sun's rays glisten and shimmer off the damp urine on the inside of his thighs.

34. John Locke's *The Social Contract* is a perennial favorite; reciting verbatim from *Brave New World* is a familiar game of one-upmanship; and anything from Ayn Rand is de rigeur.

35. David Riesman, Nathan Glazer, and Reuel Denney, *The Lonely Crowd,* p. 78.

PART II

THE ENTERTAINMENT ECONOMY ONLINE

CHAPTER 6

THE UNPRINTED WORD

A book published in 1999 was unlike any other book in recent memory for one reason: Its publication was reported on the front page of the *New York Times*. The content of the book was itself hardly newsworthy. *The Nothing That Is* by Robert Kaplan is an intelligent and well-written discussion by a mathematician that addresses the history of the concept, the history of how humans discovered the meaning, and the significance of zero. But what prompted the media coverage, however, was the fact that this erudite tome was published in a pioneering way: two-thirds appeared physically in print, and the balance was published exclusively online. A visit to the Oxford University Press' Web site is disconcerting in its unfamiliarity, for there are the "Notes and bibliography" with the advisement to "please be patient while it loads" onto one's hard drive.[1]

The unexpected marriage between the world of physical books and text that can be downloaded from an Internet site is a watershed in the incorporation of technological innovations to the business of publishing.[2] Although book, newspaper, and journal publishers struggled with—and resisted—the advent of the Internet throughout the 1990s, e-publishing is emerging as one of the more promising and creative markets of the online economy.

This is not to say that the fortunes of "e-publishers" are equally bright, per se. As the natural evolution of the online economy unfolds in the 2000s, it is necessary to review the four different business

Digitally Portable	Digitally Delivered	Internet Ready	Printer Ready
A book that can be electronically downloaded to a portable device, such as a Palm Pilot. This would allow travelers, whether for business or pleasure, to read downloaded material from anywhere. Not unlike Audio Books, most digitally portable tomes are abbreviated versions of longer titles.	Full-length books that are ordered and sent via e-mail as an attachment. Individuals can print the book on a computer screen, print it out in a loose leaf format, or both.	Books that are either read online or customized to individual specifications. An individual can select criteria from various sources into one specific book. A traveler to Paris, for instance, can request various chapters on museums, castles, and wineries from different guidebooks and have them assembled into his or her personal guidebook.	Technological innovations pioneered by IBM now make it economical to print out and bind a single copy of any book. Books stored electronically, therefore, will no longer ever be out-of-print as the minimum "run" consists of a single copy.

Figure 6.1   Online Publishing: Four Emerging Options

models that emerged for online publishers. What they have in common, however, is that each incorporates technological innovations into the publishing industry in ways that are consistent with historical precedents and reinforce real-world business models. Although mass-market book publishers are using the Internet to expand the market for books as a whole, professional, academic, scientific journal, and textbook publishers are reaching customers around the world in ways that logistics made previously impossible.

Newspapers and online journals, on the other hand, are finding that their electronic editions are seen as superfluous and as entertainment, something for which customers are not prepared to pay. The exceptions, of course, are business newspapers or professional publications that, from the start, establish user fees and the content of which is not freely available through other media. For general interest online journals, such as Salon.com and Slate.com, the observed consumer attitude is that these kinds of publications will have to be supported by advertising and distributed freely.[3]

As we shall see in the discussion of the music industry, for books both encryption and digital watermarking technologies facilitate the protection of intellectual property rights, the integrity of online copyright protection, and the payment of royalties to writers. That consumers prefer the physicality of books is one reason why "sample" chapters and digitally delivered books oftentimes result in the sale of an actual book. The result is that the e-publishing industry that is developing, moreover, is one that inspires confidence in the ability of technological innovations to expand existing markets and create new ones. A closer examination of each market is in order.

BOOK PUBLISHING: CONVERTING BOOKS TO BYTES

When Stephen King released his electronic novella, *Riding the Bullet,* in March 2000, there were more than 400,000 requests to download this work, overwhelming bn.com and Amazon.com alike. Two months later, when the Microsoft launched Reader with Michael Crichton's *Timeline,* this created an e-publishing sensation.

The viability of e-novels, however, was not settled by either Stephen King's or Michael Crichton's success with their e-novels. When Stephen King released his second online work, *The Plant,* on July 24, 2000, the *New York Times* declared "Stephen King Sows Dread in Publishers with His Latest E-Tale," asking, "Is the horror writer Stephen King leading a revolution in the way books are published, or just exploring the power of celebrity in the digital age?"

The novel, about a vampiric vine that assaults a publishing house, was posted online in installments. It could be downloaded by readers for free, but, in an honor system, visitors were asked to pay voluntarily one dollar for the right to read and download the installment. Stephen King announced that if 75 percent of readers who downloaded the story paid, he would continue to post installments. A week after *The Plant* was first posted online, Stephen King announced that 152,132 copies had been downloaded, and of those 116,200 had paid for the right to do so.

"Pay and the story rolls. Steal and the story folds. No stealing from the blind newsboy," Stephen King wrote on his eponymous Web site. Less than two months later, the novelty had worn off. Only 74,373 people downloaded the second installment of the story, and the percentage of those paying voluntarily fell far below the 75 percent minimum set by Stephen King. "We are beginning to see a widening disparity between downloads and payments," Stephen King said at the time. "There is undoubtedly some thievery and bootlegging going on."[4] By the end of the novel, online serialization proved more problematic than anyone had anticipated, and the venture became a minidisaster for the suspense writer.

In the first half of 2000, the e-publishing industry began to codify itself both in terms of technology and how publishers were aligning themselves to participate vigorously in this new market. Bn.com, for instance, became the first retailer to launch its own electronic publishing division in January 2001 when it announced it would offer an original work from suspense writer Dean Koontz. "I hope publishers realize that e-books are a real market and we are in a unique position to help writers reach readers," Michael Fragnito, publisher of Barnes & Noble Digital, told reporters at the time.[5] The foremost consideration for bn.com was the technological protocols that were becoming the industry standards. E-publications had to be converted into digital formats. These publications subsequently had to be delivered electronically to customers.

Microsoft's Reader software became the industry standard that would be used to deliver e-publications to customers via portable devices. Whether these are handheld devices or ones that are accessed through Internet accounts, the delivery of digital material to portable devices greatly expanded the market for this material.

Once an e-publication arrives to the customer, there is the matter of how the e-publication can be accessed. For publications, whether books or articles or magazines, that are delivered digitally, consumers can print physical copies from printers. In some cases, usually depending on the price paid for the material, an e-publication may only be accessible online. Customers may be permitted to read sample chapters, or an entire publication, but not be able to print a physical copy to have of their own. Others may be enticed to purchase the physical book. In addition, the technology is now available to allow readers to view books that would otherwise be out of print but that can be printed and bound into a physical book specifically for that reader. This benefits what are now "out-of-print" books, as well as creating a new industry that allows readers to assemble piecemeal chapters, maps, and information into a customized book. The most common application for customized books, for instance, is assembling disparate reading materials for a class; books can be created that include material in the syllabus of a college-level course. Outside of an academic setting,

Microsoft	Time Warner	Barnes & Noble	netLibrary
Using the Microsoft Reader software that allows for the downloading of books, Microsoft has entered into a publishing agreement with Simon & Schuster (Viacom) and Random House (Bertelsmann). Random House acquired 49% of the Internet vanity publisher Xlibris. Simon & Schuster and Random House are in the process of putting more than 40,000 back titles in digital format for e-publishing.	Time Warner Trade Publishing, a division of Time Warner, launched a separate online publishing venture called iPublish and iWrite, dedicated to securing original manuscripts for online publication. iPublish offers condensed versions of print books and serialized works published online in installments. Time Warner looks to expand the publishing market by reaching to a younger demographic market.	To expand its e-commerce operations, Barnes & Noble purchased 49% of iUniverse and entered into a marketing venture with Yahoo!. iUniverse is a vanity press for online works. The electronic books can be read on the Microsoft Reader software. Barnes & Noble plans to publish books of interest to younger audiences and students.	Dedicated to assembling and selling electronic libraries, netLibrary, the $105 million start-up, has been successful in selling to university libraries. Its sale to the University of Texas at Austin proved that if students had 24-hour access to electronic books with full-text search features, patronage rises. Students, comfortable with computers, prefer to read what is published electronically.

Figure 6.2 E-Publishing Players Seek to Expand Market by Targeting Youth

customized travel books can be assembled that reflect the interests and itineraries of each traveler.

E-publishing represents the technological breakthrough that publishers are using to expand the market for books, newspapers, and magazines. That the Internet can be used to reach young people, who can be counted to become lifelong consumers for publishers if reading becomes a part of their lives, is an opportunity to broaden the market for all kinds of written works. Indeed, the companies in the United States at the forefront of e-publishing are now more firmly established. With the announcement of comprehensive and sweeping mergers, acquisitions, and joint ventures, there are four major players competing and complementing each other. The most formidable of these is Microsoft. Although its Reader software is available to competitors, the publication of *Timeline* in May 2000 signaled its pursuit of the mass market for books with a singular determination.

That Microsoft announced an agreement with both Simon & Schuster and Random House, which together count on more than 20,000 backlisted titles, it is clear that Microsoft Reader will have exclusive access to market a formidable inventory of publishers.[6] In the same way that Ted Turner's purchase of vintage Hollywood films gave its cable network an exclusive inventory to first-rate content to broadcast, Microsoft's access to more than 40,000 titles gives it a competitive advantage however the consumer market for e-publications continues to develop in the 2000s.[7]

Time Warner is the other major corporation that has committed itself intensely into e-publishing. With the announcement that it had launched iPublish and iWrite, the media conglomerate set as its goal nothing less than the expansion of the publishing market. With the creation of a division dedicated exclusively to securing content for e-publishing, Time Warner signaled its belief that young people, familiar and comfortable with computers and reading material on monitors, constituted a vast market whose needs were not met by traditional publishing. Librarians around the country would corroborate the observation that young people represented the one constituency that read fewer books and less frequently. The same librarians, however, could also confirm that, if reading material appeared in a digital format, it was this segment of the population that downloaded the material most frequently.

Time Warner, then, has approached e-publishing as an extension of the online music and video markets that have proven to be so popular among consumers between 18 and 35 years of age. That iPublish and iWrite provide condensed versions of full-length books and publish material in installments fits nicely with the goal of expanding the traditional market for books by creating a new, younger, more technologically sophisticated audience.

This is consistent with the strategy pursued by Barnes & Noble through its equity investment in iUniverse, a vanity publisher [now defunct]. Whereas Time Warner's iPublish and iWrite have editors who perform the traditional role of deciding what material they will publish, iUniverse worked as a vanity press, where they charged a small fee to anyone who wanted to have his work published electronically.[8] The absence of editorial discretion, however, fit nicely with the nature of the medium, specifically both the democratic ideal that anyone should be able to publish anything and the simple reality that cyberspace doesn't clutter up bookshelves with unreadable tomes. For Barnes & Noble, however, the appeal of iUniverse to reach out to readers was not unlike the Internet, which allowed unknown musicians to reach audiences they would otherwise not be able to reach. The dynamics at play remain intriguing to publishers attempting to reach younger customers. The idea of mass market e-publishing becoming a "youth" industry is encouraging. It offers the opportunity to use technological innovation to expand a market in ways that were not possible a generation ago. Indeed, publishers hope to seduce young readers, using technology to conquer the barriers of national borders and language.

This internalization is best exemplified by netLibrary, which is dedicated to assembling and selling electronic libraries to institutions around the world. The ability of netLibrary to assemble products that allow, primarily, libraries at universities and colleges to serve students, has several benefits. First it allows students to access material round-the-clock, which is important not only for students a few blocks from the library that are insomniacs, but also for those who are physically in distant time zones. Second, it allows young people to access publications in a medium that they prefer over the printed page. Finally, it allows for the continuous updating of material and the cross-referencing that is not possible with traditional publications.

"The logic of electronic books is pretty hard to refute—we see it as an incremental increase in sales as a new form of books for adults and especially for the next generation of readers," Jack Romanos, president of Simon & Schuster, said in an interview. "The publisher's ultimate responsibility is to get the work to the greatest possible audience, and this is one more swing at the plate."[9]

Perhaps, but what motivated publishers was fear. It was the monumental terror that what Napster had done to music, someone somewhere would do to books. The idea of digital manuscripts circulating freely over the Internet without the consent of copyright owners was a real possibility. Thus although no one understood what the e-publishing industry would look like in, say, 2010, the speed with which publishers rushed in to stake their claims in cyberspace and extend their brands online was consistent with the belief that the Internet represented a technology that had to be embraced if publishers were to avoid the miscalculation record company executives had made by shunning it.

The unknown possibilities and market potential of the Internet, publishers were convinced, could best be developed by they themselves. Confident that with elaborate software protection and by providing economical ways for storing, distributing, and downloading digital books, publishers en masse decided to transform their back lists of out-of-print books into virtual libraries. Random House, a unit of Bertelsmann, pursued it with relentless aggression throughout 2000, determined to stake claims in the world of e-publishing. In May 2000, Random House announced an agreement with Audible to sell digitized audio books over the Internet. The new imprint, called Random House Audible, focused on smaller niche markets initially, including historical material (political speeches and news reports), specialized content (business books), and proven Random House books (John Grisham novels). That these titles could be downloaded and played over an MP3 player, furthermore, opened the possibility of allowing Random House Audible to distribute music as at future date.

To understand the competitive frenzy in its historical context, Bertelsmann was so determined to dominate publishing online that two months later, AtRandom, an exclusive digital unit dedicated to e-publishing, was announced. Launched in January 2001 with about two dozen titles, these titles could be downloaded in electronic versions, or as print-on-demand books. "This is the brave new world we want to see," Ann Godoff, president and publisher of Random House Trade Group, told the *New York Times* at the time, echoing the optimism of Bertelsmann, which was, on a different front, working to reach an agreement with the music record industry, which had lawsuits pending against Napster. "No printing, no paper and binding, no need for a sales conference or printed catalogue—we don't know the size of the market, but it could be potentially very profitable for us."[10] Or not.

Random House, cognizant of the stunning inroads made by Reed Elsevier in the field of technical and scientific publishing world online, spent the greater part of 2000 devising the groundwork for laying claim to the consumer publishing market. Even though e-publishing received tremendous attention, the actual sale of e-books among consumers remains low. Andersen Consulting expected consumer titles to account for no more than 10 percent of all e-books sold—and that wouldn't be achieved until the year 2005. When Random House announced in the fall of 2000 that it would offer electronic versions of about 100 classic works of literature, such as James Joyce's "Ulysses," it also announced that by addressing the needs of students, it could make inroads to a broader consumer market.

"The most attractive quality of e-books is their versatility," Sheana Ochoa wrote on CNN.com:

> E-books have searchable highlights, making it easier for you to relocate important sections you've marked. You can take notes without running out of margin space. An electronic dictionary allows you to click on a word and get its definition. E-books can also be read in the dark. Finally, as mentioned earlier, you can download an e-book in seconds—and there are no shipping fees.[11]

Effortless searches, dictionary definitions at a click of a button, being able to be read in the dark and downloaded instantly are all qualities ideally suited to students in high school and college. This explains why online dictionaries have met with stunning success. Merriam-Webster and Houghton Mifflin quickly joined Microsoft in the online dictionary market. "Electronic novels may be making headlines these days, but electronic dictionaries are making money," David Kirkpatrick reported in the *New York Times*. "Stifled for years by low margins and flat sales, [dictionary] publishers are salivating over digital licensing as a new source of revenue growth and promoting new features like audible pronounciations."[12]

Although Microsoft's Encarta dictionary was widely ridiculed—the illustration for "Madonna" was a photograph of pop singer Madonna Ciccone and not the Virgin Mary, for instance—the Oxford University Press made the online dictionary market a legitimate market. For an annual fee initially set at $550, researchers could access the online version of the venerable 20-volume Oxford English Dictionary. Oxford University Press planned to have the entire O.E.D., in forty volumes, online by 2010, while allowing it to be continuously updated.[13]

The development of e-publishing through 2001 conforms to a niche market within a differentiated market. "Making a mass consumer product is more challenging than developing a specialized industry," David Steinberger, president of corporate strategy for News Corp.'s HarperCollins argues. "The natural early adopters for e-publishing are the academic, professional and educational markets. Once these make it in e-publishing, a broader consumer market emerges."[14]

It is also fast becoming a developed and lucrative market. Consider the success of two companies that have developed online publishing programs for the academic community. Reed Elsevier Science, Inc., is the New York-based science division of the Anglo-Dutch textbook publisher.[15] Its professional journals include *Cell Press* and *Lancet*. Reed

Elsevier developed a program in which customers who subscribe to the print edition of their professional journals are able to choose an online component at the cost of a modest 15 percent surcharge. This allows subscribers to conduct research, search for related articles, and use the resources within the publisher's archives. At the same time, the company markets institutional online subscriptions to universities and libraries. This allows professors, scientists, and researchers to access the journals online from the university campus, research facilities, or at conferences using passwords, which, in turn, allows university and research administrators to understand what information is being used when, by whom, and how.

For professors, researchers, scientists, and graduate students, they are freed from the burden of having to have access to physical documents to conduct their work. Reed Elsevier has thus created a stunning multimillion dollar business. In 2000 revenue from its Internet-related activities and e-publishing approached $600 million, more than half of its total annual revenue.

In 1996 John Wiley & Sons, Inc. launched an online division of Wiley InterScience to publish electronically the company's journals. John Wiley has moved more cautiously into pursuing its online sales. Nevertheless, along with online book sales, John Wiley reported that in 1999 revenue from e-publishing approached $60 million. The company expects that by 2003 its total revenue from its Internet activities will be $190 million.

"Our approach to the Internet is one of listening to our customers," William Pesce, John Wiley & Sons president, said. "Our customers are the ones who told us that e-publishing was a better way of providing content. They're the ones for whom we tailor our e-publishing activities."[16]

Not unlike other book publishers, John Wiley & Sons has embarked on a program to digitize its backlist of books, offering a limited number of titles as e-books. The lessons textbook and scholarly journal publishers have learned in successful e-publishing are ones that lend themselves to the development of a broader market. Although it's news when Stephen King publishes a novel on an installment basis, this is simply the mass-market equivalent of securing paid subscriptions for a scientific journal or serial.

NEWSPAPER PUBLISHING:
SUBSCRIPTIONS FOR CONTENT

In the real world, newspapers charge both advertisers and subscribers. That the Internet failed to provide a mechanism for charging Web site visitors at first meant that to be online meant to be free of charge.

How to charge online readers took time. This was further complicated by the simple fact that the nature of this new technology confused many managers who failed to understand how the Internet would ultimately function as a business. That the most efficient model for developing an online information business was found in syndication was not immediately obvious during the first few years of the Internet. As a consequence, different newspapers pursued different strategies for establishing their brands in cyberspace.

Consider for a moment the different approaches pursued by the *New York Times* and the *Wall Street Journal*. The *New York Times* was convinced it had to provide its content free of charge. It pursued a strategy of requiring visitors to register, and, once having done so, the entire contents of the daily newspaper would be accessible. The newspaper's coverage was supplemented by providing breaking news stories from the Associated Press and Reuters. The only source of revenue, apart from banner ads, would come from charging a small fee for archived articles. This would allow the *New York Times* to develop a large customer base and position itself as a premier research site online.[17]

The *Wall Street Journal,* on the other hand, began with the assumption that its content was a valuable commodity it could not afford to devalue by being given away. From the beginning, it would charge a basic subscription to online readers. Convinced that the subscription fee could very well be considered a business expense, the *Wall Street Journal*'s online edition, in essence, was designed to reach business subscribers who were unable to secure physical copies of the newspaper. As the leading business newspaper, the *Wall Street Journal* was further aided by its ability to promote its online edition in the pages of its real-world daily.

The *Wall Street Journal* was cognizant of the reluctance of potential customers to become actual subscribers, particularly when almost everything else on the Internet was being given away. The number of subscribers remains small compared with other online newspapers, to be sure, but the *Wall Street Journal* has been building subscribers steadily as it has enhanced and expanded its content. Unencumbered by physical considerations, it can theoretically put online a limitless number of articles and stories, the diversity and depth of its online coverage offers an impressive array of choices.

The fluid nature of the Internet allows for a decentralized distribution system via networks. This flexibility affords more than one syndication model to succeed. Although they have pursued opposite approaches to their online editions, both the *New York Times* and the *Wall Street Journal* have been successful. This is all the more curious when one considers how success through the rapid expansion of the mass media online has resulted in other examples of disappointment.

ONLINE SYNDICATION AS A BUSINESS MODEL

Dear Abby became a national sensation only after it went *national.* How one woman writing one column for a Chicago newspaper, in which she dispensed common sense advice that updated Puritan values for the complexities of American life in the second half of the twentieth century, has been able to reach readers nationwide is testament to the efficacy of syndication to distribute information. The development of syndication—newspaper columns, television programs, radio shows—parallels the rise of the mass media as an industry.

Syndication as a business model has its origins in scarcity of resources. Confronted with the inability to pay to send correspondents to far-flung locations, six New York newspapers pooled their resources in the mid-nineteenth century. The nonprofit organization they created in 1848, which would send journalists to all corners of the world in order to report datelines from the actual location, was called the Associated Press. What made these innovations possible, of course, was first the telegraph and then the telephone.

The Associated Press was able to recoup the costs by charging other newspapers and publications a fee for the right to publish the stories carried over its wire. The introduction of new technologies—radio and television—further spread the demand for "content" in order to fill programming hours. A television station that was on the air for only a few hours at first could only hope to increase the hours it broadcast only when suitable and sufficient programming was available.

Consider the unique characteristic of information as a good. Whereas goods and services can be sold only once, information can be sold over and over. A case of wine is gone once it's sold; a seat on an airplane ceases to exist as a service once the airplane pulls back from the gate. In contrast, a story by an Associated Press correspondent sent via telegraph from Paris to New York can be sold over and over again to different newspapers and magazines around the country and around the world.

The nature of information and entertainment as a commercial product—"content"—required three fundamental components. Foremost, because content did not depend on the production, transportation, or delivery of a good or service, it could be sold to many customers simultaneously. The fluid nature of the distribution network introduced the element of modularity. The Associated Press stories could be carried in any newspaper at an editor's whim. A town with three or four newspapers could decide for itself which stories they carried. Because almost no newspaper published everything that came over the Associated Press wire, there was discretion. This led to the third aspect of syndication: a fragmented distribution.

The Associated Press sells its stories to 1,550 daily newspapers that jointly own it. Since its founding in the nineteenth century, the Associated Press has grown to a staff of over 3,500 in 240 bureaus around the world. The growth of syndication as a viable model for the information and entertainment industry consolidated and prospered in the first half of the twentieth century. By the time Dear Abby arrived on the scene, it was a mature industry. A columnist who enjoyed great popularity could expand readership rapidly as more and more papers entered into an agreement to carry his or her writing. In the same way that cartoons appeared nationwide through the success of the United Feature Syndicate, a natural development of aggregating and distributing syndicated content emerged as the quintessential model for the commercial dissemination of news, information, and entertainment content.[18]

The Internet is the natural evolution of the information and entertainment industry. For the Associated Press, the Internet has been a source of growing revenue. It sells its contents to almost 1,000 online companies that then post the stories on their Web sites. The growth of its online syndication service, known as Associated Press Wire, and other nontraditional sales for the Associated Press accounted for over $150 million in 2001, which constitutes about a quarter of its annual sales.[19] The ability to syndicate content online results in being able to sell the same article over and over again to either a Web site or a customer who is the end-user.

Consider a financial online company, such as E*trade. In order to build its business, it has to provide a complete array of brokerage services at a discount. In order to build a long-term relationship to existing customers as well as entice visitors to its Web site into signing on, it has to provide other services. It has to provide real-time stock quotes and financial news, advice on building portfolios, information on companies listed on the exchanges, profiles on movers and shakers, and a vast array of other information that is complementary to the interests of customers.

In the same way that a newspaper in the Midwest could boost its circulation, select news stories that from areas that were of interest to its local readership, and differentiate itself from competitors by boasting respected international news coverage because it carried overseas dispatches from the Associated Press, so can an online company such as E*trade build its business by securing its information and entertainment content from outside providers.[20]

The kind of depth and breadth of coverage afforded newspapers, the Associated Press delivers through its Wire web site. This allows online brokerage firms, for instance, to concentrate on providing trade execution services while other companies specialize in providing other content that is then assembled by editors and publishers in order to create the final product. The Associated Press has, in fact, been so successful that newspaper publishers are concerned that their own online versions of their real-world newspapers are at a disadvantage. If anyone can subscribe to the Associated Press' Wire service for content, then their dailies' exclusivity vanishes.

This is true enough, but the rules of the game have changed. Through the Internet, anyone online anywhere can register with or subscribe to the *New York Times* or the *Wall Street Journal*—or any other publication anywhere in the world that is online. This is the natural development of how technological innovations have strengthened the business of news reporting through syndication through networked distribution systems. In the same way that the modularity inherent in syndication made it unnecessary for newspapers across the country to come up with hometown versions of Dear Abby in years past, online companies can avail themselves to professional companies that can provide the aggregates required for their final product.

This is instructive, for it suggests that in the development of a successful business model for publishing online, it is important to realize that information brokers are in a specialized industry. The Associated

---

Originators   Writers, artists, and other creators of original content who provide their material for marketing and syndication.

Syndicators   Package original content for distributors. Manage relationships between creators, distributors, and the needs of the market.

Distributors   Deliver content to customers. This is done through the compiling of content aggregate from various sources that satisfy its business and editorial mission.

Consumers   Read and view the final product.

In syndication, revenues are generated through fees paid to syndicators and product sales, subscription and advertising fees paid to distributors. Syndicators pay originators. Distributors may not charge consumers when advertisers pay in exchange for more viewers of their advertisements.

Figure 6.3 Syndication as a Business Model

Press did not sell its articles directly to the public. Newspaper editors acted as intermediaries, deciding which stories they believed interested their readers and which news reports they thought their readers should be able to read.

Online publishing depends on syndication as a viable business model. Syndication consists of three steps before the final product reaches consumers. These are Originators, Syndicators, and Distributors.

Originators

Originators create original content. Dear Abby and Charles Schulz are examples of creators of content. The Internet, through its ability to make use of its vast network, makes it easier to disseminate content created by Originators. Consider Inktomi, a company that created proprietary technology that made it possible to link computers together and then function as a "supercomputer." Inktomi's technology made it possible to allow inexpensive computers, such as the ones used in most consumers' homes, to link up and have their used memory used collectively for the benefit of all. Instead of selling this technology, Inktomi chose to syndicate it, charging on a per-query basis. The result is a mechanism for creating an abundance of content that can be syndicated throughout the world in an efficient manner.

Syndicators

In the Old Economy, original content was packaged by syndicators. The Associated Press and United Features are businesses that have thrived by providing editorial review and managed relationships between the creators of content and the distributors. The Associated Press' strong move into online publishing, however, has not been exclusive. Two Internet companies that attempted syndicate were iSyndicate and Screaming Media. The compilation, collection, and packaging of digital information by iSyndicate and Screaming Media brought together original content from many sources and provided it to Web sites in standard formats on a contractual basis. The Associated Press pioneered the model, making it easy for Web sites to post its stories. That Screaming Media sought to categorize each article gave the ability to provide relevant content to each Web site that subscribed to its services.

Distributors

The companies charged with delivering the final product to customers have traditionally been the distributors. The *New York Times* and

ABC News, for instance, sell their product directly to the public. Content, in the form of news stories, articles, entertainment features, advertising, and opinion, attempts to satisfy the interests of readers and viewers. Distributors of online content include companies such as Yahoo!, CNN.com, and the NYTimes.com. That technological innovations result in markedly reduced overhead costs allows distributors to become highly specialized.

Thus although CNN.com brings breaking news of international and national interest, Squashtalk.com, on the other hand, can bring the community of squash players together by providing news on games, tournaments, interviews with players, and developments of interest to this community of aficionados. For the time being, most distributor sites are free of charge, meaning their revenue must be derived from hosting advertising (banner ads) or the sale of products (fees for downloading archived articles or the purchase of other products).

The ability of syndication to leverage abundance, develop aggregate information products for editors, thrive in loose distribution networks, and assemble continuously shifting resources is a business model that complements the specific characteristics of the Internet as a business environment.

The important role of editors, in both the real and virtual worlds, remains one of exercising their judgment and criteria in deciding what is and isn't of interest to their readers or online visitors. The proven history of syndication, however, is not entirely obvious to all. This is, in fact, where the notoriety and vastness of the Internet's networked distribution system can mislead. Consider, for instance, that for most people, "deconstruction" refers to a philosophy, and a minor art movement. But in a frantic effort to embrace a manic future, there is tremendous pressure among business consultants to present simple ideas in the jargon of buzzwords. This is why, for instance, "deconstruction" is presented as the new buzzword for, of all things, "syndication." Philip Evans and Thomas Wurster offer their unintelligible argument that with the advent of the Internet:

> Deconstruction posits a melting of the glue that binds the newspaper value chain together. The glue in this case is the economics of things—printing presses and distribution—tying together the informational content. Once other means of distribution become possible, the bundle can no longer be taken for granted.
>
> Liberated from the economics of things, journalists will be able to e-mail content directly to readers. Readers will be able to mix and match content from an unlimited number of sources. They will be able to download news daily (or several times a day) from multiple news services. They will be able to obtain movie reviews, travel features, and recipes directly from magazines, book publishers, and master chefs. Star

columnists, cartoonists, or the U.S. Weather Service can send their content directly to subscribers. Intermediaries—Internet portals, intelligent agents, formatting software, or, for that matter, editorial teams—can format and package content to meet readers' individual interests.[21]

Liberated from the economics of things? This is what businesspeople are being advised?

Presenting a business discussion in this manner is a disservice to corporate America. At a time when there are already too many demands on managers and executives, the last thing needed is for pompous pontifications that obfuscate matters. The facts are that the Associated Press, on an average day, sends one million words over its news wire. In the Old Economy, "intermediaries" are, for the most part, newspapers and magazines. To find out what's going on about town, the local section of the newspaper reports on goings on about town. To keep up-to-date on what's happening in the world of, say, outdoor adventures, Sports Afield magazine does a splendid job. Few individuals have the time to subscribe to the U.S. Weather Service to get the forecast for the zip code that interests them. Few have the interest to subscribe to movie and theater reviews by specific critics. Fewer still have the time to have customized recipes downloaded automatically.

To argue that "deconstruction" is a viable model is to forget that the individual consumer has other things to do. It is also unrealistic to expect an online company, such as E*Trade, to provide movie reviews and the weather forecast for my locality. E*Trade outsources these functions through features on its Web site that allow customers to select options resulting in a strengthening of the role of syndication. A customer, the end-user, relies on an online company, such as E*Trade, to specialize in trade execution and other brokerage services. E*Trade, on the other hand, relies on the Associated Press and the U.S. Weather Service to provide additional information that is then aggregated to the services. There is real value added in the bundling of components. In the same way that editors fill the pages of newspapers, so do online Web sites bundle disparate aggregates into a final product.

The jargon aside, what Reed Elsevier has accomplished online is a vindication of traditional economic ideas. Whereas high-profile online ventures have yet to produce the long-awaited profits, success online for Reed Elsevier has translated into greater economic power in the Old Economy. This was nowhere more evident than when Reed Elsevier announced it would pay almost $3.5 billion for the textbook business and about 500 journals published by Harcourt General.

This represents the most significant consolidation in the publishing world seen since the 1960s when Robert Maxell transformed Pergamon Press into a powerful force that controlled publications ranging from obscure, but highly profitable, scientific journals to trade books to the New York *Daily News*. The Association of Research Libraries reports that the price of the average journal has tripled since 1986, which has forced its members to reduce their acquisitions of books by 26 percent by the end of 2001. The current wave of consolidation is being led by Reed Elsevier, financed by the cash flow of its e-publishing division.

"Reed Elsevier is by far the largest journal publisher, with a list of about 1,200 titles and $1.1 billion in annual revenue from its science publishing unit," David Kirkpatrick reports. "Harcourt publishes roughly 500 journals, with about $700 million in revenue from scientific, technical and medical publishing. The combined companies would have about $1.8 billion in revenue out of a worldwide market that analysts estimate at about $6 billion."[22] The familiar nemesis of an Old Economy market imperfection that otherwise results in the elimination of choices now prospers in the New Economy.

MAGAZINE PUBLISHERS:
GENERAL INTEREST ONLINE GIVEAWAYS

Unlike real-world newspapers and magazines, journals that were created for the Internet have encountered greater difficulties to establishing themselves as viable businesses. It has often been the case that managers at online journals lack the experience necessary to manage properly their Web sites as profitable concerns. To understand the challenges of general interest online journals, one has to consider the rapid expansion of choices for readers across the board. Most newspapers and magazines now have online versions of print editions. Urban weeklies listing happenings around town, entertainment guides, and investigative reporting on local issues, from the *Village Voice* in New York to the *Bay Guardian* in San Francisco, have online editions. Cable news services have expanded coverage on the Internet, from NBC News to CNN. Almost every television and radio station maintains a Web site. Universities, professional and industry associations, think tanks, and public policy institutes offer a plethora of literature online. To these, one must add the thousands upon thousands of other organizations and enterprises in other countries that also provide information on the Internet.

There is so much information provided on any given day that it becomes almost impossible to compete for visitors. In a market where content is provided in abundance and for free, it is difficult to envision a business model where consumers pay subscription fees for a product that is, essentially, undifferentiated from what is available one click away.

Two online companies that have generated great interest and received tremendous public attention, though each has pursued a different online strategy and each has consistently disappointed analysts, are Salon.com and Slate.com. A brief overview of each company is necessary to illuminate the misguided business models pursued to develop markets that really are minor and periphery to online publishing.

Slate.com, for one, found out the hard way that one cannot give one's content away for free and then expect customers to be asked to pay for it. The reason for this resides in the nature of human psychology. The *New York Times* and *Vanity Fair,* like all newspapers and magazines, promise an illusion as much as a product. The *New York Times* sells the idea that subscribers will be well informed about the news, knowledgeable enough to form sound opinions about issues of the day, and up-to-date on cultural and social goings on. *Vanity Fair* sells the idea that readers will be informed on a variety of current events and entertained by well-written articles that trash people.

For online journals, on the other hand, that there is no hard copy that can be pulled out of a carry-on bag to share, the idea is less important than the content. And with the content being distributed free of charge, there is more disillusion among readers. There is, after all, nothing on Salon.com for which most subscribers would pay. Slate.com found this out in a humiliating manner when it began to charge, and it saw its readership vanish to such an alarming extent that it was forced to rescind charging a subscription. To be sure, both Salon.com and Slate.com have been praised for the quality of their journalism. The problem, however, is that what general interest online journalism offers is widely available; consumers have no reason to pay for entertainment that, on occasion, has unique content.

It was the irrational exuberance that surrounded the advent of the Internet that misled so many otherwise intelligent businesspeople and investors alike. That venture capitalists were prepared to write checks in the millions of dollars to young people in their late teens and early twenties who, because of their business inexperience, had not gone through the natural learning curve of their careers, meant that naïve and innocent ideas were funded. These business models were based on the bet that the number of unique visitors would be so great worldwide that banner ads and online sales would suffice to cover expenses. This was not the case. As a result, throughout 2001 each went their own way: Salon.com covered Hollywood, television, and celebrities, and Slate.com became more and more irrelevant. Online journals, in fact, are becoming a form of entertainment, publishing movie reviews, celebrity gossip, and social commentary inspired by breaking news: a youngster opens fire on his classmates at some high school, and there are a slew of pieces on guns and violence; the stock market suffers through a few volatile sessions, and there are instant pieces about the economy.

The results are Web sites that offer peripheral articles, produced instantly and shallowly, which offer assessments about public matters that are as vacuous as gossip concerning the clash of personalities during the filming of the anticipated summer movie blockbuster. It is, in other words, not a question of readers wanting free content, but the belief that if both Salon.com and Slate.com were to shut down their Web sites, their content would not be missed. The few quality writers they publish would find other outlets for their articles in other off-line media, whether it is *People* magazine or on the *Entertainment Tonight* television show.

The result is one in which, by failing to understand the principles of syndication, many online journals continue to struggle. Others have gone out of business. A few will be able to make the transition into viable enterprises. How the public, investors and observers alike, perceive these developments is important. The level of scrutiny given to a few select companies affects how the entire industry is perceived. These perceptions, in turn, affect the investment climate in any given time frame.

Scrutiny, which encompasses media coverage and publicity along with analysts' opinions, is in no small measure a product of *visibility*. This is where Internet companies resemble more closely both professional sports and the entertainment industry. Recall the importance of celebrity as an integral aspect in winner-take-all contests. Celebrity news, whether from Hollywood or Silicon Valley, consists primarily of gossip and rumor. It is one thing to follow the exploits of our favorite celebrities in the tabloid press, but it is another altogether to base investment decisions on this kind of speculation.[23]

Sociologists tell us that we pay different kinds of attention in our everyday life. A mother is more attentive to the whimper of her infant than to the wailing of a distant fire engine. There is a corresponding relationship to the varying degrees of visibility to business and industry. To understand this phenomenon more closely, it is instructive to ponder why we know who won the Tour de France in 2000 and why the best squash player in the United Kingdom is hardly known to his countrymen, let alone to Americans.

Consider how Lance Armstrong became a household word in the United States after he won both his battle with cancer and the Tour de France in 1999. The Texan cyclist first proved that he was a world-class athlete in 1993 when he won the World Championship and the Tour de France. Three years later, however, he was diagnosed with testicular cancer, a cancer that had spread to his lungs and brain. With only a 20 percent chance of recovery, his career was shelved, and he embarked on a battle that included surgery and chemotherapy. He triumphed, defying death, and returned to competitive cycling to win the Tour de France in 1999.

The compelling story of his remarkable achievement is told in his autobiography *It's Not about the Bike.* Reviewing the book in the American Library Association's *Booklist,* Brenda Barrera wrote, "It is such an all-American story. A lanky kid from Plano, Texas, is raised by a feisty single parent who sacrifices for her son, who becomes one of her country's greatest athletes."

Perhaps, but it certainly helped that cycling is a popular sport practiced by billions around the world. This is why there are cycling competitions in many countries, including the Olympics. Not all sports are this well known to the public at large. The court game of squash on the other hand, remains an obscure sport in the United States. In the United States, racquetball is more popular than squash, of course, despite the fact that it is played by more than 15 million players in 130 countries around the world with more than 50,000 courts dedicated to squash. The international appeal of this game notwithstanding, it is surprising that it is, along with racquetball, excluded from the Olympics.[24] But it is in this sport that a tale of personal triumph over tragedy is to be found.

Simon Parke, a young Englishman who was the top-seeded British player and who ranked seventh in the world, also confronted a life-threatening medical condition. In late 1995, he was diagnosed with testicular cancer for which he was operated on in early January 1996. He and Lance Armstrong faced the same life-threatening cancer at the same time. In Simon Parke's case, the follow-up chemotherapy consumed most of the rest of that year, and it was then that he withdrew from professional competition. The realization that he had been cut down at the peak of his career—and at the tender age of twenty-three—stunned the world of professional squash.[25]

In a testament to the strength of his character and his bravery, however, Simon Parke did not let cancer stop him. Far from being defeated, his determination to return to the professional athletic competition was inspirational to the entire squash community—and only months after surgery.

"I spent time with many others in the hospital who were battling greater challenges than I was," Simon Parke reflected. "I realized how lucky I was to have the chance to return to play top-level sports. This isn't going to stop me. But I am looking forward to taking a little longer now at every event to appreciate what part of the world I am in and to enjoy the experience of being there." If his personal battle gave him a broader perspective on the frailty of life, his return to the international squash circuit proved both opportune and triumphant. Simon Parke regained the position of being the best squash player in England.[26]

The realization that general interest journals online are analogous to commercial television broadcasting is a sobering one. Unlike professional, academic, and technical serials or business newspapers, Slate.com realized that their business model approximates that of giveaway weeklies or magazines, such as New York's *Village Voice* or inflight magazines that airlines make available to their passengers. Thus, left without subscribers, the primary source of revenue is advertising. In turn, the more readers delivered to advertisers, the more an online journal can charge.

Here is where technology becomes poetic, for the Internet allows precise analysis of how many read which pages and for how long. The polite fiction in publishing, that readers will read everything with equal interest, is demolished by technology. For most writers it comes as a stunning surprise to learn, for instance, that the average reader spends approximately 20 seconds on any page. The tracking of "hits" received by any site generates a count that constitutes a detailed profile of the readers to general interest online journals. Few readers read, for most skim the articles and move on.

"Insidious" and "malicious" are the adjectives used by Michael Kinsley at Slate.com to describe the realization that visitors to his site seldom read an article completely. "The click rate doesn't measure the intensity of somebody's interest," he offered, dismissing the contention that readers dismiss the content on Slate.com. "The traffic that goes to one particular article may or may not reveal how important that article is to you or your readers. It can do harm, since writers are delicate flowers." That is to say, readers' interest in Slate.com easily wilts, because it offers little of substance.

At Salon.com the situation is far different. Executive Editor Gary Kamiya admits that they "devour the counts avidly. It's become an addiction for us. We get our morning tally and we check it immediately. We look forward to seeing how we did."[27]

An article that receives 20,000 hits, for instance, is considered successful. One that generates only 3,000 hits, on the other hand, does little to impress advertisers. The pressure becomes intense, for writers feel the constant pressure to write stories that generate traffic. Not unlike the tabloid press and the free weeklies, therefore, there is a relentless pursuit of traffic to the Web site, one in which journalism is undermined. "If you put in the word 'sex' in the headline, you're guaranteed to double your hits," James Ledbetter, the television critic for *Time* said. "The daily numbers are a journalist's nightmare. What you have is a situation in which writers will come up with the most salacious angle in order to boost the number of hits they get. That's not journalism."[28]

No, it isn't, but it is entertainment, however. It is also reminiscent of gold prospectors in 1849 fighting over insignificant nuggets of gold: whereas Slate.com and Salon.com maneuver to get an overnight bump in their hits, Reed Elsevier generates more than $1.5 million in sales every 24 hours.[29]

Let us put this in perspective. In 2000, Salon.com originally expected to have revenues of about $20 million, or less than what Reed Elsevier earns in two weeks. By June 2000, revenue expectations were lowered to $14 million, or about what Reed Elsevier sells in about nine days. Compared with the amount of press coverage Salon.com receives, however, one would think that the future of e-publishing as an industry depended on the fortunes of this one company and this one business model.

"The carnage in the world of Web-based journalism continued yesterday as Salon.com, one of the highest-profile Web magazines, dismissed 13 employees in an effort to make up an expected $7 million shortfall in its $35 million budget," Felicity Barringer reported in the *New York Times*.[30] As Salon.com scrambled to rise above the financial strains of this unproven economic model, it was to become—of all things—an Old Economy company. "[I]f advertising on the Web weakens or the company cannot control its spending," Kara Swisher warned in the *Wall Street Journal* a month later, the company sought new "promising revenue streams," which included "content syndication to other Web sites and off-line publishers, the sale of downloadable audio book content, increasing focus on 'broadband' content and even the possible spinoff of its content-publishing system into a separate company."[31] This is nothing new, of course, but online syndication as a business is referred to as aggregation. "For the people who thought their content was so precious, now we could say, To whom?" said Jay Chiat, who runs the online content broker Screaming Media.[32] The intent is straightforward enough: combine the Old Economy business model of traditional journalism with the New Economy technology for content distribution.

But by selling content to off-line publishers, Internet companies such as Salon.com become an Old Economy company. "Funny how the tables have turned," noted with some amusement Brendan Coffey in *Forbes* magazine:

> Not long ago the Internet was supposed to be the death knell for print media. Now that venture capital and underwriting are drying up, struggling dot-coms are seeking more traditional forms of revenue from advertising and subscriptions—money that is more easily nabbed by traditional media properties.[33]

"It didn't take a rocket scientist in 1999 to see that there were some weaknesses with the straight-up, Web-only content model," Michael Hirschorn, cofounder of Inside.com, is quoted as saying in the article. Kurt Andersen, the other cofounder of Inside.com, which is dedicated to covering "The Business of Entertainment, Media & Technology," began to publish an off-line magazine version of itself in December 2000, six months after its initial debut online. Inside.com was heralded (at least by Andersen and Hirschorn) as part of the long-awaited transformation that melded the "Internet economy and digital technology" into an enterprise centered on the "nowness" of it all. This mediacentric approach to the Internet is confounded in its naiveté.[34]

This Web-to-print migration underscores how the laws of economics apply in cyberspace. Inside.com's capitulation to fundamental economics underscores that misguided online ventures shut down, or return to the Old Economy in due course. There are, curiously, a few companies that were launched on the Internet, have developed successful business models online, and then proceeded to establish a presence in the Old Economy as well. *Yahoo! Internet Life,* which was launched in the summer 2000 and modeled after *TV Guide,* has become one of the nation's fastest-growing serials, with a paid circulation surpassing one million. The success of Yahoo! to create a successful Old Economy magazine that complements its online Web site, however, is the exception. By appealing to youth and techies, it is able to target a receptive audience and fill a market niche.

If Salon.com is faulted by analysts for its extravagant spending and inability to bring spending in line with its revenues, the opposite is true of Slate.com. Approximately 600,000 of Slate.com's 1.5 million visitors discover the online magazine by word-of-mouth and clicks-of-links through the Microsoft Network. Michael Kinsley, Slate.com's editor, is credited with running a "lean operation," one that is "less than one-fourth of the staff of similar sites," writes Kara Swisher. "He says he is aiming to break even [in 2001] and run a site that would be able to operate as an independent operation."[35]

Hoping to break even is an odd aspiration. Recall the famed Forty-Niners who went out to strike it rich in the California Gold Rush. Their dreams of fantastic fortunes were reduced by the realities of prospecting in mid-nineteenth-century California. As they lowered their sights, what they hoped to achieve was modest success, one in which they could live decent lives and provide modestly for themselves and their families. Slate.com's Kinsley tells the *Wall Street Journal* he has "no regrets" about changing from a subscription model to an ad-sales model, noting that he is determined to keep costs in line. Salon.com's David Talbot around the same time announced the launching of a Salon Business, a business news and finance site. "There's a huge appetite for business and financial coverage online," he said in May 2000. "Salon Business will offer more colorful and critical journalism than can be found elsewhere."[36] The recriminations and turmoil among online magazines publishing resembles something out of *Macbeth*, "a tale told by an idiot, full of sound and fury, signifying nothing."[37] In instances of such impassioned fury, the comfort of perspective is welcome.

Indeed, in the same way that the gravitational pull of economics curbed the hubris of Inside.com founders Andersen and Hirschorn and brought them back to planet Earth, Salon.com and Slate.com are both entering lower and lower orbits with each passing quarter. As the 2000s unfold, both dot-coms will find themselves in a position where they will have to come out with an off-line version of their online magazines, or they will have to shut down. Yahoo!'s success with its off-line magazine, however, is not a guarantee that either Salon.com or Slate.com would be successful. Both online sites target consumers who are overwhelmed, if not overburdened, by the number of publications currently competing for their attention.

As early as 2001, it became clear that some e-publishing models were more successful than others. Consider the 2000 revenues generated by Reed Elsevier, John Wiley & Sons, and Salon.com. When the online "economy" these three companies comprise is charted graphically, it is startling. Whereas Reed Elsevier is entirely unknown to the public at large, and every press release issued by Salon.com is scrutinized by the press, the disproportionate attention paid to the insignificant impact of Salon.com on the economy in question astounds. Recall for a moment that the average find for the average miner provided an average living during the California Gold Rush. The vast fortunes generated by the Big Four, at first, escaped the public imagination completely. Everyone then told and retold stories of those who pursued their dreams of striking it rich. Everyone now analyzes and reanalyzes whether Salon.com is developing a viable business model.

The e-publishing business, however, is far ahead of where investors and the public alike are focusing their attention. E-publishing online has already emerged as a profitable niche market that will become a multibillion dollar market during the 2000s. As for the likes of Salon.com, Slate.com, TheStreet.com, and all other similar endeavors, they will generate $10–15 million in advertising sales, struggle to remain frugal, and find an equilibrium in which they become nice little businesses. The average journal will generate average revenue streams and provide average livelihoods for their employees. These, then, are respectable enterprises that will thrive in their respective market niches, but they do not warrant the attention that has been bestowed upon them by the investment community.

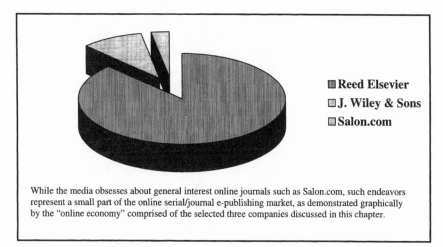

While the media obsesses about general interest online journals such as Salon.com, such endeavors represent a small part of the online serial/journal e-publishing market, as demonstrated graphically by the "online economy" comprised of the selected three companies discussed in this chapter.

Figure 6.4   E-Publishing: The "Buzz" vs. Revenue

In comparing and contrasting the high-profile antics of both Salon.com and Slate.com, the curious role played by the disparate levels of visibility—and therefore attention, if not scrutiny, each receives—of these various e-publishing enterprises is instructive. The same applies to how the print media is adapting syndication to the technological innovations engendered by the Internet. Whereas with the Associated Press' Wire service, and the brouhaha that it has caused among the newspapers around the country who believe their own Web sites are thus undermined, there has been a seismic shift in the nature of the news media that reflects the multicultural diversity of the United States. Consider California where, for the first time in 1998, the "mainstream" media reached fewer people than did the "ethnic" media combined.

The "minority" media now reaches the "majority" of people in California. The brain child of Alexandra Close at Pacific News Service, the New California Media accurately reflects diversity of these community newspapers—and the stunning reality that, together, the ethnic press reaches more Californians than do the *Los Angeles Times,* the San Jose *Mercury News,* the San Francisco *Chronicle,* and the San Diego *Union-Tribune* combined.[38] The emergence of these disparate publications as the majority media is of great consequence in society at large. In San Francisco, for instance, the mayoral race in 1999 ended in a run-off between incumbent Mayor Willie Brown and the challenger Tom Ammiano. That election was determined by how the Asian newspapers—Chinese, Korean, Japanese, and Filipino—shaped the public debate to their respective constituencies, leaving both the San Francisco *Chronicle* and *Examiner* as secondary, almost irrelevant voices in determining who would sit in City Hall.

This power is manifested in other ways. Under the leadership of Close, the New California Media has emerged as a viable business model for syndicating the writings of the ethnic media into one online service.[39] Although the business world pays attention to the divergent strategies pursued by the Associated Press, the *Wall Street Journal,* and the *New York Times,* the New California Media is at the forefront of shaping the emerging syndication business model online. As such it is now poised to reach more Americans in more languages online than the titans of newspaper publishing do in the real world. Not unlike Reed Elsevier, the New California Media is quietly establishing its market share as the single, most important content provider for the fast-becoming "majority" media in the United States.

History, does in fact, repeat itself, much the same way that during the California Gold Rush the story of a solitary miner who found one nugget was the stuff of tall tales while four merchants became robber barons before anyone realized what had happened. Reed Elsevier's stellar success in e-publishing has not gone unnoticed. Schiffrin notes that Reed Elsevier's "decision to concentrate on reference books and information retrieval represents a general trend. Publishers are talking more and more about concentrating on the profitable tip of the information pyramid. They want to make information that used to be found only in books available through new media."[40]

SUMMARY

Successful business models for publishing online have emerged consistent with *Key #1* (The Internet offers the technology to expand greatly an existing market) and *Key #3* (The nature of online economy creates both tyrannies of small decisions and prisoner's dilemmas that undermine the efficacy of a market system resulting in the New Economy affecting negatively the Old Economy).

Scientific and scholarly publications are leading the way, creating markets by being able to link professionals, researchers, and students around the world as never before in history. The logistics of informing individuals about products and the daunting task of delivering publications and books around the world have been overcome by the Internet technologies. The development of consumer and mass markets for e-publications, however, lags far behind. The obstacles to the development of these broader markets reside in the little value-added content and consumer preferences. For newspapers, such as the *New*

York Times, and for general interest online journals, such as Salon.com and Slate.com, consumers are reluctant to pay for content that is readily found in other media. In the case of e-books, even from popular authors such as Stephen King and Michael Crichton, physical books are preferred greatly over electronic versions of their works. Although journals that charge subscriptions, such as business newspapers like the *Wall Street Journal,* will be able to make their online editions profitable, consumer markets will remain a small portion of a much larger, and lucrative, e-publishing industry online for academic, professional, and research material.

NOTES

1. The Notes and Bibliography for Robert Kaplan, *The Nothing That Is: A Natural History of Zero,* can be accessed by visiting http://www.oup-usa.org/sc/0195128427/index.html.

2. Not everyone is convinced that the separating of a book's contents into two media is prudent. "If what's on the Internet doesn't last forever, then we've lost power," Jill Watts, an associate professor of history at California State University at San Marcos, was quoted as saying by the *New York Times.* "If the academic apparatus disappears, then we're moving back to an earlier period when authors weren't citing sources and could just say whatever they wanted. We're coming out of an industrial-oriented society that wanted everything to be added up and quantified into a virtual society where that's less valuable." Quoted from Doreen Carvajal, "The Book's in Print, but Its Bibliography Lives in Cyberspace," *New York Times,* May 29, 2000.

3. If relationship marketing, such as the sale of consumer products to visitors, then this constitutes discretionary income, much the same way that the sale of, say, coffee mugs with the *New Yorker* logo complements the *New Yorker*'s income, but is not the principle source of revenue.

4. The uncertainties of e-publishing made many writers weary. Mary Higgins Clark signed a $64 million deal with Simon & Schuster in May 2000, making her the highest-paid female author in the world. Although Simon & Schuster, a unit of Viacom, announced that it would release an electronic version of *Before I Say Good-Bye,* her best-seller published in 2000, it was not clear whether her audience was interested in works to be read by readers online. The misgivings surrounding Stephen King's *The Plant* raised questions about the rate at which a mass market for e-books online would develop in the first decade of the 2000s.

5. Italie Hillel, "Barnes & Noble.com Starts Digital Imprint," *The Salina Journal,* January 5, 2001. Available online at http://www.saljournal.com/stories.010501/tec_ap_bAndN.html.

6. Simon & Schuster is a division of Viacom, and Random House is a unit of the German-based Bertelsmann.

7. This is not to say, however, that media companies were not caught up in the mass retrenchment from the Internet in 2000 and 2001. Media Internet

divisions were cut back extensively. CBS laid off 24 percent of its Internet group on June 6, 2000; NBC Internet followed suit with a 20 percent reduction in its workforce on August 8, 2000; Viacom's MTVi reduced its staff by 25 percent on September 27, 2000; KnightRidder.com laid off 16 percent of its staff on December 4, 2000; News Corp. started 2001 by cutting its staff by 50 percent on January 4; and the *New York Times* Digital reduced its workforce by 17 percent on January 7, 2001.

8. Companies such as Fatbrain.com, which boasts more than $20 million in venture capital, also work like a vanity press, allowing anyone, for a fee, to self-publish anything. Both netLibrary and iUniverse believed their credibility would be undermined if they relinquished their obligation to judge the merits of the material they publish digitally.

9. David Kirkpatrick, "With Plot Still Sketchy, Characters Vie for Roles; The Struggles Over E-Books Abound, Though Readership Remains Elusive," *New York Times*, November 27, 2000.

10. David Kirkpatrick, "Random House to Establish Exclusively Digital Unit," *New York Times*, July 31, 2000.

11. Sheana Ochoa, "The Pros and Cons of E-Books," CNN.com, September 25, 2000.

12. David Kirkpatrick, "Dictionary Publishers Going Digital," *New York Times*, August 21, 2000.

13. The entry of established dictionaries into the online market has been met with tremendous enthusiasm. "The possibility that [Microsoft's] Encarta will, in fact, become the new Webster is precisely what is bothering many linguists. In a forthcoming review in Dictionaries, Sidney I. Landau, author of 'Dictionaries: The Art & Craft of Lexicography,' roundly pans Encarta's 'cumbersome, repetitive and inconsistent style' and especially what he sees as its excessive political correctness. The word 'Indian,' an example Mr. Landau notes, is described in other dictionaries as potentially insensitive but also widely used among Native Americans and inextricably woven into terms like 'Indian summer.' The Encarta issues a blanket condemnation, calling the term 'offensive' several times. In a few cases, the Encarta Web site even interrupts the viewer with a 'language advisory' before even displaying a potentially offensive word, as if it were a lewd movie. Such labels, Mr. Landau, says, reverse most lexicographers' understanding of their job—to report in neutral terms the changing shape of the language," reports David Kirkpatrick in "Dictionary Publishers Going Digital," *New York Times*, August 21, 2000.

14. Michel Marriot, "Let the Game Wars Begin," *New York Times*, April 26, 2001.

15. Reed Elsevier is the corporate parent of Greenwood Press, which publishes Quorum Books.

16. Quote provided by http://www.wiley.com/Corporate.

17. In the past, researchers would use public libraries which had back issues of the *New York Times* on microfiche, or secure the services of the newspaper's department charged with assisting in requests for copies of back articles.

18. The success of Dear Abby and Ann Landers paved the way for all other kinds of columnists, from those who specialize in celebrity gossip (Liz Smith),

to psychological advice (Joyce Brothers), to politics (Ellen Goodman), to medical health (Dean Eden), to sex advice (Dan Savage), and so on.

19. Wire also offers Web site design service for online companies. The Associated Press has also standardized how its stories are formatted, facilitating online companies to post AP stories more easily.

20. In the online brokerage business, for instance, Bridge Information Systems provided real-time stock quotes, BigCharts.com offers charts that can be downloaded, TheStreet.com distributes real-time news stories and the Associated Press and Reuters offer breaking news.

21. Philip Evans and Thomas Wurster, *Blown to Bits: How the New Economics of Information Transforms Strategy,* p. 41.

22. David Kirkpatrick, "As Publishers Perish, Libraries Feel the Pain," *New York Times,* November 3, 2000.

23. That the World Wrestling Federation launched an IPO and is a publicly traded company only blurs the distinction between investment and entertainment, a line in the sand that began to disappear with Hugh Hefner's Playboy Enterprises in the 1950s.

24. Squash isn't the only court game working diligently to become an Olympic event. As *Racquetball* magazine reports, "The International Racquetball Federation continues to make strides and see progress within the Olympic family, against tremendous odds, and it will never lose faith in its ultimate goal of being added to the Olympic Program. Racquetball's Olympic destiny continues to be 'not IF . . . just WHEN?'" The same holds true of squash. It is expected that both games will be exhibition sports at the Olympics in 2008 during the Summer Games in Athens.

25. Simon Parke was diagnosed with nonseminoma testicular cancer.

26. Simon Parke was defeated by Derek Ryan, Ireland's top-seeded player, in an upset at the tournament.

27. Rick Marin, "Online Journalists Keep Their Eyes on Daily Numbers," *New York Times,* November 11, 1999.

28. Personal communication, January 12, 2000.

29. In fact, in two weeks Reed Elsevier sells as much as Salon.com does in one year. (Slate.com does not disclose annual sales, but industry analysts believe that Slate.com and Salon.com have comparable revenue.)

30. Felicity Barringer, "Salon Dismisses 13 Workers in Effort to Fight Shortfall," *New York Times,* June 8, 2000.

31. Kara Swisher, "Read All about It: Can Web-only News Sites Ever Pay Off?" *Wall Street Journal,* July 17, 2000.

32. Warren Berger, "The Cool Thing About Aggregration," *Wired* 8.10, October 2000. Available online at http://www.wired.com/wired/archive/8.10/chiat_pr.html.

33. Brendan Coffey, "Publish or Perish," *Forbes,* November 13, 2000.

34. "Don't think I'm a geek," Michael Hirschorn said at the press conference announcing the launching of Inside.com. "But I consider Napster to be an epochal event." With that said, "geek" is not the noun that came to many analysts' minds.

35. Kara Swisher, "Read All about It: Can Web-only News Sites Ever Pay Off?" *Wall Street Journal,* July 17, 2000.

36. "Salon.com Relaunches New Sections and Redesigns," *The Write News*, May 26, 2000. Available online at http://writenews.com/2000/052600_salon_business.htm.

37. William Shakespeare, *Macbeth*, act 5, scene 5.

38. It is astounding to realize that, since 1999, more people throughout the Los Angeles metropolitan area read *La Opinion*, the Spanish-language daily, than read the *Los Angeles Times*.

39. The New California Media can be reached at www.ncmonline.com and its membership consists of: African American: *Black Futurists, Final Call, City Flight, KSBT Soul Beat TV, Net Noir, S.F. Bay View, Sun Reporter;* Arab: *Cairo Times;* Asian: *ABS-CBN International—The Filipino Channel, Asia Inc., Asian Week, Calitoday, China Crosstalk, Filipinas, KPST TV 66 (Chinese), KTSF Channel 26, Korean Television Network of SF, Little Saigon TV, Little Saigon Radio, Nikkei West, Nichi Bei Times, SaigonUSA, Sina.com, Singtao Daily, Thoibao Daily, Trikone, Vietnam Daily, World Journal, Zhong Guo Daily Journal;* Community Resources: *Mecresources.com;* Indigenous Peoples: *AIROS, Biopiracy News, Four Winds, Indian Country Today, Indigenous Environmental News Network, International Indian Treaty Council News, The First Perspective, The Eastern Door, Tribal Link;* Indian: *India-West, India Currents, IndoLink:* Iranian: *Iran Today;* Irish: *Irish Herald;* Latino: *El Andar, Frontera Magazine, KDTV-Univision, KPIT TV 66, La Oferta, La Opinion, La Prensa, Latinolink, Nuevo Horizonte;* and Multiethnic: *ColorLines, Maynard Institute,* and *Pacific News Service.*

40. Andre Schiffrin, *The Business of Books,* p. 117.

CHAPTER 7

LIKE MUSIC TO MY HARD DRIVE

To paraphrase Madonna's hit single, music brings the bourgeoisie and rebel together. Her words were prescient, for on October 30, 2000, Bertelsmann announced an agreement in which it would drop its suit for copyright infringement against Napster. This represented a significant shift in how the music industry saw the Internet, from shunning new technologies as a threat to the music industry to seeing it as a means through which the market for music could be expanded worldwide. The adversarial stance taken by the music industry and some musicians who believed their intellectual property rights were being violated through the unfettered distribution of their songs over the Internet, at first clouded the development of the business of distributing music to consumers via the Internet. "We invite other record and publishing companies, artists and other industry members to participate in the development of a source membership-based service," Thomas Middlehoff, chairman and CEO of Bertelsmann, said when the agreement was announced.[1]

That an agreement was announced at all was a milestone in corporate America's acceptance of the Internet as a business tool. It also promised to put an end to a lawsuit against Napster that was placed in December 1999 by five major record companies who were determined to shut down the online start-up.[2] The agreement envisioned transforming Napster from a "freewheeling Internet phenomenon" with 38 million users into an online company that would allow users to download music on the Internet but would compensate recording artists and music companies that owned the rights to those songs. Middlehoff's decision to embrace Napster as a company the way he embraced Napster founder 20-year-old Shawn Fanning, underscored the benefits the Internet offered the music industry. "The Internet is a wake-up call for the recording industry," Thomas Middlehoff of Bertelsmann said at the news conference announcing the deal. "The Internet is part of the future, an it is a part of our business."[3]

Observers were taken off guard by the unexpected and stunning announcement. Only three months prior, a federal judge had granted the recording industry's request to shut down Napster when he issued a preliminary injunction against the online company. Having found Napster guilty of "wholesale copyright infringement," the Recording Industry Association of America hailed the decision as a victory in their efforts to protect the integrity of copyright law and the intellectual property rights of musicians and companies.[4] The record industry was as concerned about technology itself. "Prodded by the explosive growth of Napster, and the difficulties of blocking copyrighted material on any file-sharing service, the labels have been actively examining methods of copy-protecting CDs," Charles Mann reported in Salon.com on March 28, 2001.[5]

Opposition to anything that challenges the status quo is a familiar pattern, of course. An industry resists a technology by which it feels threatened. When the emerging technology threatens to change the playing field by upsetting the prevailing business model, adversarial positions are staked out. Should the innovations have widespread implications, industry leaders rush to embrace the emerging technologies, usually through alliances, acquisitions, or mergers with the companies that were at the forefront of adopting the technological innovations. Madonna was right about the bourgeoisie and the rebel coming together. To understand how cooperation of this nature puts an end to acrimonious conflicts, one need go further back in time and recall the words of Plato:

> And what about lawsuits and mutual accusations? Won't they pretty much disappear from among them, because they have everything in common except their own bodies? Hence they'll be spared all the dissension that arises between people because of the possession of money, children, and families. . . . They'll be free of all these, and they'll live a life more blessedly happy than that of the victors in the Olympic games.[6]

Bertelsmann's deal with Napster consisted of a $50 million loan with the option of securing equity. The loan, which solved immediate cash flow problems for the besieged upstart, allowed Napster to begin developing the technology and services that will allow users to pay for the music they download. By embracing Napster, Bertelsmann positioned itself to create a platform that will allow it to market its media products—music, books, magazines, videos, and films—across the spectrum of the entertainment economy online. To put in proper context the forces that came together and resulted in Thomas Middlehoff and Shawn Fanning embracing each other at the doorstep of the Essex House in New York on a cool fall day, it is instructive to consider the development of the technologies that have made it possible for music to play such a central role in the emerging entertainment economy online.

CONFLICTS AND ANIMOSITY WITHIN
THE MUSIC INDUSTRY

The business of selling music has long been characterized by conflicts between the musicians who create the product and the record company executives who sell it to the public. As is often the case in human affairs, each partner feels he does all the work for half the credit. Musicians believe they create the intellectual property from which record executives make fortunes; David Geffen did not buy a Gulfstream jet from the money he earned singing songs. The music industry counters that its ability to market and promote talent is what makes them commercial successes; however brilliant Mozart may have been, he ended up distraught, starved, and destitute because he lacked the right manager.

In situations where there are these conflicts, it is not unexpected to find animosity. The possibilities opened up by the Internet—giving performers the ability to reach audiences and thereby circumventing record companies altogether—threatened to change the way the music industry operated, for both musicians and executives. Chuck D, the lead rapper in the Public Enemy, articulated the sentiment of many musicians when he argued that he:

> believe[d] that artists should welcome Napster. . . . I believe [the music industry] . . . has hurt the artist more than someone passing a song around free of charge. Not that most artists ever have much say about how their work is marketed and sold anyhow. Most contracts only guarantee artists a few cents in royalties from each record sold. And if a song doesn't become a hit, the label can cease selling it but still own rights to it forever. . . . [R]ecord companies [thus] created the concept of disposable artists; with jacked-up marketing and promotional costs, record companies stopped nurturing career artists.[7]

When rappers "dis" their labels and rock stars denounce their contractual "enslavement" to the whims of corporate America—Prince had the word "slave" written on his face to protest his contract to Warner—the music business remains one that is characterized by rampant discontent and discord. These animosities and conflicts between creative artists and business managers are the source for the phenomenon that swept music as an online business dominated by Napster and MP3.com.

"The Internet has been very cool for us," Ken Peterson of the band mi6 is quoted as saying. "We just want to play. But a record deal contract—yeah, that would be awesome."[8] If consumers have benefited from being able to trade and download music from the Internet without paying for it, then bands have been able to gain exposure—and gain fans. MP3.com, which was sued separately by the music industry for copyright infringement, predated Napster by several years in pioneering an online business model. For unknown and struggling musicians, the technology offered by MP3.com allows them to distribute their music as files freely, getting exposure and building a following. There has also been a payoff for these musicians. The traffic generated has been tremendous: the music industry has expanded and broadened in ways that had previously been impossible using traditional marketing and promoting.

When MP3.com began in May 2000 paying a small fee to the artists every time their music was downloaded, the *New York Times* reported that the company "expanded its monthly Payback for Playback pool to $1 million, it has become a source of significant revenue for those at the top of the MP3.com heap, and an incentive for the 75,000 or so others to promote their music."[9]

These developments raised concerns among music executives in the second half of the 1990s. There were questions, for instance, regarding how some artists went about "promoting" their music. "There's a popular nymphet named Tiffany who includes airbrushed nude photos on her home page, and whose blatantly smutty songs include one called '90 Seconds of Ecstasy,'" Janelle Brown wrote in Salon.com. "For every fan of download-brokering and tricking the [Payback for Playback] system, however, there are plenty of purists who feel such practices are polluting MP3.com."[10] In the same way that Stephen King threatened to bypass publishers entirely and sell his novels to readers directly, the Internet has the potential of allowing musicians to market their music to listeners without a record company contract.[11] Venture capitalists identified the opportunity as something unique. "The Internet offers recording artists the ability to reach fans directly in a way that has never been possible before," Roger McNamee, a managing director of Integral Capital Partners in Silicon Valley, explained.[12]

The Web site Garageband.com was launched in September 2000 precisely to develop online market opportunities for musicians who did

---

✔ *Netradio.com*: Launched 1995, owned by Net Radio Corp., 3 million visitors each month.

✔ *Spinner.com*: Launched 1996, acquired by AOL May 1999, plays 24 million songs each week.

✔ *Wiredplanet.com*: Launched 1999, traffic statistics unavailable.

✔ *Sonicnet.com*: Launched 1999, owned by MTVi Group, 350,000 visitors each month.

✔ *Icast.com*: Launched 2000, owned by iCast.com, 1.3 million visitors each month.

Figure 7.1   Streaming-Music Web Sites: Redefining Radio Online

not have record deals. Royalty payments, introduced by MP3.com in November 1999, were quickly adopted by other online music sites, such as Broadcast.com and Shoutcast.com. Compensating artists each time their songs are downloaded is the business model adopted by Web sites that distribute music legally over the Internet. It is not surprising that Bertelsmann, realizing that whether Napster was successfully defeated in court for copyright infringement was itself *immaterial:* a new business model for the creation, distribution, and marketing of music had emerged. How technology threatened to undermine the concept of intellectual property and copyrights would ultimately determine whether this business model was sustainable.

EVOLUTION OF ONLINE INTELLECTUAL PROPERTY RIGHTS: THE IMPORTANCE OF OPEN SOURCE AND COPYRIGHT

The conflict that surrounded the emergence of an online music industry is, at its most fundamental level, a question of protecting property rights when the market itself came into existence through the transfer of what critics called inappropriable social benefits. Recall that in Chapter 2 we discussed how the construction of the Intercoastal waterway by the Army Corps of Engineers resulted in enormous profits for private developers who built homes and condominiums along the Florida coast, another instance of how publicly funded goods (real estate out of swamps and marshes) benefited private investors (who built condominiums). The same occurred with the emergence of the online music industry. Many of the Internet technologies were developed by research projects funded by the government, which were then transferred over to the private sector without compensation to taxpayers who paid for government research and development.

The importance of the Internet can be likewise measured in the growing consensus that the software to make it grow needs to be distributed free of charge. Commercial software companies have considered source code—the fundamental blueprints for software programs—to constitute proprietary information. Not unlike pharmaceutical companies that invest hundreds of millions of dollars to develop new drugs, the formulas for which are then patented, software companies have considered software source code as private information, divulged only under strict licensing agreements. The growth of the online economy continues at such a breakneck pace that there are simply not enough qualified programmers to meet the demand for developing software.

As a result, leaders within both the private and public sectors are calling for open source. In a report submitted to the Clinton White House in the second half of 2000, the members of the President's Information Technology Advisory Committee recommended that open source software become "an alternate path for software development." This would mean, in other words, that software programs be distributed free of charge and that its source code be distributed freely in order to allow other programmers to study and modify the original program.

There have been two open source software programs released successfully. Apache and Linux were developed under the radical and iconoclastic approach championed by open-source advocates. Apache software enables computers to operate Web sites. Linux controls, on the other hand, the operating systems of computers. Apache is used by approximately 65 percent of the Web server software market, whereas Linux accounts for 40 percent of the Web server operating systems market. The closest competitor is Microsoft, which controls about 20 percent of each market.

What has made Apache and Linux successful is the ability of the Internet to allow programmers to collaborate with each other, regardless of where they are physically located. Interested and like-minded techies can work together on specific problems and challenges, each contributing to the improvement of the entire software system. This communal effort reflects both passion and practicality. "I am increasingly coming to the conclusion that the Internet and open-source initiatives are the free marketplace way of dealing with the extremely complex software issues we are facing," Irving Wladawsky-Berger, a member of the presidential advisory committee and IBM executive, said. Others in business agree.[13]

"Open source is where you'll find a lot of the passion in software these days," Rajiv Gupta, the general manager of Hewlett-Packard's e-speak, said. "Appealing to that passion certainly helps software companies in the war for talent. We're starting to get help from volunteers who contribute to the code, similar to what happened with Linux. They think it's cool, and they think it's good for society. As a result, by the way, e-speak development didn't cost Hewlett-Packard nearly as much as it would have if we'd decided to keep it proprietary."[14]

E-speak is software program that facilitates the creation of business relationships for e-commerce through the "halo" effect, which is the generation of goodwill among customers. Hewlett-Packard spent millions of dollars to develop e-speak, which transcends the industry boundaries imposed by B2B and B2C hubs. For Hewlett-Packard, e-speak provides the standards and an open environment on the Internet that fosters the development of e-commerce. The strategy behind giving the source code for free is that it allows Hewlett-Packard to expand the market for other products and services. The costs of developing, marketing, and delivering Hewlett-Packard products are reduced once e-speak dominates Internet e-commerce. In the same way that Apple Computers created a generation of loyal followers through its strategy of making its computers available to students inexpensively, the proliferation of open-source programmers makes it possible to ensure that the companies that actively promote open source are the ones that will dominate the Internet online economy.

Critics have pointed out that open source is radical insofar as it transfers into the public domain what has, in a capitalist market economy, always been intellectual property. Is it possible for a corporation to relinquish its property rights and still participate in a market economy? Carly Fiorina, Hewlett-Packard's president, seems to think so. "E-speak represents a risk, but we have to encourage invention and innovation. Hewlett-Packard is determined to expand the market for its products and services. If this is one road to achieving that end, then we are committed to this business model."[15]

This business model, in fact, has been called, rather flippantly, "The Doughnut Economy," in which the "emptiness" of core consists of intellectual property that is available to everyone because it is in the public domain. The material that "surrounds" the see-through core consists of the value-added, proprietary products and services that are derived from what remains in the public domain.[16] The intellectual conflicts in the software industry are intriguing, if for no other reason than they are characterized by the absence of hostilities. To be sure, intelligent and articulate individuals have different opinions about the viability of open source. But it is arresting to witness public presidential advisory committees and Fortune 500 companies in agreement on what was once a radical notion.

That a consensus can emerge without recrimination or litigation stands in sharp contrast to how intellectual property rights and the online economy are being discussed by musicians, music companies, fans, and Internet companies. The question that open source answers, in essence, is that a market economy can accommodate the development and distribution of intellectual property freely to attract the talent and accelerate the development of that property in order to create progress. The emerging uneasy coexistence between what properly belongs in the public domain and what constitutes proprietary know-how is confusing if for no other reason than the simple fact that the boundaries are not completely well defined. This fluidity confuses many, and issues become unclear.

"Copyright protects not just the financial interest of people who create artistic or intellectual property, but the very existence of creative work," argues Jack Valenti, chairman of the Motion Picture Association of America. "At a time when this country is bleeding from trade deficits, the copyright industries have a surplus balance of trade with every country where copyrighted works are sold or licensed. These businesses are a national treasure, one that every other nation views with envy. The Internet marauders argue that copyright is old-fashioned, a decaying relic of a non-Internet world." He then uses an analogy. "Suppose some genius invented a magic key that could open the front door of every home in America and wanted to make keys available to everyone under a canopy sign that read, 'It's a new world—take what you want.'"[17]

Imagine the horror that has gripped the music industry when they read calls for the destruction of private property and anarchy. "No law can be successfully imposed on a huge population that does not morally support it and possesses easy means for its invisible evasion," writes John Perry Barlow in *Wired* magazine, regarding copyrights and intellectual property rights. "Even during the heyday of copyright, we got some pretty useful stuff out of Benoit Mandelbrot, Vint Cerf, Tim Berners-Lee, Marc Andreesen, and Linus Torvalds, none of whom did their world-morphing work with royalties in mind," he adds, showing total ignorance of the distinction between appropriable and inappropriable property rights. "Following the death of copyright, I believe our interests will be assured by the following practical values: relationship, convenience, interactivity, service, and ethics."[18]

This is as absurd as arguing that because the U.S. Army Corps of Engineers was responsible for transforming swamps into real estate by building the Intracoastal, all beachfront property in south Florida should rightfully remain in the public domain. It may be a New World, but it is not entirely so unfamiliar and alien. What John Perry Barlow advocates—eliminating intellectual property rights altogether—is a recipe for dystopia. It is one, however, that will happily not come to pass for it is simply unsustainable. But it is nonetheless disconcerting to see techies advocate such irresponsible ideas. Classical economics provide the means by which the Internet economy can be understood. There is reassurance in knowing that, although it may be a whole new ball game, it isn't an incomprehensible one. Armed with the lessons presented in Part I of this book, it is now possible to discuss the Internet itself—and the online economy—in a way that that is both familiar and instructive.

Jack Valenti objects, in essence, to the incomplete nature of technology. Although the Internet allows for the efficient distribution of copyrighted material online, there is not a corresponding mechanism for preventing copyright violations and producing reliable accounting for determining royalty payment to musicians. With the rhetoric found in the pages of *Wired* magazine, and the daunting speed with which Napster and MP3.com and other Web sites appeared for the expressed purpose of sharing (or stealing, depending on one's perspective) Web sites spread across the Internet, recording industry executives and artists felt under siege.

Metallica responded by filing suit against Napster on April 13, 2000, in order to prevent more than 335,000 fans from sharing music files over the Internet. Metallica band members James Hatfield and Jason Newsted stated that they would like to sell a few albums, and that, in principle, it was unfair for their music to be traded back and forth by hundreds of thousands of people for free. Napster stated that they were in compliance with the Digital Millennium Copyright Act of 1998, which required them to expel users who were "infringing." This is not unfamiliar in the off-line world—photocopy businesses post warnings on their copiers against violating the "fair use" provisions of the copyright laws, and they, in theory, are required to prevent someone from making a photocopy of an entire book. Napster, which had been found by a court not to qualify as an Internet Service Provider (ISP), closed more than 300,000 of its online music sharing accounts on May 11, 2000.[19] Despite the good faith efforts of Napster after it settled its lawsuit, what it—and Bertelsmann—found out was that once Pandora's Box has been opened, it is very difficult to regain control of the situation. Throughout 2001, the Recording Industry Association of America (RIAA) continued to make demands on Napster, arguing that it failed time and time again to filter material that was copyrighted from its service. "Virtually all of the music that we noticed [of copyright infringement] to Napster, that they claimed they have filtered out, is still available on their system," RIAA president Hilary Rosen complained in mid-2001.[20] Not that Napster was the only online site on which copyrighted material was freely traded. There was WinMx, Swapoo, Splooge,

Networked Information Sharing		
	Launch Date	**Description**
Freenet	*March 2000*	Open-source programming project that allows individuals to distribute any kind of digital information on the Internet anonymously.
Gnutella	*March 1999*	A product of America Online's Nullsoft division. Currently managed by programmers for downloading images, music, software, text and videos.
Gnarly	*March 2000*	Open-source program that allows users to download files in any format, inclusive of MP3, Microsoft Word, Microsoft Excel graphics and Zip files.

Centralized Information Sharing		
iMesh	*August 1999*	The company, backed by American and Israeli investors, plans to create a distribution system for all kinds of digital files on a pay-per-use basis.
Napster	*May 1999*	Provides a centralized directory of MP3 music files that allows free sharing among individuals. Copyright infringement suit filed by music industry for willful violation of property rights.
Scour Exchange	*April 2000*	Allows individuals to exchange files with graphics, music, and video. Michael Ovitz and Ron Burkle purchased controlling interest of company. Plans to sell music and advertising online.
Wrapster	*March 2000*	A centralized directory that allows individuals to use Napster to exchange and download music and software files.

Figure 7.2 Networked vs. Centralized Information Sharing

Toadnode, Imesh, Aimster, and Filetopia—not to mention the open-source Gnutella—which made file-sharing possible by virtually anyone who wanted to set up his or her own Web site for that purpose.

Regardless of the particulars of the arguments offered by RIAA, a consensus emerged by 2001 that copyright law, on principle, applies in cyberspace. The objections of industry leaders, such as Jack Valenti, and musicians, such as James Hatfield and Jason Newstand, were validated by courts. At the same time, technology was fast emerging that addressed their concern. Digital downloading of music (as well as books, films, and videos) could be accomplished through encryption technology that prevented unauthorized users from accessing copyrighted material. Of equal importance, digital watermarking technologies were being introduced that safeguarded the integrity of accounting, essential for the payment of royalties to musicians, writers, and filmmakers.

The Secure Digital Music Initiative (SDMI) is the music industry's effort to develop a technology that allows for the "watermarking" of digitalized files. In December 1998, the technology was announced as ready to begin being marketed in September 2000. This was then postponed to December 2001. The SDMI sought to allay the fears of music industry executives and musicians alike. An initiative of the five major recording companies—Bertelsmann, EMI, Sony, Seagram's Universal, and Time Warner's Warner Music—consider that it took the industry four years after Aerosmith released "Head First," a full-length commercial song released exclusively over the Internet, before executives acknowledged the potential of this new medium. Throughout 1999 and 2000, of course, the record industry was consumed by lawsuits against MP3.com and Napster, delaying the industry's efforts to enter the online music industry in earnest.

As 2001 unfolded, the two favored strategies were variations of licensing and subscription services. By licensing their songs to Web sites such as Launch.com, the record companies assessed the market potential of licensing itself as a viable business model for the Internet. Another approach centered on various subscription programs. The most ambitious of these involved Universal, EMI, and America Online (which was then merging with Time Warner). Matters of pricing, marketing, and distribution in various digitized formats were in a state of flux during the inception of these competing business models. At the core, however, was the technical problem of protecting the integrity of copyrighted material and other intellectual property rights. The SDMI fought for encryption technology that could be modified depending on the fees paid by the consumer.

Watermarking technology was favored for watermarks, once embedded in a digitized file or a compact disc, determine how a song may be copied and played and who is entitled to a royalty payment for the rights exercised. When this technology comes into wide use in the 2000s, there will be other, but more manageable concerns, such as fair use. Someone who buys a physical book can lend it to others to read without having to pay for that right, or that person can read it over and over again without having to pay in excess of the original purchase price. The same should apply for digital music. Indeed, the SDMI seeks to make content available to consumers while protecting the intellectual property rights of copyright holders.[21]

Although SDMI's security, when first introduced in 2000, could be compromised by skillful hackers, SDMI demonstrated the resolve to work within the framework of the technological innovations the Internet had created in order to expand the market for music. This was evident to any adult with teenagers in her household. "[I]t's too simple to say that every MP3 represents a lost sale. For a year I've watched my son use Napster to sample bands he's heard about but never actually heard, then rush out and buy their compact discs. Napster may have been free, but the music on Napster emptied his bank account."[22] Microsoft recognized how the future or merchandising music was changing. In September 2000, Microsoft purchased MongoMusic for a reported $65 million, which was impressive considering that MongoMusic had neither products nor customers. It had, however, the ingenuity of its programmers. The acquisition of MongoMusic was, in fact, the logical step in Microsoft's aggressive development of technology to manage the digital distribution of music online. That Microsoft would enjoy a considerable competitive advantage should MongoMusic develop a technology that was compatible with the Microsoft Windows Media format was not lost on media companies.

Digital Watermark	Authorized Device	MS Audio	DigiBox
A digital watermark adds information to a music file. This allows an authorized individual to download and play it back. It also allows the same individual to make copies, consistent with "fair use" rulings concerning copyrighted materials. The digital watermark, however, prevents pirating because should an individual make an unreasonable amount of copies that are subsequently sold or distributed, once a pirated copy is located, the digital watermark identifies the individual that violated "fair use" provisions. This would allow copyright owners to identify pirating, safeguarding the system for all parties.	Sony is developing the use of an authorization device that is embedded in chips inside a computer. This device would allow for an individual who is authorized, meaning who has paid for the right to download music, to play back the encrypted music. The drawback with this approach, however, does not allow for the "fair use" provisions to which consumers who purchase copyrighted works are entitled to have. There are also privacy concerns for each individual user. Furthermore, the use of encryption lends itself to being circumvented by hackers who could subsequently distribute or sell the music files.	Microsoft Audio envisions compressing music files that can be played back on Windows Media Player. The files would remain "locked" until an individual pays for the right to listen to music. This would presumably be either through a credit or debit card payment. The nature of the payment would determine the configuration in which the music would be released. For example, an individual that agrees to see a banner ad may be entitled to listen to the music once, whereas another person who purchases the music with a credit card would be allowed to multiple playbacks and copying the music file.	Universal Music Group is developing an online music distribution program that would allow individuals to pay for the music they want to download from the Internet. Although it remains in early stages of development, this strategy can be centered around one of two approaches. The first would allow individuals to download music they pay for in such a way as to allow for "fair use" personal playbacks. The second approach is to consider the Internet to be roughly analogous to the radio—a small fee, or commercial messages, may be included by way of compensation.

Figure 7.3   Protecting Music Copyright Online

Bertelsmann's alliance with Napster was, to no small degree, a response to Microsoft's challenge: The announcement created frenzied speculation that the $50 million loan to Napster would boost development of encryption software technologies that would transform Napster into a viable, which is to say responsible, business that could enjoy widespread application in many consumer markets. In addition to the watermark developed by SDMI and the initiatives undertaken by Microsoft, a software program called the International Standard Recording Code was proposed as one type of software for tracking copyrighted material as it moved across the Internet. All these technological innovations seek to create digital fingerprints that can provide accountability in order to determine who is using the material, who is entitled to be paid for this use, and how to ensure that proper residuals and royalties are collected and distributed.[23]

Confusion abounds, and it is confusion precipitated by a failure to understand fundamental principles of economics. At the height of the media frenzy that surrounded the RIAA lawsuit against Napster, for instance, Bruce Forest, a music pioneer who was the director of media and entertainment services for Viant Corporation, an Internet consulting firm, voiced the same kind of misunderstanding held by the public at large.

"Go on to Napster and watch the chat," he said in an interview with Allison Fishman, a writer for *Revolution,* a music magazine. "Half the people there know so little about the technology that they don't even understand what they're doing. They don't understand file sharing, and they don't care about aggregation, peer distribution, or monetization. They care that they're getting free shit."[24]

And what does he recommend the major record companies, such as Sony, do about this? His response is one word: Monetize.

Monetize?

Monetize, after all, is what central banks do when they increased money supply in order to pay off debt denominated in their national currency. The result is inevitable hyperinflation; in Latin America, for instance, countries that have monetized their debts have experienced astronomical inflation rates.[25]

Perhaps what Bruce Forest is recommending is to *commercialize* the online music industry. Here, then, is the problem the online economy has encountered: Too many people pontificating about it lack a fundamental understanding of rudimentary economics. This has been compounded because the impulse to replace simple words with buzzwords proves too often irresistible. The result is the proliferation of jargon that obfuscates simple economic principles.[26]

Consider how buzzword-babble suffused discussions of the music industry online. "No [music] company is going to make big money by selling CDs, because digital technology transforms one copy into 1 million copies," John Ellis illuminates in *Fast Company,* a publication that is published so fast there is apparently no time for editors to reflect and think about its content. "[R]ecording companies . . . [must] reinvent themselves," John Ellis explained, "as what Evans and Wurster call 'navigators,' and as what others call 'infomediaries.'"

Infomediaries is a word invented by Evans and Wurster and embraced by the media. In this article, John Ellis continues parroting the nonsensical jargon to describe an Old Economy business model that works very well online. He explains that "[t]echnology is now conspiring to make it more possible—and, ultimately, more likely—that great creative talent, or at least very popular creative talent, will finally be compensated adequately. Companies that enhance that value proposition will prosper. Companies that don't will be deconstructed."[27]

What nonsense is this? Does he mean that the vast distribution possible on the Internet will make syndication the primary business model for rewarding those who come out on top as the winner-take-all contests proliferate? Why obfuscate a situation that is already complicated as it is? The answer is as old as the Enlightenment. Michel de Montaigne made the following observation about pompous and artificial speech: "Just as in dress it is the sign of a petty mind to seek to draw attention by some personal or unusual fashion, so too in speech; the search for new expressions and little-known words derives from an adolescent schoolmasterish ambition."[28]

The idea that can be better expressed in plain English is that the alliance between Bertelsmann and Napster shares certain of the elements of a winner-take-all contest, but there are other economic ideas at work. To put these developments in perspective, it is necessary to consider the apparent paradox of what the record industry said it wanted, to put online companies like Napster and MP3.com who have entered into the competitive frenzy, and develop the technology necessary to become dominant players in the online music industry.

Metallica denounces file-sharing software, while Eric Clapton invests in CantaMetrics, a company that is developing fingerprints for digital music files. Bertelsmann files a lawsuit against Napster, only to rush to be the first to enter into an alliance with it. "It preserves traditional protection for copyrights," the editors of the *New York Times* opined when the Napster deal was announced.

> If followed by the rest of the industry, the deal would allow Napster to develop its file-sharing technology without facing the threat of being shut down or fined heavily for fomenting copyright infringement. The deal also offers long-term benefits to consumers, although they will lose their free ride. . . . Protecting copyrights is important to the general public. File-

sharing technologies threaten to remove the financial incentives that encourage musicians to compose, authors to write and newspapers to publish. In the long run, unfettered distribution of copyrighted materials hurts everyone. Yet crushing Napster has never been a good answer. File-sharing technologies have exciting potential for consumers as well as artists and authors. That is why a voluntary solution is best.[29]

Economists understand contradictions in consumer behavior very well because it suffuses every aspect of our lives as agents in a market economy. The conflicts and recriminations surrounding the online music industry involve attempts to reconcile what consumers (say they) want, what musicians (say they) want, and what record company executives (say they) want. This is complicated because what each party actually ends up doing is oftentimes different. In order to gain a greater understanding of how the music industry is evolving in the entertainment economy online, it is necessary to digress briefly and understand the economics of why we often do things that are different from what we say we want to do.

STATED PREFERENCE VERSUS REVEALED PREFERENCE

Throughout the twentieth century, economists were puzzled by the peculiar discrepancy between what consumers said and what consumers did. This has not changed. When asked, consumers say one thing but then end up doing something altogether different. Why do they misrepresent their true opinions and intentions? Do people lie? Economists, for the most part, are generous, which is why intentional deception is ruled out as a satisfactory reason. There had to be another explanation for this consistently observed behavior. The consensus that emerged to reconcile the apparent contradiction between what people say and what people do, moreover, has been codified in the theory of Stated Preference and Revealed Preference.

A common experiment used to illustrate the phenomenon at work is to ask individuals to conduct informal surveys of people who are about to enter a supermarket. Consumers are then approached and asked what they *intend* to buy, not what may be on their shopping list (if they have any). The responses are considered *expressions* of good intentions: vegetables and fruits, fresh pastas, skinless chicken, lean beef, and so on. At the end of the day, the store manager is asked what items were actually *sold* that day. A very different picture then emerges. In the United States for the year ending March 29, 2000, vegetables and fruit did not make it in the Top Ten list of items sold at supermarkets nationwide. Cigarettes, soft drinks, beer, frozen meals, ice cream, and salty snacks, however, did.

Convenience Stores		Supermarkets		Drug Stores	
Category	*Sales ($mm)*	*Category*	*Sales ($mm)*	*Category*	*Sales ($mm)*
1. Cigarettes	$34,839	1. Carbonated Beverages	$12,634	1. Cigarettes	$1,866
2. Beer	$11,188	2. Milk	$10,136	2. Vitamins	$1,373
3. Carbonated Beverages	$10,938	3. Cheese	$7,574	3. Cosmetics	$1,242
4. Candy	$3,932	4. Fresh Bread/Rolls	$7,389	4. Internal Analgesics	$979
5. General Merchandise	$3,174	5. Cigarettes	$6,969	5. Cold/Allergy/Cough	$774
6. Fluid Milk Products	$2,994	6. Cold Cereals	$6,957	6. Liquor	$759
7. Salty Snacks	$2,944	7. Salty Snacks	$6,306	7. Beer/Ale	$711
8. Auto Products	$1,846	8. Beer/Ale	$6,248	8. Chocolate Candy	$675
9. Publications	$1,707	9. Frozen Meals	$5,349	9. Skin Care	$646
10. Sweet Snacks	$1,577	10. Ice Cream	$4,375	10. Carbonated Beverages	$635
Source: CS News Industry Report 2000		*Source: IRI Infoscan, year ending 3/29/00*		*Source: IRI Infoscan, year ending 3/29/00*	

Figure 7.4   Revealed Preferences

"I can resist anything except temptation," Oscar Wilde is famous for saying. Economists recognize the nature of temptation in human affairs. Every day people enter supermarkets with the noblest of intentions, but as they walk up and down the aisles they give in to temptation. Broccoli can hardly compete with chocolate chip cookies. That people say they *intend* to purchase vegetables and fruits, but end up buying salty snacks and soft drinks makes no difference to supermarkets. Store managers are indifferent to any moral obligation to challenge why shoppers purchase what they purchase. (John Kenneth Galbraith, of course, is appalled at the distortions in consumer demand manifested at the retail level; Milton Friedman, on the other hand, is pleased with the restraint displayed by retailers.)

That store managers resist giving in to the temptation to express one opinion or another is because it is very easy for them to look at the day's sales and have their stock replenished accordingly. Because supermarkets have the ability to modify their purchases on a daily basis, they can easily adjust the products on their shelves to reflect changes in consumer choices. Whether the next morning's delivery trucks are filled with broccoli or chocolate chip cookies, after all, really makes no difference: supermarkets stock what sells.[30]

The discrepancies between stated and revealed preferences, however, are not always inconsequential or benign. Consider what happens outside of the arena of supermarkets, and stated preferences are at odds with revealed preferences. City officials oftentimes rely on detailed analysis of what residents say they want done about public transportation. They then make serious proposals and considerable investment of public funds that reflect these expressed desires of their community and move forward to implement these elaborate plans, which result from years of analysis and hard work. But what if the majority of residents consistently says they want more mass transit, then after years have been invested to secure funding, build elaborate transit systems, and the ribbon-cutting ceremony is done, no one rides the buses or boards subway trains?

Now consider a pharmaceutical company that conducts elaborate market research to find out how doctors would best prefer to treat their patients. The data are collected on the physicians' expressed preferences about products available, and the costs of different alternatives, attitudes toward these various treatment options, and concerns about side effects of medicines are carefully analyzed. Years are invested in the development of new products that reflect these concerns. What happens when, having diligently spent tens of millions of dollars, the new product is introduced, only to find that doctors end up ignoring the product that was developed specifically to address their expressed concerns and preferences?

Writing in the *Transportation Research Record,* K. Morikawa, T. Ben-Akiva, and M. Yamada argue that it is necessary to incorporate a methodology for taking into account the differences between revealed preference and stated preference among urban commuters. "The empirical study of intercity travel demand demonstrates the practicality of the methodology by accurately reproducing observed aggregate data and by applying a flexible operational prediction method," they report.[31] Transit officials, in essence, need to consider that things such as surveys and opinion polls are inadequate indicators of which mode of transportation commuters will ultimately take when all the choices they say they want are in fact available to them. Policymakers are understandably frustrated when commuters say they want reliable public transportation, local governments invest billions of dollars in mass transit system, and, once completed, people change their minds and drive to work anyway.

To be sure, the discrepancy between Stated and Revealed Preference has repercussions throughout the entire economy. More than a question of whether supermarkets are selling chocolate chip cookies in greater quantities than they are selling broccoli, it affects everything from how elected officials and municipal bureaucrats approach mass transit problems to how pharmaceutical companies determine which medicines to develop. Indeed, it affects not only the nation's economy, but also virtually every other aspect of our public and private lives.[32]

In the realm of politics, consider the insidiously confusing role opinion polls now play in public life and debate. If one considers polls to constitute a statement of the public's stated preference, what voters actually do when they draw the curtains closed behind them in voting booths and then cast their ballots is in fact their revealed preference.[33] The 1980 presidential election between Jimmy Carter and Ronald

Reagan is one of the more startling instances of how the discrepancy between stated and revealed preference affects the nation's life in recent times.

"Most studies of American voting behavior also fail to find evidence of a major realignment of voter allegiance toward the Republicans," Thomas Ferguson and Joel Rogers wrote in *The Atlantic Monthly* in May 1986, reflecting on the aftermath of the 1980 presidential election. "The most carefully conducted studies of 'policy voting' in 1980, for example, concluded that the vote was more a negative referendum on Carter than an endorsement of Reagan's policies."[34]

The authors nonchalantly note that the campaign "reached a crescendo in 1979–1980, when the fall of the Pahlevi regime in Iran, the seizure of the American embassy in Tehran, and the Soviet invasion of Afghanistan were repeatedly cited as proof that U.S. military capabilities were seriously weakened."[35] This, coupled with the economic difficulties the United States encountered at the time, the authors make it seem, is what made Ronald Reagan's victory appear both natural and inevitable.

Ferguson and Rogers wrote this six years after Jimmy Carter had been defeated. The polls they analyzed were based on the revealed preference data compiled long after the fact. This is like surveying what retailers have sold and then arguing that of course it is natural and inevitable to expect that drug stores sell more cigarettes than medicine and that supermarkets sell more soda pop and beer than vegetables and fruit. Why would anyone have any doubts?

Well, there *are* doubts because it *is* counterintuitive. Supermarkets sell more soft drinks than milk? Drugstores sell more cigarettes than medicines?

That Jimmy Carter was defeated by such an overwhelming and decisive margin surprised everyone because the opinion polls did not predict such an outcome. In the same way that most people find it surprising to learn that drug stores sell more liquor and beer than prescription medicines, the differences between stated and revealed preferences catch us by surprise and leave us with very embarrassing public works projects. This is why mass transit systems around the country from Miami to Los Angeles lack sufficient passengers to cover marginal operating costs long after residents in the same urban centers clamored, voted, and paid for the very rapid transit systems they once vigorously demanded but are subsequently loathe to use.[36]

What Ferguson and Rogers failed to consider in their essay is that on Election Day in November 1980, it was not clear which candidate would win, for opinion polls put Jimmy Carter and Ronald Reagan in a statistical tie. "Although polls have successfully predicted the winner in presidential races since 1952," Norman Bradman writes, "they have also indicated that races are very close, even too close to call, when they turned out not to be as close as predicted (e.g., the Carter-Reagan election in 1980). Large deviations in predictions about the margin of victory, which are not uncommon, and failure to predict winners in state or local races, may be enough to remind people of the fallibility of polls and keep us from being too complacent about their power."[37]

Bradman is closer than Ferguson and Rogers to understanding more fully the principles behind stated and revealed preference, but he nevertheless fails to distinguish properly the implications for public debate and public policy. The polls he references indicated, in fact, that the presidential race was too close to call with any degree of confidence. The outcome, however, produced a resounding landslide for Ronald Reagan.

What happened in 1980 was that people liked Jimmy Carter and were looking for a reason to vote for him. They were expressing to pollsters their heartfelt intentions simply because voters in democracies around the world want to think their leaders are good people. This is one reason why incumbents enjoy a competitive advantage in tight races. The results of these opinion polls therefore reflected the noble intentions of the electorate (Stated Preference). When Election Day arrived and people stepped inside the voting booths and closed the curtains behind them, however, they couldn't bring themselves to vote for him (Revealed Preference).

Musicians, fans, and the record companies have been struggling to reconcile with conflicts that emerge when technological innovations have widened the gap between Stated Preferences and Revealed Preferences. What frustrates rapid transit planners, pharmaceutical companies, and political pundits is, at the core, what has convulsed the online music industry. Discussions about copyrights and digitized music files are secondary in nature to the underlying need to bring Revealed Preferences closer in line with all parties' Stated Preferences. The narrowing of the gap between preferences is a powerful economic principle that, in the second half of 2000, began to be addressed in earnest by the online music industry and the off-line recording and media conglomerates. The introduction of digital rights management as a business strategy represents a sensible way of resolving this dilemma.

DIGITAL RIGHTS MANAGEMENT

The online economy is being shaped by the challenges posed by the efforts to overcome the natural conflicts between Stated and Revealed Preferences. It is a process in which established companies in the music industry realize that if they fail to establish a formidable dot-com presence, they will become dot-gone. This is one reason why, a year after Time Warner and Sony announced that they would merge the operation of Columbia House, which they owned jointly, with the troubled online music store, CDnow, Warner announced that it would enter the digital-download market in an "aggressive" and "forceful" manner. With an inventory of classic rock artists, such as Fleetwood Mac and Neil Young, Warner had a firm foundation upon which it could market more contemporary artists, including R.E.M and Matchbox Twenty.[38]

The announcement of Bertelsmann, Warner, Sony, and Microsoft legitimized the emerging online music industry.[39] What they had so vehemently resisted and decried was now embraced as the business model that would expand existing markets, open new ones, and bring about the kind of breakthroughs that will invigorate and sustain a viable business model. The havoc of misguided techies at startups such as Gnutella and Scour aside, it astounds me to see the speed with which the music industry distinguished between the public domain and private property rights.[40]

In the first decade of the twenty-first century, the online music industry will continue to develop consistently and within the framework economists have developed to understand the phenomenon of Stated versus Revealed Preference. If understanding the business issues surrounding intellectual property rights and the Internet has been difficult to grasp, it is, in part, because of the nature of the technology itself. An appropriate analogy is found in mathematics, where the concept of "zero" poses similar challenges. "Zero and infinity always looked suspiciously alike," Charles Seife writes. "Multiply zero by anything and you get zero. Multiply infinity by anything and you get infinity. Dividing a number by zero yields infinity; dividing a number by infinity yields zero. Adding zero to a number leaves the number unchanged. Adding a number to infinity leaves infinity unchanged."[41]

The same holds true of how industries threatened by technological innovations act at first. The inherent contradiction between what are inappropriable rights belongs in the public domain (open-source software), and the property rights (copyrights) have sorted themselves out. Rob Lord, a brilliant techie who was one of the original employees of Nullsoft, said in defense of the assault on copyrights, "We're legitimate nihilistic media terrorists, as history will no doubt canonize us."[42]

Considerations of legitimate illegitimacy aside, the emergence of "digital rights management" represents an erudite characterization of Internet technologies. Online music moved from piracy to the evolution of a viable business model once Napster began to comply with court orders preventing the unfettered distribution of copyrighted material among its users and commenced to charge fees in 2001. An online music industry in which musicians and copyright owners are compensated for their intellectual property, however, is not the end of the story.

In a curious development that further complicates matters, the success of the music as an important component of the entertainment economy online has been clouded by questions about the content of songs. In the 1980s, Tipper Gore led the Parents' Music Resource Center and lobbied successfully for the music industry's "Parental Advisory" stickers one finds on CDs.

Although critics complained that this represented an unconstitutional attempt to coerce the music industry to engage in self-censorship, this raised the question not of First Amendment rights, but, rather, of the recalcitrant nature of certain market imperfections that resulted in the proliferation of choices we don't want. To be sure, the music industry has, for almost two decades, agreed to monitor itself and remove violent or overly sexual lyrics from the music it offers. As we shall see in our discussions in the remaining three chapters of this book, however, with the widespread use of the Internet technologies, there is a corresponding proliferation in market imperfections. It is appropriate that we now examine how it is that one kind of market imperfection led to an abundance of unwanted choices. If the tyranny of small decisions impacted our lives by eliminating choices, it is necessary to consider how the supply of unwanted choices impacts our lives both as individuals and as a society.

A discussion of the online music industry is not complete without addressing the social impact of music on youth. Because youngsters and young people derive so much pleasure from music and because these are segments of the population that are not fully rational—and therefore require paternalistic measures to safeguard their emotional development—as a society, we recognize the limitations of the marketplace to ensure that all our concerns as a society are adequately addressed. Indeed, no economic system is perfect, which is the precise reason that the inevitable imperfections of any given system prove daunting. It was clear, for instance, that the tyranny of small decisions creates an environment in which individual choices become a de facto referendum on the availability of all the choices from which one chooses, with the end result being the elimination of some of those choices. The resulting deprivation in the selection is genuine for it denies a community of options it wants to have, however infrequently it chooses to make use of them. As Alfred Kahn first pointed out, commuters in Ithaca faced a serious quandary when passenger train service was discontinued.

To prevent our social lives from becoming desolate landscapes, the sales of subscriptions, such as season's tickets, were introduced as a remedy. By covering the marginal operating costs of something a community values, whether it is supporting professional baseball or a symphony, we guarantee that the kinds of choices we want are available to us—whether we attend every ball game or concert.

Thus, we know how to prevent the market imperfection of the tyranny of small decisions from becoming a market failure. This is important for, as Amazon.com continues to demonstrate with alarming speed, technological innovations that made the online sale of books possible have created an unintended referendum on the continued viability of independent bookstores as a choice. The stunning decimation of independent booksellers, not to mention independent travel agents, is evidence of how the tyranny of small decisions is making a market imperfection into a sobering referendum that is changing the basic industries by which we have come to define ourselves in fundamental ways that affect our community lives and the choices we have.

In our society we value learning and we treasure books. Libraries and bookstores are fundamental pillars in our civic pride, community lives, and resources for helping us raise our children so that they become educated, productive, and responsible members of our nation. There are, of course, remedies to arrest and reverse these unintended consequences of market imperfections.[43]

As we have seen, the greater the gap in the discrepancy between Stated Preference and Revealed Preference, the more choices that are made available that result in an inferior communal outcomes. This is a case where more is definitely not better. Recall how Bobby Hull way back in 1969 understood the essence of a prisoner's dilemma: Sometimes having a choice is no choice at all. The investment in offering choices that no one genuinely wants results in enormous waste. The market imperfection that we understand to be the gap between Stated Preference and Revealed Preference results in empty trains running in Miami and in pharmaceutical companies with excess inventories of unwanted medicines.[44]

This discrepancy affects all areas of our lives, private as well as public. In summer 2000, the dismal television show *Big Brother* was broadcast on CBS. What made this program, in which total strangers agreed to live together in a confined space with television cameras filming them continuously, such a disappointment was to witness how bland our lives become when people endeavor to deny healthy and normal conflicts. Comparing the American version of the program that stands in contrast to the hits the show has become in European nations, critics have wondered why CBS's version produced such stultifying and unsatisfying television.

"The Americans acted as if they were in some celibate, selfless commune, and just happened to be wearing body mikes," Caryn James wrote in the *New York Times*. In her meandering analysis of why the show proved so boring, she touched on what economists have long known: "The success of confrontational reality shows exposes the gap between our noblest self-image and our mischievous delight in others' conflicts. What the public says it wants and what it watches are two different things."[45]

Earlier I noted that in a democracy one has the right to be a jerk. The corollary, of course, is that in a market economy one has the right to make stupid mistakes. Adam Smith's invisible hand is not required to be graceful and sometimes it comes back to slap us in the face, both as individuals and as a society. Superfluous choices are one of the dilemmas endemic to open democratic societies. This paradox arises from the values market economies embrace and champion. The underlying assumption of modern democracies is that free will exists. We believe individuals must be free to exercise their own will, and they must be held accountable for their actions. As a society we take it upon ourselves as a common responsibility to educate children so that they can grow up to become productive and responsible members of societies. In economic terms, the affirmation of free will is found in Smith's invisible hand theory, of course.[46] But the gap between Revealed Preference and Stated Preference, in essence, is the difference between what we want in *principle,* but not in *practice,* and this falls outside of Smith's invisible hand theory.

Go home and watch this paradox come to life: We want free speech in principle, but we don't want to have unwelcome solicitations from pornographic or violent Web sites in our email Inbox.[47] Here, then, is the somber reality of the challenges we, as individuals and a society, confront: How can we eliminate unwanted options without infringing on our principles?

Economists are accomplished at devising mechanisms by which market imperfections can be corrected and our choices preserved. But no one has been able to figure out how to prevent market imperfections from creating unwanted choices that waste resources. It's impossible to conduct an exit poll *before* elections. It's very difficult to measure the difference between what people *think* they want and what they *do* want before billions are invested in rapid transit systems, medicines, or anything else.[48]

On a human level, it is challenging to reconcile the importance of freedom of speech with the reality that that speech threatens to bring objectionable material into our homes. The first attempt to censor the new technology that made possible movies and films occurred in 1922 when Postmaster General William Hays was appointed by President Harding to run the newly formed Motion Picture Producers and Distributors of America (MPPDA). The codes enacted by the Hays Office were circumvented by filmmakers who could, by demonstrating an overall positive moral lesson, portray topics and situations that would otherwise be banned. No one was satisfied with the results. Hollywood producers were loath to comply with the codes set by regulators. Moralists were appalled at the continued distribution of material they deemed obscene. In 1934, 12 years after the Hays Office was empowered, religious leaders came together to form the League of Decency in order to pressure Hollywood executives into self-censorship lest they face a boycott of all their films.

One actual boycott was carried out, and that was sufficient for Hollywood to capitulate. Studios began to self-censor and self-regulate themselves, which delighted the League of Decency.[49] At the same time, however, what no one realized was that filmmakers intent on producing films as violent or "immoral" as they wanted to make with complete abandon went underground. It was in the 1930s that the underground market in stag films emerged as an industry.

Hollywood and music industry executives who are not responsible for the challenges market imperfections create in fueling the proliferation of unwanted choices are nonetheless summoned to testify before Congress, as if either industry or government could erase the exasperating gap between Expressed Preference and Revealed Preference. Recall the prisoner's dilemma: Although every hockey player would individually want to wear a helmet, his decision is predicated on the actions of the other players against whom he plays. Unless there is a rule that requires *all* players to wear helmets, then *no* player will wear a helmet.

When music executives testify before Congress, state their positions, and then agree to conform to some code of conduct on a voluntary basis, they face a dilemma. Absent an enforcement mechanism, an individual studio executive who complies with a restriction (hockey players who wear a helmets voluntarily) is at a disadvantage because other executives will gain a competitive advantage by not complying with a voluntary restraint (hockey players who refuse to wear helmets). Officers at companies that deliberately engage in actions that harm their business are guilty of dereliction of duty.

This is the paradox of Smith's theory, for here is a case where we, pursuing what is in our best interest individually, make decisions that, over time, lead to inferior collective outcomes. The market imperfection that offers unwanted choices, in other words, makes it necessary for parents—not Hollywood or Congress—to decide the films minors watch, the music to which they listen, and the Web sites they access on the Internet. Technology oftentimes makes our lives more and more complicated.

It is therefore both disingenuous and fruitless to frame these arguments in moral terms for two reasons. Market imperfections are amoral, which is to say they are value-neutral.[50] The other reason is that when presenting the dilemma as a question of morality, one confronts one of the fundamental principles of democratic life: freedom of speech. Thus the First Amendment creates a barrier that no amount of political rhetoric can overcome, creating a tautological absurdity from which there is no escape, unless we abolish the First Amendment. What we confront here, then, is an instance in which the collective outcome of an economic fact of life causes outrage, an outrage about which we feel helpless.

Robert Frank pointed out that there are times when individuals can achieve a better communal outcome if they entered into agreements in which they volunteered to have their choices restricted. "The libertarian who insists that the right not to be restricted cannot, as a matter of principle, ever be negotiated away," he wrote, "shows contempt for the rights of people to resolve such issues for themselves."[51]

But it is one thing to agree to limit one's freedoms within clearly defined parameters: Protective helmets must be worn (facing forward) by players on the ice rink while a game is in process. This simple regulation defines who must wear a helmet, where he must wear a helmet, and when he must wear a helmet. Freedom of speech is also restricted when it is to incite violence or endanger life and property. One is free neither to rally a mob into looting nor to scream "Fire!" in a crowded theater for the purposes of securing a seat. But what occurs when speech creates no imminent danger?

The ubiquitous nature of the Internet now is an integral and undeniable part of our lives. In the same way that radio waves penetrate physically through our bodies, the Internet sweeps through our conscious. Thus, we feel particularly vulnerable when offensive choices invade the intimacy of our home lives. Elected officials would serve us better if they were more understanding of the dilemma the Internet has now thrust in our lives in the most intrusive manner. For this to occur, this kind of public debate needs several elements. First is the public recognition that it isn't a matter of Hollywood marketing sex and violence to youngsters. Second, there then must be the recognition that certain market imperfections have been exacerbated by technological innovations in a way that a disturbing array of choices are made available to us that we may not want, either for ourselves or as a society. Finally, we need to accept the difficulties that arise from resolving conflicts between the First Amendment and the absence of an enforcement mechanism into which everyone concerned will enter voluntarily.

If it weren't bad enough that we are loath to abandon the one principle that allows us to speak, think, and argue freely, economists have proved quite useless in finding a viable resolution for constricting the unwanted choices that arise from such market failures. Indeed, the conflict between different values in an open society is one that can produce disturbing demarcations in ideological positions, and at times result in recalcitrant schisms. Historian Gertrude Himmelfarb argues that society then confronts the threat of a "polarization," a polarization that stands to undermine the nature of civil discourse. The result is an ethics and morality gap that divides society. Himmelfarb believes that:

> The cultural divide helps explain the peculiar, almost schizoid nature of our present condition: the evidence of moral disarray on the one hand and of a religious-*cum*-moral revival on the other. This disjunction is apparent in small matters and large—in the fact, for example, that both gangsta rap and gospel rock are among today's fastest-growing forms of music; or that while raunchy talk shows are common on television, moralistic ones are on the radio; or that while a good many people were tolerant of President Clinton's sexual infidelities, many others purchased enough copies of William Bennett's *Death of Outrage* (most of whom presumably share his outrage) to have kept it on the best-seller list for months.
>
> This polarization . . . has larger ramifications, affecting beliefs, attitudes, values, and practices on a host of subjects ranging from private morality to public policy, from popular culture to high culture, from crime to education, welfare, and the family. In some respects, it is even more divisive than the class polarization that Karl Marx saw as the crucial fact of life under capitalism.[52]

Technological innovations propel social polarization forward. Consider the peculiar way in which something as innocuous as a song is impacted by various technologies. The Federal Communications Commission (FCC) has guidelines under which radio and television stations may broadcast their programs. The FCC prohibits certain words and images from being broadcast or telecast. MTV therefore has to "bleep" words and "blur" images in order to comply. No such restrictions apply to material available on the Internet. Consider how Third Eye Blind was accused of glamorizing drug abuse in 1999 and Eminem was denounced as promoting hate-speech in 2000. The exact lyrics at the center of these controversies are reproduced here to let the reader decide the merits of each argument. Let us first consider Third Eye Blind and then Eminem.

Stephan Jenkins, an English major who graduated from the University of California at Berkeley, is the lead singer of Third Eye Blind, a band based in San Francisco. In 1999, one of the top songs in the country was "Semi-Charmed Life," which he wrote. This song included the following lyrics:

The sky it was gold, it was rose
I was taking sips of it through my nose
And I wish I could get back there
Some place back there
Smiling in the pictures you would take
Doing crystal meth
Will lift you up until you break
It won't stop
I won't come down, I keep stock
With a tick-tock rhythm and a bump for the drop
And then I bumped up
I took the hit I was given
Then I bumped again
And then I bumped again.[53]

MTV, mindful of the political storm surrounding music lyrics, censored its broadcasts, erasing references to drug use when the music video was played. But youngsters, who could read the lyrics provided with the CD, could also download the music online (or play it) while watching the video on television. MTV's decision made no sense; MTV was supposed to be for them, and not subject to their parents' approval. The music video was recorded on a VCR, and thus youngsters could see the video while they played the uncensored music.

The following summer, Marshall Mathers, known as Eminem, caused a sensation with the lyrics in his hit song "The Real Slim Shady." The profanity and violence caused a controversy, particularly because his words were interpreted as being misogynist and homophobic. The use of obscenities forced MTV to bleep some of the lyrics, but Eminem was unapologetic. The last refrain before the final chorus stated that there were a million others just like him who cuss like him.

Shock value is an age-old tactic for creating a buzz—and making sales. Art critic and historian Robert Hughes described how artists, since the Industrial Revolution, have attempted to "shock" the public in order to make their point.[54] But neither Stephan Jenkins nor Marshall Mathers intends to shock. "Artistic freedom," "First Amendment rights," and "censorship" have become the tired refuge of the intellectually dishonest and the lazy, for adopting this politically correct pose is convenient. But what we have, in fact, is the natural process in the cyclical patterns in vulgarity in entertainment. This is the price of democracy. Tim Berners-Lee, the inventor of the World Wide Web, acknowledges as much:

Since the Web is universal and unbounded, there's all sorts of junk on it. As parents, we have a duty to protect our young children from seeing material that could harm them psychologically. Filtering software can screen information under control of the reader, to spare the reader the grief of having to read what he or she deems junk. . . . But when someone imposes involuntary filters on someone else, that is censorship.[55]

Not everyone sees it that way. In his defense of efforts by European governments to regulate content on the Internet, for instance, Erkki Liikanen, a Finnish member of the European Commission, argued that "it's our basic assumption [in Europe] that when you do business in an area, you have to respect local laws just as you do offline. And the medium [of the Internet], because of the way it operates, presents certain difficulties that present a challenge to industry to resolve through self-regulation."[56] How "self-regulation" differs from "self-censorship" or how "self-regulation" constitutes a competitive disadvantage for the firms self-regulating are not clear. What is clear, however, is that censorship is, ultimately, futile. When Warner Brothers pulled "Cop Killer" from Ice-T's album, *Body Count,* in 1992, the vilified rapper defended his political right to rap about killing police officers to denounce alleged police brutality against minorities. "When I started out I was signed to Warner Brothers and they never censored us," he told Mick Heck, an interviewer from Rock Out Censorship. When asked if he thought that his song was attacked for the sake of creating controversy about music, he argued that, "'Cop Killer' was a protest record. . . . It was a record of anger and some people didn't understand it. . . . I didn't need people to come in and really back me on the First Amendment. I needed people to come in and say 'Ice-T has grounds to make this record.' I have the right to make it because the cops are killing my people."[57]

If the societal conflicts are framed not in terms of artistic expression, freedom of speech, or censorship, what emerges is the observation that the Internet is being used for social discourse. The last time the media was used to make social commentary by creating controversy was when John Lennon and Yoko Ono released their *Two Virgins* album and staged a "love in" in their Manhattan apartment as part of a peace protest against the Vietnam War. Had the Internet been available in the early 1970s, Lennon and Ono would have, undoubtedly, broadcast their "love in" to millions of online voyeurs on the Internet.

The blessed absence of controversial war, moreover, makes it more challenging for artists in the 2000s to engage publicity with an equal sense of urgency. Eminem, like Madonna a decade before him, is interested in pushing the public's buttons and questioning the assumptions in society.[58] A talented young man, who did not enjoy as many advantages growing up as many others in his generation, the conviction in his lyrics is poignant. Consider the song, "Who Knew," in which he sings about taking drugs, committing rape, ridiculing gays, and condemning parents who lack parenting skills. It is clear that Eminem is aware that his songs are entertainment, a way for adolescents to live vicariously through the music and find a release for their fantasies. The music industry in the entertainment economy online has changed the rules of the game.

The "Parental Advisory" stickers on CDs have been rendered irrelevant; the Parents' Music Resource Center has been obliterated by the technology of the Internet. Third Eye Blind and Eminem are two examples of how, in a misguided attempt to restore a familiar order, technology is changing the way we live our lives and how we deal with each other. They are pushing the envelope without a doubt, but as we shall see in the next chapter, the result is counterintuitive for it is socially redeeming.

SUMMARY

The adversarial role between the music industry and online music sites that characterized the 1990s ended when online music providers and the technological innovations that ensured mechanisms for providing a reliable business model that would compensate copyright owners for their intellectual property combined. This is consistent with what one can expect by a market that is characterized by *Key #2* (The online economy is characterized by the proliferation of winner-take-all contests and by the exacerbation of both market imperfections and market failures) and *Key #4* (The online economy can create conditions in which inferior societal outcomes will prevail unless regulatory remedies are in place to balance private wants and public needs).

That the music industry in the entertainment economy online had expanded into broader demographics by 2001 served to accelerate the entry of record companies into the digital-downloading market.[59] The paradoxes that suffuse the music industry's relationship with the Internet, moreover, were consistent with the discrepancies economists have observed in other consumer markets, most of which can be explained by the theory of Stated versus Revealed Preference. Music executives, musicians, and Internet entrepreneurs now recognize that the same technology that has made the online music industry possible offers, in fact, greater protections for copyrights and intellectual properties. The online music industry is evolving in ways consistent with business strategies that strive to diminish the gap between what one says and what one does, creating more efficient markets in the process.

NOTES

1. "Bertlesmann and Napster Form Strategic Alliance," Napster.com, October 31, 2000.

2. The plaintiffs consisted of Time Warner, Sony, Universal Music Group, EMI, and Bertelsmann's BMG subsidiary. The Recording Industry Association of America represented the first four plaintiffs.

3. Personal e-mail communication from http://www.napster.com/pressroom.

4. "The industry has not embraced the usage of file sharing," Andreas Schmidt, CEO of Bertelsmann E-Commerce Group, said in New York. "We are getting together with Napster, and we are going to change all that. But this agreement is important. We have to reinvent ourselves as a digital company, not as a media company. Somebody [in the industry] had to step up to the plate and take the leadership position. With this deal, we've done that" (Charny, "Napster Deal Comes with A Price Tag").

5. Charles C. Mann, "Napster-Proof CDs," Inside.com. Available online at http://www.salon.com/tech/inside/2001/03/27/cd_protection/print.html.

6. Plato, *Republic,* Book V, 360 B.C.E.

7. Chuck D, "'Free' Music Can Free the Artist," *New York Times,* April 29, 2000. Other musicians hold similarly dim views of their business relationships with record companies. Prince, who filed suit against Warner Brothers, went so far as to claim that he was a "slave" of the industry.

8. Amy Harmon, "Unknown Musicians Find Payoffs Online," *New York Times,* July 20, 2000.

9. Ibid.

10. Janelle Brown, "Whoring for Download," Salon.com, November 30, 2000.

11. The income potential is considerable. The *New York Times* reported the case of Ernesto Cortazar, a 60-year-old Mexican composer who earned in excess of $100,000 from MP3.com in one year alone ($80,000 from the music fans downloaded and $20,000 from the sale of merchandise, such as T-shirts).

12. John Markoff, "Bridging Two Worlds to Make On-Line Digital Music Profitable," *New York Times,* September 13, 1999.

13. Steve Lohr, "Code Name: Mainstream," *New York Times,* August 28, 2000.

14. As quoted in http://www.ciionline.org interview.

15. Personal communication, May 2000.

16. "In a donut economy no one owns the intellectual property, which rests in the center. Value lies in the ring of innovation wrapped around this core," Clay Shirky wrote in "The Genome's Open-Source Approach" in *Business 2.0,* June 13, 2000. Making the case that the human genome project could best move forward if programmers were free to contribute, he argued that the Internet was a fine model to emulate for biotech research. "In the case of the Internet economy, the intellectual property at the center consists of the free Web server and browser and the protocols they were built around–HTML and HTTP," he wrote. "Innovation in the New Economy came about when these freely available assets were employed to deliver products or services desir-

able enough to draw attention and eventually cash from consumers. Donut economies lower barriers to entry because anyone can use the IP [Intellectual Property] in the center without having to pay fees or ask permission." (Why people insist on ridiculous metaphors remains a mystery as frustrating as the human genome project.)

17. Jack Valenti, "There's No Free Hollywood," *New York Times*, June 21, 2000.

18. John Perry Barlow, "The Next Economy of Ideas: Will Copyright Survive the Napster Bomb?" *Wired*, October 2000, pp. 240–242. The individuals named worked on public projects, or state-financed institutions, each with the understanding that the rights to the intellectual property they developed would revert to their institutions or employers. These, in turn, had contractual obligations with funders. Linus Torvalds, for instance, knew that his work on Linux was to remain in the public domain. Benoit Mandelbrot, a Polish mathematician, had his work financed by institutions of higher learning and their funders. Tim Berner-Lees and Marc Andreessen, whose work led to the development of the World Wide Web, had their salaries paid by their respective institutions, and they designed the protocols that makes the World Wide Web possible to be free of charge, to remain in the public domain, and to open to constant innovation and evolution, much the way, say, the English language remains in the public domain. Vint Cerf, a pioneer in technological innovations, contractually, has his work remain property of Worldcom. In each case cited, the work developed is financed by taxpayers or shareholders with the legal framework that whatever intellectual property each researcher develops remains inappropriable by private individuals.

19. In a separate lawsuit, MP3.com was found guilty of willfully infringing the copyrights of Universal Music Group by Judge Jed Rakoff of Federal District Court in Manhattan. MP3.com was ordered to pay $25,000 for each of the Universal Music Group compact discs included in its MyMP3.com service, damages that amounted to $100 million. MP3.com set aside $150 million until the matter was settled with Seagram, the owner of Universal Music Group. "Some companies operating in the area of the Internet may have a misconception that because their technology is somewhat novel, they are somehow immune from the ordinary applications of laws of the United States, including copyright law. They need to understand that the law's domain knows no such limits," Judge Rakoff was quoted in Amy Harmon's article, "Judge Rules Against MP3 On CD Copying."

20. Telephone news conference held on March 28, 2001, as reported by the Associated Press.

21. The volatile nature of technology was more than evident when, one month after the SDMI was announced, CNN reported on October 24, 2000, that "[r]esearchers at Princeton University, Xerox PARC and Rice University said they were able to remove invisible security measures placed on four music files by the Secure Digital Music Initiative–a group of 200 music, telecommunications and consumer electronic companies. . . . The claim, if true, strikes at the heart of efforts to protect copyrights and prevent people from listening to music for free using technology such as Napster. 'I believe all four of these schemes would have been cracked by pirates if they had been

deployed,' said Edward Felten, an associate professor of computer science at Princeton."

22. Charles C. Mann, "A Whole New Vision for Napster," *Yahoo! Internet Life,* June 2001.

23. Some of the encryption programs being developed, for instance, center on creating automated systems that develop mathematical formulas to identify specific files, thereby making it possible to track song, book, and video files that have not been embedded with a watermark.

24. Allison Fishman, "Swamp Thing," *Revolution,* November 2000, p. 71.

25. Bolivia, where the government a generation ago printed money so relentlessly the exchange rate at one point exceeded more than one million-to-one dollar, had to replace its currency because it was then worthless. Inflation in that country exceeded that of the Weimar Republic, which created such chaos in Germany that it facilitated the political ascendance of the National Socialist, or Nazi, party.

26. Consider the disconcerting impact on others that the non sequitur in the representation of the online evolution of syndication as a business model has termed "deconstruction" by Philip Evans and Thomas Wurtster in their book, *Blown to Bits: How the New Economics of Information Transforms Strategy.*

27. John Ellis, "That Explosion You Just Heard Is the Music Business," *Fast Company,* October 2000, p. 338.

28. Michel de Montaigne, *The Complete Essays,* Book I, Essay 26, translated by M.A. Screech, p. 194.

29. "The Napster Deal," *New York Times,* November 2, 2000.

30. It may not make a difference to a retailer, but there are, of course, public health considerations if everyone is eating chocolate chip cookies exclusively.

31. "Forecasting Intercity Rail Ridership Using Revealed Preference and Stated Preference Data," *Transportation Research Record,* No. 1328, pp. 30–35.

32. In our personal lives, the stakes are incredibly high. When a couple takes a vow to be faithful (Stated Preference), the sense of betrayal and hurt when there is infidelity (Revealed Preference) is enough to tear a union asunder. Hurting someone who loves you, like being hurt by someone you love, is the most personal and devastating consequence that occurs when Stated and Revealed Preferences are in conflict. Few relationships can withstand the rupture in one's trust that results should a promise for monogamy (Stated Preference) become the reality of adultery (Revealed Preference).

33. This is why not all polls are alike: exit polls are far more accurate because they measure how people *actually* voted, and not how they said they *intended* to vote.

34. Thomas Ferguson and Joel Rogers, "The Myth of America's Turn to the Right," *The Atlantic Monthly,* May 1986.

35. Ibid.

36. It is unsettling, for example, to see bumper-to-bumper traffic on the congested South Dixie Highway in Miami while the Metrorail trains zoom by overhead, empty.

37. Norman Bradburn, "Watching the Polls: Elections, the Media and Polling," *Chicago Policy Review,* 1, no. 1 (fall 1996).

38. On July 13, 1999, Nobuyuki Idei, of Sony, and Gerald Levin, of Time Warner, announced that CDnow would be merged with Columbia House. "The first business that will benefit the most from the Internet will be the revolution in music," Gerald Levin predicted in Saul Hansell's article, "Sony and Time Warner Make Music Deal." On September 10, 2000, when Warner announced its entry into the digital-download market, it confirmed its belief that the technological innovations developed by RealNetworks and Preview Systems would ensure that it would be able to compete aggressively in the market with technology that would be compatible on whichever platform any individual customer would use, a tacit recognition that Warner had fallen behind.

39. Sony Music Entertainment and Seagram's Universal Music Group announced their joint subscription service in the fall 2000. Online companies, such as Scour, the start-up that was sued for copyright infringement, agreed to settle claims against it by liquidating its assets to Listen.com. Scour had made headlines when it was launched in Los Angeles because it was backed by Michael Ovitz, the famed Hollywood agent and former president of Disney.

40. Gene Kan of Gnutella, defending his efforts to provide open source software that would allow anyone anywhere to download anything off the Internet without paying for it, said, "First off, there are many like me. And secondly, what would [the music industry] get? There would be little potential for recovering any financial damage, there is absolutely zero potential of shutting down Gnutella and in any case Gnutella is nothing but a communications protocol. It'd be like suing English" (Brown, "The Gnutella Paradox").

41. Charles Seife, *Zero: The Biography of a Dangerous Idea,* p. 131.

42. Nullsoft developed Shoutcast.com, one of the first audio streaming technologies. Rob Lord's approach to the Internet is expressed on Nullsoft's Web site, http://www.nullsoft.com.

43. Predatory pricing, unfair competition, and antitrust legislation all represent a body of remedies that have been used successfully to ensure that the playing field remains level and healthy competition is maintained in the marketplace.

44. What makes these market failures all the more frustrating is that they impact society in significant ways. The money could have been invested in other forms of rapid transit, such as more highways and expanded bus routes in south Florida. It is also a continuing aggravation: whenever anyone in Miami-Dade County makes a purchase, the sales tax paid is a reminder of the subsidy the Metrorail requires; whenever politicians attempt to address rapid transit, the disaffected electorate resorts to cynicism. In health care, the gaps between Expressed Preference and Revealed Preference contribute to distortions, creating a system in the United States, for instance, where preventive maintenance is undermined while costly options proliferate—oftentimes costly precisely because they are unwanted. (If it is any consolation, there are other countries where the situation is worse than in the United States. The proliferation of market imperfections in France, for instance, has resulted in a country where people are overmedicated and hypochondriacs are found everywhere.)

45. Caryn James, "Nice Is Not Enough," *New York Times,* September 29, 2000.

46. In other societies, the idea that we do best collectively when we are free to pursue our interests in the marketplace unencumbered, is often presented as a "superorganic" theory of culture, or the Gaia theory of life.

47. Indeed, when I began research on this book, I secured a laptop computer to use exclusively on the research for this project. I did this to avoid those cookies from compiling a disturbing profile of my hard drive, one in which my other work would be interrupted by unwanted solicitations from gambling, video, and adult sites.

48. Any parent understands this phenomenon intimately well. "You *think* you want another bowl of chocolate ice cream. But you really don't," I said during the course of writing this chapter to a certain five-year-old boy, before acquiescing to his request. It is not surprising that later that evening he came to me in my study complaining he couldn't sleep because his tummy hurt. "See? At the table you *thought* you wanted more ice cream, but you were just being gluttonous and now your tummy aches." Children grow and become adults, but that doesn't mean that we are then endowed with what economists call Perfect Knowledge, an idea that makes "hindsight" irrelevant in the economic sphere.

49. The League of Decency disbanded in 1965, one reason cited for the escalation in aggression, violence, and sex in films since the mid-1960s.

50. True enough, Shakespeare admonished that nothing is either good or bad, but thinking makes it so.

51. *Choosing the Right Pond*, p. 225.

52. Gertrude Himmelfarb, *One Nation, Two Cultures,* pp. 117–118.

53. "Semi-Charmed Life," words and music by Stephan Jenkins, copyright EM Blackwood Music, Inc. and 3EB Publishing.

54. For a fascinating discussion, see Robert Hughes, *The Shock of the New.*

55. Tim Berners-Lee and Mark Fischetti, *Weaving the Web,* p. 134.

56. U.S. Senator Patrick Leahy dismissed such arguments. "Governments, basically, should resist trying to develop special rules for the Internet. There are model ways of doing Internet regulation, but to think that government, any government here or in Europe, is going to develop a whole set of rules for the Internet, they're making a bad mistake." These views are exchanged in Amy Zuckerman, "Continents Clash on Content," *New York Times*, April 18, 2001.

57. Rock Out Censorship is a grassroots organization, whose Web site is http://www.theroc.org.

58. Social critic Camille Paglia, writing in *TV Guide* (October 21–27, 2000), summed up her assessment of Eminem by calling him "the enema for the stale, saccharine platitudes and pieties that kids are force-fed these days by their [politically correct] teachers and counselors. It's clear from his huge popularity that Eminem has tapped into a rising tide of rebellion among middle-class white kids who are sick and tired of the canned, humanitarian schmaltz of their antiseptic, namby-pamby, culture-starved schools."

59. Media Metrix reported that at the end of 2000, adults over the age of 50 constituted 20 percent of the visitors to online music sites.

CHAPTER 8

"SURRENDER OR DIE YOU FOOLISH MORTALS!"

Anyone anywhere with access to the Internet can download Ultravixen, one of the world's leading online video games. It is a video game that has young men around the world spellbound. Ultravixen, in fact, introduces them to the world of online video games that combine violence and sex, fantasy and sadism in an interactive video game that astounds in its power to become part of the vernacular of an entire generation of young men and women. Youngsters who visit the Web site are enticed to come in play the game by being presented with this sexually explicit language:

> A beautiful college student is snatched out of time by the evil sex fiend OverLord and thrust into a future of erotic slavery. She escapes and vows vengeance, assuming a new identity. ULTRAVIXEN—a super-hot sci-fi sex star whose powerful SuperClimaxes can warp both time and space.
>
> The dark OverLord has been using a vast network of time portals to torture and enslave young girls in his maniacal, mechanical sex machines. Now, UltraVixen must use her tremendous sexual powers to seal the time portals and bring the dark OverLord to his knees. There's just one catch. She needs YOU to master the incredible array of erotic tools and weapons that will unleash her SuperClimax and destroy the evil sex machines forever. The fate of the universe is in your hands.[1]

Critics of online video gaming point to the violence and explicit sexuality that is offered almost exclusively to adolescent males. Parents, educators, and policymakers alike are concerned about the impact this violence-and-sex as entertainment has on youngsters and young adults. That this market is growing by leaps and bounds—everyday there are more Web sites with Ultravixen-like characters—further intensifies the concerns and debate about what should be done about these forms of entertainment. In the first part of this book, recall how I described Paulina Borsook's devastating description of techies as "cypherpunks," whom she characterized as immature men reveling in a teenage boy's love of the dark, ghoulish, and apocalyptic. On a social level, these socially awkward men, she claimed, held an adolescent's view of sexual relations and a Hobbesian view of politics and society.

At first glance, the idea of a Hobbesian "war of all against all" that includes, with no apologies, outrageous sexual violence resembles one of the most popular online video games. After sex and music, online video games are the most popular destinations for young people in the entertainment economy online. The escalation of violence in entertainment films has not gone unnoticed. Writing in the *New Republic,* Gregg Easterbrook criticizes an entire genre of filmmaking that depends on violence:

> [The film] *Scream* opens with a scene in which a teenage girl is forced to watch her jock boyfriend tortured and then disemboweled by two fellow students who, it will eventually be learned, want revenge on anyone from high school who crossed them. After jock boy's stomach is shown cut open and he dies screaming, the killers stab and torture the girl, then cut her throat and hang her body from a tree so that Mom can discover it when she drives up. A dozen students and teachers are graphically butchered in the film, while the characters make running jokes about murder. At one point, a boy tells a big-breasted friend she'd better be careful because the stacked girls always get it in horror films; in the next scene, she's grabbed, stabbed through the breasts, and murdered. Some provocative send-up, huh? The movie builds to a finale in which one of the killers announces that he and his accomplice started off by murdering strangers but then realized it was a lot more fun to kill their friends.[2]

This essay was prompted by the massacre at Columbine High School on April 20, 1999, when two teenage students, Eric Harris and Dylan Klebold, carried out a military-style assault on their classmates, killing 13 before taking their own lives. This was the worst incident of school violence in American history, and it opened a national debate on the kinds of violence to which young people are exposed to by the entertainment media.

Parents and policymakers alike were stunned at these events, and social critics began to debate the impact of violence in the entertain-

ment media on society at large. The escalation in violence committed by youngsters continues to cast a cloud over the music, film, and
video industries, and generated laser-sharp scrutiny of Hollywood by
elected officials in Washington and parents' groups nationwide.

"Almost none of those interviewed said they wanted Washington to
censor Hollywood, or even Hollywood to censor itself," the *New York
Times* reported in an article decrying Washington's interference in how
they raise their children.[3] If in the previous chapter we saw the lyrics
to which youngsters listen that they download from the Internet or
found in CDs—and about which parents, religious leaders, educators,
and policymakers show concern—in this chapter we examine the extraordinary violence that pervades video games.

As we shall see later on, people are complex beings and there is
no strong case for a cause-effect between violence in the media and
violence in society. But first, however, in order to understand how the
video gaming online develops, let us first consider how a market is
impacted when it is politicized. Media and entertainment violence continues to be treated as a public policy issue, one in which the need to
protect children and young adults is at odds with First Amendment
rights and the underlying principles of a free marketplace. With social
scientists, lobby groups, and politicians weighing in, certain distortions
interfere with the normal development of this market. As we shall see,
flawed science is often used to justify misguided public policy, and this
exacerbates distortions in the marketplace. This is of concern if for no
other reason than, as we have seen in our discussion of winner-take-
all contests, the nature of the Internet is such that it magnifies market
imperfections in unexpected ways.

VIDEOS AND THE ECONOMICS OF FLIGHTS OF FANCY

There are four major companies that together produce the videos
that dominate the market, both online and off-line. The violence and
sadism of Ultravixen is an exception, however, and the products produced by Nintendo, Sony, Sega, and Microsoft relegate themselves to
games of fantasy and science fiction.[4] Although these games involve
extreme forms of violence, as we shall see later on in this chapter, this
is not necessarily an objectionable thing.

The size of the market for videos and the economic power their le-
gions of followers command can be best understood by considering
what happened when Sony released its eagerly awaited PlayStation 2
on October 26, 2000. Not unlike the sensation that came with the release of the fourth installment in the Harry Potter series, stores across
the United States opened at the stroke of midnight to let customers
buy Sony's PlayStation 2, which had been heralded as the video game

Nintendo	*Gamecube* and *Game Boy* IBM PowerPC microprocessor
Sony	*Playstation 2* Custom chip developed by Toshiba
Sega	*Dreamcast* Proprietary microprocessor
Microsoft	*X-Box* Intel-based video game system

Figure 8.1 Video Gaming: Who's Who in the Real World

technology of the twenty-first century. This is how a Sony press release described the scene in downtown San Francisco at the Metreon, an urban entertainment center where Sony has a store:

> With only 500,000 units available in its first shipment, the [PlayStation 2] console sold out at most retail outlets across North America by early this morning. To commemorate the launch and to give their customers first access to the console, several retailers opened their doors at 12:01A.M. this morning. The PlayStation store at the Metreon in San Francisco had a large turnout, with over 300 people—some camping out since early Wednesday morning. At midnight, Sony ushered in the PlayStation 2 era with a countdown. Surprisingly, despite the grave shortage and the fact that most of the people looking to buy a PlayStation 2 were turned away at virtually every retailer, the launch came off without any significant glitches. . . . "Retail outlets [around the U.S.] reported today that they were sold out of PS2 consoles by 9 A.M. this morning," said Matt Gravett, game analyst for PC Data. "It's a definite measure of the hysteria around the PS2 that people are willing to buy software with no guarantee that they'll have hardware to play it. They're all revved up with no place to go."[5]

Think of the size of this market: with 500,000 units selling out within a matter of days, at the retail price of $300 each, the PlayStation 2 brought in $150,000,000 in its *initial* shipment.[6]

This is the revenue generated by *one* company with *one* game in *one* shipment to *one* country. During the 2000 holiday season, subsequent shipments of 800,000 additional units were sold in the United States, making total revenues generated by Sony's PlayStation 2 a monumental $390,000,000. Sony, with the span of a few short years, had replaced Nintendo as the video of choice among American youngsters. (Sales of PlayStation 2 consoles topped the 10 million mark in March 2001, and Sony confirmed that its plans to ship 20 million units for the 2001–2002 business year starting April 2001 to be on target.) It is not difficult to understand why Sony, which did not enter the video game market until 1995, in a span of five years was able to have sales to the video game market account for almost a third of the entire company's profits.

In 2000, Sony made $2.75 billion in profits from its PlayStation products. The revenue streams are considerable, and the profits at stake are enormous. During the same time, Nintendo and SegaNet split an additional $3 billion in profits from video games between them. Microsoft, cognizant of the potential of the Internet to expand this market considerably, decided to enter the video game market in 2001, eager to establish a formidable presence in a youth-oriented market.[7] This proves instructive, for it demonstrates how strategies must constantly be revised to reflect the level of competition, technological changes, and how consumer preferences evolve.

Youths enamored with hand-held Nintendo 64 in the early 1990s— it was impossible to walk through an airport terminal in any major American city and not see kids playing these games while sitting at departure gates and lounges with their bored parents and guardians— were replaced with youngsters enraptured with PlayStation 2 as the 2000s began.[8]

Other players were cognizant of the breathtaking speed with which the video game market was evolving. In August 2000, Sega announced a $150 million marketing campaign on behalf of SegaNet, its new online gaming Web site. "A year after staging a comeback of sorts with its Dreamcast video game console, Sega now bets that being first in the online gaming arena will give the third-ranked console company an early advantage over bigger rivals Sony Computer Entertainment of America and Nintendo of America, as well as Microsoft's X-Box," Tobi Elkin reported.[9] The media blitz, launched during the MTV Music Awards broadcast on September 7, 2000, showcased the built-in modem of its Dreamcast console, which allows online play via SegaNet's Internet service. This technology allows players in different parts of the country (or world) to play an interactive game with each other via the Internet.

Sony's PlayStation 2 and Sega's Dreamcast were in mortal competition as each sought to remake the market shares their products enjoyed in the burgeoning market that, for the first time, shifted to the

Internet. "The challenge for us," said Joe Culley, vice president of marketing at Sega, "is how do you talk about SegaNet as a new property and make people understand that Dreamcast and a SegaNet account deliver a new experience."[10]

Nintendo, of course, was not about to be pushed aside by either Sony or Sega and, at the Spaceworld video game trade show in Tokyo, introduced Gamecube in August 2000. The reaction from people at that trade show was one of great enthusiasm. Powered by an IBM microprocessor, Nintendo's Gamecube was an anticipatory move to position itself strongly before Microsoft could launch its X-Box and less than two months before Sony's PlayStation 2 hit American stores.

"It's like three giant planets colliding," Greg Galanos, managing director of Softbank Venture Capital in Silicon Valley, said, characterizing the collision between Sony, Nintendo, and Microsoft. "The potential impact of Microsoft in 2001 and beyond is unknown at this time, but the dominant players are ready to compete for this very, very lucrative market."

Electronic Arts, the largest independent video game software company, for its part, is coming over the horizon, intent on competing with the major industry players. Despite the fact that Electronic Arts lost $42 million on sales of $155 million in just one-quarter in 2000, this company was confident that online video gaming is the way of the future. "You'll interact with other people. You'll get to date, marry, murder—it's all here," John Riccitiello said. "By the end of the 2001, these games will start to look like legitimate competition on television."[11]

Electronic Arts has invested $700 million in developing video games, half of which was spent on its online gaming products and its Web site. Ea.com, in fact, entered into an exclusive agreement with America Online to operate AOL's game channel.[12] That, coupled with the success of SSX, a snowboarding video game, has positioned Electronic Arts to compete effectively against the corporate giants.[13] Although detractors pointed out that Electronic Arts' offerings were more difficult to use at first, the distribution that AOL offers on the Internet shifts the focus; Ea.com will benefit from the traffic generated by AOL, which is key to its marketing and branding strategies.

The forceful entry of these companies into the video gaming market in the entertainment economy online is fueling its tremendous growth. Consider that the worldwide market for online video games is expected to surpass the $6 billion mark by the end of 2002, and some analysts believe that when Microsoft enters the market and video streaming becomes feasible, the market will approach the $15 billion by 2005.[14] The entire worldwide in-home entertainment market was $20 billion in 2000, with video games, rental films, cable television, and pay-per-view dominating this market.[15] The technological innovations being brought to the market stand to dwarf these figures.

As if in a mad race to bring greater technologies to the market, Intertainer and Akamai Technologies announced plans to bring video-on-demand to customers with high-speed Internet connections. Pioneering the development of Internet-based streaming video, analogous to interactive broadcasting on the Web, the alliance included the licensing rights to the media conglomerates, including Sony Music, Warner Brothers, DreamWorks SKG, and Columbia. Intertainer is a privately held company, owned, in part, by Microsoft, NBC, and Sony. In fact, Microsoft's stake in Intertainer amounted to $56 million six months after Intertainer announced in July 1999 that it supported Microsoft's TV platform initiative, a protocol that is expected to set the standard for interactive television.

A formidable challenge, however, is emerging in the form of direct competition from Blockbuster. In a profitable alliance with Enron, the bankrupt utility and energy conglomerate, Blockbuster plans to deliver movies via digitized video stream to its customers directly. Even though Blockbuster has a first-rate distribution system and phenomenal brand recognition, it is at a competitive disadvantage in that it has no direct Internet service, which will require a considerable investment in time and money to launch. The importance of Blockbuster's entry into the video-on-demand market, however, signals fierce competition and corporate America's conviction of the considerable potential of this market.[16] Intertainer/Akamai and Blockbuster are pioneering the expansion of the video-on-demand market during a time when technological innovations are shifting the video game market more firmly into the entertainment economy online. This, of course, includes the market for consumers who have wireless Internet access.[17]

As 2001 unfolded, natural market forces began to shape how video-on-demand penetrated the consumer market. That the four giants of the video game market—Sony, Nintendo, Sega, and recent-arrival Microsoft—embraced the technology and the youth market and constituted a major commitment to the growing online video gaming and videos on-demand market. Afraid of being left out, Miramax became the first Hollywood studio to offer a full-length feature film on the Internet. "Guinevere," starring Sarah Polley and Stephen Rea, could be downloaded at various Web sites for $3.49. Industry concerns over DivX software, which, by virtue of being the favorite of hackers and movie traders, stands to become the standard for digital video compression online were brushed aside. Creating a market was the foremost concern; piracy and copyright issues could be dealt with at a later time.

The August 2000 Spaceworld trade show in Tokyo, however, heralded a welcome shift from the resistance and adversarial stance that many companies had taken over to the embrace of the market potential of the Internet technologies. This was the first time when I heard industry leaders shift the public policy debate from denouncing the threat of copyright infringement and piracy and began to talk about the strategies for "digital rights management" and the promise of Microsoft's encryption technology that prevents unauthorized copying or distribution of digitized video-on-demand. The emergence of digital rights management as a corporate strategy, as we saw in Chapter 7, legitimizes the industry. Furthermore, video gaming entails developing products that appeal primarily to young men, who constitute the overwhelming consumers.[18] The content of these video games remains a political issue.

WELFARE ECONOMICS AND VIDEO VIOLENCE

Video gaming online continues to grow at a double-digit rate, and the Internet is propelling the expansion of this market with unprecedented speed. Technological innovations, furthermore, make the simulation of games more intense and real. Companies such as Alias|WaveFront are the forefront of innovative graphic technologies that make the special effects in video games and films breathtakingly real. Youngsters around the world are awed by these graphics and live to play these video games, download video-on-demand, and seek ever-greater thrills. In a market where the profits are enormous, that is witnessing the expansion of the market with the entrance of Microsoft, and the Intertainer/Akamai and Blockbuster alliances, the online video gaming is becoming more entrenched in society.

All one has to do is consider a film such as *Fight Club*, starring Brad Pitt and Edward Norton. The violence in this film was of such enormity that it repulsed the public at large—and it flopped at the box office. But this commercial failure reflects the tastes of the *general* movie-going public. Among young men, the movie was an unqualified hit. Indeed, it was so sensational that *Fight Club* is now a video game. Thus we see how a movie can become a successful franchise, one based on marketing extraordinary violence to young men. The "Fight Club" video game, in fact, has satisfied a niche so completely, there are now several editions of the video on the market.

The question for us, as consumers, parents, and citizens, becomes how to reconcile the choices a market economy offers and the societal impact that exposure to violence may have on youth. It is therefore necessary to understand if, and how, exposure to violence in the media affects our behavior. The questionable work on the impact of the broadcast media on the development of people by Brandon Centerwell, unfortunately, continues to shape the public's perceptions and misperceptions about how the violence and sexuality portrayed in videos and films influence youth.

In order to gain a clear perspective, let us turn our attention to the work of social scientists who examined the impact of television in the 1950s, 1960s, and 1970s. Their insights into how television viewing affects viewers offer a map to find our way as a society through the unfamiliar terrain of the Internet technologies. What we shall see, in fact, challenges the conclusions offered as facts to the American public in the 1990s and 2000s. This is important for, as the online video gaming and video-on-demand market prospers, policymakers need to know the truth.

Indeed, if Centerwell makes the case against videos by extrapolating one (unsound) study that examines the impact of introducing television in a given society, then let us now review the work of other, more reasonable, and thorough social scientists who pioneered the study of how television influences viewers. The following discussion is a digression, but given the level of rhetoric surrounding the debate about the impact of violence in the media on youth, I believe a thorough review of the matter is crucial to helping consumers and policymakers reach informed and thoughtful opinions on the development of this market.

OF BAD SCIENCE AND QUESTIONABLE PUBLIC POLICY

In his opening remarks during the Youth Culture and Violence hearing of May 13, 1999, held in the aftermath of the assault by two teenagers at Columbine High School in Littleton, Colorado, Chairman of the Committee of the Judiciary Rep. Henry Hyde stated:

> Some people point to the near saturation level of violence in the movies. [O]ur kids flock to and ask whether movies and TV programs that display extreme violence anesthetize the moral sensibilities of both adults and teenagers. Others criticize the violent nature of video and computer games that allow kids to simulate killing, and ask whether violent video games that glorify death desensitize our youth and lead to violent behavior. Furthermore, concerns have been raised about easily accessible information on the Internet that can be corrupting and dangerous, including Web sites and chat rooms that provide explosive-making instructions and expose children to inflammatory rhetoric and violent philosophies.[19]

Parents, students, mental health professionals, and representatives from the entertainment industry testified before this congressional body. In response to the testimony offered by witnesses who argued that exposure to violence on television, films, and video games desensitized young people and conditioned them to violence, Jack Valenti, chairman of the Motion Pictures Association of America, offered:

> The statistics are revelatory. Fewer than one percent of homicides involving school-age children occur in and around schools, according to the Centers for Disease Control. Since 1992 the annual death toll from school shootings has ranged from twenty to fifty-five, says the National School Safety Center. There were forty-nine deaths in the last school year. Forty-three percent of all schools had no crime at all in the 1996–1997 school year, said the Department of Education. . . . In 1997, the murder rate in the USA was the lowest in thirty years. . . . The FBI reports that the number of persons under eighteen in the U.S. is some 70 million. The rate of arrests for violent crimes in this category, has declined from its high water mark in 1994 at 51% to 41%. . . . This also means that 99.59% of young people under eighteen . . . were not into violent crime. The children of this country do not deserve being all herded into a category that labels them as something they are not. They are not all killers. They are not all brooding, menacing figures, filled with hatreds, emotional abnormalities which house a defective mythology. Though all children more or less inhabit the same entertainment and community enclaves, ninety-nine percent of them are decently formed good citizens.[20]

Supply is supply and demand is demand, Valenti essentially argues, and neither has anything to do with what is morally right or wrong. Critics of media violence often cite "numerous" scientific studies that establish a link between being exposed to violence as entertainment and subsequently engaging in violent acts.

The *New York Times* itself entered the fray in a rather irresponsible way by fanning the hysteria shaping the public debate. Indeed, the newspaper of record published a front-page article titled "How the Studios Used Children to Test-Market Violent Films" in the fall of 2000. "[C]onfidential marketing documents submitted by nine movie studios to the government commission that investigated the marketing of violent entertainment to children and teenagers, who are frequent moviegoers," the *New York Times* reported.[21] Suggesting there was an industry collusion to develop marketing campaigns that were duplicitous, the *New York Times* implied that Hollywood did this to counter conclusive scientific evidence establishing a causal relationship between violence in entertainment and aggressive behavior.

The public at large has been led—and misled—to believe that there are thousands of such studies that offer evidence of causal linkage, or a cause-and-effect, relationship between violence in the media and violence in society. In fact, from 1970 to 2000, there were only about

220 studies worldwide. The findings of but *one* of these studies appeared in an article titled "Exposure to Television as a Risk Factor for Violence," by Brandon Centerwall published in the *American Journal of Epidemiology*. In that article, Centerwall wrote:

> Following the introduction of television into the United States, the annual incidence of white homicide deaths increased by 93%, from 3.0 homicides per 100,000 white population in 1945 to 5.8 homicides per 100,000 in 1974; in South Africa where television was banned, the incidence of white homicide deaths decreased by 7%, from 2.7/100,000 white population in 1943–1948 to 2.5/100,000 in 1974. As with US whites, following the introduction of television the incidence of Canadian homicides increased by 92%, from 1.3/100,000 in 1945 to 2.5/100,000 in 1974.[22]

This researcher was so confident in his conclusive establishment of a causal linkage between exposure to violence on television and the explosion of violence in society they were taken at face value by other scientists.

When other researchers attempted to duplicate the results, however, they were in for a surprise. Studies of similar statistical information from France, Italy, Japan, and Germany were carried out to establish definitive and irrefutable evidence of a causal relationship between violence in the media and violence in society. If it could be established that in other societies there had been a corresponding increase in the murder rate that was directly linked to the introduction of television, then Centerwall's findings would be validated. They were not.

Other scientists were unable to conduct studies that duplicated Centerwall's results. His study, however, became political—and notorious—for it was criticized for being fundamentally flawed by other social scientists. Franklin Zimring and Gordon Hawkins, two legal scholars at the University of California at Berkeley, for instance, were unable to duplicate Centerwall's findings using statistics compiled in other industrialized countries. In Italy, for instance, homicide rates remained the same even as television usage spread throughout Italy. And to the dismay of social scientists, in France, Germany, and Japan, murder rates *declined* as television viewing *increased*. Their findings were published in their 1997 book, *Crime Is Not the Problem,* which refuted fundamental assumptions about the causal linkage between media violence and actual violence.

Reviewing the book in *Booklist*, Mary Carroll notes:

> London and New York City have nearly the same number of robberies and burglaries each year, but robbers and burglars kill 54 victims in New York for every victim death in London. Why are the risks so much greater

that victims will be killed or maimed in the United States? And what can be done to bring the death rate from American violence down to tolerable levels? The authors show how the impact of television and movie violence on rates of homicide is wildly overrated, but emphasize the paramount importance of guns. By making the crucial distinction between lethal violence and crime in general, the authors clear the ground for a targeted, far more effective response to the real crisis in American society.[23]

In other words, playing violent video games or watching violence on television and in movies does not result in a corresponding rise in crime at large. What does this say about the message human beings pick up from the violence in the media to which they are exposed? What is even more revealing is how Centerwall responded to criticism of his work.

The U.S. surgeon general weighed in with a study that refuted widely held assumptions. "We clearly associate media violence to aggressive behavior," Surgeon General David Satcher said on January 17, 2001. "But the impact was very small compared to other things. Some people may not be happy with that, but that's where the science is."[24] This, of course, confirms yet again what Norbert Elias and Eric Dunning had written in *Quest for Excitement* years before.

"I'm a scientists [sic], and it's not my role to set guidelines," Centerwall said, by way of defending the indefensible conclusions of his flawed study. "My role is just to lay out the facts. The public is intelligent and resourceful, and I leave it to them to ponder this information and decide what they want to do about it individually or as groups. But I do believe that parents must set limits on how much TV their children watch, in the same way they set boundaries for other behavior."[25]

It is clear that accusing Hollywood of being responsible for violence in society is an urban myth. It is fueled by bad science. It is, in essence, the social science equivalent of the scandal that surrounded Martin Fleischmann and B. Stanley Pons, of the University of Utah, scientists who in 1989 stunned the world with their announcement that they had achieved cold fusion, when other scientists were unable to duplicate their results. "It seems clear that in such a scenario, the scientist's foremost concern should be to avoid lapsing into self-deception and pathological science," James R. Wilson, of the North Carolina State University, said eight years after this scandal embarrassed the world of physics.[26]

The response to Centerwall has been more circumspect; politicians and lobbyists embrace him while other researchers distance their work from his. Centerwall may not be a *mad* scientist, but he is a *bad* scientist. He is also unfortunately a very influential scientist. Consider how his arguments suffuse the interpretive analysis of the narrow studies offered by psychologists Craig A. Anderson and Karen Dill. They approach the question of the impact of media violence on youngsters with an openly biased perspective:

> There are good theoretical reasons to expect that violent video games will have similar, and possibly larger, effects on aggression. The empirical literature on the effects of exposure to video game violence is sparse, however, in part because of its relatively recent emergence in modern U.S. society. About 25 years ago, when video games first appeared, popular games were simple and apparently harmless. In the 1970s, Atari introduced a game called Pong that was a simple video version of the game ping pong. In the 1980s, arcade games like Pac-Man became dominant. In Pac-Man, a yellow orb with a mouth raced around the screen chomping up ghosts and goblins. At this point, some eyebrows were raised questioning whether young people should play such "violent" games. In the 1990s the face of video games changed dramatically. The most popular video game of 1993 was Mortal Kombat. . . . This game features realistically rendered humanoid characters engaging in battle. As the name of the game implies, the goal of the player in Mortal Kombat is to kill any opponent he faces. Unfortunately, such violent games now dominate the market. Dietz . . . sampled 33 popular Sega and Nintendo games and found that nearly 80% of the games were violent in nature. Interestingly, she also found that 21% of these games portrayed violence towards women.[27]

This *is* interesting, to be sure. But does it mean anything? What is even *more* interesting and meaningful, however, is that the FBI reported that violent crime continued to *decline* precisely during the two decades that video game violence increased.[28] This is evidence that the arguments put forth by Elias and Dunning in *Quest for Excitement,* that young men live vicariously through sports and entertainment violence and that this constitutes a healthy way for society to channel natural male aggression, are strengthened by statistics that show a correlation between declines in real-world crime when there is an increase in the violence in video, film, and music.

"The nation's violent crime rate fell by more than 10 percent during 1999, reaching the lowest level since the Justice Department's Bureau of Justice Statistics (BJS) started measuring it in 1973," the Justice Department said in a press release on August 27, 2000. "The 1999 data indicated that 54 percent of all violent crime victims in 1999 knew their attackers," suggesting that Americans were at greater risk of being victimized by friends and family with whom they had disagreements than they were from strangers.[29] Two months later the FBI reported that the murder rate in 1999 fell to a 33-year low.[30]

One wouldn't know that violent crime in the United States in every category measured by law enforcement officials was falling from reading Craig Anderson and Karen Dill. In fact, these researchers, who present their arguments with indefinite antecedents, multiple qualifiers, and skillful circumlocutions, are irresponsible when they conclude that:[31]

> Playing violent video games often may well cause increases in delinquent behaviors, both aggressive and nonaggressive.[32] However, the correlational nature of Study 1 means that causal statements are risky at best. It could be that the obtained video game violence links to aggressive and nonaggressive delinquency are wholly due to the fact that highly aggressive individuals are especially attracted to violent video games. Longitudinal work along the lines of Eron and Huesmann's work on TV violence . . . would be very informative.[33]

Stop for a moment and let us consider what happens when politicians listen to social scientists such as Anderson and Dill. Despite their qualified conclusions—x "may" lead to y instead of x "does" lead to y—there is no evidence that exposure to video games, television violence, or offensive films have almost no discernible impact on the behavior of teenagers or young adults.[34]

This is lost on Democrats and Republicans alike. Recall when Tipper Gore's founding of the Parents' Music Resource Center successfully lobbied for parental advisories to be placed on records and CDs. Her rants against music and video games continued for years and culminated with the publication of her book, *Raising PG Kids in an X-Rated Society.* That book irresponsibly described the Dungeon and Dragons video game as "satanic." This video game was accused of being directly responsible for more than 50 deaths each year. To her credit, Tipper Gore has since disavowed her work with the Parents' Music Resource Center.[35]

But the damage was done. Immediately following her book, media entertainment companies implemented a program of "self-regulation." This, however, lasted less than 24 months, and by 1985, media violence was on the rise and according to police departments around the country crime began to decline. The next sustained increase in crime commenced after 1990 and lasted through 1993. This time it was a Republican attack on the media industry—led by Bob Dole—who held a series of hearings and decried Hollywood and the music companies in well-publicized speeches. Indeed, in his presidential campaign of 1996, *Time* magazine columnist Peggy Noonan took Bob Dole to task by chiding, "[E]very time your staff tried to make you show passion, you wound up pounding the lectern—'Have you no shame, Hollywood.'" Pressure to self-regulate and self-censor lasted about 36 months, which is when crime increases. Then violence in videos, films, and song lyrics continued to rise—with a corresponding fall in crime.

There is no attempt by ideologues, however, to find an explanation for the sustained reduction in crime and violence precisely when video games become more violent. It is counterintuitive to note that since the mid-1990s as the Internet has come into widespread use, with its online violence and pornography, it has become one of the factors contributing to the decline in crime since 1993.

It is, in fact, curious to suggest that the violent video games (like the incendiary lyrics of Eminem's songs) do calm the savage breast and have a *healthy* impact on youth and society. In fact, when the work of Anderson and Dill is examined more closely, there is a disturbing element of intellectual dishonesty.

When they mention "longitudinal work," Anderson and Dill, for instance, refer to a chapter titled "Aggression and Its Correlates over 22 Years," by Leonard Eron.[36] He, in fact, argues that after examining crime rates over a two-decade period, even though early aggressive behavior is a good predictor of violent behavior later on in life, the propensity to resort to violence runs in families, and there is very little evidence to establish a causal linkage.[37]

It is unfortunate to see bad science avail itself to good science, all the while creating confusion among the public at large. When the world is stunned by mass murders in American high schools and the U.S. Congress holds hearings on violence marketed as entertainment, it is reasonable to question the marketplace that creates these kinds of choices for consumers. When bad science is thrown into the equation, matters are complicated further.

Consider the unwarranted pressure exerted on retailers to stop carrying certain kinds of video and computer games, or to ban the sale of such products to minors. Stores are thus placed in the improper position of discriminating to whom they sell their products without being legally required to do so, as is the case with alcoholic beverages, tobacco products, or pornography.[38]

K-mart's capitulation to threats by politicians and special interests groups, however unfortunate it may be, is understandable. When self-aggrandizing politicians make sweeping political statements based on rhetoric, and not fact, it can be rather unsettling. "The entertainment industry is encouraging young people to defy and deceive their parents," Senator Mike DeWine, R-Ohio, said before Congress when the Federal Trade Commission issued a report detailing how the entertainment industry markets to minors.[39]

The assertion that children are masters at manipulating their parents is not disputed, however. Then again, politicians are expert at manipulating their (adult) constituencies.[40] A clarification is in order before proceeding further. Consider the perspective on video violence offered by psychiatrist Michael Brody, who is a member of the media committee of the American Academy of Child and Adolescent Psychiatry, and a voice of reason in a debate otherwise populated by alarmists. "Kids who are sitting in front of their PC playing games all the time are not playing with other kids; they aren't doing anything physical," he warns by way of recommending moderation.

His concern is not that violent video games will make kids become violent, but that the lack of exercise will affect their health adversely and the playing online alone will stunt the development of their social skills. The danger videos represent is that kids spent too much interfacing with computers instead of interacting with their peers, and that these are sedentary activities that take away from the time they have to engage in physical activity. This is consistent with the findings of sociologist and historian Norbert Elias. "Sure," Brody explains, "kids need a way to zone out, but they also need a balance."[41]

VIOLENCE, CLIMATES OF HOSTILITY, AND MEDIA ENTERTAINMENT

The same technological invention that allows us to pick up a receiver, dial a few numbers, and summon emergency medical, fire rescue, or law enforcement assistance also allows us to receive unwanted telemarketing solicitations that interrupt our lives. If we discuss the important and positive role telephones play in saving the lives of those who are in imminent danger, it is only fair that we also address the frustration we experience when we are imposed upon by insistent telemarketers. In this same vein, if the discussion in this book champions how our lives are enriched by the ability of the Internet to create an online entertainment economy, one in which we can view books, music, films, interactive video games, and so forth, it is only proper to address the emergence of *violence* as a form of *entertainment.*

The use of the Internet to spread hate-speech has long been associated primarily with the proliferation of groups advocating Aryan supremacy through violence. In Germany, for instance, there are more than 360 white supremacist hate groups using the Internet to advance their causes. Rudiger Hesse, the spokesman for Germany's domestic security agency, stated that "right-wing extremists have made extensive use of the Internet since mid-1997 as a means of communication," which alarmed officials precisely because some sites incited violence and provided instructions on how to make bombs.[42]

There is scientific work on how the media operate in the real world to allow us to understand that how information is presented shapes our thoughts and actions. Rose Goldsen, the late sociologist at Cornell

University, was one of the leading authorities on how human beings assimilate information from television broadcasts. In her landmark book, *The Show and Tell Machine,* she provided a sweeping critique of the ways all of us, but particularly the young, absorb information and interpret messages seen on television.[43] "What is clear is that we are all capable of absorbing messages from television and, in many instances, the meaning of those messages is unintended by television programmers or executives," Goldsen argued.

> When the Soviet Union, for example, wanted to broadcast news footage of violence on American campuses in the 1960s and 1970s, their intention was to convey to their people the idea that capitalist societies were violent, where the police brutalized unarmed civilians. This message would have been consistent with Marxist philosophy of the class struggle of the proletariat against the bourgeoisie, of course.[44]

Goldsen studied the mechanisms by which human beings processed information to discern unintended meanings and subliminal messages. Soviet television programmers, she explained with relish,

> were completely undermined because while viewers did see police violence against student protesters in the U.S., France, the U.K., wherever, they also saw that these young men and women who were arrested or beaten were wearing Levi's jeans and cowboy boots. In other words, the message the Soviet people got was that in capitalist societies even the *underdogs* were privileged and wealthy enough to wear high status clothing and boots. The television images they showed on Soviet television were terrifying in the graphic violence they depicted, but they were also images of unrivaled material wealth, which stunned people who were living day-in and day-out with compelling deprivation.[45]

Goldsen concluded that it was possible to establish a direct cause and effect link between what people saw in the media, and how their beliefs and behavior changed as a result. These are subtle processes, however, for the simple reason that human beings are complex creatures and human relations are multilayered with meanings. "What is certain, however, is that there is a process of 'desensitization' in which we become numb to certain things," Goldsen believed.

> It is enough to watch a television commercial for tires that contrast one car negotiating its way safely through a thunderstorm drive past another distressed vehicle with a flat tire, its hazard lights on the driver soaking wet, to cause a problem for society. The subliminal message that is reinforced over and over again that it is acceptable to drive past someone in need without looking back, satisfied that it isn't you who's stranded on the side of the road. Over time this process of "desensitization" erodes

our ability to empathize with others. The fabric of society is weakened when citizens become indifferent and apathetic to their fellow beings.[46]

Goldsen was prescient. She could have been speaking about the findings reported in early 2000 by the Stanford Institute for the Quantitative Study of Society that discussed the social alienation of Internet users in the United States who suffer as their interactions with family and friends continue to decline over time. This occurs when isolation (surfing the Internet) is a more valued activity than communal activities (interacting with friends and family). If children learn that it is acceptable to be callous, then that is because children are influenced in unexpected ways by the technology and media to which they are exposed. One safely concludes that technology, as much as the media, *defines* certain social contexts in antisocial ways.

The impact, over time, of this learned callousness can be alarming. But there is a strong argument that vicariously living out "inhumanity" through violent and fantasy video games, youngsters can become more responsible citizens. But this is counterintuitive: to hear Anderson and Dill, no one would have expected American youngsters to respond so altruistically in the aftermath of September 11, 2001. When Goldsen published her work, however, the "long-term" was not known.

CBS was stunned by the findings of Goldsen's pioneering work in the 1970s. CBS responded in several ways, more notably by creating the *Fat Albert and the Cosby Kids* television show.[47] Each episode, with a finely tuned message, was shown to children whom researchers interviewed and studied in order to determine how they reacted to the content of that program. CBS released studies demonstrating that children who watched this show learned good moral messages.

"That's fine," Goldsen said. "But this only demonstrates what I've been saying: that children pick up messages from television in a value-neutral way. In this case these are good moral lessons, but this is one half hour in an entire broadcast week. What about the other messages they are picking up, the *unintended* messages? What are children learning or not learning about right or wrong, up or down?"[48]

Internet surfing now competes with television watching as a favorite activity among youngsters. If it is difficult to fine-tune the precise message a viewer will receive from television, it becomes more ambiguous when one considers that the Internet is a medium that is open creating various contexts, many of which offend our values as individuals and as a society. Broadband is broad indeed.

Discussing the sociocultural aspect of stereotypes, for instance, sociologists Richard Ashmore and Francis Del Boca write that "[i]ndividuals are socialized into a particular culture, and, through social rewards and punishments, led to act in accordance with cultural dictates. Further, by accepting cultural stereotypes, individuals reinforce and thereby help to perpetuate the exiting cultural pattern."[49]

Peer and parental pressure, then, affect how youngsters determine what they should believe and how they should behave.[50] These cues are, increasingly, transmitted online, through chat rooms, music and video sites, and Web sites that complement television viewing. MTV, for instance, encourages viewers to log on to MTV.com simultaneously. Ashmore and Del Boca further argue that "[h]umans internalize social values and norms and are largely motivated to seek social approval by conforming to these values and norms."[51]

To understand how the Internet as a technology is changing how we learn, recall how Deborah Tannen argued that "frames" created structures of expectations that provide context to our understanding of the world. The Internet comes into our homes and thus into our lives. If *prejudiced speech,* which is a form of violence and hate, is marketed as *online entertainment,* one in which the subliminal pressures for acceptance through conformity are ever present, it desensitizes us to think that would otherwise be repugnant and rejected.

Not unlike television that can desensitize through the repetition of a given message, the Internet contributes to creating what critics call "climates of hostility." "With words we govern men," Benjamin Disraeli observed. The corollary, of course, is that the context in which words are presented govern the forces that shapes hate. This refers to the emergence of an environment in which certain groups of people are defamed, degraded, intimidated, or feel threatened. Most often this includes the use of stereotypes as a way of identifying, classifying, and targeting certain members in a given community. Ashmore and Del Boca note that

> [a]t the societal level, stereotypes also serve a value-expressive function (e.g., negative images about the mentally retarded reinforce cultural values concerning intelligence and self-reliance). For the individual, expressing stereotyped beliefs is an affirmation of part of a system of benefits that one accepts as one's own. And, by expressing these shared view the individual gains social acceptance.[52]

To understand how these subtle processes work in the real world, consider the emergence of a "climate of hostility" against Hispanics in New York as a consequence of Hispanics outnumbering African Americans as the largest minority in New York City. There is a backlash against this Hispanic ascendance in New York. This is evident in, for instance, an escalation of prejudiced speech against Hispanics in New York. Prejudiced speech gives permission to members of one community to engage in violence, whether psychological or physical, against another. It creates a threatening environment. Such a "climate of hostility" is analogous to the Broken Windows theory developed by criminologists George Kelling and James Wilson.

These law enforcement officers observed that if broken windows in a neighborhood were not replaced, this was interpreted as public disorder and a sign of marked social decline. This, in turn, constituted an open invitation for criminals and delinquents to escalate the violence experienced in that specific community. Wilson and Kelling write:

> Muggers and robbers, whether opportunistic or professional, believe they reduce their chances of being caught or even identified if they operate on streets where potential victims are already intimidated by prevailing conditions. If the neighborhood cannot keep a bothersome panhandler from annoying passersby, the thief may reason, it is even less likely to call the police to identify a potential mugger or to interfere if the mugging actually takes place.[53]

Broken windows do not have to be shattered glass panes. It also refers to the climate of hostility that emerges when a community is characterized by disorder that creates an environment for crime. "Disorder demoralizes communities, undermines commerce, leads to the abandonment of public spaces, and undermines public confidence in the ability of government to solve problems; fear drives citizens further from each other and paralyzes their normal, order-sustaining responses, compounding the impact of disorder," Kelling and Catherine Coles argue.[54]

In their influential essay, "Social Status, Cognitive Alternatives and Intergroup Relations," J. C. Turner and R. L. Brown report their findings that oftentimes members of high-status groups tend to exhibit greater bias, discrimination, and hatred against others when they conclude their social superiority is legitimate but perceived to be threatened by new arrivals.[55]

To understand the escalation in aggression against Hispanics in New York, consider the disturbing examples set by *Harper's* magazine. Edited by Lewis Lapham, a former San Franciscan, throughout the 1990s *Harper's* increased its rhetoric against Hispanics. Consider the following sentence published in *Harper's*: "[Mexico] is here [in the U.S.]. It has arrived. Silent as a Trojan horse, inevitable as a flotilla of boat people, more confounding in its innocence, in its power of proclamation, than Spielberg's most pious vision of a flying saucer."[56]

The imagery used by the writer conjures up a surreptitious and calculated invasion of the United States by the Hispanic people. The tone is alarming precisely because this human migration is characterized as a military invasion, one that is represented as a de facto action, both

Low ←	AGGRESSION			→ High
Acts Against				
Avoidance	**Defamation**	**Property**	**Assault**	**Murder**
Limited or Selected Total	Verbal Jokes Labeling Name Calling Accusations Written Jokes Labeling Name Calling Accusations	Graffiti Light Damage Heavy Damage Destruction	Verbal or Written Physical	Limited Genocide

Figure 8.2 Aggression and Racial Animus

complete and final. To characterize Hispanic immigration in military terms constitutes, in sociological terms, defamation (written accusations) for it incites negative views about Hispanics. Speech that is cloaked in inflammatory terms against one group of people is uniformly considered a form of aggression by social scientists.[57] Other articles, in a similar vein, have been published in the pages of *Harper's* throughout the 1990s. Each one has alarmingly escalated the rhetoric against the Hispanic people.[58]

What alarms, however, is to see hate-speech suddenly become linked to and accompanied by an unprecedented escalation and intensification of aggression directed against Hispanics. Witness the article by Earl Shorris, "The Last Word," which was published in the August 2000 issue of *Harper's*. In that article, which ostensibly discussed the demise and disappearance of indigenous languages around the world, Earl Shorris wrote:

> The situation requires a few words of history: The decline [of the Maya in Yucatan] had gone on for many centuries. The Maya city-states had ravaged one another in terrible wars of betrayal and fire. Then the Spaniards invaded, burning the painted books, destroying culture for the sake of culture. The Maya resisted the Spaniards, attempted to secede from Mexico . . . Henequen, the agave fiber used to make rope and sisal matting, had finally been the worst enemy in this part of the peninsula.

> The Maya descended into the depths of colonialism. The planters
> . . . brought overseers to the peninsula to work the Maya like beasts in
> the fields all day and lock them into cells at night; they devoted them-
> selves to silencing the language as a defense against rebels and other
> heretics; and all the while the henequen fields displaced corn and beans
> and squash of the Maya farmers and the forage food and medicinal
> plants of the low jungle. Then the market for Mexican sisal collapsed in
> the mid-twentieth century and with it the economy of the henequen area.
> The people lived on government welfare until in the late 1980s President
> Carlos Salinas de Gortari ended the welfare, and nothing remained.[59]

The deliberate publication of falsehoods constitutes social aggression.
As Milton Kleg, the director of the Center for the Study of Ethnic and
Racial Violence writes:

> Accusations consist of charging a group with some evil act or plot.
> . . . They are designed to create fear. . . . As an economic and social
> weapon against racial and ethnic minorities, accusations are extremely
> effective when combined with stereotypes. Making accusations that fit
> the traditional stereotype of a group increases the credibility of the ac-
> cusation—it fits what is already framed in one's perceived reality.[60]

Harper's magazine, in essence, contributes to fostering a climate of
hostility in which hate speech precedes hate acts. "This town of 15,000
people gives many mixed messages to the brown-skinned men—wel-
comed as workers but shunned as neighbors—who line up in front of
the 7-Eleven at a central intersection looking for day work," Tina Kelley
wrote in the *New York Times* reporting from Farmingville, New York.
"But there was nothing ambiguous about the message delivered Sunday night when two white men picked up two laborers, took them to
a secluded, abandoned factory in Shirley and then hit one in the back
of the head with a crowbar and slashed the other's neck and wrists with
a knife."[61]

Critics of the Internet who decry the violence of online video games
fail to accept the subtle ways in which human beings process information. Conservatives often argue that this new technology represents
another, more malevolent, and ominous, kind of breakthrough, one that
threatens to legitimize violence.[62] But the facts, however counterintuitive they may be, suggest otherwise. It is not immediately clear,
for instance, that *Harper's* magazine contributes to an escalating climate of hostility that legitimizes real violence against a group of people
defamed by writers published in its pages. Indeed, Rose Goldsen's pioneering work identified subtle ways in which prejudiced speech is
spread unintentionally through television.

Current studies of Internet users reinforce the observations made by
David Riesman, Nathan Glazer, and Reuel Denney in *The Lonely*

Crowd: Internet users become alienated, suffer from more frequent bouts of depression, and become isolated. This weakening of the social fabric makes them more susceptible to hate speech. "The most important thing to keep in mind," Goldsen pointed out, "is that young people are more influenced by their peers than by their parents. The pressure to conform, to fit in, to be accepted, to be cool are the driving factors in decisions they make. They may end up making stupid decisions they will regret later on, but they commit these errors because they are emotionally immature and vulnerable. What they see on television and radio, for example, affects them in ways we don't fully understand."[63]

Not unlike telephones, which bring us both a necessary convenience for modern life as well as great frustration when they do not work properly, the versatility of the Internet technologies are creating unwanted choices that impact our lives. If it is difficult to identify readily how a publication like *Harper's* apparently fosters such racial animus that it contributes to the climate of hostility that makes bias crimes possible, how are we as a society ever going to be able to manage hate online?

Societies around the world continue to debate, in ever more exasperated terms, how aggression is marketed at youth everywhere through television, music, and film, of course. But the emergence of violence as entertainment online further complicates the situation in ways that are almost overwhelming. The subliminal process that desensitizes television viewers is accelerated by the Internet technologies. The impact of "virtual" hate is more insidious because we do not fully understand how hate-as-entertainment affects the climate of hostility.

It is, likewise, alarming to see how the video gaming and video-on-demand in the entertainment economy online is being vilified in pursuit of narrow political objectives inconsistent with both First Amendment protections and the healthy operation of the market economy. Indeed, the same kind of aggression and violence that Goldsen first identified as a problem in television programming in the 1960s and 1970s is now seen in the emergence of violence as an industry in the online economy in the 2000s. The data, however, indicate that the sustained decrease in crime is a result of young men living out their aggression vicariously through video games and violence in the media and entertainment.

That violence in video games (and other forms of entertainment) constitutes a *beneficial* form of channeling the natural aggression in adolescent males is not new. Norbert Elias and Eric Dunning make this argument in their book, *Quest for Excitement.* Violence as entertainment, curiously, has its origin in the evolution of representative democracy. With the development of parliamentary government, they point out, it became necessary to "civilize" aggression. In the political life of democracies, when one side loses, they must be prepared to hand over power to the winning faction in a peaceful, civilian transition:

> Among the chief requirements of a parliamentary regime as it emerged in England in the course of the eighteenth century was the readiness of a faction or party in government to hand over office to its opponents without the use of violence if the rules of the parliamentary game required it, for instance if an important vote in Parliament or an election in society at large went against it.[64]

Organized sports, then, emerged as a substitute for aggression. The ability to play games and develop good sportsmanship, which meant winning with grace and losing with honor, was instrumental in the "pacifying and civilizing" effect athletic competition had on young men—who at that time held a monopoly on participating in politics. As the rule of law came to dominate society, so did the importance of games and competitions.

The complementarity between the breaches of violence-control at sports events and ordinary social existence of young outsiders from the working classes is, in that respect, no less revealing than the complementarity between the more controlled pleasurable excitement provided by the firmly regulated battles of a leisure sport and the well-tempered control of emotions that becomes second nature, an almost inescapable characteristic of the social habitus of the members of more complex societies in all nonleisure activities.[65]

Sports, games, and other competitions that involved regulated violence, physical skills, and personal risk-taking, then, become healthy mechanisms by which natural aggression is socialized and the individual is civilized. This is why Valenti is correct in asserting that the fantasy violence of the entertainment industry allows for youngsters to live out their violent fantasies vicariously. If this weren't the case, then why would we enjoy going to horror movies, looking forward to being scared?[66]

It is because there is pleasure in knowing we have survived a risk, endured a test. There is a natural high that comes from the rush of adrenaline when we are genuinely terrified. Boxing, football, adventure sports provide, as Elias and Dunning state, "an important source of meaning, status and pleasurable emotional arousal."[67] How that arousal is channeled in a socially acceptable and benign way is important; video game violence is one mechanism we have for ensuring that young men learn how to express aggression vicariously.[68]

In conversations with youths that are "obsessed" by violent video games, a young man reported that video game violence, for him and his friends, is "the ideal release from the stress and pressures from our lives. Playing these video games gives us the opportunity to blow things up, shoot things up and control make-believe characters, and it is OK. Spending an hour playing a game where we can take over the whole world and scoring over the villains *prevents* violence. It's like watching 'Cops' on TV, you know. Once you see that stuff, it's out of your system—and it's easier to do my homework and take out the garbage and be left alone by my parents."[69]

Sophisticated teenagers are masterful of constructing self-serving arguments, such as why getting them cars will free their moms from the chore of having to chauffeur them around town. So hitting the old man up for $100 to buy video games is going to make taking out the garbage easier to take, making for a more pleasant domestic life? But there is an element of truth to the escape video game violence offers to adolescent males.

Living out violence vicariously in this manner is consistent with the work of sociologists Goldsen, Elias, and Dunning. An unintended comparison is possible by contrasting the crime rates between the United States and Japan. In the United States, where political pressure coerces video game producers to engage in self-censorship, violence is rampant. But in Japan, however, where video games are far more violent and sexually explicit than what is available on the American market, it appears that as a society the Japanese have found a benign and healthy release for the natural aggression of male youth. Japanese companies such as Nintendo, Capcom, Konami, and Square Soft produce thousands of games that are never sold in the United States, fearing a backlash because of the violence or sexuality portrayed. "Japanese games often push further into the realms of sex and violence than American products," David Kushner reported in the *New York Times.* "When Japanese game developers are deciding whether to market a title in the United States, a factor they consider is how it will be rated by the industry's voluntary ratings group, the Entertainment Software Ratings Board."[70]

The work of Goldsen, Elias, and Dunning, then, offers a reasonable explanation for the apparent contradiction found in realizing that violent crime decreases when there is an escalation in the level of violence in entertainment: Violent video games (like the antisocial lyrics of Eminem) *prevent* violence instead of inciting it. Indeed, *The Show and Tell Machine* and *Quest for Excitement* should be required readings for every member of Congress, member of the print and broadcast media, school board and PTA member, and civil rights organization. They offer the answer into a phenomenon that would otherwise remain perplexing: It is by channeling natural male aggression through benign forms of fanciful entertainment that Japan has the most violent and sexuality explicit video games in the world while enjoying the lowest violence of any industrialized nation on Earth.

SUMMARY

The video gaming and video-on-demand industry is at the center of a political firestorm, one that clouds the potential of an otherwise explosive industry. This is to be expected in a market that is characterized by *Key #1* (The Internet offers the technology to expand greatly an existing market) and *Key #5* (The technological nature of the "New Economy" facilitates the polarization of society, one in which pathological consumer behavior creates not only economic distortions but also exacerbates unhealthy alienation among people at risk).

The seamless evolution of video gaming to the online entertainment economy, however, has propelled video games into one of the fastest-growing industries on the Internet. Videos online, video-on-demand, and streaming technologies to allow for the downloading products stands to transform and expand the entire in-home entertainment industry from a $20 billion market in 2000 to an estimated $40 billion by 2007. The speed with which online video gaming has grown, however, has brought it under greater scrutiny by educators, parents, social critics, and policymakers. What otherwise were once considered innocuous pastimes are now blamed for increased violence in society at large. As we have seen, however, since the emergence of the market—which coincided with the widespread use of the Internet—there has been a corresponding decline in violent crime, evidence that the fantastic violence of video games fulfills a fundamental need among (male) youth to find benign and healthy releases for aggression. That the growth of this robust market is threatened by individuals who are prepared to advance their political agenda by targeting the entertainment industry clouds the prospects for this market and undermines the integrity of First Amendment protections.

NOTES

1. See the UltraVixen Web site at http://www2.ultravixen.com/index2.html.
2. Greg Easterbrook, "Watch and Learn," *New Republic,* May 17, 1999.
3. Jacques Steinberg, "Parents Say Censoring Films Is Their Job, Not Politicians'," *New York Times,* September 28, 2000.
4. As 2001 began, the market share of the video game company was Sony, 55 percent; Nintendo, 30 percent; SegaNet, 17 percent; and Microsoft's X-box's scheduled launch in 2001 threatened to change the entire market. Competition online, furthermore, became more complicated with the announcement of the alliances at Blockbuster, and between Intertainer and Akamai, both of which announced their entry into the streaming video market, which would facilitate the downloading of games and films from the Internet, thereby expanding greatly the role of videos and films in the entertainment economy online.

5. Sony's press release is available at http://www.station.sony.com/stationbreak/;$sessionid$YVZ1OVQAAELOMQBFREPUE0I.

6. To understand how intense the demand for the PlayStation 2 was, consider that while the suggested retail price was $300, consumers desperate to secure the console entered in bidding wars on the online auction Web site, eBay.com, and paid as much as $1,500.

7. Profits would be higher if the video game industry could prevent piracy. Industry sources indicate that an estimated $3 billion in profits are lost each year from the sale of pirated programs. This is one reason why Sega, Microsoft, Nintendo, and Electronic Arts have banded together; Business Software Alliance estimates $11 billion in sales are lost worldwide, and that 40 percent of all video games sold outside the United States are illegal.

8. Technology does offer blessings: it is now common to see youngsters enthralled with their PlayStation games sitting, still and quietly, in their seats for the duration of an entire flight.

9. Tobi Elkin, "Sega Gambles on Internet to Extend U.S. Comback," *Advertising Age,* September 4, 2000.

10. Isao Okawa, Sega Corporation's president and chairman, confirmed his desire to leave the hardware business altogether on January 24, 2001, when Sega confirmed officially it was considering halting production of its Dreamcast game console.

11. Matt Richtel, "A Video Game Maker Hits Reset; Electronic Arts Bets on Future of Web-Based Interaction," *New York Times,* August 21, 2000.

12. AOL's presence in the online video market expanded when it teamed up with Sony to offer PlayStation service. "Sony Computer Entertainment is teaming with America Online to offer high-speed Internet access, hoping the deal gives Sony's PlayStation 2 an edge over rival consoles by Microsoft and Nintendo," Leslie Gornstein of the Associated Press reported on May 15, 2001.

13. Shifts in technology and marketing are changing the industry. Musicians such as MixMaster Mike and Marilyn Manson, for instance, are entering into licensing agreements with video companies, with the expectation that they will benefit from the "synergies" between music and videos in helping to develop brands combining music and images.

14. These figures are consistent with analysis on the video game market provided by Dresdner Kleinwort Benson Securities.

15. Betsey Schiffman and Kathleen Cholewka, "Enron, Blockbuster Partner for Movie Mania," Forbes.com, July 20, 2000.

16. Telecommunications company AT&T entered the video-on-demand in July 2000. "AT&T threw its weight behind streaming media by launching a digital media platform that it said will eventually serve 10 million simultaneous streaming media Internet users," Kate Gerwig reported in "AT&T Launches Streaming Video Plan," on July 11, 2000, in Tele.com. "The AT&T ecosystem network services platform will be jointly created, marketed and distributed with a long list of partners that include Microsoft, Inktomi, and RealNetworks as a way to enable other companies to create, manage, and distribute audio and video to millions of users over the Internet."

17. SciFi.com, for instance, announced games that can be played on Palm Pilots and other wireless devices. These games can be downloaded, free of

charge, from SciFi.com's Free Zone. "Gaming is truly one of the most inter-active ways of entertaining audiences, and portable devices give users the freedom to be entertained when and where they choose. It's also a way to extend our brand beyond the television and PC," said Ben Tatta, senior vice president of USA Interactive Entertainment.

18. The proliferation of video games is so fast-paced that three excellent sites, Bluesnews.com, Games.ign.com, and Station.Sony.com, provide up-to-the-minute information on news, information, and developments.

19. The entire transcript of the hearing is available at http://commdocs.house.gov/committees;judiciary;hju62441.000/hju62441_0.HTM.

20. Ibid.

21. The alarmist tone of the New York Times article suggested that an in-dustry conspiracy had been exposed, roughly analogous to the tobacco industry's deliberate concealment of scientific evidence that nicotine caused cancer. The New York Times reporting, I believe, rushed to render judgment, much the same way that its coverage into allegations against Los Alamos scientist Wen Ho Lee contributed to a climate of hostility against Asian Ameri-cans and created a poisoned atmosphere. The biases fostered by the media contributed to actions by the Justice Department that were subsequently de-nounced by the courts. See Doreen Carvajal, "How Studios Used Children to Test-Market Violent Films," New York Times, September 27, 2000. Curiously, this article contradicted another front-page article published in the New York Times the day before. "The proliferation of electronic entertainments [sic] con-verges with other trends that isolate children from adults," John Leland reported. "Bigger houses, smaller yards, longer commutes and the rise of re-gional high schools all limit the opportunities for generations to mix," he wrote. Despite forces that "fracture" the family, however, the article stresses the role of parents to limit the alleged negative influence of video violence. See John Leland, "Family's Choices Can Blunt the Effect of Video Violence," New York Times, September 25, 2000.

22. Brandon Centerwall, "Exposure to Television as a Risk Factor for Vio-lence," American Journal of Epidemiology, 129/4, April 1989, pp. 643–652.

23. Franklin Zimring and Gordon Hawkins, Crime Is Not the Problem: Le-thal Violence in America.

24. The study was ordered by Congress and the Clinton administration in the wake of the Columbine High School shootings. The report, Youth Violence: A Report of the Surgeon General, is available from http://www.surgeongeneral.gov/library/youthviolence/sgsummary/summary.htm. The surgeon general's statement that some people might not be happy about the scientific facts begs the question, What kind of people, other than mystics or ideologues, would be unhappy about scientific findings?

25. Frederick Case, "Murders Again Tied to TV Violence," (Seattle) Times, May 8, 1990.

26. A complete discussion of this scientific scandal is found in John R. Huizenga, Cold Fusion: The Scientific Fiasco of the Century.

27. Craig A. Anderson and Karen Dill, "Video Games and Aggressive Thoughts, Feelings, and Behavior in the Laboratory and in Life," Journal of Personality and Social Psychology 78, no. 4 (April 2000), pp. 772–790.

28. The FBI report on crime between 1973–1999 shows a decline in the long term, but there are two intriguing jumps in violent crime. Crime, in fact, increases during 1973–1980, and only begins to decline after 1981. It is during the 1980–1982 time frame when video games came into widespread use. That young people were then able to find an outlet for their aggression vicariously through video games may account for the decline, for during the time when violence in video games increased, there was a stunning decrease in real-world crime. If one notes that during these same years there was an increase in the violence offered as entertainment in the media, then one can see how a backlash against violence produced an increase in violence: crime jumped in 1983 when the music industry began to self-censor.

29. The report also revealed the explosive fact that "a gun was present but not necessarily used in about 1 percent of such incidents [of sexual assault or rape]." The report was authored by Callie Marie Rennison and a copy can be secured by visiting http://www.ojp.usdoj.gov/bjs.

30. "Eighth year of Crime Decline Puts Murder Rate at 33-Year Low," CNN.com, October 16, 2000.

31. Corporate America, so often accused of duplicity, has no monopoly on accusations of being shameless as Craig Anderson and Karen Dill demonstrate. "The [advertising] agency knew that I'd been making speeches about Asian children sewing sneakers for sixty cents a day, and they wanted me to say, 'Another shameless attempt by Nike to sell shoes.' Can you imagine that? I mean, the way those people think? I sent back an email saying no, and they gave the money and the line to Spike Lee," Ralph Nader said he replied when Nike approached him with the proposition of him appearing in their ads. This, in all likelihood, is the same question entertainment executives ask themselves of researchers such as Anderson and Dill.

32. An important consideration overlooked is the context in which video games are played. "The proliferation of electronic entertainments converges with other trends that isolate children from adults. Bigger houses, smaller yards, longer commutes and the rise of big regional high schools all limit the opportunities for generations to mix," John Leland summarizes the observations made by William Damon, director of the Stanford University Center on Adolescence in "Family's Choice Can Blunt the Effect of Video Violence," in the *New York Times*, September 25, 2000.

33. Craig A. Anderson and Karen Dill, "Video Games and Aggressive Thoughts, Feelings, and Behavior in the Laboratory and in Life," pp. 772–790.

34. See Norbert Elias and Eric Dunning, *Quest for Excitement: Sport and Leisure in the Civilizing Process,* which makes the persuasive case that experiencing violence vicariously through fantasy and games is a healthy part of socializing children and allowing adults to deal with life's frustrations through harmless outlets for aggression.

35. "The 2000 Campaign: The Vice President's Wife," published in the *New York Times,* May 19, 2000.

36. L.D. Eron, L.R. Huesmann, E. Dubow, R. Romanoff, and P. Yarmel, "Aggression and Its Correlates Over 22 Years," in *Childhood Aggression and Violence,* eds. D. Crowell, I. Evans, and D. O'Donnell, pp. 249–262.

37. The question whether there is a genetic component to violent behavior, or if it is environmental, or a combination of both, remains unknown.

38. Bad science has negative economic consequence and imprudently narrows consumer choices. Consider K-Mart's decision to require proof of age for the purchase of violent video and computer games in September 2000. Fearful of a backlash by parent groups, K-Mart announced that this decision was, in the words of company spokesperson Frank Buscemi, the "self-regulation that everyone was hoping for, so it's not done for us." The Entertainment Software Rating Board has six ratings for videos and computer games. These are EC for early childhood, E for six and older, T for thirteen and older, M for seventeen and older, AO for adult only, and RP for rating pending.

39. Ian Christopher McCaleb, "Lawmakers, Health Professionals Blast Entertainment Industry for Marketing Adult Material to Children," CNN.com, September 13, 2000.

40. Once bad science is presented as fact before a congressional committee, it takes a life of its own. Consider testimony given before the Senate Committee on the Judiciary chaired by Senator Orrin Hatch of Utah. "Children, Violence and the Media: A Report for Parents and Policy Makers," dated September 14, 1999, states on p. 10, "Studies indicate that violent video games have an effect on children similar to that of violent television and film. That is, prolonged exposure of children to violent video games increases the likelihood of aggression. Some authorities go even further, concluding that the violent actions performed in playing video games are even more conducive to aggressive behavior." A review of the "sources" cited in the Congressional report, however, identifies the work of Mark Weitzman, who authored "Technology and Terror: Extremism on the Internet" (*National Council of Jewish Women Journal*, Winter 1998/99, p. 24). This article was published, without the benefit of peer review, in the quarterly of a political organization. In other words, Mark Weitzman's personal *opinion* was published by an organization that lobbies Congress and was presented as scientific *fact* and subsequently quoted as such by politicians.

41. Roberta Furger, "Does Shoot-'Em-Up Software Lead to Aggressive Behavior?" PCWorld.com, November 2, 1998.

42. "Neo-Nazi Web Sites Reported to Flee Germany," *New York Times*, August 21, 2000.

43. Rose K. Goldsen, *The Show and Tell Machine: How American Television Works and Works You Over*.

44. Private communication, March 1983.

45. Ibid.

46. Ibid.

47. Another program, "Big Blue Marble" showcased kids from different cultures in shorts broadcast between television programs. "Big Blue Marble," while aiming to create greater sensitivity to other cultures by focusing on children from different parts of the world was, itself, a product with sinister origins. It was sponsored by ITT after that company's lobbying of officials at the CIA and the Nixon White House to overthrow the government of Salvador Allende in Chile was exposed.

48. Personal communication, October 1983.

49. Richard Ashmore and Francis Del Boca, "Conceptual Approaches to Stereotypes and Stereotyping," in *Cognitive Processes in Stereotyping and Intergroup Behavior,* ed. David L. Hamilton, p. 23.

50. Goldsen's work on how peers influence youngster's behavior, attitudes, and beliefs was reaffirmed with the publication of *The Limits of Family Influence* by David Rowe in 1994.

51. Richard Ashmore and Francis Del Boca, "Conceptual Approaches to Stereotypes and Stereotyping," p. 23.

52. Ibid., p. 24. The authors go on to argue that, "[w]e believe that cumulative additions to social scientific understanding of stereotypes are most likely to derive from the following two-part strategy. First, . . . it is necessary to seek connections between these perspectives [psychodynamic, cognitive and sociocultural orientations]. Second, each orientation should be developed and elaborated. . . . Progress in understanding stereotypes and stereotyping would benefit greatly from a similar clarification of the other two perspectives" (p. 31).

53. James Wilson and George Kelling, "Broken Windows: The Police and Neighborhood Safety," *The Atlantic Monthly* (March 1982), p. 34.

54. George Kelling and Catherine Coles, *Fixing Broken Windows,* p. 242.

55. J. C. Turner and R. L. Brown, "Social Status, Cognitive Alternatives and Intergroup Relations," in *Differentiation Between Social Groups: Studies in the Psychology of Intergroup Relations,* ed. H. Tajfel.

56. Richard Rodriguez, *Days of Obligation.*

57. In the 1990s, Richard Rodriguez's rhetoric escalated to the point whereby in one article published in *Harper's,* he described a young Mexican worker at a ski resort as lustful of our "blond" young women. His implication clearly was that Mexican immigrants were more likely to commit rape than young men in the general population at large. This is perhaps one reason Richard Rodriguez has been criticized so harshly by the Hispanic and Latino communities in the United States, for he has been accused of being "self-hating" and "self-loathing." His writings are described as "inflammatory," and Richard Rodriguez has been ostracized for the most part by many leaders within the Hispanic and Latino communities in the United States.

58. In *Harper's* one can see prejudiced speech against Mexicans escalate in conjunction with the rising Mexican immigration to the New York metropolitan area. Indeed, throughout the late 1980s and 1990s, in *Harper's* one finds inflammatory speech (Richard Rodriguez, "Across the Borders of History," [March 1987]) escalating into accusatory speech (Richard Rodriguez, "Mixed Blood," [November 1991]), which finally becomes defamation and libel (Earl Shorris, "The Last Word," [August 2000]).

59. Earl Shorris, "The Last Word," *Harper's* (August 2000), p. 41.

60. Milton Kleg, *Hate Prejudice and Racism,* pp. 179–180.

61. "Sympathy for Migrant Workers After Attack," *New York Times,* September 21, 2000.

62. There are two excellent Web sites dedicated to identifying and helping filter hate groups online. In the United States, the Anti-Defamation League operates http://www.adl.org/hate-patrol/info. In Canada there is http://

www.media-awareness.ca, which provides a wide range of information on groups that preach racial hatred. The approaches taken by these groups, however, do have their limitations. It is easy to identify the hate speech message from an Aryan supremacist organization, but it is far more difficult to prevent the kind of hate speech found within the pages of *Harper's* magazine.

63. Personal communication, April 1984.

64. See Norbert Elias and Eric Dunning, *Quest for Excitement: Sport and Leisure in the Civilizing Process,* p. 28.

65. Ibid., p. 58.

66. It certainly is curious to come to the conclusion that violent entertainment, in part, has made it possible for us live in representative democracies.

67. Norbert Elias and Eric Dunning, *Quest for Excitement: Sport and Leisure in the Civilizing Process,* p. 257.

68. Elias and Dunning make the fascinating point about sports in ameliorating relations between the sexes in their analysis of "football hooliganism." They write: "It is noticeable, furthermore, that, whilst rugby players, when the subculture of their male preserve was at its height, tended to mock, objectify and vilify women *symbolically* through the medium of rituals and songs, women do not figure in the songs and chants of football hooligans at all" (p. 257).

69. In a self-deprecating touch that is refreshing, these young men call themselves "vidiots," which is, they explained, what happens when "idiots" is added to "videos."

70. "We buy games at incredible mark-ups, all in the pursuit of the hottest and the newest," Kevin O'Connor, a 25-year-old, told the *New York Times.* See David Kushner, "For Hard-Core Gamers, the Lure of the East," *New York Times,* March 22, 2001.

CHAPTER 9

THE WHEEL OF MISFORTUNE

Since 1999 online gambling is growing at annual rate of 25 percent in the United States. It is expected to become a $150 billion industry by 2010. What accounts for this phenomenal explosion of gambling in the entertainment economy online?

Gambling online can be described as "pathological" insofar as it is fueled by compulsive consumer behavior that is not rational. Pathological patterns are evident in certain kinds of consumer behavior. More often than not these behaviors have economic consequences. If enough consumers are chemical dependents who seek out the stimulants found, for instance, in alcohol, then the production, marketing, and retailing of alcoholic beverages can be expected to be a vibrant and robust component of that economy. If these chemical dependencies become outright addictions, secondary remedial markets then emerge. The industry to help individuals treat alcoholism as a disease is a growth industry in many countries around the world.

Alcohol provides a succinct example of how a personal challenge can contribute to a specific societal malaise. It also demonstrates how markets emerge to satisfy demands that are, on the surface, at conflict with each other. Alcoholism is a symbiotic industry: producers of alcoholic beverages generate consumer demand for alcoholism treatment programs.[1]

There are numerous consumer markets for these kinds of pathologies. In the discussion of the pornography economy online in the next chapter, we shall see how sexual pathologies for fetishes, perversion,

	1997	1998	1999	2000	2001
Adult Home Internet (in millions)	46	81	121	145	159
Percentage of Users Conducting Online Transactions	15%	18%	21%	24%	27%
Potential Internet Gambler (in millions)	0.9	14.5	25.4	34.8	43.0
Per Capita Expenditure	$146	$154	$155	$160	$165
Potential Internet Gambling Revenue (in millions)	$1,009	$2,182	$3,922	$5,555	$7,080
Estimated Actual Internet Gambling Revenue (in millions)	$0	$51	$811	$1,520	$2,330

Figure 9.1   Internet Gambling Worldwide

and outlaw sex have produced an unprecedented growth in the industry for satisfying demand for fetishes.[2] In this chapter, however, we discuss the economic impact of psychological factors that manifest themselves in pathologies and the development of gambling, as both an addiction and an industry, in the entertainment economy online.

To understand the intrinsic nature of gambling online, it is instructive to understand the subtle psychology of collecting. This is because instead of collecting *winnings,* what the consumers truly want is to collect *thrills.* Individuals who are rational understand the mathematical probabilities against them when they gamble. It is illogical to gamble with the expectation that one will win over the long term. But human beings are not expected to be rational all the time. There is pleasure in seeking thrills and the satisfaction that comes from overcoming formidable odds.[3] It is perfectly rational to give in to the temptation of an emotional high. Internet technologies are making widely available the kinds of thrills inherent in games of chance.

One motivational factor when examining the undeniable appeal of gambling online, then, is to understand why individuals want to collect thrills. Let us first turn to the act of collecting, for if we understand why human beings collect things in general—including the accumulation of experiences and thrills—it will facilitate developing a model to understand and predict gambling online. Economists prefer theoretical models that can be expressed in mathematical formulas because they use concepts that are not under contention. Everyone around the world understands the values numbers represent. An economist can look at a series of numbers and offer an opinion, much the same way that an accountant can put the books in order.

It is possible to examine this without offering marketing and sales advice. (To do so would be to make "policy" or "strategy" recommendations.) Once economists meander into the realm of social science, after all, the fields of sociology, psychology, anthropology, and politics beckon across an unfamiliar landscape, a landscape often filled with land mines.

In this book I have discussed only two economists who ventured in the realm of social science, Milton Friedman and John Kenneth Galbraith. Each one has argued economics from well-defined philosophical perspectives, offering specific policy recommendations. Most economists do not have the inclination to navigate the world of politics and remain respected by their colleagues, or the talent to do so successfully.[4] All one has to do is look at the fate of MIT economist Rudiger Dornbusch, who has earned the scorn and ridicule of leaders in several countries by using his role as a critic of the International Monetary Fund as a platform from which to pontificate his political ideas.[5] It is in the proper realm of social science and politics, however, that human beings conduct their economic lives. We must now turn to psychologists in order to understand how pathological impulses give rise to entire industries.

William Lambert, one of the pioneers in cross-cultural psychology, has long observed that game theory facilitates testing the validity of theories. If one assumes that the human mind is the same around the world, then when humans are confronted with puzzles, it becomes far easier to discern the thought processes that are used to arrive at solutions. Games of chance are puzzles about probability, more often phrased in terms of "luck," "feelings," and gut instincts.

"Throughout the 1950s and 1960s when cross-cultural psychology was in its infancy, evaluation results were very strange," Lambert said. "The tests showed a tremendous gap in the scores of Westerners and people from other cultures, suggesting that non-Westerners were stupid or mentally impaired. How could such disparities among people possibly exist? One knew *instinctively* that there was something very amiss—not with people, but with our method of testing them. But when we approached cross-cultural psychology from a different perspective—assume the human mind is the same across cultures—then psychologists began to make progress in understanding how culture affects human development and why societies are structured the way they are. This approach has added tremendous rigor to the discipline and it helped completely change the way we understand the world."[6]

If one can understand how humans in various cultures approach gambling, then one can make significant inroads in understanding how human beings think in general about the business of gambling as entertainment in the online economy. To understand how they think about the passion of collecting experiences, risks, and casino winnings, first consider the work of New York psychoanalyst Werner Muensterberger. In his authoritative work on the psychological profile of the personality traits of collectors, the desire to possess becomes pathological. Muensterberger reports:

> Obtainment in whatever way—bought, found, or even acquired by scheming or tricky means or thievery—works like a mood regulator and provides the owner with a potential sense of success or triumph, and occasionally of grandeur, as is the case with the winner at the gaming table.[7]

If the factor that motivates collectors is the need for acclamation, then collecting can be understood as an endeavor undertaken as a *quest.* Collectors, in essence, set out on a quest to acquire—whether the object of their desire is baseball cards or winning hands at blackjack.

The *addictive* nature of collecting thrills among gamblers is, in fact, heightened by the desire to succeed in their quest. Muensterberger suggests that feelings of insecurity and inadequacy are at the root of addictive pathologies when he writes:

> The compelling concern to go in search, to discover, to add to one's store, or holding, or harem, is not generated by conscious planning. Rather, every new addition, whether found, given, bought, discovered, or even stolen, bears the stamp of promise and magical compensation. It can as well be understood as a momentary symbolic *experiment* in self-healing of an ever-present sense of frustration. The successful *experiment* is usually followed by a short-lived sense of elation, of triumph and mastery. . . .
>
> [Collectors] like to pose or make a spectacle of their possessions. But one soon realizes that these possessions, regardless of their value or significance, are but stand-ins for themselves.[8]

What Muensterberger suggests, in other words, is the phenomenon economists refer to when they discuss the discrepancies that abound in consumer behavior when the gap between Stated Preference and Revealed Preference is considerable. Collectors say they pursue the acquisition of *things,* but what they really seek, is to find (and heal) *themselves.* Gamblers, likewise, *say* what they're after is the jackpot, but what they really want is the adrenaline rush that comes from the *thrill* of playing.

It is this need to collect thrills that is the single-most important motivating factor that leads to obsessive compulsive disorders. Muensterberger reports that "most characteristically, there is always an addictive component—a potential but always present unconscious modality of affect linked to a powerful reparative need."[9]

The premise offered is consistent with explanations of compulsive behaviors that give rise to disorders. Writing about George Bland, a compulsive thief of rare maps, Miles Harvey describes the obsessive nature of collecting by noting that collectors are "aware that for the aficionado, as for the adventurer, the journey is better than the destination."[10] Muensterberger is aware of danger of obsession when he argues:

> In some instances collecting can become an all-consuming passion, not unlike the dedication of a compulsive gambler to the gaming table—to the point where it can affect a person's life and become the paramount concern in his or her pursuit, over-shadowing all else: work, family, social obligations and responsibilities. We know of numerous cases in which moral standards, legal considerations, and societal taboos have been disregarded in the passion to collect.[11]

What do collectors have to say for themselves? Are they aware of the pathologies that drive them to embark on these pursuits?[12] "This is anything but complacency," Muensterberger writes of collecting, "because most collectors are aware of the temporality of their ingrained longing for magic security."[13] Gillett Griffin, who was the director of the Art Museum at Princeton University, for instance, has written widely in defense of collectors, once notably in *National Geographic*. Analyzing the motivations for his own impulse to collect, he writes:

> I feel that I am not the owner, but only the custodian of the works, which I have assembled, and my goal has been to pass them on to the world in an ordered way, so that they will add to the knowledge of present and future generations. And this, I believe, is the true goal of the serious collector: to assemble disparate works of art, put them in a meaningful order and to bring to the attention of the world the beauty and integrity of the art of civilizations which we are just beginning, through archaeology, iconography, and epigraphy, to understand.[14]

It is clear that collectors of things do not understand the pathologies that drive them to collect any more than collectors of thrills understand completely why they incur risks, whether these are physical by jumping out of airplanes or financial by going for broke at a gaming table.

Muensterberger, however, offers an insight that will help us understand more fully why gambling on the Internet is now such a powerful sector of the entertainment economy online. He explains that:

> Collecting, then, emerges as an instrument designed not only to allay a basic need brought on by early traumata and as an escape hatch for feelings of danger and the reexperience of loss. However, because it is an effective device for relief from these pressures, it is felt as a source of pleasure and wish fulfillment.[15]

If the suggestion is that collectors collect because they are unconsciously overcoming some unresolved trauma, then collecting thrills by gambling on the Internet has a tremendous future.

The world is full of dysfunctional people. This is why overcoming traumas, as well as inferiority complexes and insecurities, is a growth industry. Consider the situation of a friend who was psychologist in private practice in San Francisco during the 1990s. In the midst of a sustained economic expansion and the stellar growth of the Internet technologies, throughout northern California middle-aged well-to-do women who did not have careers outside their homes felt insecure. Their feelings of inadequacies were fueled by the belief that they themselves were worthless as human beings and the only reason people had an interest in them was because of who their husbands were, or the money they had. These insecurities manifested themselves in one peculiar way: Women who lead lives of leisure and material overabundance do not have a need to learn to drive, for instance, because there is always someone to chauffeur them around or to run their daily errands. As a result there were many women in the swank neighborhoods of Pacific Heights and Russian Hill who experienced such anxiety about commandeering an automobile that it paralyzed them. This psychologist friend, in fact, began to specialize in treating these women by helping them overcome their anxieties. In therapy sessions that, on occasion, lasted more than a year, these women were taught to establish a sense of self-worth by learning to drive. A skill that most people in the United States mastered by the time they graduated from high school represented a major achievement for these patients. And if they admitted their anxieties to others, they ran the risk of being ridiculed. There is little sympathy for a woman who owns two Mercedes and a Ford Durango who is incapable of driving any of them.

"Therapy" was deemed successful when these women achieved a more healthy sense of self-esteem, self-worth, and self-respect evidenced by passing their driving test. Then again, whether they ever actually drove was beside the point. It is clear to see, then, how insidious the nature of pathological disorder can be, for it becomes a source of shame and guilt, making it more difficult for individuals to seek out professional therapy.

It is also filled with well-intentioned people who, for a variety of reasons not fully understood, engage in behaviors that can become obsessive, addictive, and self-destructive. That men and women are free to engage in activities that undermine their well-being is on a social level frustrating, of course. Then again because ours is a market economy, their actions result in consumer behavior that economists study. It may very well appear perverse that market economies endeavor to create efficiencies in activities that result in pathologies, but such a conclusion is a value judgment.

Let us assume that recreational gambling can lead to pathological disorders. Let us further assume that the emergence of a gambling economy online has, by its very existence, the potential of spreading the medical disorder known as pathological gambling.[16] Working within the parameters of these definitions, the discussion of gambling online is an analysis of a market consisting of pathological consumer behavior.

ONLINE GAMBLING AND SOCIETY

In the National Gambling Impact Study Commission (NGISC) report issued in June 1999, the authors noted both the pathological aspect of recreational gambling and the explosive growth of the gaming economy online. The Commission noted with alarm that:

despite the fact that pathological gambling is a recognized medical disorder, most insurance companies and managed care providers do not reimburse for treatment. The Commission recommends to states that they mandate that private and public insurers and managed care providers identify successful treatment programs, educate participants about pathological gambling and treatment options, and cover the appropriate programs under their plans.

It is instructive that the Commission approached the subject of problem gambling as a public health matter. By framing chronic gambling in the real world as a medical problem—the Commission naively recommended that duly authorized gambling operations "conspicuously post and disseminate the telephone numbers of at least two state-approved providers of problem-gambling information, treatment, and referral support services"—it set the stage for its dim view of gambling in the virtual world. In fact, the report's section that addressed the Internet was adamant in its belief that online gambling constituted a threat to society:

5-4 The Commission recommends to the President, Congress, and the Department of Justice (DOJ) that the federal government should prohibit, without allowing new exemption or the expansion of existing federal exemptions to other jurisdictions, Internet gambling not already authorized within the United States or among parties in the United States and any foreign jurisdiction. . . .

5-5 The Commission recommends to the President and Congress that because Internet gambling is expanding most rapidly through offshore operators, the federal government should take steps to encourage or enable foreign governments not to harbor Internet gambling organizations that prey on U.S. citizens.[17]

The Commission concludes by observing that "policymakers may wish to impose an explicit moratorium on gambling expansion while awaiting further research and assessment."[18]

Not unexpectedly, the gambling industry, in both the private sector and by state-run lotteries, condemned the Commission's findings, conclusions, and recommendations.[19] Others outside the federal government have been critical of the social impact of gambling in American society. In their study of the impact the introduction of a state lottery in South Carolina would have on the people of that state, for instance, John Hill and Gary Palmer examined how state lotteries had affected other states. "When lotteries are legalized," they concluded, "the number of problem and pathological gamblers increases dramatically. Crime also increases as gambling addicts seek more money to bet on the lottery. Hundreds of millions of dollars in social and economic costs are lost annually as a result of problem and pathological gamblers."[20]

The Interactive Gaming Council, based in Vancouver, British Columbia, argues that any effort to regulate online gambling by nations will prove futile. "Technology is changing so fast that it will be impossible to criminalize an activity that is legal in more than fifty countries around the world," Sue Schneider, chair of the Interactive Gaming Council said. "The U.S. Congress would be wiser to legalize and regulate online gambling than to try to impose an ill-conceived and unenforceable ban. Any ban will only serve to frustrate American gamblers and make them vulnerable to fraud and abuse by unscrupulous and illegal Web sites that will set up business outside the law."[21]

The dilemma policymakers confront was evident in the failure of the U.S. Congress to pass a measure to curb online gambling in July 2000. The measure, sponsored by Robert Goodlatte, R-Virginia, sought to ban most forms of online gambling.[22] Although strongly supported by the Nevada gambling industry and religious groups, efforts seeking to ban online gambling prove difficult to devise because of the ethereal nature of the technology. The Internet Gambling Prohibition Act, sponsored by Senator Jon Kyl (R-Arizona) would be impossible to enforce in a wired world where enforcement overseas is problematic.

Another obstacle to banning gambling on the Internet resides in how gambling is defined. Health professionals define the demand side as individuals who have an obsessive compulsion that can become pathological and therefore addictive. But how is the supply defined? This has increasingly become a more difficult question to answer because the thrills (and chemical reactions in the brain) associated with traditional forms of gambling are increasingly seen in other kinds of activities not usually considered games of chance.

Consider the following account given by a San Francisco attorney describing his online day trading, the practice of "rapid-fire" buying and selling stocks online:

> "During conference calls and drafting sessions, I would sneak out to check my portfolio," said the lawyer, who asked that his name not be used because he did not want his firm to know about his trading or his family to know about his debts. But, he said, he could not resist the potential payoff. "I was a gambler sitting at a table in Las Vegas," he said. "My palms got sweaty thinking about how much money I could make."[23]

If one replaces the word "portfolio" with "winnings," then the statement could have been made by a pathological gambler. If either word is replaced by "thrills," then the speaker displays the unresolved childhood trauma Muensterberger identified as the chief motivation that accounts for why collectors collect.

In their efforts "to allay a basic need brought on by early traumata," gamblers resort to compulsive gambling because each new bet "is an effective device for relief." The most direct way of finding out if this is accurate is to ask gamblers why they gamble. In a study conducted by the Addiction Research Institute (ARI) in Melbourne, Australia, callers to a confidential hotline designed to assist pathological gamblers, part of the intake included asking questions to determine why gamblers believed they gambled. The findings of the survey appear in Figure 9.2, and they are remarkable not in what they reveal, but in the stark differences between the sexes. Whereas men identify pleasure, excitement, and financial gain as their chief motivating factors, in contrast, women identified boredom, anxiety, and loneliness.

The survey raises questions about how men and women see themselves in the economic arena: whereas men pursue something (pleasure, excitement, money), women strive to avoid something else (boredom, anxiety, and loneliness). This offers a wealth of information about how men and women see themselves and their roles in society. Do men seek "pleasure" because they are "bored"? Do women wish

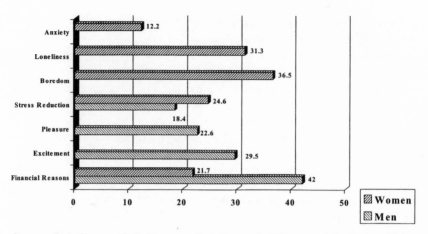

Source: G.J. Coman, G.D. Burrows, B.J. Evans, in "Stress and Anxiety as Factors in the Onset of Problem Gambling: Implications for Treatment," Stress Medicine (1997), pp. 235–244.

Figure 9.2   Why Do You Gamble?

to ameliorate feelings of loneliness by seeking "excitement"? It is clear that men and women are saying the same thing, only using different words.

What gamblers, in fact, are doing is trying to reduce the unease in their lives through a diversion that may subject them to a disease. "First, the central nervous system of the problem gambler becomes habituated to the gambling behavior," The Wager, a joint publication of the Division on Addictions at Harvard Medical School and the Massachusetts Council on Compulsive Gambling, reports.

> Once habituated, the gambler experiences stress and tension when not gambling. To relieve the stress and tension, the gambler continues to gamble. Changes in stress levels are accompanied by changes in the body's chemistry. In particular, levels of cortisol and neurotransmitters such as norepinephrine are sensitive to both external and internal stressors.[24]

The same physiological changes measured in pathological gamblers are seen in day traders. Are, then, the financial stock exchanges disguised casinos where people gamble?[25] One can argue convincingly that "market analysis" and "risk assessment" are sophisticated ways of hedging one's bets. The dynamics of Wall Street parallel to an uncanny degree the behavior observed among pathological behavior. Rituals to secure "luck," the irrational evocation of the power of instinct, and the willingness to dismiss failure, are seen among both groups of people. One can also find a striking observation about the long-term effects. In both gambling and day trading, one finds individuals who suffer emotionally after an extended period of time.

What people in business normally refer to as "burn out" is oftentimes stress or clinical depression. In pathological gambling, it was thought that people who are depressed gamble in order to improve their state of mind. The reverse is also true. The data suggest that pathological gambling, not unlike day trading, causes depression, rather than depression being the condition that leads people to gamble in the first place.[26] This cycle then leads to greater dependence on the behavioral patterns that lead to disorder. The general public first became aware of the pathological nature of online gambling when newspapers began to report on working-class people who were encountering financial difficulties because of their losses to online casinos.[27]

THE ANTHROPOLOGY OF ONLINE GAMBLING

What health professionals label an "addiction," marketers hail as "brand loyalty." This statement is not intended to be facetious, but rather, it is to recognize how, in response to heightened competition, business executives are availing themselves of social scientists in order to gain insights into consumer behavior and to develop interdisciplinary marketing programs. "With ethnography, a consumer is viewed using products in his or her natural environment," Marvin Matises, a principal with Galileo Idea Group, a firm that specializes in developing new-product concepts for consumer product companies, writes in *Brandweek*. He continues to praise the incorporation of the discipline of anthropology in marketing in order to understand more completely consumer behavior and needs:

> Perhaps the greatest benefit of such an ethnographic approach is [the] marketer's ability to view the consumer actually using the product, taking the concept of a "taste test" to a whole new realm. Rather than having a consumer test a product and provide feedback, consumers are using the product where and when they are most comfortable.[28]

What has been commonplace among Western academics, who secure funding to film people in other cultures going about the business of living their lives, which is then edited and packaged for broadcast on programs such as *Discovery* or *National Geographic Presents*, is now being used by marketing executives who film American consumers using plastic storage containers in their own kitchens—in order to develop a better plastic storage container.

An interdisciplinary approach to consumer marketing offers significant insights and has its advantages in product placement. "Whether
you think ethnography is a science or an art form, the consensus is
that it works," Matises concludes. It may be that certain kinds of consumer behavior may be classified by health professionals as pathological disorders, but that does not deprive the economic consequence of
pathological consumer behavior of validity as a market. The application of anthropological techniques in marketing the entertainment
economy online is making it possible for individuals who may be susceptible to developing a gambling disorder to participate in a vibrant
economy that enables their pathology.[29] This is a legitimate concern
on a macroeconomic level and for policymakers to investigate. For the
gambling business community, however, most consumers are able to
engage in some sort of gambling without suffering ill effects. In the
United Kingdom, for instance, almost 90 percent of the adult population engages in some form of gambling, betting, or lotteries in the
course of a year. Of the millions of people who travel to Las Vegas,
most enjoy themselves in thoroughly harmless gambling that does not
affect their mental health.

ONLINE GAMBLING AND THE BUSINESS OF
COLLECTING THRILLS

It is an intriguing proposition to characterize gamblers as collectors
of thrills. That consumers are willing to participate in such irrational
and risky diversion in such numbers as to constitute an industry as
large as gambling has become raises questions. Las Vegas is less than
a 90-minute flight from San Francisco. It is a short distance to travel
to spend a week at the Treasure Island at the Mirage resort.[30] Treasure Island, like most other casino resorts in Las Vegas, bills itself as
an entertainment destination. There are theme-restaurants, theater per-
formances, spectacles (pirates engaging in battle on Buccaneer Bay),
spas, and, of course, the ubiquitous casinos. Millions of travelers from
the world over journey to Las Vegas on holiday, have splendid vaca-
tions, and return home with memories they cherish.

During the week that I spent there, being in Las Vegas was similar
to being in Cancun: the number of problem gamblers, and the problems they created, in the former were comparable to the difficulties
problem drinkers, particularly during Spring Break, posed for authorities in the latter. In other words, problem gamblers in Las Vegas were
well within the statistical norms predicted by analyses of distributions
of pathological gamblers in the general population. Although it cannot be denied that there was a core segment of problem gamblers
whose conduct was both compulsive and pathological, their number,

in terms of percentages, was small.[31] What astounded was the healthy, which is to say, harmless, manner in which most visitors to Las Vegas approached gambling; it was a form of recreation and entertainment, not a desperate bid for instant wealth.

In the course of speaking with dozens of gamblers, hotel managers, and residents of Las Vegas, it became clear that this was a sustainable, mature industry. The Nevada gambling industry has been successful in creating the kind of entertainment destination that does a remarkable job of safeguarding visitors from the ill consequences gambling may entail. The extensive selection of entertainment options does cater to families, and it is clear that the safeguards regulation provides are an integral part of minimizing, if not preventing, the possible negative impact from gambling. Without regulation, online gambling enables pathological gambling, which becomes more acute for its development will depend on attracting vulnerable segments of the population. This is the exception in Nevada. Visitors to Las Vegas make the conscientious decision to indulge the fantasy of their holiday; and Las Vegans make their livings by working, not by gambling.

This is stark contrast to the general perceptions of Las Vegas by the public at large. The San Francisco attorney who confessed to *New York Times* reporter Amy Harmon that he approached day trading as if he were a pathological gambler—"I was a gambler sitting at a table in Las Vegas. . . . My palms got sweaty thinking about how much money I could make"—would be an atypical sight. The profile of the average gambler in Las Vegas, in fact, is that of a more well-adjusted individual than a sizable percentage of consumers who habitually purchase tickets from lotteries run by the various states.[32] Casinos in Nevada are solid businesses in the business of providing entertainment and diversion to middle-class consumers in safe, friendly, and innocuous diversions. It is undoubtedly an industry that has the potential for expanding its market by establishing a formidable presence in the entertainment industry online.

The Nevada gambling industry, however, opposes online gambling. It mistakenly sees it not so much as unwelcome competition, but as a threat to its continued success as an industry. The first objection arises from the absence of government regulation of online gambling, according to the Nevada gambling industry. Whereas casinos in the real world are regulated by state and federal agencies, count on physical locations that can be inspected by government authorities, and are required to collect taxes on disbursements paid to winners, none of these safeguards are in place for online casinos. They remain, for the most part, outside the jurisdiction of state and federal authorities.

A second objection arises from the unfair competitive advantage that online gambling sites potentially represent. That they operate within a business realm whose jurisdiction has not been established—to say nothing of a body of regulations that constitute a playing field—constitute a marked advantage as the entertainment economy online continues to evolve. This is, of course, the same complaint voiced by other industries against online merchants. Retail department stores, for instance, have expressed concern over their relative disadvantage vis-à-vis online merchants for the simple reason that retailers in the real world are required to collect applicable sales taxes whereas online purchases are exempt.[33] In due course over the present decade, however, Nevada gambling executives express reservations about the medium-term impact of online gambling on their industry. Not unlike the uncertainty and adversarial nature surrounding the music industry's approach to online music, Nevada casinos have trepidation about online gambling. As we saw, the music industry clothed their concerns as copyright issues, when the true essence of the conflict was one of the gap between Stated and Revealed Preferences. The Nevada gambling industry similarly presents its objections in terms of the absence of regulatory governing bodies, when it is a reluctance to extend its brands and marketing savvy onto the Internet.

The third issue raised by the Nevada gambling industry is a matter of public welfare. Although in the real world, casinos, lotteries, and sports betting facilities can ensure that players are of legal age, can identify problem gamblers on an ongoing basis, and have procedures to identify fraud, these objectives are far more difficult to meet online. The use of an adult's credit card can make it possible for minors to gamble online. The anonymous nature of the Internet makes it possible for problem gamblers to adopt different "handles" online that makes it possible for pathological gambling to take place unnoticed. Finally, the use of various credit card numbers and offshore accounts makes it possible for fraud to take place. Unauthorized charges to secure credit, or the use of offshore accounts to transfer funds, not only makes it possible to engage in fraud and money laundering, but also undermines the public's confidence in an industry where safeguards are absent. In the same way that recording artists are reluctant to produce music if their intellectual property can be used without their being compensated, consumers are reluctant to partake of an industry if they are fearful. In a stunning incident, Jonathan Lebed, a 15-year-old boy, was accused by the S.E.C. of stock manipulation and carrying out a scheme that earned him $273,000 in illegal profits.[34]

These concerns address, primarily, the concerns of casinos. Indeed, that Nevada casinos have been vocal in their opposition to the gambling industry online has given the American public the erroneous impression that the Las Vegas–style casinos are the primary forms of online gambling. Sports betting and lottery Web sites account for a significant part of the multibillion-dollar gambling economy online. Millions of recreational gamblers are able to enjoy placing bets and participating in games of chance without becoming addicted, much the same way that most people can drink alcohol without becoming addicted.

In 2000, the 750 online casinos took in approximately $20.3 billion in wagers of which payouts to players were estimated to amount to $1.02 billion.[35] An estimated 350,000 Americans are believed to have wagered online in 2000. Others are more exuberant in the figures they offer. Venture Tech, a company whose mission is "to establish state-of-the-art international gaming Web sites and provide secure and exciting real-time casino systems to its gaming subscribers," believes the gambling industry in the United States consists of a $600 billion-a-year market, netting the industry over $40 billion in profits annually.

An industry with $40 billion in profits is evidence of the undeniable fact that many people are in the market for "collecting" thrills. This has not gone unnoticed. Tom Grey, who directs the National Coalition Against Legalized Gambling (NCALG), scoffs at suggestions that online gambling is benign. "Gambling is a form of 'entertainment' in which five percent of participants will 'entertain' themselves into bankruptcy, destroying their lives and families in the process."[36] Venture Tech, on the other hand, claims that credible estimates put gambling in all forms around the world in excess of $1 trillion, evidence that billions of people are able to gamble without becoming problem gamblers.

There is evidence to support this view. In much the same way that the medical community reversed itself in the 1990s when study after study revealed that people who consumed alcohol in moderation were healthier than those who abstained completely, researchers have documented that people who gamble once in a while have higher self-esteem than those who abstain altogether.[37]

The medical community now endorses the recommendation that a glass of red wine several times a week can be beneficial for most people. It can likewise be argued that buying lottery tickets, betting on a sports game, or taking a vacation that includes discretionary occasional gambling can be part of a healthy lifestyle. No one denies that excessive drinking leads to alcoholism, and there are mechanisms in place designed to help consumers from becoming problem drinkers. The emergence of the gambling economy online brings the potential of enticing individuals or vulnerable groups.

The unintended irony is that, in this instance, those who oppose gambling in principle are on the same side as the Nevada gambling industry. The same concerns raised about the negative societal impact of unregulated gambling, where minors and those susceptible to pathological gambling are left to their own devises, are familiar to welfare economists. In fact, economists are familiar with the costs to society as whole when groups of people are marginalized. Comparing data concerning pathological gambling among indigenous people in North Dakota and New Zealand, for instance, R. A. Volberg compared the Sioux and Chippewa in North Dakota and the Maori in New Zealand and established a correlation of higher rates of pathological gambling among native people than in the surrounding Caucasian populations.[38]

If vulnerable members of society throughout the general population are tempted into participating in a diversion that will become addictive, there are legitimate issues for policymakers to address. Although the draconian attempt to ban Internet gambling altogether is as misguided as it is destined to fail, the issues surrounding the advent of these technologies must be addressed forthrightly.

The Nevada gambling industry nevertheless remained adamant in its opposition to Internet gambling until 2001. The most familiar and compelling argument raised in opposition to an unregulated gambling industry online centers on the belief that this is an activity that properly belongs to adults. Not unlike drinking, smoking, and pornography, gambling is an activity that society deems inappropriate to minors who are viewed as consumers too immature to make responsible decisions. The Nevada casinos correctly point to the difficulties in keeping those who are not of legal age from being able to gamble. Whereas casinos in the real world can easily ensure that only adults sit at the tables or play the slot machines, the anonymity of the Internet makes it impossible to guarantee that underage players are not gambling online. That most online casinos require simply a valid credit card number to absolve themselves of legal liability does not end the matter. An underage individual can use a parent's or adult guardian's credit card to establish false proof of age, purchase credits to play, and incur debt that can become the legal obligation of the cardholder.

The Nevada gambling industry can use the inability to prevent minors from playing at online casinos as one kind of fraud. The absence of regulation, in fact, offers consumers little protection that online casinos operate fairly and ethically. Whereas the gambling industry is subject to rigorous regulation by states, it is imperative for gambling, on principle, to remain credible. If unregulated operators are not subject to scrutiny by legal authorities, consumers have no assurance that the games aren't rigged against them, or that there are enough winners being paid sums that are consistent with industry norms. The anonymous nature of the Internet facilitates the fraudulent use of someone else's credit cards.

In the real world, there are rules to prevent consumers whose judgment has been impaired by alcohol or medication (prescription or illegal) to gamble. There are also regulations in place to ensure that online gambling sites are not used to launder money or funds secured through illegal or fraudulent means. The essence of the Internet technologies makes it difficult to prevent organized crime from using online casinos as a front for defrauding the public at large. Indeed, there are enough problems policing the gambling industry in the real world, where regulators meet face-to-face and where casino operators can monitor the players to their satisfaction.

If these issues were not compelling enough, the Nevada gambling industry points out that there is the serious matter of taxation. Without the regulation of online gambling, it is impossible to tax the winnings of players or the profits of operators. Without regulatory oversight to ensure there is an accountability—and that the proper tax laws within the various, if not overlapping, jurisdictions are respected—the credibility of the gambling industry online is undermined.

The operators of online casinos argue that their ventures, by virtue of taking place in cyberspace, are not subject to any government's jurisdiction. Earlier in this discussion I argued that the proper definition of what belongs to the New Economy is a transaction that is completed in its entirety online. Arguments against online gambling fail to convince, for the "real" world nature of how online gambling operates challenges our current understanding of the jurisdiction of nation-states.

To the claim that "cyberspace" defies jurisdiction by its very nature, critics point to the simple fact that to access the Internet, consumers rely on telephone communications. Therefore, the Wire Wager Act comes into play. This federal law prohibits the use of a wire transmission facility, such as telephone lines, to foster gambling. Title 18 of the United States Code states that:

> (a) Whoever being engaged in the business of betting or wagering knowingly uses a wire communication facility for the transmission in interstate or foreign commerce of bets or wagers or information assisting in the placing of bets or wagers on any sporting event or contest, or for the transmission of a wire communication which entitles the recipient to receive money or credit as a result of bets or wagers, or for information assisting in the placing of bets or wagers, shall be fined under this title or imprisoned not more than two years, or both. . . .
>
> (d) When any common carrier, subject to the jurisdiction of the Federal Communications Commission, is notified in writing by a Federal, State, or local law enforcement agency, acting within its jurisdiction, that any facility furnished by it is being used or will be used for the purpose of transmitting or receiving gambling information in interstate or foreign commerce in violation of Federal, State or local law, it shall discontinue or refuse, the leasing, furnishing, or maintaining of such facility, after reasonable notice to the subscriber, but no damages, penalty or forfeiture, civil or criminal, shall be found against any common carrier for any

act done in compliance with any notice received from a law enforcement agency. Nothing in this section shall be deemed to prejudice the
right of any person affected thereby to secure an appropriate determination, as otherwise provided by law, in a Federal court or in a State or
local tribunal or agency, that such facility should not be discontinued
or removed, or should be restored.[39]

In addition, there is the Professional and Amateur Sports Protection Act
that makes it illegal for an individual to sponsor:

> operate, advertise or promote, pursuant to the law or compact of a gov-
> ernmental entity, a . . . betting, gambling, or wagering scheme based,
> directly or indirectly . . . on one or more competitive games in which
> amateur or professional athletes participate, or are intended to partici-
> pate, or on one or more performances of such athletes in such games.

The right of Congress to regulate—or ban—gambling online is not in
question. But gambling on the Internet, however, becomes more popular everyday.

Herein lies another contradiction. Although it can be argued that,
on technical grounds, Internet gambling is a violation of federal laws,
the American public overwhelmingly supports its legalization and regulation. In Figure 9.3, a survey conducted by MSNBC.com is consistent with the sentiment documented time and time again. Americans,
though made cognizant of the dangers of gambling, are convinced that,
for most people, gambling is a benign pastime.[40] It is intriguing, thus,
to see roles reversed: the gambling industry opposed gambling on the
Internet whereas the public, desensitized by a generation of playing
state lotteries, are enthusiastic about the possibilities of greater, and
more accessible, gambling. The case can be made that the gambling
industry errs by resisting Internet casinos and sports betting. Instead
of seeing the gambling economy online as a threat their business, they

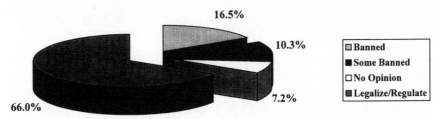

Source: Adapted from http://www.msnbc.com/modules/FlexSurvey/gambling.asp?
step=2.

Figure 9.3   What Should be Done About Internet Gambling?

should recognize their self-interest, and see it as a way of expanding the market in a responsible way.

ONLINE GAMBLING AS A BUSINESS MODEL

In the week that I spent at Treasure Island in Las Vegas, I was astounded by the ease with which state-of-the-art technologies were incorporated continuously by casinos. The care with which they developed, and protected, their brands was exemplary. The cacophony of entertainment options, and the meticulous and effortless way in they are marketed, is simply exhausting. It was therefore puzzling to witness the steadfast opposition to online gambling, particularly given the fact that the industry is expected to reach, by decade's end, the $150 billion threshold. From a marketing perspective, online gambling represents an ideal opportunity to expand the franchises of the dominant players in the Nevada gambling industry. In the same way that other entertainment conglomerates, such as the Walt Disney Company, have expanded the markets for its brands by opening parks in Europe and Japan, the Nevada gambling industry has the opportunity to expand its brands to consumers who will never travel to Las Vegas. Native American nations, for instance, are moving toward establishing a dominant presence in the online gambling market. "We're a rural gaming operation here in rural Northern Idaho and the market is limited," says David Matheson, the Coeur D'Alene tribe's chief executive officer of gaming. "So if you can't get them to visit your site on the paved highway, then you might as well use the high-tech highway."[41]

Herein lies the natural competitive advantage that the Nevada gambling industry can enjoy: brandscape. This is one of those frivolous vanity words made up by marketing executives intent on creating hype. "To assist in our understanding of brand depth, and to get a better picture of the competitive environment in which brands co-exist on and off the Internet, we have created a model called the 'brandscape,'" Marc Braunstein and Edward Levine argue in *Deep Branding on the Internet.*[42] Brands "coexist" the way foxes and chickens coexist: uneventfully until the former devour the latter.

Brands do not coexist, in fact. They compete. One of the unintended consequences of the Nevada gambling industry's objections to online gambling is of the erosion of credibility among consumers of the entire gambling industry, online and off-line alike. When one sector of a market operates under a cloud, the entire industry suffers. When one airliner crashes, passengers around the world are apprehensive, regardless of which carrier they are flying. If online casinos operate under a cloud, this darkens the value of the brands of Nevada casinos. Consider that the traits Braunstein and Levine point out are consistent with traditional marketing techniques to build strong brand loyalty entail "associat[ing] the name with the many positive attributes that increase [a brand's] overall value: customer awareness; preference and loyalty; the ability to compound higher prices; and demand for the brand from prospective allies and licensees."[43]

This is true, but only to a point, and it is not universal. Thomas Frank, a critic of the "new economy," mocks the idea that brands should be venerated. "A brand's meaning is as complex and as contested as socially constructed as, say, gender," he writes.[44] One can argue that there are times when a successful branding campaign does not enhance a company's revenue stream. Pets.com's enormously popular Sock Puppet made this Web retailer a household name in 2000, but it ultimately proved inconsequential.[45] "Pets.com discovered that, absent an effective business model, brand visibility doesn't translate into purchase intent," Brandweek declared.[46] Purchase intent, or actual sales, for that matter, should have been mentioned.

Then again, where gambling is concerned, there is brand value to games of chance. State governments throughout the United States, by running high-stake lotteries, have been rather successful at removing the social stigmas associated with gambling and in desensitizing consumers to the idea of getting something for (almost) nothing. The result is a pool of consumers ahead of both the industry and policymakers when it comes to proposals that greatly expand the market for gambling.

Throughout the United States and around the world, there are hundreds of millions of people who will find it far easier to travel to cyberspace than to a casino in Las Vegas. For low stakes games of chance, the members of the Nevada gambling industry count on some of the more respected brands in the world that have stellar reputations. Braunstein and Levine aptly point out that "[m]any of the so-called brands that emerged in the earliest years of the Internet were pressured into existence using vast sums they had not earned; consequently, they were quick to vanish when the funds ran out."[47]

One of the more important obstacles that online gambling must overcome if it is to grow to its true potential—$20 billion of a $600 billion market represents one-third of 1 percent market share—is to win the confidence of consumers. If consumers do not recognize the brands of the companies with whom they do business, they tend to be skeptical. When they realize that online operators are not regulated, they become reluctant to participate. The confidence in the gambling industry online is tenuous, and there is reason for consumers' misgivings. Consider that in Las Vegas, an average slot machine will pay back about 97 percent of the money players put into it, leaving the house with a 3 percent margin. These are fair overall odds for recreational consumers: play one machine long enough, and most of your money will be returned.

This is not the case with gambling online, which is why consumers do not trust the cyber house. The lack of consumer confidence and the absence of a regulatory mechanism for supervising how operators run their online casinos are an impediment to the industry. In the void created by the absence of licensing for the industry, there are discomforting opportunities for abuse. Defrauding consumers is as much of a concern as the potential for online casinos being used to launder money. A market characterized by the absence of goalposts and referees is one in which chaos unfolds. This is not in the interests of the Nevada gambling industry, policymakers, or consumers.

The development of an industry that has the potential of providing entertainment for millions is being undermined by both the lack of political will to establish ground rules and by the opposition to the Internet by the Nevada gambling industry. The speed with which online gambling was making inroads into American culture was such that the *New York Times* reported on the unexpected consequences. "Rolling dice can seem unreal when a computer does it," Matt Richtel wrote. "But the money that changes hands can be all too real."[48] What is clear, however, is that a technology once unleashed cannot be abandoned, particularly when it stands to greatly expand an industry on a global basis. The challenges are twofold. First, Congress must enact laws that create a level playing field for the industry in ways that are consistent with the laws of other nations. Once a workable regulatory framework is in place, it will be easier to prevent fraud, collect taxes due, and ensure that the industry develops in a manner that is equitable and instills consumer confidence. Second, the Nevada gambling industry must embrace further the technology as the natural evolution of its industry. With the unrivaled brands, expertise, and reputation its members enjoy, Las Vegas casinos, in addition to the Principality of Monaco, stands to establish a formidable presence in an industry that is destined to be an ever-growing part of entertainment on the Internet. The undeniable logic of this conclusion began to make itself clear to the Nevada gambling industry in 2001.[49]

SUMMARY

Gamblers are, in essence, collectors who accumulate thrills. The psychological profile of the vast majority of gamblers is not different from the benign traits often associated with collectors. An industry that develops to satisfy such a market is one characterized by *Key #1* (The Internet offers the technology to expand greatly an existing market) and *Key #4* (The online economy can create conditions in which inferior societal outcomes will prevail unless regulatory remedies are in place to balance private wants and public needs).

The emergence of the Nevada gambling industry as a mature and stable economic sector, however, is evidence that for the vast majority of consumers, recreational gambling is an innocuous form of entertainment. The emergence of gambling online, on the other hand, has been marred by the unregulated nature of the industry and consumer misgivings about Internet security. It is nevertheless growing on a worldwide basis at daunting speed.

The Nevada gambling industry, not unlike the music industry, is resisting the expansion of the market for gambling through the Internet technologies. This represents a missed opportunity for the industry. What emerges as a sweeping concern for nations around the world is the realization that the technological innovations that made online gambling as an industry possible targets segments of the population that are most at risk for pathological gambling. For policymakers, the challenge is to address the negative societal impact of pathological gambling while asserting its responsibility to regulate, tax, and supervise gambling online.

NOTES

1. Alcohol and alcoholism have widespread ramifications, to be sure. Law enforcement and the criminal justice system grapple with the violence and criminal behavior produced by chemical dependencies on alcohol. Families are torn apart by alcoholism. Religious institutions, social organizations, and the business communities struggle with the destructive impact of alcoholism throughout society.

2. Pathological behavior is, at times, encouraged by national policy. Consider the peculiar development in France, where, in a misguided attempt to be overly generous in providing health care to the French, France has become a nation where the consumption of prescription medications is the highest in the world. Overmedication itself contributes to health problems, of course, while creating sweeping distortions throughout the French economy.

3. If we were governed by rationality exclusively, most cost-benefit analyses would rule out having children. Fortunately, there is no monetary value attached to the pleasure we derive from loving our children, which is why we are happy to have them, even if, in pure economic terms, it is a dubious undertaking, one filled with many risks and no guarantee of success.

4. Cornell economist Robert Frank is wise to offer narrow and specific policy recommendations from the editorial pages of the *New York Times* for if he were more vocal in advocating specific policies, he would appear partisan. MIT economist Paul Krugman, on the other hand, has stepped on not a few land mines in his twice-weekly column in the *New York Times,* suggesting there are such things as too much publicity and quality suffers when there are deadlines to put out columns. Indeed, during the presidential race of 2000,

I joked with colleagues that Krugman's column should have been renamed from "Reckonings" to "Biases."

5. The merits of his views are not at question, but rather it is the idea that an economist should dictate specific political actions that raised eyebrows. In his criticism of the international debt crisis that gripped the developing world in the 1980s, Rudiger Dornbusch, for instance, argued that the "IMF set itself up to save the system, organizing banks into a lender's cartel and holding the debtor countries up for a classical mugging." Such rhetoric was as valid as it was stunning, and therein lies the danger for economists who run the risk of telling Emperors they have no clothes. See *Dollars, Debts and Deficits* (Cambridge, Mass.: MIT Press, 1986), p. 140. Lester Thurow is another economist who makes specific policy recommendations that are consistent with a specific political ideology, a fact that diminishes his objectivity to a degree.

6. Private communication, April 1983.

7. Werner Muensterberger, *Collecting: An Unruly Passion,* p. 254.

8. Ibid., p. 13.

9. Ibid., p. 44.

10. Miles Harvey, *The Island of Lost Maps: A True Story of Cartographic Crime,* p. 259.

11. Werner Muensterberger, *Collecting: An Unruly Passion,* p. 6.

12. An intriguing glimpse into the minds of collectors is found by visiting Yahoo!'s directory of collecting sites (http://dir.yahoo.com/Recreation/Hobbies/Collecting/), which lists such collectibles as air sickness bags, lunch boxes, and thimbles.

13. Werner Muensterberger, *Collecting: An Unruly Passion,* p. 254.

14. Gillett G. Griffin, "Collecting Pre-Columbian Art," in *The Ethics of Collecting Cultural Property: Whose Culture? Whose Property?,* ed. Phyllis Mauch Messenger, p. 114.

15. Werner Muensterberger, *Collecting: An Unruly Passion,* p. 47.

16. Psychologist Eric Geffner, a therapist specializing in pathological gambling, explains that compulsive gambling is a medical disorder because the brains of pathological gamblers are physically different under a microscope than those of people who do not gamble. "We call it a hidden disease," he explained in Barbara Jamison-Estrada's article, "Gambling: The New American Landscape," because unlike other pathological addictions, such as alcoholism, pathological gambling is "difficult to identify."

17. National Gambling Impact Study Commission Report Recommendations, June 1999. See Chapter 4, "Problem and Pathological Gambling," and Chapter 5, "Internet Gambling."

18. The entire NGISC Report is available online at http://www.ngisc.gov/index.html.

19. The lottery for the State of New Mexico (http://nmlottery.com) was typical in its condemnation of the NGISC Report. "As with any broad-based study, there are findings with which we agree and some with which we disagree," David Miller, New Mexico lottery chief executive officer, said. "Although New Mexico has a relatively new state lottery, we have been cognizant of society's concerns and have addressed them responsibly and with the toughest legislative oversight and scrutiny by our board of directors," he continued, noting

that "New Mexicans with questions or concerns about any aspect of problem gambling have been able to call a toll-free number that reaches counselors at a multi-state mental health and addiction information center." He concluded by warning that "[f]ederal involvement is not necessary in the day-to-day operations of a quasi-private/quasi-government agency charged with raising funds through a low-stake entertainment process."

20. John Hill and Gary Palmer, "Going for Broke: The Economic and Social Impact of a South Carolina Lottery," South Carolina Policy Council Education Foundation, March 2000. The authors characterized public debate in South Carolina as driven by politics. "The lottery is not a harmless form of entertainment as hyped by South Carolina politicians," they noted. "[The lottery] comes with real costs for society and taxpayers." The entire report is available by accessing http://www.scpolicycouncil.com.

21. Personal communication, October 31, 2000.

22. An earlier measure in the U.S. Senate, sponsored by Jon Kyle, Republican of Arizona, passed on a voice vote in November 1999.

23. Amy Harmon, "'Casino Mentality' Linked to Day Trading's Stresses," *New York Times,* August 1, 1999.

24. "Stress, Anxiety & Why Gamblers Gamble," *The Wager* 5, no. 27. Also available online at http://www.thewager.org.

25. "In late November [1998], the North American Securities Administrators Association Inc., which consists of all state and provincial regulators in the United States, Canada and Mexico," Gretchen Morgenson wrote, " warned investors against day trading, calling it a form of gambling, not investing." See "Day Trading Not Usually Worth Risk," *New York Times,* July 31, 1999.

26. J.A. Thorson, F.C. Powell, and M. Hilt, "Epidemiology of Gambling and Depression in an Adult Sample," *Psychological Reports* 74, pp. 987–999.

27. Matt Richtel, "Bettors Find Online Gambling Hard to Resist," *New York Times,* March 29, 2001. For instance, this was one of the newspaper articles to report on the dire circumstances associated with pathological gambling online. "A novice gambler," Matt Richtel reported, "she started playing slot machines over the Internet in February. When her spree ended . . . she . . . contemplated plunging her Grand Am, and herself, into the Pacific [Ocean]."

28. Marvin Matises, "Send Ethnographers into New-SKU Jungle," *Brandweek,* September 25, 2000, pp. 32–34.

29. Pathological gambling is classified as an impulse-control disorder (ICD) in which gamblers display criteria for bipolar, manic, hypomanic disorder or cyclothymia. For more information, see "Impulsivity, Personality Disorders and Pathological Gambling Severity," *Addiction* 93 (6), pp. 895–905.

30. No payment for any travel, transportation, hotel, meals, and expenses on my behalf were accepted. As with any other company mentioned in this book, no endorsement is made or implied, and I have no financial interest in any of the companies mentioned.

31. Lost souls are found the world over: Cancun has a permanent population of American expatriates who spend their retirement pensions drinking.

32. The most significant socioeconomic factor contributing to this observation is based on the median household income of a gambler on holiday in

Las Vegas and that of the household incomes of consumers who play state-run lotteries.

33. Proponents point out that deferring the collection of sales taxes on e-commerce transactions constitutes a tax break that will encourage investment in and development of Internet technologies. Others further point out that mail-order businesses are also exempt from collecting sales taxes in states other than where they are physically located; if L.L. Bean hasn't driven Eddie Bauer out of business, they maintain, there's no reason to believe that an e-commerce company will drive Federated Stores out of business.

34. Gretchen Morgenson, "S.E.C. Says Teenager Had After-School Hobby: Online Stock Fraud," *New York Times*, September 21, 2000.

35. Online gambling is growing at an annual rate of 25 percent per year. By 2010, it is expected to be a $150 billion industry in the United States. For comparative purposes, consider that in 2000 all forms of gambling in the United States—casino, sports, lottery, and illegal—were estimated to approximate $500 billion in total wagers.

36. Tom Grey quote from http://www.ncalg.org/pages/conf_working.htm.

37. D.C. Reitzes and J. Boles, "Exploring the Links between Gambling, Problem Gambling and Self-Esteem," *Deviant Behavior: An Interdisciplinary Journal 18*, pp. 321–342.

38. R.A. Volberg and M.W. Abbott, "Gambling and Problem Gambling Among Indigenous Peoples," in *Substance Use & Misuse* 32 (11), pp. 1525–1538.

39. This statute can be found online at http://caselaw.findlaw.com/scripts/ts_search.pl?title=18&sec=1084.

40. Recent efforts to quantify the social costs of pathological gambling consist of attempts to put a price on the employment-related costs, bad debts, thefts, police and judicial costs, and health and welfare expenses. In "The Social Costs of Gambling in Wisconsin," *Wisconsin Policy Research Institute Report* 9 (6), pp. 1–44, W.N. Thompson, R. Gazel, and D. Rickman put the cost, per problem gambler, at $9,468.72 in 1996.

41. "American Indians Eye the Internet for Casino Growth." Available online at http://www.casinos-gambling.com/n16.htm.

42. Marc Braunstein and Edward Levine, *Deep Branding on the Internet*, p. 69.

43. For an inexplicable reason, Marc Braunstein and Edward Levine mistake sound marketing and brand development for some sort of science experiment. Good brands, they write, are the product of "heat and pressure applied over time." This is a recipe for making lots of charcoal and a few diamonds, but brands?

44. Thomas Frank continues, "and it was the job of account planners to monitor and study the brand's relationship with us in its every detail. As corporate figures of every kind were learning to understand markets as the ultimate democratic form, as an almost perfectly transparent medium connecting the people with their corporation, Planners functioned, or believed they functioned, as interpreters of and advocates for the popular will." Thus "Account Planners" become the high priests of the New Economy, or so, Frank

ridicules in *One Market under God: Extreme Capitalism, Market Populism, and the End of Economic Democracy,* published by Doubleday in 2000.

45. Despite a $21 million advertising campaign in 2000, Pets.com ceased taking orders on November 10, 2000, and commenced liquidating its assets, making it, at that time, one of the largest publicly traded online retailers to go out of business.

46. "Death of a Spokespup," *Brandweek,* December 11, 2000, p. 42.

47. Marc Braunstein and Edward Levine, *Deep Branding on the Internet,* p. 76.

48. Matt Richtel, "The Casino on the Desktop," *New York Times,* March 29, 2001.

49. "In a sharp reversal, several of Las Vegas' most powerful casinos no longer want to ban Internet gambling, and some are starting Web sites and exploring technology that could eventually offer wagering in homes, offices or anywhere there is a computer wired into cyberspace," Matt Richtel reported in the *New York Times* on May 17, 2001. Noting that some "politicians and industry analysts have a more skeptical view of the casinos' motives, asserting that the casinos are seeking to control a lucrative field that they have realized they cannot legislate out of existence," Matt Richtel reported how reluctantly the Nevada gambling industry had begun to capitulate to a technology it could no longer ignore. See "Las Vegas Casinos Shift Stand, Backing Internet Wagering," by Matt Richtel, *New York Times,* May 17, 2001.

CHAPTER 10

PORNOGRAPHY FOR EVERYONE

To understand how the pornography economy online works, it is first necessary to understand why the ivory trade threatened the very existence of elephants and why tour operators to the Galapagos Islands have little difficulty filling their tours. The economic idea that describes the demand for online pornography, poached ivory, and ecotours to the Galapagos Islands is called *price elasticity of demand*. A brief digression is in order before we can discuss the pornographic economy online intelligently.

Soon after Cathay Pacific introduced service between San Francisco and Hong Kong, I flew across the Pacific on one of their flights. I spent a few days in Hong Kong before continuing on to Bangkok, Thailand. While exploring both cities on pedestrian strolls, I was struck by the quantity, both in variety of offerings and sheer abundance, of ivory carvings. What intrigued me most, however, was the pricing for ivory. In both Hong Kong and Bangkok, I queried merchants about the *uniformity* of high prices I had observed. One of them explained that "no matter what we charge, we can always sell our entire inventory every year. It is true that prices have risen rapidly this decade, but that has not had an impact at all on sales."

A few years later I traveled to the Galapagos Islands. Others who went on the same journey were divided into the well intentioned and the well heeled, or both. For some, traveling to the Galapagos was a bold affirmation of their concern for nature, endangered species, and natural history. (Charles Darwin, developing his theory of evolution, visited the Galapagos Islands when the *Beagle* sailed there in 1835.) For others, traveling to these desolate islands in the Pacific Ocean off the coast of Ecuador was a matter of status, something one could boast about at cocktail parties upon returning home.

Trips to the Galapagos are limited to a certain number of visitors, one measure intended to protect the islands as a sustainable habitat for the endemic species. Over the course of the trip, one of the scientists operating this tour mentioned that he was surprised by the simple fact that, though they had raised their prices recently by a considerable amount, bookings had not trailed off at all. "It doesn't matter what we charge, it seems," she said, "because we are completely booked for the entire season. And to think we were afraid that a price increase was going to result in our having trouble filling all the spaces."

Economists have long been curious to understand how the demand for a good or service fluctuates in response to changes in the price of that good or service. The elasticity of demand for a good or service determines the range within which prices will fluctuate within the short term. This phenomenon is known as the price elasticity of demand, which is defined as the percentage change in quantity demanded divided by the percentage change in price.

Consider Figure 10.1. When the cost of a good or service is P_1, the quantity sold is Q_1. If the price suddenly drops to P_2, the quantity sold increases to Q_2. This is an idea that everyone understands instinctively: If the cost of those high-tech scooters drop from $99 to $29, then a considerably greater number of youngsters will be scooting around parks, in playgrounds, throughout pedestrian walkways, and on city sidewalks. How consumers respond to change in prices affects our lives every day, of course, and not just on discretionary items for our children. Supermarket managers, for instance, know that when broccoli goes on sale, they will sell much greater quantities than they normally do otherwise.

In the examples provided, however, just how much does the price of a scooter or a pound of broccoli have to drop before quantities sold increase coincidentally? And is there a point where it no longer makes sense to drop prices further? Is there an optimal price that would generate enough demand to sell the entire inventory on hand? The answers to these questions are important because it helps create efficient markets: goods and services are priced optimally to the demand that can be generated in a sustainable manner.[1]

There are certain factors that impact price elasticity of demand. These consist of availability of substitutes or complements, relative prices of competitors, whether the good or service is a necessity or a luxury, personal characteristics of consumers, and the time perspective of purchases. If the price of Coke skyrockets, there's always Pepsi.

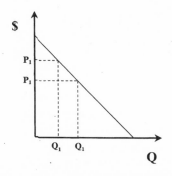
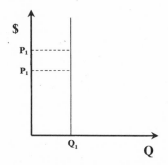

In the chart on the left, when price falls from P₁ to P₂, the quantities—and total revenues—increase from Q₁ to Q₂. This is a graphic representation of what consumers know instinctively: the lower the price of an item, the more likely it is to sell in greater quantities. Price elasticity, then, measures how sensitive consumers are to the price of a good or service. The chart on the right, however, represents a good or service that is price inelastic, meaning that a change in the price does not affect the quantity sold. Elephant ivory during the 1970s was a product which, regardless of how much the price rose, all available supply sold. As a result, both the Asian and African elephants became endangered species. In the discussion presented in this book, the revenues generated by online sales of adult entertainment are consistent with a price inelastic commodity. As a consequence, pornographers know that this price inelasticity allows them to engage in "dynamic pricing," which is a method of maximizing revenue by charging a premium price given that consumers are insensitive to price increases.

Figure 10.1   Price Elasticity vs. Price Inelasticity

If one airline raises its fares between New York and London, there are many other carriers competing on that route. If the price of Beluga caviar becomes exorbitant, then one can readily live without it. If a passenger has time on his hands, he may care about paying a premium to take a taxi when the bus will do. If one won't arrive home until after Christmas, then one can take advantage of sales by waiting until December 26 to shop for some gifts.[2]

What happens, however, when demand does not conform to these expectations? Recall the desperate parents who paid hundreds of dollars for Beanie Babies from scalpers when the suggested retail price was just few dollars at a toy store, or concert-goers who pay ten times the face value of a ticket to attend a specific performance. What ivory sellers in the 1980s in Hong Kong and Bangkok and ecotour operators to the Galapagos Islands in the 1990s observed, with some bafflement, was the phenomenon of situations in which demand is indifferent to the prices.

Economists are aware that there are instances when demand for the product or service is indifferent to the cost. The graph denotes a situation in which the quantity sold is the same, regardless of whether the cost of the product or service is P_1 or P_2. Economists, such as Milton Friedman, for the most part, are satisfied to note such observations and do not say much more than, "Isn't that interesting?"[3] Others, such as Kenneth Galbraith, however, take a dimmer, proactive view and are quick to consider price inelasticity of demand in moral and ethical terms.

It is not necessary to point out that pornography, as a consumer industry, has numerous detractors who take offense expressly on moral and religious grounds. Economists often look at decisions about morality as instances that can be best understood as situations in which consumer choices are characterized by price inelasticity of demand. Before addressing the contentious commodity of pornography, let us first put these arguments in perspective by considering the moral arguments against price inelasticity observed in the worldwide market for ivory.

Throughout the 1960s the price for raw ivory fluctuated between $3 and $10 per pound. During this decade new manufacturing technologies were developed and refined that made it possible to produce, on a mass scale, ivory carvings. What had once been sculptures made one by one were now transformed into machine-made collectibles produced in factories. One result was that ivory carvings were no longer status symbols for the wealthy, but easily within the grasp of ever-larger numbers of consumers around the world.

Asian cultures have historically prized ivory carvings because they are signs of social status and wealth. With the greater availability of ivory carvings, moreover, in short order connoisseurs throughout the Middle East, Western Europe, and North America were eager to begin their own collections of ivory carvings. Prices thus began to rise steadily. By 1975 one pound of raw ivory had risen to $50. Twelve years later it had tripled to $150. The rise in consumer demand during the 1970s resulted in the fact that all the ivory that came on the market in any given year found ready buyers.

Ivory, however, is not like most other products. If the sale of scooters rises from one thousand to one million, for instance, manufacturers can dedicate another manufacturing plant to produce them. But ivory comes from elephants—which cannot be manufactured. In fact, throughout the 1970s and 1980s the demand for ivory continued to rise with such speed that the Asian (*Elephas maximus*) and African (*Loxodonta africana*) elephants became endangered species.[4] Listed in the Convention on International Trade in Endangered Species (C.I.T.E.S.), the number of African elephants was halved from 1.3 million in 1979 to 600,000 in 1989. It was then that alarmed world leaders enacted a global ban on the commercial trade in ivory that went into effect immediately.

The outcry over the carnage of elephants around the world had been presented in moral terms by conservationists. The outrage was such that the ban proved effective; few were willing to violate the ivory ban for humanity had been sufficiently shamed. By the late 1990s, some elephant populations had been replenished in the wild; conservationists expressed concern that elephant herds had grown too large and that, in certain countries, there were too many elephants. In 1997, for instance, Zimbabwe's elephant population was estimated at 65,000, or twice what that nation's ecosystem could hold in a sustainable way.

There was an instructive paradox at work here. Technological innovations in manufacturing had created a demand for ivory carvings that could not be sustained without threatening the very existence of elephants. The other consideration was that a total ban on the commercial trade in ivory created an overpopulation of elephants in the wild, a situation that put other species at risk for it upset the natural ecosystems of various habitats throughout Africa and in India, Sri Lanka, Thailand, and Sumatra.

The situation was further complicated by the use of moral—and not economic—arguments. When David Barritt, African director of the International Fund for Animal Welfare (I.F.W.A.) described the situation in the late 1990s by saying, "We're looking at greedy businessmen,"[5] he showed both a vigorous sense of moral outrage and an appalling lack of understanding of the fundamental laws of economics.

Barritt objected strenuously to the sale proposed by Zimbabwe, South Africa, and Congo of stockpiled ivory in their government warehouses.[6] These three nations had petitioned the C.I.T.E.S. in 1997 to allow them to sell 30 tons of ivory in government warehouses annually to Japan in order to satisfy the consumer demand for ivory. Barritt nonetheless objected, arguing that because it is impossible to determine the provenance of ivory on the world markets, should C.I.T.E.S. authorize the sale of the stockpiled ivory by these three African nations, it would unleash illegal poaching. "If we fail to keep the worldwide ban in place," he said, "the elephants of Africa are imperiled."[7]

"Greed" is an unfortunate word if for no other reason than the simple fact that what we are confronting is a situation in which a specific economic phenomenon—price inelasticity of demand—creates a curious situation. Unlike ecotours to the Galapagos Islands, coveted tickets to rock concerts, or toy fads during Christmas, however, in certain situations morality takes center stage.[8] It is, in fact, by appealing to our passions, our sense of decency, and our concern for the welfare of other species that the world community is moved to come together, agree on a ban in the ivory trade, and enforce it with such rigor that elephant populations around the world rebounded.

The same sense of outrage and passion that saved the elephant is seen when pornography is denounced. But if a technological innovation in *manufacturing* created a crisis for the elephant, it is technological innovations in *communications* that has created a series of markets that together constitute a pornography economy online.

Whereas in the real world, pornography is subject to the traditional concern of manufacturing and distributing, the online economy circumvents these obstacles through technology innovations.[9] In the same way that the mass manufacture of ivory carvings made it feasible for people everywhere around the world to covet what had previously been beyond their economic reach, the Internet has created a pornographic economy online that defies the price elasticity of demand characteristic by making it a product characterized by price *in*elasticity.

Consider once more Figure 10.1 that depicts the price elasticity of demand. Prior to the Internet, the market for pornography was one in which demand was not particularly sensitive to price. Consumers were prepared to pay a premium to get what they wanted. Hugh Hefner built his empire by selling fantasies about sex, potency, and a certain virile lifestyle, which he personified. As we shall see in this chapter, because only so many magazines could be displayed in any newsstand and because of restrictions on the sale of adult material, the supply was limited. Not unlike ivory carvings, only a certain amount of pornography could be manufactured, packaged, distributed in any given year, or in any given jurisdiction.

Whereas the world community could ban the commercial trade in ivory, democratic countries around the world, however, cannot prohibit commerce in pornography.[10] One reason for this is that, given a limited supply, price does not curb demand; when it comes to sex, people are prepared to pay whatever it takes to get what they want. Adult entertainment online, however, can increase the supply, theoretically, infinitely. That the technology of the Internet makes the efficient distribution possible also increases by quantum leaps the supply of ever more specific fetishes and deviant sexual practices available.[11] This is why in 2001 the pornographic economy online constituted a $20 billion market. Adult entertainment online is, without a doubt, the most lucrative market on the Internet.

The rise of the availability of pornography in our lives has alarmed many. When Barritt described commercial trade in ivory in terms of "greedy businessmen" he did a disservice. Instead of addressing the market peculiarities of specific commodities for which demand is price inelastic, he framed the discussion in terms of emotion and not reason. Critics of the pornographic economy online often favor this approach, presenting their arguments in terms of morality and the social ills engendered by obscenity. The civic stage is filled with men and women debating the merits of pornography and how its negative impacts can be mitigated while not compromising our commitment to free speech.

In his authoritative discussion of how the media's use of crime as entertainment impacts the public and affects the criminal justice system, for instance, Ray Surrette decries the ability of pornography to normalize "aggression towards women for some men in sexual and other interpersonal encounters and increasing the tolerance for aggression toward women in the larger culture."[12]

Although pornography can lead to disorders when one becomes obsessed and addicted to the stimulation it offers, as we shall see, pathological disorders can arise from anything. It is therefore inappropriate to approach an examination of the pornographic entertainment economy online from a moralistic perspective. Why people want what they want and whether they should want what they want are not the concerns of economists. Instead of entering into polemics that are inevitable when religious, moral, and ethical approaches are therefore applied to social issues, economists prefer to adhere to the neutrality of the price elasticity of demand.

Armed with a fundamental understanding of the price elasticity of demand, it is clear that the stellar growth of the pornography economy online is a value-neutral phenomenon, one that has little to do with morality and much to do with the nature of economics. This realization is fortuitous for it permits us, unlike our predecessors who were inclined to pontificate, to engage in an objective and dispassionate analysis of the most profitable segment of the entertainment economy ever created.

RECOGNIZING THE ECONOMICS OF PORNOGRAPHY WHEN YOU SEE IT

Things begin to come together now, and the ideas introduced reinforce each other in splendid ways. Recall that in explaining the proliferation of violence and sexual themes in music, music videos, and entertainment, I argued that that was an instance in which a specific market imperfection resulted in the proliferation of choices we do not want. As we shall see, the same characteristics of the worldwide demand for ivory that brought the African and Asian elephants to the brink of extinction, now forces pornography on the Internet to operate essentially in the same fashion.

When one throws into this equation (1) the legal framework that offers constitutional protection to pornographic material, and (2) technological innovations that confer privacy to activities that previously carried significant social stigmas, then all the ingredients are ready for an explosive recipe. There is an undeniable correlation in the psychology, emotion, and values that define how pornography as an industry operates in contemporary societies. Indeed, in order to understand better how these perspectives come together to flesh out a comprehensive portrait of pornography on the Internet, let us examine the key distinct components of this pornographic economy online.

HISTORY OF PORNOGRAPHY IN AMERICA

St. Augustine defined certain ideas about the world that continue to impact how human beings live their lives. In his *Confessions,* perhaps the most influential religious autobiography in Christianity, he presented a worldview that reverberates to this day. "Not in rioting and drunkenness, not in chambering and impurities, not in contention and envy, but put ye on the Lord Jesus Christ and make not provision for the flesh in its concupiscence," he said, quoting a verse from the Epistle to the Romans in the New Testament.

The imperative of this statement was one of the defining influences in his life. In his teachings, he argued that in order for men and women to attain a state of grace, they had to renounce the material world. For human beings to give in to the temptations of the flesh was a form of evil. That our bodies consist of living matter from which we derive pleasure through sex is itself a source of corruption, according to St. Augustine. Sex itself was not evil, of course, but taking undo pleasure from it made us unclean before God. These ideas influenced centuries of Christians throughout Europe. The early Protestants who settled in the New World embraced the austerity of these ideas, for it celebrated modesty and humility.

That "puritanical" has become an adjective widely used to describe individuals advocating modesty and restraint is derived from the philosophical agreement of the Puritans with the teachings of St. Augustine on sexual matters. Although sex was recognized as crucial to creating the bond of intimacy in the institution of marriage, the Puritans frowned upon acts that cheapened and devalued what they believed should exist only in moderation and only between a married couple.

The American colonists were few in number, and it was a rather easy matter to regulate social conformity in small, rural communities. This kind of regulation of society's mores became impossible as immigrants arrived in New England and the beliefs of the various people grew more diverse. In time, however, the economic prosperity that made the American colonies successful brought ever greater numbers of immigrants from other areas of Europe and the world, and made it more difficult to regulate what people would do, say, think, or distribute.

It is therefore amusing that a strong and convincing case can be made that, in fact, the first pornographer in the American Colonies was none other than Benjamin Franklin. In 1745, the ribald revolutionary-to-be wrote an essay that was so notorious its publication was banned altogether.

"Advice to a Young Man on Choosing a Mistress," in which one finds the immortal line "and lastly—they are so grateful," was published in England and smuggled back into the American colonies. Whatever scandalous, obscene, and pornographic material made their ways to the colonial cities of New York, Boston, Philadelphia, and Washington was done on an ad hoc and informal basis, mostly from seaman arriving from other ports.[13] In keeping with the Puritan worldview of their founding settlers, the American colonies—and subsequently the United States—conducted its civic life consistent with the moral teachings of St. Augustine, at least, where pornographic material was concerned.

It was not until the mid-1800s that pornographic material began to circulate openly in the United States. Rank and file soldiers in both the Union and Confederate armies consumed pornography in unprecedented quantities and varieties. That young men expected to have pornography as a fundamental diversion in their lives challenged the prevailing mores of American society in the second half of the nineteenth century. It was a scandalous idea, one that moralists pointed to when they denounced the evils armed conflict had on civilian society.

The public outcry was such that the Young Men's Christian Association (Y.M.C.A.) was compelled to spearhead an antiobscenity campaign, working to stamp out "degeneracy" among young men in Reconstruction America. The Y.M.C.A. lobbied legislators to pass laws to protect children and women from exposure to pornographic materials. Walter Kendrick reports that one man, Anthony Comstock, was so passionate in his outrage over pornography that he was successfully recruited by the Y.M.C.A. to help persuade Congress to outlaw the sale and distribution of obscene material in 1865.[14]

Comstock had the gift of oratory, and he put it to effective and persuasive use. He saw himself as the moral guardian of American virtue, and he convinced enough other people that this was his mission in life with such passion that in 1873 he was appointed special agent of the U.S. Post Office once the Comstock Law, named to honor his tenacity, was enacted.[15] This allowed him the legal authority to carry out his own agenda—which he did for 42 years—in which he attempted to impose his puritanical ideas on the whole of society.[16]

With inexplicable energy and enthusiasm, Comstock, who gave American vernacular the term "Comstockery," emerged as the most powerful moral censor in the history of the United States. His work continued well into the twentieth century. This had the effect of making pornography scarce—and that much more desirable because of its illegal nature. That the nation's morality was safeguarded by preventing the U.S. Post Office from delivering obscene material worked well as long as the nation was largely rural and disjointed across the continent. The establishment of networks, however, changes everything for it alters how things are distributed. In the same way that seamen smuggled smut into the American Colonies, once the U.S. Post Office's monopoly on transportation ended, so did the effectiveness of the Comstock Law that then prevailed.

Sociologists Marshall Clinard and Robert Meier summarize Anthony Comstock's work:

> In the United States there was little enforcement of either state or federal obscenity laws until about 1870, after the passage in 1865 of the first mail obscenity act, and, in New York, after legislation enacted to prohibit the dissemination of obscene literature. Enforcement of existing statutes increased largely because of the efforts of one man, Anthony Comstock . . . this crusader became a special agent of the Post Office in charge of enforcing the law. States with no previous obscenity legislation passed their own laws, and by the end of the century some form of general prohibition on the dissemination of "obscene" materials was on the statute books of at least 30 states.[17]

A crusading zealot and laws on the books slowed down the emergence of pornography as an industry, but it did not stop it. Attorney and author Frederick Lane, in fact, argued that:

> Each new development [in transportation technology] had the pleasant effect for pornographers of lowering the overall cost of distribution and offering less risky alternatives to the use of the U.S. mails. Most railroads and steamboat companies, for instance, offered shipping services that were beyond the reach of Comstock's attention, as were the services of privately owned shipping companies. . . . With the advent of the private automobile, it became even easier to ship materials without risking the wrath of the postal inspectors.[18]

As is the case in all other areas of our economic life as a society, the establishment of networks gave impetus to commercial development of pornography as an industry.

WINNER-TAKE-ALL PORNOGRAPHERS

Robert Frank and Philip Cook noted that "in winner-take-all markets . . . pay distributions will be more spread out—often dramatically so—than the underlying distributions of effort and ability."[19] When the industry in question is new, moreover, the pay distributions will be more greatly distorted. Recall how technological innovations in the manufacturing process for ivory carvings greatly expanded the market for ivory products.

The role that sea captains performed for centuries, railroad conductors began to play. Packages with all manner of obscenity were easily transported for a fee from one train stop to the next, all far from the scrutiny of postal authorities. Wherever trains spread, so did the ability to distribute pornographic material. And private shipping companies extended the reach of obscene material even farther, making it possible for everyone to have access to material the U.S. Post Office deemed immoral.

Ideas about morality began to change as well. The Victorian worldview was transformed by the grisly brutality of the new machines of war. World War I unleashed upon humanity machine guns and mass killing of soldiers. The horrors of the conflict that failed to end all wars were immortalized by poets and writers.

The desire of life to engender life clashes with the memory of the death unleashed upon the world at the beginning of spring of 1914. The individual discontent and social cynicism that two world wars— with a Great Depression in between—created was one that fostered a more jaded public. That public, furthermore, consisted of soldiers and veterans who had relied on pornography to pass the time away while on duty.[20] In the same way that scofflaws became folk heroes during Prohibition, the commerce in pornography raised fewer eyebrows. The ability of Comstock Law to legislate morality was greatly reduced, eventually becoming impossible once efficient distribution networks that operated parallel to the U.S. Post Office were in place.

Pornography, then, was ready to become an industry once World War II was safely concluded. That pornography as a commercial enterprise was new meant that the first entrants would secure enviable market positions. That the entire enterprise of commercializing pornography met with social resistance meant that it would become a winner-take-all market, one in which a little talent would result in a disproportionate reward. The United States in the 1950s and 1960s was ready for a winner-take-all contest for the adult magazine industry. This is how Lane describes the ascendance of Hefner in American life:

> The combination . . . of an enormously successful sexual entrepreneur . . . a well-attended sexual revolution, and a steady flow of technological innovations to increase the privacy of pornography consumption have significantly reduced or eliminated much of the stigma attached to pornography.[21]

Hefner's successful *Playboy* was further accelerated by technological innovations.

Color magazines, films, video recordings, telephones, and other forms of private communication made it possible for people to engage in all kinds of private matters that could remain secret. Had it not been for a subpoena from Kenneth Starr, for instance, it is highly likely that

Hillary Clinton would never have found out about her husband's phone sex with a certain White House intern.

Films, video, color printing, and telephones changed how the world communicates. Lane notes that:

> The social impact of these new technologies has been profound. By eliminating inconvenient, potentially embarrassing, and occasionally unnerving trips to urban adult movie theaters, such innovations as cable television, the VCR, and later the CD-ROM have helped the pornography industry to dramatically expand its potential pool of customers. . . . The potential privacy of talking to a phone sex operator or watching an adult movie in one's own living or hotel room has made it a much more palatable activity for millions of people, most of whom would never have considered going to an adult movie theater.[22]

No one was in a better position than to establish a significant market position and come out on top in this winner-take-all contest than the enterprising Hefner. This is how Lane summarizes Hefner's success in the pornographic industry:

> By any objective measure, Hefner's success was stunning: The first issue of *Playboy* in December 1953 sold more than 50,000 copies in a little more than four weeks. At 50 cents an issue, Hefner grossed more than $25,000 in his first month, which enabled him to pay back his investors and still print a second issue. Within two years, he was selling more than 600,000 copies per month. Just 13 years after founding *Playboy* in his living room, Hefner's personal worth crossed the $100 million mark.[23]

Hefner's ability to generate such wealth is a reflection on the inelasticity of demand for sexual titillation. Throughout the 1950s and 1960s, as the dominant supplier, *Playboy* was in a position to increase prices steadily and still sell the entire supply. Not unlike bewildered conservationists who were astounded at the speed with which the African and Asian elephants became endangered, social critics throughout the second half of the twentieth century were stunned at the proliferation of pornography in American society.[24]

Hefner's *Playboy* had one major competitor, Bob Guccione's *Penthouse*. Together these men had a virtual duopoly on the pornographic entertainment industry in the United States, which would not be challenged until Al Goldstein and Larry Flynt, whose respective magazines, *Screw* and *Hustler,* broadened the market by publishing more graphic material. It would take two developments to transform adult entertainment into a truly mass market. The first would establish the legal basis for pornography to exist as a legitimate business. The other would be a series of technological innovations that ended the duopoly of *Play-boy* and *Penthouse*—and with it the winner-take-all contest outcome of the industry—by transforming it into an online entertainment economy. In order to understand how pornography has become such an integral part of the entertainment choices adults have, let us first consider the legal status of pornographic entertainment.

THE LEGAL PROTECTION FOR PORNOGRAPHY

In 1973, the U.S. Supreme Court in *Miller v. California* established the legal standard that provided the foundation for pornography as an industry. It would, however, take two more decades before technological innovations made it feasible for the court's decision to engender the pornographic economy online. In that decision, the Supreme Court weighed in on how obscenity was to be defined under American law. The standard the court defined the standard for obscene as:

> (a) whether the average person, applying contemporary community standards would find that the work, taken as a whole, appeals to the pru-rient interest; (b) whether the work depicts or describes, in a patently offensive way, sexual conduct specifically defined by the applicable state law; and (c) whether the work, taken as a whole, lacks serious literary, artistic, political, or scientific value.[25]

The legal conclusion that for pornography to be obscene it had to offend the "average person, applying contemporary community standards," resulted in a fragmentation of the consumer market for this material.

Imagine if every community issued its own currency for "community standards"; businesses have to know the "exchange rates" in each jurisdiction. What offends community standards in a rural community in the Midwest is a different question altogether in New York.[26] As a consequence, throughout the 1970s and 1980s there was a proliferation of pornography catering to diverse interests and countless community standards. Adult material published by *Playboy* and *Penthouse* could be easily marketed throughout the United States; *Screw* and *Hustler* had to struggle to expand their retail distribution network because their material offended many consumers. Pornography that catered to more narrow sexual interests gave rise to an array of products for these niche markets.

Market barriers separated producers and consumers, such as the stigma of being seen in unsavory, red light districts to secure these products sold in hard-core adult stores and were the major factor that prevented the market from expanding. "We had so many problems getting our product to customers," Goldstein said, echoing the concerns voiced by other pornographers from the 1970s and 1980s. "The last thing a middle-class man wanted was to be seen by someone coming out of an adult bookstore. And the national chains refused to carry our stuff. Anyone can walk in to a 7-Eleven and pick up *Playboy,* a pack of cigarettes and a stick of gum, but to get my magazine, it was an effort."[27]

Two years later, Sony Corporation introduced the videocassette recorder, and pornography moved quickly from the seedy red light districts to the privacy of one's home. Publishers became producers of films, and the market for adult entertainment exploded; in 1970, the federal government estimated the market for hard-core pornography at $10 million annually in the United States. Thirty years later, hard-core pornography on the Internet alone was estimated at $2 billion.[28]

Technology was the catalyst that transformed a *$10 million* market into a *$2 billion* one in the span of one generation. That consumers of sexual persuasions and of all sexual interests could indulge their interests without running the risk of stigma surrounding pornography was fundamental. Videos made pornography a mass-market industry. Lane reports that the release of *Deep Throat* in 1973 generated $100 million in sales for its producer Gerard Damiano. The film cost $25,000 to make.

Any market where such astounding rates of return are possible invites competitors. The traditional barriers to entry into the market (in the form of difficulties to widespread distribution to customers) had been rendered immaterial by technological innovations. "It was so frustrating," Goldstein recalled. "I spent a fortune securing the rights of Americans to have the material they want, and then they invent video cameras and everyone can become a player in the industry. Is that an ironic twist?"[29]

If the VCR overcame the barriers that had prevented pornography from becoming mass-market, there was still the occasional risk of being seen in the adult section of the video store. In 1999, Adult Video News reported that Americans rented 711 million hard-core sex films, which translates to 2.5 videos per capita, considered a remarkably low figure by people in the industry.

This indicated that not only was there tremendous potential to grow the market, but also that the last remaining barrier, specifically criminal prosecution for shipping obscene material across state lines, had to be addressed. Indeed, the mosaic of community standards made it a risky proposition to send materials across some state lines. Kink Video in San Francisco, which specializes in gay fetish films, for instance, refuses to ship its videos to about a dozen states. "Some states in the South are too risky," says Tony Top. "We're not going to ship anything where the material is illegal. How do we know the person at the other end is not a law enforcement official?"[30]

The next set of technological innovations—cable programming and the Internet—gave impetus to the market forces that greatly expanded the market for pornographic entertainment. Through pay-per-view and Internet sex sites, the entire market exploded in the mid-1990s. *Wall Street Journal* reporter Thomas Weber noted in 1997 that:

> Cyberporn is fast becoming the envy of the Internet. While many other Web outposts are failing, adult sites are taking in millions of dollars a month. Find a Web site that is in the black and, chances are, its business and content are distinctly blue. That has legions of entrepreneurs rushing to cash in, from former phone-sex marketers gone digital to new-media mavens to a onetime stripper whose thriving Web site brings in so much revenue that she has given up the stage and nude photo shoots.[31]

Three years later the *New York Times* took notice, reporting that "[s]purred by changes in technology that make pornography easier to order into the home than pizza . . . the business of selling sexual desire through images has become a $10 billion annual industry in the United States."[32] The market continues to expand in giant leaps, grossing around $190 million in pay-per-view programs and almost $4.8 billion in videos.

PORNOGRAPHY AS AN ONLINE BUSINESS

Now that we have surveyed the evolution of pornography as a consumer market in the United States, we can discuss with confidence how the Internet has greatly expanded this industry. The growth of pornography as an online industry is consistent with the trends in American society. Internet technologies are only one of the developments that have made possible the rapid expansion of pornography as an online business. The other two components are the deregulation of telephone services, which makes it possible to reach a mass market in a cost-effective manner, and the exemplary entrepreneurship of pornographers who have been at the cutting edge of marketing and salesmanship.

The perspective offered by a distance in time affords a more precise understanding of the social issues surrounding pornography in American culture. Discussing the matter, consider the how the Commission appointed by Lyndon Johnson approached this matter from the perspective of public policy:

The Commission believes that much of the "problem" regarding materials that depict explicit sexual activity stems from the inability or reluctance of people in our society to be open and direct in dealing with
sexual matters. This most often manifests itself in the inhibition of talking openly and directly about sex. Professionals use highly technical
language when they discuss sex; others of us escape by using euphemisms—or by not talking about sex at all. Direct and open conversation about sex between parent and child is too rare in our society. Failure
to talk openly and directly about sex has several consequences. It over-
emphasizes sex, gives it a magical, nonnatural quality, making it more
attractive and fascinating. It diverts the expression of sexual interest out
of more legitimate channels. Such failure makes teaching children and
adolescents to become fully and adequately functioning sexual adults
a more difficult task. And it clogs legitimate channels for transmitting
sexual information and forces people to use clandestine and unreliable
sources.[33]

The report, concluding that federal laws against the distribution of
pornography should be repealed, was submitted to the Johnson White
House in 1970. Thirty years later it is possible to evaluate how the
Commission's recommendations have or have not been implemented
for the sake of the generation born after the Commission's work was
concluded.

There is broad agreement concerning the need to decriminalize sex
laws in order to have a more honest legal system that reflects the diversity of human sexuality. Sociologists Marshall Clinard and Robert
Meier made this point one year after the Johnson Commission issued
its report. Decrying that:

The proliferation of state obscenity statutes coincided with the decline
in the direct influence of the church over community life, the beginnings
of free universal education, and the increase in literacy. . . . As sex has
moved into the mass media, it has taken on a new relevance [that] has
meant that it has entered the area of the politically relevant. This situation has drastically altered the relation between sex and the law. Actually, the law can do little to inhibit sexual behavior when it is desired by
a substantial segment of a society. Where sexual morality has moved
from a degree of public consensus to the private area of consenting
behavior between adults, laws regulating its expression appear to be
antiquated. . . . Those who have studied the operation of sex laws have
maintained that the area regulated by these laws is far too wide and that
only those sex acts that should be punishable are those which involve
the use of force or duress; adults who take advantage of a minor; and
public sex acts.[34]

The market has moved far ahead of the law, moving at Internet-speed
to create a thriving market.

At the beginning of this chapter, I discussed the concept that economists call the price elasticity of demand. For most consumer goods, as the price falls, total revenue increases, for a greater supply is sold. There are a few goods and services—such as ivory carvings and ecotours to the Galapagos Islands—that do not conform to this, simply because the available supply cannot satisfy the demand in the marketplace. Such goods and services are said to be price inelastic.

The reason why this economic tool was introduced into this chapter is because it illuminates the phenomenon observed in the second half of the 1990s. With the emergence of pornography as a mainstream industry, the market has divided into two distinct markets. One market offers conventional pornography, and the other specializes in fetish and perverse material.

Recall for a moment that the tyranny of small decisions resulted in the elimination of choices that made people in a community feel deprived. Technology changes the nature of some markets, especially when it affects barriers to entry of new suppliers and expands greatly the distribution network to reach consumers. If infinite broadband holds the promise of infinite distribution, then supply becomes abundant. It may not be possible to download a piece of ivory from the Internet onto one's home computer, but it certainly is to access pornographic videos, magazines, and graphics online. That pornography is no longer scarce means that the elasticity of demand shifts and behaves like most other consumer products: as price falls, total revenues increase.

This is not the end of the story. When we surveyed the development of gambling on the Internet, it was clear that pathological consumer behavior shaped the development of that industry. The Internet has the ability to bring together like-minded individuals who would otherwise not be able to find each other easily. This means it is possible to have an online community emerge where marginal fetishes thrive. There are, of course, moral and legal questions raised by this ability. It is one thing, for instance, to have a community of individuals who are aroused by tickling finding one another, but what happens when pedophiles can anonymously communicate with each other and traffic in child pornography?

Economists sidestep these questions by simply pointing out that what we have here is a highly segmented consumer market. The two broadest categories of online pornography are "mainstream" and "fetish." Mainstream pornography is quickly becoming saturated (the price elasticity of demand returns curve is consistent with other consumer products). On the other hand, marginal pornography, that which depicts fetishes or illegal sexual interests, emerges as a viable and robust market, one in which the price inelasticity of the demand curve denotes a profitable market. The price inelasticity of fetish desire is one in which the more extreme the market niche (or fetish), the higher the price it demands. As we shall see, there has now been a significant segmentation in the pornographic industry online. The larger market is mainstream sex, i.e. heterosexual, nonkinky, nonviolent sex, which struggles to become a profitable business in the face of fierce competition and oversupply. The other market, consisting of deviant sexual desire, fetish interest, and illegal sexuality (involving children, narcotics, and animals) is resulting in the proliferation of niche Web sites that cater to all manners of perversity—consistent with the Supreme Court's ruling on the fluid definition of obscenity.

At this point it is opportune to address the moral ambiguities surrounding these markets, which is, in effect, a professional disclaimer. Economists are peculiar in that otherwise intelligent people at times display an appalling lack of common sense. Robin Lakoff pointed out that "egghead professors" are likely to be scorned, pitied, and ignored for failing to exhibit a fundamental grasp of how the world works. The reason for this lies in the fact that economists are inclined to look at the larger macroeconomic picture, failing to understand how things work on a microeconomic, which is to say individual, level.

Consider two countries. The Gross National Product (GNP) of both Country A and Country B is $100 per year. Ten people live in Country A, and 10 people live in Country B. On a macroeconomic level, then, both countries are analytically identical. Both Country A and Country B each has a GNP of $100 and a population of 10, meaning that the per capita income is $10 per person annually. Economists, however, are mistaken to conclude that both countries are interchangeable if they fail to look more closely at other facts. What if in Country A, one person makes $12, eight make $10 each, and one person only makes $8. Such a society has a large middle class, with 10 percent of the population living in relative wealth and another 10 percent living in relative poverty. It is, overall, a fairly equitable society where most people enjoy a fair share of what their economy produces. In the real world, Country A would probably be called Switzerland.

Let us say, however, that in Country B, one person makes $90, and each of the remaining nine people make only $1 a piece. This is a society with a dismal distribution of income, where 10 percent of the population has access to 90 percent of the nation's wealth, leaving the overwhelming majority of the people to languish in poverty. In the real world, Country B would be called Haiti or Bangladesh.

Economists, however, step back and insist that, from a macroeconomic perspective, both County A and Country B are identical. This is the infuriating nature of mathematics, how numbers can mislead and deceive. Most economists shrug their shoulders and refuse to take a moral position on the merits of how Country A and Country B go about the business of distributing the economic bounty they produce among their citizens. Milton Friedman is content to state that we should not grant freedom for madmen or children. John Kenneth Galbraith is outraged that Country A and Country B can be compared with each other exclusively on macroeconomic criteria and be pronounced interchangeable. In defending the market economy, Friedman offers argument that the only tenable restriction on individuals is when they are incapable of being responsible individuals. Then again, within the parameters of a market economy, we do believe in freedom for pornographers.

The essence of this proposition has been updated by Alan Greenspan, who, in his comments in Mexico City in mid-November 2000, expressed his concern that a "notable shortfall in economic performance from the exemplary standard of recent years runs the risk of reviving mistrust of market-oriented systems, even among conventional policymakers. Thankfully, such views are not widespread, and most fall quickly to the force of reason."[35]

In other words, those concerned with the microeconomic distribution of wealth within a society will, should there be an economic downturn, exert pressure for government intervention. Even though activists in Seattle and Washington, D.C., challenge the indifference of policymakers to income distribution simply because the 1990s was a period of sustained growth, the globalization of markets will face greater resistance when the United States is in a recession. Gathering storm clouds will darken the continued expansion of the laissez-faire and cavalier development of the online economy.

Of greater importance, as witnessed during the turmoil that engulfed the dot-com world since mid-2000, is how the laws of economic gravity pulled things into place. Profit and loss statements are unforgiving of unworkable business models; a company can bleed so much red ink before its bled dry. By the same token, successful business models that employ new technology soon develop in ways that conform to classical economics. The pornography industry in the entertainment economy online developed successful business models for the Internet.

Rose Robbins has, for many years, been an attorney who has earned my confidence. When I approached her to make introductions to prominent individuals in the pornography industry, she was kind enough to make arrangements. Thus, one evening, I walked over from Casa Casuariana over to Washington Avenue for dinner at Bang, an appropriately named restaurant that was then a swank spot in South Beach.[36] It was here that Robbins introduced me to Goldstein, the outspoken publisher of *Screw* magazine.

The Nixon Justice Department sued Goldstein in 1973 on obscenity charges; the lawsuit was filed in Wichita, Kansas. Goldstein was to be made an example in order to send a clear message to other alleged pornographers. In litigation that wound its way through the legal system, however, Goldstein emerged as a champion for free speech and an advocate of First Amendment rights. If the Nixon White House sought to differentiate between socially acceptable pornography (*Playboy*, *Penthouse*) and outright obscenity (*Screw*, *Hustler*), the lawsuit against Goldstein transformed him into a martyr, galvanizing prurient elements within liberal circles that opposed Nixon. Ultimately defending himself almost bankrupted Goldstein, even though he was subsequently vindicated by the Supreme Court.

In the three decades that he, along with Flynt, has worked to expand the boundaries of free speech, Goldstein has emerged as a leading authority on pornography in America.[37] "This is really a close-knit family," is how he characterized the world of pornographers. "We've been ostracized by society, and that's why we've had to look out for each other. We all know our kids' birthdays and we are friends, even if we compete against each other," he explained.[38]

A week after our dinner, we met again at his condo in Boca Raton. A month after this, he introduced me to over a dozen people in the adult entertainment business over brunch at a trendy restaurant on Santa Monica Boulevard in Los Angeles. The producers, directors, photographers, actors, actresses, writers, and publishers assembled could very well be a middle-aged group of friends getting ready to set off on a drive to Palm Springs for a weekend of golfing. In the conversations that ensued, and in the ones that followed with people involved in the adult entertainment industry in San Francisco and California, certain trends emerged that illuminate the development of the market for pornography in the entertainment economy online. As we shall now see, an examination of pornography online entails both the Internet technology and San Francisco civic values.

MAINSTREAM PORNOGRAPHY AND PRICE ELASTICITY OF DEMAND

As we have seen, the total consumer market for pornographic material continues to expand greatly because technological innovations make distribution possible. The apparent contradiction in this market, since 1998, has been the downward pressure in the prices of mainstream pornography—Web sites that used to charge $29.95 a month now charge $9.95—while there has been an explosion in the Web sites that concentrate on extreme sex, outlaw sex, and fetishes. Of greater consequence, titans throughout corporate America have entered the pornography market.

AT&T Corporation offers hard-core sex to consumers through its Hot Network cable service. A wholly owned subsidiary reaches two-thirds of the 1.5 million hotel rooms throughout the nation that offer pay-per-view pornography to their guests.

Marriott International and Hilton Hotels together provide pornography in over one million of their rooms. General Motors offers pornography to almost 9 million Americans who subscribe to DirecTV, with annual sales surpassing the $200 million mark. Cable companies such as EchoStar, On Command, and LodgeNet provide pornography to their customers. Media conglomerates, including Time Warner and News Corporation, have thriving businesses selling pornography.

Recall in Chapter 3 how we saw externalities at work: When we consider the actions of others in deciding what we do, consumer behavior is changed. When a hotel guest checks in and enters his room, if he sees adult entertainment as one of the amenities offered by the hotel, it becomes a legitimate choice. If other hotel guests presumably demand so much pornography that the hotel offers it as a matter of course (no different than a well-stocked minibar), then it must be socially acceptable. This is not unlike a five-year-old boy who, seeing other kids with Razor scooters, assumes that having one is natural.

In addition to the companies that produce and market pornography, Visa, MasterCard, and American Express generate over $1 billion in revenue from sex-oriented e-commerce charges made by consumers. None of these companies discuss publicly their adult entertainment businesses. "Big business America has come in and taken over the big bucks of the porn industry," Goldstein laments. "It's just another piece of big business. Now *that's* indecent!"

Corporate America is, indeed, awash in the pornography business. The corporate "takeover" of mainstream pornography, however, is precisely the reason why the market now conforms to standard price elasticity of demand. The competition in the market for mainstream sex, which I define as all forms of heterosexual sex and "vanilla" homosexual sex, is so intense, that the few publicly traded companies that specialize in the adult entertainment are experiencing difficulties.[39] Rick Cabaret International (RICK), New Frontier Media (NOOF), and Nuweb Solutions (NWEB) trade on the NASDAQ, where they struggle. RICK and NWEB are penny stocks and throughout 2000 NOOF tumbled for a 52-week high of 12-3/8 to around 2-1/2 in the last quarter of 2000, consistent with the realities of the highly competitive business environment. Playboy Enterprises, in fact, postponed an initial public offering of its online division in November 2000, citing lack of investor enthusiasm for dot-com companies.[40]

This malaise is attributable not to lack of interest in adult entertainment online, but to a saturation of mainstream pornography. Although

Playboy.com reported that the number of page views almost doubled between September 1999 to September 2000, reaching a reported 152.8 million hits in that month alone, the overwhelming choices available for most consumers far exceeded the tame offerings on this premier Web site. After four years, the Playboy Web site only managed to have 65,000 paying subscribers for its "extras"—celebrity nude photos, streaming videos of parties at the Playboy mansion, and access to the magazine's archives. Social critic and novelist Tom Wolfe is not surprised by the acceptance of pornography in American culture. He notes that:

> By 2000 . . . [t]he word "pornography" had disappeared down the memory hole along with "proletariat." Instances of marriages breaking up because of Web-sex addiction were rising in number. . . . In 1999, the year before, this particular kink—sadomasochism—had achieved not merely respectability but high chic, and the word "perversion" had become as obsolete as "pornography" and "proletariat." Fashion pages presented the black leather and rubber paraphernalia as style's cutting edge.[41]

There are dissenters, of course. Writing in the editorial page of the *Wall Street Journal,* Holman Jenkins disagreed. "This is still a pariah business, and you can participate in it or you can participate in mainstream commerce, but you can't do both," he states, ignoring that Wall Street has underwritten the IPOs of three online pornographers and that major mutual funds are institutional investors in the pornographic economy online.[42]

He is correct, however, in pointing out the ambiguity that the Supreme Court has created by defining "obscenity" as a standard that is relative to community standards. Jenkins ponders, "Obscenity law rests on the legislatibility of a certain baseline of taste, what the courts have recognized as 'community standards.' It says we don't want this in our faces."[43] How this might fare in a broadband world, where something that's anywhere is everywhere, would be a thorny issue for the courts to figure out, and maybe they'd throw up their hands and give up.

The new generation of cyber-pornographers have moved far ahead of whatever "community standards" might mean in cyberspace. Consider Flying Crocodile, a Seattle-based online pornography company founded in 1997 by Andrew Edmond, who was 23 years old at the time. Flying Crocodile's flagship property, SexTracker.com, has grown from a $30,000 investment in 1997 to a company with revenues in excess of $20 million in 2000. "We have had to whittle down 250 fetishes and make it a no-brainer for the user to get through the site and consume the product," Edmond explains. "Truth is, it's very complex. Pornography is just as sophisticated and multi-layered as any other marketplace. We operate just like any Fortune 500 company."[44]

In 2001 there are an estimated 60,000 Web sites that comprise the mainstream pornography industry in the entertainment economy online. As competition continues to intensify, the introduction of video-on-demand promises to increase the number of choices consumers have, and the downward pressure on prices and membership dues will continue to fall. When media conglomerates, international hotel chains, and producers "whittle down" and package adult entertainment for mass consumption, the resulting product is bland, mainstream pornography for everyone. The goal of AT&T, Hilton, General Motors, Time Warner, and producers such as Playboy Enterprises, Vivid Entertainment, and Flying Crocodile hope to achieve is to be able to purvey generic adult entertainment in the major categories that interest the average consumer. When AT&T, for instance, agreed to carry Vivid Entertainment's Hot Network on its digital system, the market for pornography expanded overnight. The same drive that expanded the cable market for pornography at the end of the 1990s—Cox Communications, Insight Communications, Hughes Electronics' DirecTV (controlled by General Motors), and Cablevision Systems all became players in the pornography market—is now being used to expand the market for adult entertainment online.

An unregulated market that strives to meet the demands of a market that comprises teenage youths clandestinely downloading adult content, exhausted businessmen spending a night in a hotel room far from home, and an older couple pursuing their own interests, and anyone else for that matter, not only invites additional entrants into the industry, but also creates temptations as competition exerts downward pressure on prices any single company can charge. Total revenue for the industry rises, but that sum is distributed among a greater number of merchants. "The No. 1 complaint we get is that it's not explicit enough," an executive whose company carries the Hot Network explained.[45] If the companies entering the market far exceed the growth in demand, or if a few companies establish a formidable market share, most other companies are relegated to smaller percentages of the total industry revenues.

The trick of the trade for online pornographers is to seduce consumers. This is a difficult thing to accomplish, however. In the musical *Cabaret*, the emcee beckons with "Willkommen, Bienvenue, Welcome. . . . Leave your troubles outside." He then enchants and guides through an entertaining story, all the while cognizant that his goal is to separate the patrons from their money. "A mark, a yen, a buck or a pound," he sings, while the customer orders more drinks—and linger a while longer. When the show is over, and the customers are spent, he bids farewell by pointing out, "Meine Damen und Herren—Mesdames et Messieurs—Ladies and Gentlemen. Where are your troubles now? Forgotten? I told you so. We have no troubles here."

However, that is not to say that the mainstream pornography industry online itself is not without trouble. Technology is the culprit; the fluid nature of jurisdiction over the Internet provides a cover for consumer fraud. In 2000, a quarter of all porn Webmasters were based in Europe, 20 percent in Asia and the remaining 55 percent were in the United States and Canada.[46] Online consumer fraud takes the form of un-authorized charges on an individual's credit cards.

In the most notorious case ever successfully prosecuted in the state of California, Kenneth and Teresa Taves and Dennis Rappaport were ordered by U.S. District Court Judge Audrey Collins to pay $37.5 million in September 2000 for illegally billing customers for subscriptions to visit adult sites on the Internet. "The operators apparently bet that as many as 900,000 consumers billed wouldn't notice the charges or would be too embarrassed to contest them once they found the charges were associated with an adult Web site," Jerry Guidera and Jonathan Friedland reported in the *Wall Street Journal.* "Many of the consumers didn't even own computers, [the Federal Trade Commission] said."[47]

The temptations are too great, particularly during a time when the worldwide market for pornography is growing tremendously simply because of technological innovations. Consumer fraud will grow as new entrants set up shop in the market and as established companies are forced to reduce prices and membership fees in order to remain competitive. This is the natural development of most consumer goods and services.

In relation to the size of the overall market, however, consumer fraud is not epidemic. It is true that the industry is plagued by some unscrupulous merchants who seize upon the fact that some people will not dispute an unauthorized charge out of embarrassment.[48] Since 1995 the most important players in adult entertainment have become Fortune 500 companies, which offers consumers assurances that industry operates aboveboard and that they have greater protections and venues for remedies in disputes.

There is a trade-off to all of this, however. As the production of adult entertainment becomes a corporate enterprise, offerings are standardized. In the course of reviewing the material available over a 20-year period, it is clear that pornography has become a genre, like Westerns or horror films.[49] The kind of mainstream pornography available online conforms to the kind of standardization inevitable when taste is a commodity: ice creams, denim jeans, and toothpaste are offered in easily recognizable choices, and so is genre pornography, such as cheerleaders, lesbian three-ways, kinky vamps, and so on across the spectrum of what corporate America offers.

To be sure, the conformation of mainstream pornography facilitates it being produced, packaged, and marketed, much the same way that standardized cereal products can be branded and marketed nationwide. When an industry matures in this way, however, although it can meet most consumer demand in an efficient manner, it allows for entrants to satisfy niche preferences. Folgers is very successful at offering a variety of coffees, such as its Breakfast Blend, which satisfy demand of most people, but someone who wants "Caffe Toscana" has to refer to a specialty retailer, such as the San Francisco Bay Coffee Company.[50]

The nature of the demand for the goods and services offered by niche producers, moreover, allows for certain price inelasticity of demand: Although consumers may balk if a can of Folgers goes up, someone who wants a specific coffee is prepared to pay a premium.[51] A similar phenomenon is evident in the development of the pornography industry. At its most benign, consider the failed experiment in exhibitionism conducted by Josh Harris, founder of Jupiter Communications and Pseudo.com. "It was Manhattan's most outrageous bohemian-chic blowout, a booze-saturated salon that ran nonstop for the entire month of December 1999," Charles Platt wrote in *Wired*.[52] Titillation for voyeurs was the high-camp experiment, one that attempted to duplicate Andy Warhol's Factory, only this time, anyone anywhere could log onto http://www.WeLiveInPublic.com to take a peek. With 32 cameras mounted throughout the SoHo loft, Josh Harris attempted to live with Tanya Corrin, his girlfriend, their entire lives in public without one second of privacy for 100 days. "By day 60 I had to get out," Corrin, wrote in the *New York Observer* in February 2001. Not unlike other experiments that rely on exhibitionism online, the marketing of fetishes and fetish desire requires refined skills. An examination of the economics of perversion and fetishes—the niche markets of pornography—appears in the next chapter.

SUMMARY

The fastest-growing industry in the entertainment economy online is pornography. As with online gambling, online adult entertainment is characterized by *Key #1* (The Internet offers the technology to expand greatly an existing market) and *Key #4* (The online economy can create conditions in which inferior societal outcomes will prevail unless regulatory remedies are in place to balance private wants and public needs).

Within the first decade of its existence, this proved to be such a pioneering and profitable industry that corporate America entered the mainstream pornography market with the full force of Fortune 500 companies. As a result, pornography online has fragmented into two distinct markets. The mainstream online pornography industry is now dominated by a few companies dedicated exclusively to providing content, and others who provide the distribution system. A parallel market, one for fetish desire and perversion, however, continues to grow rapidly as it identifies—and endeavors to satisfy—specific niche markets.

NOTES

1. In the Figure 10.1, let us replace numbers. If P1 is $10 and Q1 is 60 units, then when the price falls by 50 percent and P2 becomes $5, if the number of units sold rises to 100, then the price elasticity of demand for this good can be determined. If sales rise from 60 to 100 when the price is reduced from $10 to $5, then the price elasticity of demand is 1.33 (40 divided by 60 is 2/3; and 2/3 divided by 1/2 [percentage of price drop from $10 to $5] = 1.33). But suppose we began the other way around? Suppose we had increased the price from $5 to $10 and then witnessed a sales fall from 60 to 100 units. A price increase of 100 percent resulted in a sales decrease of 40 percent (40 lost units divided by 100), meaning that the price elasticity then is 0.4. If we begin at the higher point and cut prices, our price elasticity is 1.33, but if we start at the lower point and raise prices, the price elasticity is 0.4. What is happening is that price elasticity changes continuously along the demand curve. In other words, there is consumer resistance to prices as they continue to increase, a phenomenon normally referred to as "sticker shock." The formula can be written as $D = -(DQ/DP) \times (P/Q)$.

2. To understand how the price elasticity of demand changes over time, consider what happens when taxi rates rise abruptly because of, for instance, a sharp increase in the price of gasoline. Consumers may have no choice in the short term and simply resign themselves to paying higher rates. But over time, they may take other forms of public transportation or make arrangements for other transport. Demand becomes more elastic over time in response to how prices affect a consumer's economic choices.

3. Except for John Kenneth Galbraith, of course, who would offer criticism of why things aren't the way they should be, which is presumably one reason why the government should intervene in one way or another.

4. The carnage was grisly, to be sure, but fueled by the simple fact that an adult male elephant's tusks were worth in excess of $40,000 in the late 1980s.

5. Peter Hawthorne, "The Horns of Plenty," Time.com, June 9, 1997. Available online at http://www.time.com/time/magazine/1997/int/970609/environment.the_horns_of_.html.

6. The estimated value of all the ivory warehoused by the government around the world was listed at $8.5 billion according to conservationists.

7. Not every conservationist agreed, however. John Hutton, who runs the Zimbabwe program for the Africa Resources Trust pointed out, "elephants

must contribute to the local and national economies of these nations. The elephant is not endangered in this part of Africa any longer." There are, however, 33 additional African countries with elephant populations. Ensuring that commerce in ivory is regulated properly while preventing the return of armed ivory gangs is a challenge.

8. There are, of course, critics who argue it is "immoral" for anyone to spend hundreds of dollars for a Beanie Baby toy while children go to bed hungry. Then again, our communal sense of outrage is far less at footage of adults fighting like children for a stuffed toy, than it is seeing a majestic elephant shot down by poachers.

9. Magazines, books, videos, and adult toys have to go from point A to point B, which means that local laws and ordinances determine the physical and legal parameters within which pornography as an industry in the real world can take place and develop, such as "red light" districts.

10. Totalitarian regimes, of course, can censor and ban speech that is offensive to the government, which is why it is only in undemocratic societies that pornography is unavailable.

11. Price inelasticity of demand increases as the nature of the sexual deviancy increases; the more arcane fetishes and outlaw sexual practices, the more expensive it is to get satisfaction. The pornographic economy online, for instance, makes individuals with unusual interests, such as urolangia, pedophilia, and bestiality, to identify other like-minded individuals who share the same interests. The "community" that emerges oftentimes results in markets for specialized goods and services, which, because their cost increases the more perverse they become. In the markets for "extreme" pathological sexual desire, the greater the price for a specific sexual deviancy, the greater the supply will be offered. This poses serious problems in some instances, such as law enforcement officials combating the international market in child pornography. The most notorious case involved a conspiracy known as the Wonderland Club that involved trafficking in over 750,000 images of child pornography to a dozen countries from London, where the operations were headquartered.

12. Ray Surrette, "The Media as a Cause of Crime," in *Media, Crime, and Criminal Justice.*

13. Sea captains, on the other hand, profited handsomely from charging a premium to American colonists who ordered material unavailable in New England. Seafarers have historically engineered novel ways of circumventing trade embargoes, smuggling, and in nurturing nascent black markets.

14. Walter Kendrick, *The Secret Museum: Pornography in Modern Culture,* pp. 133–134.

15. To understand how human beings are of two minds when it comes to pornography, consider the irony in the passage of a law that prohibited the U.S. Post Office from delivering obscene material: Benjamin Franklin, after all, was the first postmaster general—and the first pornographer in Colonial America.

16. Anthony Comstock was also the secretary of the Society for the Suppression of Vice, a tantalizing clue to the social position to which he aspired among his fellow Victorians.

17. Marshall Barron Clinard and Robert F. Meier, *Sociology of Deviant Behavior.*

18. Frederick Lane, *Obscene Profits,* p. 16.

19. Robert Frank and Philip Cook, *The Winner-Take-All Society,* p. 17.

20. In an interesting aside as to how pornography in the military impacted civilian society, consider that the pin-up models soldiers during World War II painted on the bombs they dropped gave rise to the word "bombshell" to describe an attractive woman.

21. Frederick Lane, *Obscene Profits,* p. xiv.

22. Ibid., pp. xv–xvi.

23. Ibid., p. xvi.

24. It is mistaken for social and religious critics, such as Pat Robertson of the Christian Coalition, to point to the stellar growth of the pornography industry as evidence of moral decay among Americans. Peculiarities of price elasticity of demand are value-neutral phenomenon, which reflect certain characteristics and not matters of morality or conscience.

25. U.S. 15, 24–25 (1973).

26. The Supreme Court's ruling also raised the tantalizing possibility: If a community has no standards, is nothing obscene?

27. Personal communication, December 4, 1995.

28. Frederick Lane, *Obscene Profits,* p. 115.

29. Personal communication, June 1996.

30. Tony Top is the industry name for one of the owners of Kink Video.

31. Thomas Weber, "The X-Files," *Wall Street Journal,* May 20, 1997.

32. Timothy Egan, "Erotica Inc.: Technology Sent Wall Street Into Market for Pornography," *New York Times,* October 23, 2000.

33. *Report of the Commission on Obscenity,* President's Commission on Obscenity, 1970, p. 53.

34. Marshall Clinard and Robert Meier, *Sociology of Deviant Behavior,* pp. 532–537.

35. Richard Stevenson, "Global Trade Strengthens Economies, Greenspan Says," *New York Times,* November 15, 2000.

36. It has since gone out of business, so my mention of this restaurant cannot be seen as an endorsement, but simply to point out at an amusing coincidence.

37. One unintended effect of the Nixon Justice Department's lawsuits against *Screw* magazine is that it allowed Larry Flynt's *Hustler* magazine to increase its market share. "If it weren't for my legal expenses defending myself, I would have been bigger than *Hustler,*" Al Goldstein said over dinner. "Flynt's got more money that I do," he explained. "But fuck him. At least I'm not shitting into a plastic bag!" he added, referencing the assassination attempt against Larry Flynt that left him both confined to a wheelchair and with a colostomy bag.

38. This sentiment is shared by the new generation of adult entertainers and pornographers, most of whom no longer believe the appellation of "pornographer" has any stigma or negative connotations. Jonathan Silverstein, president of Cybererotica commented on cybererotica.com, "I've never worked

in an industry where the competition socializes with each other. We're all friends." Critics point out that that's because they are all ostracized.

39. "Vanilla" homosexual sex refers to ordinary sex among same-sex couples. That this is "mainstream" is evidenced in the fact that Gay.com and PlanetOut.com, both "vanilla" Web sites targeted at the masses within the gay/lesbian/bisexual/transgender community, agreed in November 2000 to merge. With over $55 million in start-up capital, after several years, both companies have failed to turn profitable; merging is one way of reducing overhead while combining marketing in order to turn their fortunes around.

40. Vanguard and Oppenheimer mutual fund families, for instance, are two of the larger institutional investors who hold RICK, NWEB, and NOOF stock.

41. Tom Wolfe, *Hooking Up*.

42. Holman W. Jenkins Jr., "What's Worse, Imaginary Violence or Real Sex?" *Wall Street Journal*, September 20, 2000.

43. Ibid.

44. "Tricks of the Adult Trade," celebritywebmasters.com, November 1, 2000. Available online at http://www.celebritywebmasters.com/industrynews/november0100.html.

45. Sally Beatty, "Cable Operators Find New Profit in Pornography," *Wall Street Journal*, November 28, 2000.

46. This information is based on a survey conducted by Greg Geelan of YNOTMasters.com, an online directory for pornographers in the entertainment economy online.

47. "The court finds that the FTC has proven by a preponderance of evidence than 90.8% of the total 'sales' amount the defendants caused to be deposited into their merchant accounts was unauthorized," Judge Audrey Collins wrote in her decision. Jerry Guidera and Jonathan Friedland, "Porn Web Site is Ordered to Pay $37.5 Million for Billing Illegally," *Wall Street Journal*, September 8, 2000.

48. This is no different from other forms of consumer fraud, such as outfits that prey on the elderly or poor who use heavy-handed marketing to deceive consumers into purchasing unwanted, unnecessary, or overpriced goods or services.

49. How mainstream pornography is produced—photo shoots shot, films directed—is a surprisingly tedious and monotonous process.

50. Mass merchandisers, furthermore, have concerns marketing to specific market niches. How this is evolving can be seen in the inconsistent manner in which, say, Yahoo! treats pornography and hate-literature. "But is an association with porn even more dangerous than an association with Nazi merchandise, which Yahoo! continues to defend?" Damien Cave pondered in Salon.com. See "The Porn Crusaders" by Damien Cave, http://www.salon.com, May 11, 2001.

51. This is the difference between a "beverage" and a "drink." Coffees that are "beverages," such as American coffee, can be sipped over the course of an extended period of time. Coffees that are "drinks," such as Cuban coffee or Italian espresso, on the other hand, are consumed in one sitting.

52. Charles Platt, "Steaming Video," by Charles Platt, *Wired* (November 2000).

Chapter 11

End of Privacy and
Fetish Desire Online

"Privacy is dead, deal with it."
                    Scott McNealy, CEO of Sun MicroSystems, 2000.

This book does not offer a discussion of how the online economy is accelerating the erosion of privacy in the United States and around the world. An analysis of this phenomenon, one that threatens an individual consumer's sense of security and safety, requires an entire book. "Privacy protects us from being misdefined and judged out of context in a world of short attention spans, a world in which information can easily be confused with knowledge," writes Jeffrey Rosen, the legal affairs writer for *The New Republic,* in his superb book, *The Unwanted Gaze.* "In such a world, it is easy for individuals to be victimized by the reductionist fallacy that the worst truth about them is also the most important truth."[1]

As an economist, however, this is an opportune moment to discuss the erosion of privacy in the digital age regarding the most intimate part of a consumer's life. It is in the pursuit of aberrant sexual desire— fetishes and perversions—where it is seen how, through the price inelasticity of demand, one can document the fundamental concerns consumers have about online privacy. By understanding how price inelasticity of demand changes as privacy is eroded, it is possible to see how pathological consumer behavior—online sex addiction—now characterizes the market for perversion.

Indeed, if mainstream pornography online now conforms to the standard price elasticity of demand, then what we have in the market for perverse and fetish pornography is nothing less than the Twilight Zone of economics. Indeed, the price elasticity for fetish demand is inverted in a peculiar way that illuminates the socioeconomic forces shaping the Internet Age. What one finds is that as consumers become jaded, desensitized, or simply bored by mainstream sex, a secondary market in online pornography sites opens that centers around fetish erotica.

Whereas the kind of pornography one finds at a Marriott Hotel or on DirecTV's menu is ordinary, the films, products, chat rooms, and online services for fetish erotica is a bazaar of the bizarre. The diversity and perversity of this industry is as sweeping in its imagination as it is fragmented into niche markets. The epicenter of this fetish demand in the pornography industry online is San Francisco, with important production enclaves in New York and Los Angeles. Since the 1960s, San Francisco has cultivated a libertine image, encouraging sexual expression, deviance, and tolerance. When gay liberation advanced in the 1970s, the "open love" of the Flower Power generation gave way to the civic embrace of the gay, lesbian, bisexual, and transgender community, which in San Francisco city government is collectively referred to as, in a nonjudgmental way, the "queer" community.

To be sure, there have been concerns along the way. Diane Feinstein, one of California's senators in Washington, D.C., expressed her own reservations while a supervisor in San Francisco, by pointing out that, "One of the uncomfortable parts of San Francisco's liberalism has been the encouragement of sadism and masochism. . . . The gay community is going to have to face it. There's a need to set some standards. The right of an individual to live his life-style in a way he or she chooses can become offensive."[2] Senator Feinstein was, obviously, not familiar with the Supreme Court decision about "community standards."

If one arbitrarily thinks of postal zip codes as one way to define communities, then a casual census of the community one finds in any given zip code offers an overview of the prevailing standards. Zip code 68005 corresponds to Omaha, Nebraska. One can presume that the community standards of the people who live there to be quite different from those who live in 10011, which corresponds to the Chelsea district in New York City. What may be obscene to the people living in zip code 68005 may very well be a good Halloween show to the people in 10011.

For San Francisco, so close to the technological revolutions of Silicon Valley, zip codes 94103 and 94114 correspond, respectively, to the SoMa and Castro districts. The former is home to wholesalers, residential neighborhoods for low-income people, and immigrants, as well as a thriving nightlife, including the city's leather, fetish, and sadomasochistic scenes. The latter is a center of the city's gay neighborhood. Together, consistent with the Supreme Court's rulings, these communities have, in essence, no standards for sexual conduct: Anything goes, and therefore nothing can be reasonably considered obscene. San Francisco is therefore at the forefront of driving the development of the online market for fetish erotica.

With local luminaries such as Richard Hunter of Mr. S Leather & Fetters U.S.A., Chris Ward as the director of outlaw-sex videos, and the renowned dominatrix Mistress Midori, the fetish and perverse communities are found in, or have significant dealings with, San Francisco. Hunter is a pioneer in the online e-commerce of fetish erotica, hardcore gay adult videos, and the sale of adult entertainment online. Ward, a director and producer of acclaimed outlaw-sex videos for Hot House, has branched out into his own production company, Raging Stallion Studios. Mistress Midori, a celebrity throughout the fetish community, is at the cutting edge of sadomasochistic sex play.

"It's taken us quite a while to get our site up and running," Hunter says. "But we are very pleased with the business it's generating. The traffic is incredible, the orders are considerable and after making this serious investment, it is paying off." Hunter, whom I first met when his company was first exploring the possibility of establishing a Web site— and whose patience was tested through several technological convulsions euphemistically called "upgrades" by the developers of his company's online presence—has been profiled on an HBO special, consults to Hollywood filmmakers, and is one of the more successful entrepreneurs in the fetish market on the Internet.[3]

The same holds true for director, producer, and actor Ward. "This is tremendous fun, and we're giving people what they want," Ward reported. "The videos are phenomenally successful. And wherever I go around the country for circuit-events, there is such interest." Chris Ward gained notoriety with the filming of a trilogy for Hot House. In "exhibitions" given at sex clubs and sex parties at venues for fetish events, Ward has developed a cult following of admirers.[4] As evidence of the demand for this, consider that he has since opened his own production company, Raging Stallion Studios, reaching to ever more well-defined market niches within the fetish community.

"There are so many opportunities to reach people who are interested in domination," Mistress Midori offers over dinner in San Francisco. "The Internet is allowing people everywhere to realize that they are not alone in having these ideas and fantasies. Not all of them will live them out, but we can try!"[5] Mistress Midori, who has been the subject of numerous articles and photoshoots, remains one of the most celebrated after-hours personalities in San Francisco's fetish community.

Hunter, Ward, and Mistress Midori are three of the leading pioneers who have helped shape the character of the fetish community on the Internet. Each one specializes in a different area of fantasy sex and fetish erotica, to be sure, but they are members of the growing community of a distinct market, one that becomes more and more lucrative the more extreme it becomes.

In the graph provided on page 273, the criteria indicate that what were once marginalized and rare activities become robust markets. Individuals, for instance, who engaged in fetishes (e.g., eroticism of women's shoes), perversions (e.g., deriving sexual pleasure from urine), and outlaw sex (e.g., sexual acts with children) cannot only find each other, but also participate in commerce.

At one point, of course, one crosses the threshold from health to pathology. Not unlike a person who slips from being a social drinker into an alcoholic, there comes a point where healthy eroticism becomes obsessive. Rose Goldsen was wary of how consumers were affected by the media and how our social interactions changed as a result of the technology around us. Interfacing with machines affects how we interact with others. This wariness, of course, now seems charming in an antiquated way, by which I mean that, in the 2000s, the obsession with branding consumer products has become a marketing obsession. In the discussion presented on gambling, we saw clearly how a recognized psychological disorder, pathological gambling, became the basis for an industry in the entertainment economy online. The proliferation of pornography on the Internet, particularly the Web sites that cater to extreme fetishes, give rise to the following question, Is it brand marketing, or is it a mental disorder?

TOO MUCH OF A FUN THING: CYBERSEX ADDICTION

Nowhere is the role of pathological consumer behavior strongest than in the explosion of the pornography entertainment industry on the Internet. Whereas pathological gambling is pathological gambling regardless of whether it takes place in a Las Vegas casino or gambling online, the pervasiveness of online pornography is so complete that it has given rise to a new psychological disorder: cybersex addiction.

The "accessibility and anonymity of the Internet," Jane Brody reports in the *New York Times,* "are fueling a brand new psychological disorder—cybersex addiction—that appears to be spreading with astonishing rapidity and bringing turmoil to the lives of those affected."[6]

Long before the public was made aware of this disorder, mental health professionals were alarmed. "One reason that cybersex can be so dangerous for a sexual addict is that it entails many of the characteristics that recovering addicts try to avoid: isolation, fantasy, objectification, anonymity, and sexual images," writes Geral Blanchard in "Cybersex and Sexual Addiction," a position paper of the National Council on Sexual Addiction and Compulsivity (NCSAC). "The Internet . . . does provide a form of sexual acting out that can lead to the progression of sexually addictive behaviors. Censorship in any form other than self-censorship, is not viewed as a productive way to assist sexual addicts in their misuse of the Internet."

Geral Blanchard further warns that:

> All sexual addicts are responsible for their behavior and the consequences of their sexual acting out. While the Internet may provide easy access to sexualized information, the Internet cannot be blamed for the addiction or a relapse. . . . Sexual addicts who are not in recovery have lost their freedom of choice. They are no longer free to choose whether or not they engage in sexual activities. While this does not excuse sexual addicts from their behavior, it does speak to the nature of addiction. Those who are experiencing discomfort as a result of their Internet use should seek consultation with a professional knowledgeable about sexual addiction.[7]

Because there are few outward symptoms to the casual observer, the diagnosis of sexual addiction is not easily made. Psychiatrist Jennifer Schneider, however, notes that:

> Addiction to sexual activities can be just as destructive as addiction to chemical substances. Addicts may jeopardize their marriage and family relationships, allow their job performance to deteriorate, and endanger themselves and their partner through multiple sexual exposures. Even though they realize the consequences, they cannot control their compulsions without appropriate treatment.

The insidious nature of this pathological disorder is that it is difficult to identify:

> Sex addicts describe a euphoria with sex similar to that described by drug addicts with drug use. This may be an effect of endorphins and other endogenous brain chemicals, whereas the drug-induced state is externally produced. . . .
> Like alcoholics and other drug addicts, sex addicts' behavior engages in distorted thinking, rationalizing, and defending and justifying their behavior while blaming others for resulting problems. They deny having

a problem and make excuses for their behavior. . . . Sex addicts, like alcoholics and other addicts, often come from a dysfunctional family in which parents were chemically dependent, sexually addicted, abusive, or otherwise emotionally unavailable.

The report concludes by offering a course of treatment in which:

the sexual addiction model enables physicians to understand the self-destructive behavior of patients whose actions may otherwise appear inexplicable. When a person is preoccupied with sex and continues to engage in compulsive sexual activity despite adverse consequences (e.g., loss of marriage, job, health, freedom), he or she is a sex addict. Treatment allows sex addicts to stop their compulsive behavior and improve their relationships.[8]

On the question of *how* an individual first becomes addicted to sex, the NCSAC takes a formal position. Ralph Earle and Marcus Earle articulate the position by noting:

Compulsive sexual thoughts and/or behavior leads to increasingly serious consequences, in both the addict's internal and external worlds. The consequences may include severe depression, often with suicidal ideation, low self-esteem, shame, self-hatred, hopelessness, despair, helplessness, intense anxiety, loneliness, moral conflict, contradictions between ethical values and behaviors, fear of abandonment, spiritual bankruptcy, distorted thinking, remorse, and self-deceit. . . . Many sex addicts suffer from broken relationships. . . . Sexual activities outside the primary relationship result in loss of self-esteem to both partners as well as severe stress to the relationship. The sex addict is frequently absent, resulting in a loss of time in parental role modeling. . . . Many sex addicts are also addicted to alcohol and other drugs. When multiple addictions coexist, untreated sex addiction complicates recovery from chemical dependency and makes relapse to drug use more likely.[9]

The condition becomes chronic for reasons not fully understood. "Although behavioral addictions involve no external drugs preliminary research has suggested that they cause changes in brain chemicals, like the release of endorphins, that help to perpetuate the behavior," Brody reports. "The sexual stimulation and release obtained through cybersex also contribute importantly to the continued pursuit of the activity."[10]

That is to say, the pornography industry in the entertainment economy online lends itself to confusing a pathology with "customer loyalty" and successful "branding." Is it possible that an online customer that spends an hour everyday at a Web site concerned with a particular fetish is doing so to the detriment of his relationship with his family and friends? Or that he is going into debt in order to pursue an obsessive interest?[11]

Perversion substitutes for human companionship and intimacy. Diane Ackerman argues as much in her account of love in human history and biological evolution. She notes that:

> Love is an act of union or merging with a beloved, which is sought greedily by most, but there are some for whom that is a frightening thought. What if they get suffocated, swallowed up, dismantled? Intimacy takes high-wire courage; it's dangerous. Once could be humiliated, lose face, be forced to relive old traumas. . . . [But perversion dehumanizes sexual partners and o]nce they're dehumanized, the would-be partners pose no threat. But there is still the sexual excitement. Most often, unknown to the players, this is a revenge drama.[12]

The gratuitous violence of Quentin Tarantino's *Pulp Fiction,* for instance, is one in which gullibility and innocence substitute for an affected and cultivated hipster stance. What we have emerging in the secondary market of the online pornography business is a market for sexual pathologies.

The market for sexual pathologies will only grow in the 2000s. There are two reasons why this is so. First, there is a vested interest to encourage the development of markets for sexual pathologies. The other is the erosive nature of the Internet on our privacy. In the former, market forces will continue to generate overwhelming choices for all kinds of

---

✔ Engaging in a certain behavior more and more often over time.

✔ Continuing desire for a certain behavior to the point of obsession.

✔ Spending much time in activities necessary for the behavior, participating in the behavior itself or recuperating from the effects of the behavior.

✔ Obsessive thoughts about the behavior.

✔ Limiting other activities, such as social, occupational, or recreational activities, in order to pursue the desired behavior.

✔ Need to increase the intensity or frequency of the behavior in order to achieve the desired effect, or experiencing diminished satisfaction at the previous intensity or frequency of the behavior.

✔ Restlessness if unable to engage in the desired behavior.

At least two criteria must be met for diagnosis.

Figure 11.1   Criteria for Addictive Sexual Disorders

perversions and sexual niche markets. In the case of the latter, it will become more difficult to exercise self-discipline considering that even if one struggles to avoid temptation, temptation has a way of finding one.

Let us consider the economic incentives to nurture a market for sexual pathologies. Richard Scruggs, the attorney who won the $368.5 billion settlement for the states in their suit against the tobacco industry in 1997, understands the perverse nature of human self-interest. "There wasn't enough money in the world to satisfy some people," he said, explaining the difficulty of reaching a settlement with the tobacco companies.

> The problem is that here are people invested in the fight, okay? I mean, like, some people in Palestine or Northern Ireland don't want the wars to end. . . . We did not anticipate the self-interest of some of the health groups in perpetuating their existence and fund-raising. Because bashing big tobacco was their fundamental way to raise money . . . some groups like the American Lung Association saw their fund-raising threatened by a tobacco solution.[13]

The idea that the American Lung Association felt threatened by the prospect of fewer Americans getting lung cancer from smoking cigarettes over the course of their lifetimes is an arresting one. It is more than an idea. It is an industry. Industries develop to serve markets, and whether those markets exist to offer solutions or create problems is immaterial. If the tobacco industry can be accused of promoting a product that creates health problems, then there are other industries, such as fund-raising organizations and the medical profession, whose self-interest lies in the continuation of these problems.

Economists remain detached from discerning the motivations and self-interest of parties. *Prevention* and *Men's Health* magazines, for instance, are in the business to promote the health of their readers—a business that would be significantly reduced if consumers resisted eating fast food, exercised regularly, and refrained from smoking or drinking in excess. If we accept the idea that the American Lung Association has a vested interest in people being outraged at the tobacco industry and that the editors of *Men's Health* magazine recognize that if consumers followed the advice found in their magazine, their publication's fortunes would be diminished, however, then we can understand the proliferation of niche markets in the pornography industry online. In 1995, there were fewer than 1,000 Web sites with sexually explicit material. In 2000, there were more than 60,000. These commercial enterprises are on the Internet seeking customers. There is no reason to think their marketing efforts will wane as the market expands on a global scale.

Of equal importance is the systematic erosion of privacy engendered by the Internet technologies. "In this brave new world, every transaction you make adds that much more information to the universal data bank known as the Internet," commentator Robert Scheer explains. "The point of Aldous Huxley's *Brave New World* was that the public would come to accept totalitarian intrusion as a part of the normal fabric of life, as something that was actually good for them."[14]

Attorney Jeffrey Rosen, writing in *The Unwanted Gaze,* explains that our ability to form intimate relations is undermined by the violation of our privacy. He argues persuasively that:

> [t]here are the personal costs of the erosion of privacy. Privacy is important not only, or even primarily, to protect individual autonomy but also to allow individuals to form intimate relationships. . . . Friendship and romantic love can't be achieved without intimacy, and intimacy, in turn, depends upon the selective and voluntary disclosure of personal information that we don't share with everyone else. Behind the protective shield of privacy, two individuals can relax the boundaries of self and lose themselves in each other. Because of their mutual self-exposure, friends and lovers are uniquely vulnerable to each other, which is why a serious fight in a friendship or a marriage can quickly escalate to a nuclear exchange.[15]

Privacy makes us feel secure, which is why its violation is so invasive to our sense of safety. Anyone whose home has been burglarized is familiar with how violated one feels when a private space has been ransacked by a stranger. This violation is a trauma. Thus Rosen expresses his own bewilderment at the apparent indifference of Americans to the erosion of their privacy:

> [T]ransactions in cyberspace tend to generate detailed electronic footprints that expose our tastes and preferences to the operators of Web sites, who can then sell the information to private marketers. But to the frustration of professional privacy advocates, Americans don't always seem terribly concerned about the possible misuse of click-stream data. Many of us use credit cards for the most intimate on-line purchases. We willingly accept cookies, and we don't take the time to cover our electronic tracks with cumbersome anonymity providers.[16]

A decade before Rosen wrote these sentences, a techie had boasted about the software that made cookies possible over dinner in San Francisco's Chinatown. "The program launches itself, collects tons of data, then seals itself up and returns to the originator," he said, crushing a Chinese fortune cookie open.

There is little to arrest, let alone reverse, this trend. This is due as much to the law as it is to the technology that makes it possible.

"Because the Fourth Amendment is rooted in notions of private property . . . judges have had trouble regulating forms of electronic surveillance that don't clearly invade property rights," Rosen explains, noting that efforts to protect the privacy of citizens is not an easy matter. "There are, however, limits to the degree that personal data can be conceived of as private property, especially because property rights can be sold."[17] By 2000, the Internet's *mis*fortune cookies had become entrenched as part of our lives. This is how Robert Scheer describes these electronic Trojan horses:

> New spying is like a high-powered vacuum cleaner; one that scoops up every bit of information it comes across, even the extraneous or incomprehensible stuff. That's what Echelon and the FBI's Carnivore—and perhaps unreported private systems—can do: Grab everything, because the cost is so low. Carnivore simply places a black box with your ISP and snarfs up all e-mail traffic. Supercomputers do the sifting and the sorting. Needles in haystacks become simple to find, simple to compare with other needles.[18]

He laments, finally, that when "it comes to privacy, Americans are the most unprotected citizens in the world."[19] On that simple fact, the online pornographic industry relies, as more technological innovations come online.

SUMMARY

The most compelling threat to the privacy of consumers arises from the parallel market for fetish desire and perversion online. *Key #1* (The Internet offers the technology to expand greatly an existing market.) and *Key #4* (The online economy can create conditions in which inferior societal outcomes will prevail unless regulatory remedies are in place to balance private wants and public needs.) apply in these niche markets.

NOTES

1. Jeffrey Rosen, *The Unwanted Gaze: The Destruction of Privacy in America*.

2. Randy Shilts, *The Mayor of Castro Street*, p. 198.

3. Richard Hunter, for instance, provided all the equipment in the S & M thriller, *8MM*, which starred Nicolas Cage. Mr. S Leather & Fetters U.S.A. is the premier fetish store and Web site (http://www.mr-s-leather-fetters.com) based in San Francisco.

4. One consequence of my inquiries is that I now have these adult tapes autographed by the directors or stars. "They'll be worth something someday on eBay," one advised, cheerfully.

5. Mistress Midori operates her Web site with her partner and manager Michael Manning at http://www.fetishdiva.com.

6. Jane Brody, "Cybersex Gives Birth to a Psychological Disorder," *New York Times,* May 16, 2000.

7. Geral Blanchard, "Cybersex and Sexual Addiction," National Council on Sexual Addiction and Compulsivity, available at http://www.ncsac.org.

8. Jennifer Schneider, "How to Recognize the Signs of Sexual Addiction: Asking the Right Questions May Uncover Serious Problems," National Council on Sexual Addiction and Compulsivity, available at http://www.ncsac.org.

9. Ralph Earle and Marcus Earle, "Consequences of Sex Addiction and Compulsivity," National Council on Sexual Addiction and Compulsivity, available at http://www.ncsac.org.

10. Jane Brody, "Cybersex Gives Birth to a Psychological Disorder," *New York Times,* May 16, 2000.

11. Two influential tomes to review concerning the psychological disorders associated with perversion are Robert Stoller's *Pain and Passion: A Psychoanalyst Explores the World of S & M* (1991) and his *Perversion: The Erotic Form of Hatred* (1986).

12. Diane Ackerman, *A Natural History of Love,* pp. 247–248.

13. "Making the Case for Racial Reparation: A Forum," *Harper's* (November 2000).

14. Robert Scheer, "Nowhere to Hide," *Yahoo! Internet Life* (October 2000), p. 101.

15. Jeffrey Rosen, *The Unwanted Gaze: The Destruction of Privacy in America,* p. 215.

16. Ibid., p. 197.

17. Ibid., p. 181.

18. Robert Scheer, "Nowhere to Hide," p. 101.

19. Ibid.

Conclusion

In 1869, the Empire Express united the nation in a transcontinental railroad from coast to coast. For the next six decades, a vast network of iron rails crisscrossed the landscape, facilitating the industrialization of the nation's economy and the settlement of the American continent. By 1929 there were, in fact, 163 "Class I" railroads. Then, a massive consolidation reverberated through the industry. In the ensuing six decades after reaching its apogee, through mergers, acquisitions, and bankruptcies, the number of railroad companies plummeted. By the year 2000, the Association of American Railroads reported that in excess of 90 percent of all rail freight throughout the United States was handled by the *seven* remaining "Class I" railroads. This is natural in the course of market economies. In the first decade of the American automotive industry, for instance, 346 companies went out of business, or were acquired by their competitors.[1]

When I sat down to write the first draft of this manuscript in May 2000, a major consolidation of the dot-com world began. "The investment climate has changed a hundred and eighty degrees," Henry Blodget, an analyst at Merrill Lynch, said at the time.This was an unexpected about-face. During Christmas 1999, after all, any company with a "dot-com" at the end of its name was drowning in venture capital. Throughout spring 2000, it became clear that the business models being invented by the likes of Razorfish had "dot-comed" to nothing.[3] Throughout the summer of 2000, more and more dot-com companies failed, or were acquired, or postponed their IPOs, or ceased operations.[4] By the end of 2001 Merrill Lynch had let go Henry Blodget.

Indeed, in the fall of 2000, surveying the dot-com debris that littered the business landscape, Birinyi Associates estimated that from their respective 52-week highs, by the time the November 2000 presidential elections rolled around, the combined market value of the 280 stocks that comprised the Bloomberg U.S. Internet Index had fallen from $2.948 trillion to a mere $1.193, representing a loss of $1.755 trillion between March and September 2000.[5]

The speculative bubble burst. Not unlike the bitter conflicts that dominated the emergence of other economic networks in centuries past, the effervescence of extravagant claims has, oftentimes, undermined the judgment of investors, businesspeople, policymakers, and the public at large. The loss in the valuation of the dot-com stocks in a period of six months approximates the federal budget of the U.S. government for fiscal year 2000, evidence that reason had ceded to anarchy. The frenzied acclamation that once surrounded the introduction of pioneering Internet technologies, in fact, led otherwise intelligent investors, blinded by dreams of instant wealth, to discount the probability that a particular venture should end in failure.

Wall Street took notice when POP.com announced in September 2000 that it had laid off most of its staff. Launched in October 1999 and backed by Microsoft's Paul Allen, Dreamworks' Jeffrey Katzenberg, and Imagine Entertainment's Ron Howard, it had been hailed as the birth of the New Media Era. It may have been new, but it confronted old problems.[6] It is clear that when companies build business models on vapor, their bubbles will burst without a trace. This disappointment is the logical outcome of human enterprise under irrational conditions.

A colleague who read Part I of this book commented that what I had written was "a devastating critique of the dot-com world," insofar as it addressed the need for a "unified corpus that explained the e-commerce narrative." Internet enthusiasts advanced to investors and the public alike. If the discussion presented here became an unexpected "dot-coming" of age story, it did so because I have attempted to offer a unified theory affirming the use of classical economics in explaining our world. The discussions in this book have been precisely an attempt to reconcile contradictory desires when dualities mix and converge in this Brave New Online World.

This story began with an account of the dinner conversations I had at the Huntington Hotel in San Francisco in the late 1980s. It ends in the late 1990s with drinks at the Mark Hopkins where the idea for this book—examining the online economy by applying the laws of classical economics—was born. The distance between the Huntington and Mark Hopkins hotels is one city block. We have, however, traveled far and wide in strolling from one place to another. True, we have meandered here and there along the way, but in the process, we have gained a new-found confidence in our knowing that the fundamental laws of economics apply as technological revolutions go by.

Whether the discussion has addressed why pharmaceutical companies spent millions to determine which medicines they should develop, or why five-year-olds in Barcelona want Razor scooters, each digression has added depth to our understanding of how our market economy—with all its imperfections—works the way it works. We have seen how the complex and intricate nature of the human mind offers counterintuitive answers to questions that affect us all. The causal relationship between violence in the media and violence in society, for instance, exists, like cold fusion, only in bad science. And when bad science meets poor public policy, distortions occur that undermine the healthy development of an industry.

The question of health itself, economic and human, is salient to the Internet. In the last two chapters, we saw how the alienation inherent in technology fosters certain kinds of pathological consumer behavior with compelling social consequences, for they lead to inferior communal outcomes. However pathological collecting may be, for instance, it remains rather benign in the real world. When the collection of thrills through online gambling emerges as an unregulated and unbranded industry, however, it lends itself to an economy that harms an individual, his family, and society. The same holds true in the fragmented world of online pornography. That the corporate takeover of mainstream pornography makes it available virtually everywhere itself is of concern. What alarms, however, is the explosive growth in the markets for fetish desire and perversion, which is creating distortions in consumer behavior, with all the inferior societal outcomes that this entails.

To make these arguments in a succinct manner, I have taken an interdisciplinary approach to the discussions presented. These perspectives have been necessary in order to illuminate how the Internet affects our lives, and not just in the economic realm. Although I have attempted to demonstrate how this one single technological innovation that has magnified market imperfections as intensely as has the online economy, the distortions are spilling over into our civic lives, which is why there is comfort in knowing that, when we are faced with a puzzle, there is an economic principle at work.

It was not at first apparent, for instance, to see how Amazon.com's impact on independent booksellers was a case of society being impoverished through the tyranny of small decisions. The acrimonious debate that engulfed the online music industry, likewise, was more a conflict that arises when the gap between Stated Preference and

Revealed Preference widens because of a technological innovation. Other economic principles, such as the price elasticity of demand, pathological consumer behavior, and how well-intentioned but misguided policymakers can, at times, interfere with the development of markets in ways that are healthy for business and society, offer insights that challenge our preconceptions and make us think in new ways about our economy, families, and business.

These arguments resonate because, by bringing economic principles into a discussion of how the entertainment economy online is developing, it is liberating to see how things fall into place and make sense. This is reassuring, for it makes it easier to understand how the Internet affects the economy and impacts our world as it enters our lives. When Missouri Governor Mel Carnahan died in an airplane crash in 1999, then-Senator John Ashcroft, the incumbent whom Governor Carnahan was attempting to defeat, shut his campaign for an entire week out of respect for the late governor. "It's the right thing to do," Senator Ashcroft told a reporter while being interviewed on national television.[7]

If we're all trying to do the right thing, then why do so many wrong things get done?

Economists have no maps or guides to illuminate our way through the treacherous terrain that lies beyond the limits of economics. The principles of market economies, however, suggest solutions and help us orient ourselves when confronted by the new and unfamiliar. The entertainment economy online offers the highest of the highs and the lowest of the lows. Humanity now struggles to map out the future that is a path in between. Indeed, as we establish landmarks on this new landscape, it is crucial to recognize that the quandary we now confront is as old as human history itself. The Bible, after all, teaches that it was the acquisition of forbidden knowledge that resulted in Adam and Eve's loss of innocence and subsequent banishment from the Garden of Eden.

The ancient Greeks expounded upon this cautionary tale about the dangers found in unintended consequences. Of all the denizens of the Greek pantheon, in fact, it is Pandora who speaks to us as we attempt to come to terms with the impact of the Internet on our lives. It was none other than Pandora who unleashed upon the world pandemonium, much the same way the Internet has, at the beginning of the twenty-first century, introduced mass confusion into ours. It took Zeus to bring order to the unsettled world of the ancient Mediterraneans. For us, on the other hand, it is not classical mythology but classical economics that now reign in the apparent chaos. It is comforting, then, to realize that questions that baffle us may very well have simple, straightforward answers.

"What is not forgivable," *Business Week* opined once the dot-com mania was over, "is that many analysts were revealed to be no better than circus barkers who brought investors into the tent to pump up the investment banking side of their Wall Street employers."[8] A certain sense of *Schadenfreude* (the German idea of rejoicing with delight at the misfortune of others) gripped those who had been left out of the dot-com boom of the 1990s.[9]

Throughout San Francisco in the nineteenth century, people re-counted with glee that John Sutter died penniless in 1880—as did many of the Forty-Niners who took over his land. Those start-up up-starts got exactly what they deserved when their paper millions van-ished into nothing, was the open sentiment in San Francisco. The lesson for us of the California Gold Rush of 1849 and the Silicon Gold Rush of 1999, then, is to avoid their mistake now that the online economy evolves along sound economic principles and tested busi-ness models: What's the point of having any kind of Gold Rush if no one is going to make a fortune?

A second generation of Internet start-ups, ones with business plans, mindful of the fundamental laws of economics and with realistic ex-pectations, is emerging. Even as the NASDAQ fell—for every IPO that increased in value in 2000, there were two that ended the year below their offering prices—careful venture capitalists were making signifi-cant investments, chastened by the early failures.[10] "Most first movers end up lying facedown in the sand, with other people coming along and learning from their mistakes," Marc Andreessen explains the ob-vious to readers of *Fast Company* magazine—five years too late to be of any help for the millions who lost over a trillion.[11] The failures of the dot-com meltdown of 2000–2001, however, have given rise to the emergence of a sustainable online economy. It is as if the New Economy's most enthusiastic champions had learned from Friedrich Nietzsche who implored:

> Examine the lives of the best and most fruitful people and peoples and ask yourselves whether a tree that is supposed to grow to a proud height can dispense with bad weather and storms; whether misfortune and external resistance, some kinds of hatred, jealousy, stubbornness, mis-trust, hardness, avarice, and violence do not belong among the *favourable* conditions without which any great growth even of virtue is scarcely possible.[12]

That the fundamental truths of economic theories have survived the dot-com mania of the 1990s is reassuring, for it means that the wild wild west days of the World Wide Web are over, allowing us all to get down to business.

NOTES

1. "Cadillac," "Chevrolet," and "Buick," for instance, were independent companies that were subsequently acquired by General Motors. Other companies went out of business, one reason no one drives a Rainier convertible.

2. Howard Kurtz, "Who Blew the Dot-Com Bubble?; The Cautionary Tale of Henry Blodget," *Washington Post*, March 12, 2001.

3. "I think this definitely is not a fad, what's occurring right now," Jeff Dachis, a co-founder of Razorfish, a leading Internet company in New York's Silicon Alley, told Bob Simon of *60 Minutes* in a broadcast on February 2000. "This is absolutely real; this is a revolution; we're packing rifles; and this is going to be something that's going to change the course of the way the world is functioning," he added. That *60 Minutes* segment has become a classic among critics of the dot-com world, who delight in deconstructing the arrogance, naiveté, and outright idiocy of Razorfish.

4. In a survey of what it termed the most "spectacular crashes," the November 27, 2000, issue of *Adweek* identified Redrocket.com, BBQ.com, Digital Entertainment Network, Toysmart.com, Pixelon, Pop.com, Pseudo.com, Ingredients.com, Freeinternet.com, and Modo.net as unmitigated disasters. After Pseudo.com filed for bankruptcy, for instance, it was revealed that the company spent $32 million in venture capital, and its remaining assets were sold for a mere $2 million to INTV, a New York Internet company, which was deemed a fair market price by the courts.

5. Failures of dot-com companies unfolded with such breathtaking speed beginning in the second half of 2000 that an entrepreneur launched a Web site to chronicle their demise. Spoofing the high-tech "Fast Company" magazine, Fuckedcompany.com caused quite a stir when the owners attempted to sell it on eBay.com, the auction Web site.

6. Similar problems plagued other Hollywood luminaries. San Francisco–based Shockwave.com, which successfully recruited director Tim Burton, itself was retreating from the market by the end of 2000.

7. The late Missouri governor defeated the incumbent senator in a peculiar case of a dead man defeating a living one in a political race.

8. "Getting Over the Dot-Con," *Business Week,* December 11, 2000, p. 142.

9. For the sadists who want to delight in *Schadenfreude,* pick up a copy of *Digital Rush: Nine Internet Start-Ups in the Race for Dot-Com Riches* (New York: AMACOM) by Jonathan Aspatore. "The time to be part of an online venture is now," he writes on the first page of a book published in November of 2000, as the Internet stocks began to crash. "There has never been a better time to raise money from financing sources such as venture capitalists," he explained. The book, which declares on the inside jacket that "[t]he only rule for Web success is that there are no rules," asks the reader to suspend disbelief and pretend that the laws of economics have themselves been suspended. *Digital Rush* will make anyone with common sense laugh out loud.

10. Without expressing any endorsement of any kind, consider that *Business Week* reported in its December 11, 2000, issue that four e-commerce sites favored by venture capitalists in the wake of the NASDAQ debacle included eyestorm.com, guggenheim.com, kick.com, and liveplanet.com.

11. George Anders, "Act II: What's Still True—And What Was Never True—About the Internet," *Fast Company* (February 2001). The dot-com debacle offered its own levity, for in San Francisco self-referential confessionals by the self-indulgent became a literary genre. "On a Monday morning just five short weeks ago, I had to tell my employees that they didn't have jobs anymore," Jennifer Jeffrey wrote in "The Day I Killed My Dot-Com," published online by Salon.com on December 12, 2000. "On a Sunday morning, at a cavernous performance space in the heart of San Francisco's Mission District, a group of social workers, artists and community activists sit around on flea-market furniture to plan a counterattack on the infiltrating enemy—the hordes of well-heeled newcomers, many of them dot-com yuppies, gentrifying the neighborhood," wrote Carole Lloyd in "I'm the Enemy!," published online by Salon.com on October 29, 1999. Thus the pampered and idle who enjoy nothing more than in speaking at length about the mundane minutiae of their problems found a creative outlet for the tragically boring, but predictable, stories of their dot-com failures.

12. Friedrich Nietzsche, *The Gay Science,* p. 19.

BIBLIOGRAPHY

Ackerman, Diane. *A Natural History of Love.* New York: Vintage Books, 1995.

Anders, George. "Act II: What's Still True—And What Was Never True—About the Internet." *Fast Company,* February 2001.

Anderson, Craig A., and Karen Dill. "Video Games and Aggressive Thoughts, Feelings, and Behavior in the Laboratory and in Life." *Journal of Personality and Social Psychology* 78, no. 4 (April 2000).

Annenberg Public Policy Center. "The Internet and the Family 2000." May 2000.

Ashmore, Richard, and Francis Del Boca. "Conceptual Approaches to Stereotypes and Stereotyping." In *Cognitive Processes in Stereotyping and Intergroup Behavior,* ed. David L. Hamilton. Mahwah, NJ: Lawrence Erlbaum Associates, 1981.

Bain, David Haward. *Empire Express: Building the First Transcontinental Railroad.* New York: Viking Press, 1999.

Barlow, John Perry. "The Next Economy of Ideas: Will Copyright Survive the Napster Bomb?" *Wired,* October 2000.

Barringer, Felicity. "Salon Dismisses 13 Workers in Effort to Fight Shortfall." *New York Times,* June 8, 2000.

Beatty, Sally. "Cable Operators Find New Profit in Pornography." *Wall Street Journal,* November 28, 2000.

Bender, Kandace. Personal interview, February 12, 2000.

Berger, Warren. "The Cool Thing About Aggregration." *Wired* 8.10, October 2000.

Berners-Lee, Tim, and Mark Fischetti. *Weaving the Web.* San Francisco: Harper San Francisco, 1999.

"Bertlesmann and Napster Form Strategic Alliance." Napster.com, October 31, 2000. Available online at http://www.napster.com/pressroom/pr/001031.html

Blanchard, Geral. "Cybersex and Sexual Addiction." National Council on Sexual Addiction and Compulsivity. Available online at http://www.ncsac.org.

Bodow, Steven. "The '99ers." *New York*, April 2, 2001.

Borsook, Paulina. *Cyberselfish: A Critical Romp through the Terribly Libertarian Culture of High-Tech*. New York: Public Affairs, 2000.

Bradburn, Norman. "Watching the Polls: Elections, the Media and Polling." *Chicago Policy Review* 1, no. 1 (fall 1996).

Braunstein, Marc, and Edward Levine. *Deep Branding on the Internet*. CITY: Prima Communications, Inc., 2000.

Brody, Jane. "Cybersex Gives Birth to a Psychological Disorder." *New York Times*, May 16, 2000.

Bronson, Po. *The First $20 Million Is Always the Hardest*. New York: HarperTrade, 2000.

———. *The Nudist on the Late Shift*. New York: Broadway, 2000.

Brown, Janelle. "The Gnutella Paradox." Salon.com, September 29, 2000. Available online at http://www.salon.com/tech/feature/2000/09/29/gnutella_paradox/print.html.

———. "Whoring for Download." Salon.com, November 30, 2000.

Carvajal, Doreen. "The Book's in Print, But Its Bibliography Lives in Cyberspace." *New York Times*, May 29, 2000.

———. "How Studios Used Children to Test-Market Violent Films." *New York Times*, September 27, 2000.

Case, Frederick. "Murders Again Tied to TV Violence." (Seattle) *Times*, May 8, 1990.

Cass, Dennis. "Let's Go: Silicon Valley!: Wherein the Author Stalks the Flighty Webhead in His Habitat." *Harper's*, July 2000.

Cave, Damien. "The Porn Crusaders." Salon.com, May 11, 2001.

Centerwall, Brandon. "Exposure to Television as a Risk Factor for Violence." *American Journal of Epidemiology* 129/4 (April 1989).

Chancellor, Edward. *Devil Take the Hindmost: A History of Financial Speculation*. New York: Farrar, Straus & Giroux, 1999.

Charny, Ben. "Napster Deal Comes with A Price Tag," ZDNet UK, November 1, 2000. Available online at http://news.zdnet.co.uk/story/0,,t269-s2082305,00.html.

Chuck D. "'Free' Music Can Free the Artist." *New York Times*, April 29, 2000.

Clinard, Marshall Barron, and Robert F. Meier. *Sociology of Deviant Behavior*. New York: HBJ College & School Division, 1997.

Coffey, Brendan. "Publish or Perish." *Forbes*, November 13, 2000.

Dash, Mike. *Tulipomania: The Story of the World's Most Coveted Flower*. New York: Crown Publishers, 2000.

"Death of a Spokespup." *Brandweek*, December 11, 2000.

Dornbusch, Rudiger. *Dollars, Debts and Deficits* Cambridge, MA: MIT Press, 1986.

Earle, Ralph, and Marcus Earle. "Consequences of Sex Addiction and Compulsivity." National Council on Sexual Addiction and Compulsivity. Available online at http://www.ncsac.org.

Easterbrook, Gregg. "Watch and Learn." *The New Republic*, May 17, 1999.

Egan, Timothy. "Erotica Inc.: Technology Sent Wall Street into Market for Pornography." *New York Times*, October 23, 2000.

Eisenhower, Dwight D. State of the Union speech, February 1956.

Elias, Norbert, and Eric Dunning. *Quest for Excitement: Sport and Leisure in the Civilizing Process*. New York: Blackwell Publishers, 1986.

Elkin, Tobi. "Sega Gambles on Internet to Extend U.S. Comeback." *Advertising Age*, September 4, 2000.

Ellis, John. "That Explosion You Just Heard Is the Music Business." *Fast Company*, October 2000.

Eron, L. D., L. R. Huesmann, E. Dubow, R. Romanoff, & P. Yarmel. "Aggression and Its Correlates Over 22 Years." In *Childhood Aggression and Violence*, ed. D. Crowell, I. Evans, and D. O'Donnell. New York: Perseus, 1987.

Evans, Philip, and Thomas Wurster. *Blown to Bits: How the New Economics of Information Transforms Strategy*. Cambridge, MA: Harvard University Press, 1999.

Ferguson, Thomas, and Joel Rogers. "The Myth of America's Turn to the Right." *Atlantic Monthly*, May 1986.

Fishman, Allison, "Swamp Thing." *Revolution*, November 2000.

Frank, Robert. *Choosing the Right Pond*. New York: Oxford University Press, 1987.

———. "The Cost of Governing Less." *New York Times*, August 26, 2000.

———. "The Rules Nasdaq Forgot." *New York Times*, March 17, 2000.

Frank, Robert, and Philip Cook. *The Winner-Take-All Society*. New York: Penguin, 1996.

Frank, Thomas. *One Market under God: Extreme Capitalism, Market Populism, and the End of Economic Democracy*. New York: Doubleday, 2000.

Fraser, Jill Andresky. *White-Collar Sweatshop: The Deterioration of Work and Its Rewards in Corporate America*. New York: W. W. Norton, 2001.

Friedman, Milton. "The Role of Government in a Free Society." In *Private Wants and Public Needs*, ed. Edmund S. Phelps. New York: W. W. Norton & Company, 1965.

Furger, Roberta. "Does Shoot-'Em-Up Software Lead to Aggressive Behavior?" PCWorld.com, November 2, 1998.

Galbraith, John Kenneth. "The Dependence Effect and Social Balance." In *Private Wants and Public Needs*, ed. Edmund S. Phelps. New York: W. W. Norton & Company, 1965.

———. "Evading the Obvious." *New York Times*, October 12, 1998.

Gerwig, Kate. "AT&T Launches Streaming Video Plan." Tele.com, July 11, 2000.

"Getting Over the Dot-Con." *Business Week*, editorial, December 11, 2000.

Gilder, George. C-SPAN *Booknotes*. Television broadcast, September 24, 1989.

———. *Telecosm: How Infinite Bandwidth Will Revolutionize Our World.* New York: Free Press, 2000.

———. *Wealth and Poverty.* Oakland, CA: ICS Press, 1993.

Goldsen, Rose K. Personal interview, March 1983.

———. *The Show and Tell Machine: How American Television Works and Works You Over.* New York: Dial Press, 1978.

Gornstein, Amy. "AOL, Sony to Offer PlayStation Service." Salon.com, May 15, 2001.

Greenspan, Alan. Speech delivered at the Bank of Mexico, Mexico City, November 14, 2000.

Griffin, Gillett G. "Collecting Pre-Columbian Art." In *The Ethics of Collecting Cultural Property: Whose Culture? Whose Property?*, ed. Phyllis Mauch Messenger. Albuquerque: New Mexico University Press, 1999.

Guidera, Jerry, and Jonathan Friedland. "Porn Web Site is Ordered to Pay $37.5 Million for Billing Illegally." *Wall Street Journal,* September 8, 2000.

Hall, Alan. "The Old Economy Is the New Economy." *Business Week Online,* November 13, 2000. Available online at http://www.businessweek.com.

Hamel, Gary. "Bringing Silicon Valley Inside." *Harvard Business Review,* September–October 1999.

Hansell, Saul, "An Ambitious Internet Grocer Is Out of Both Cash and Ideas." *New York Times,* July 10, 2001.

———. "For Amazon, a Holiday Risk: Can It Sell Acres of Everything?" *New York Times,* November 28, 1999.

———. "Sony and Time Warner Make Music Deal." *New York Times,* July 14, 1999.

Hansen, Alvin. "Standards and Values in a Rich Society." In *Private Wants and Public Needs,* ed. Edmund S. Phelps. New York: W. W. Norton & Company, 1965.

Harmon, Amy. "'Casino Mentality' Linked to Day Trading's Stresses." *New York Times,* August 1, 1999.

———. "Judge Rules Against MP3 On CD Copying." *New York Times,* September 7, 2000.

———. "Unknown Musicians Find Payoffs Online." *New York Times,* July 20, 2000.

Harvey, Miles. *The Island of Lost Maps: A True Story of Cartographic Crime.* New York: Random House, 2000.

Hill, John, and Gary Palmer. "Going for Broke: The Economic and Social Impact of a South Carolina Lottery." South Carolina Policy Council Education Foundation, March 2000.

Himmelfarb, Gertrude. *One Nation, Two Cultures.* New York: Vintage, 2001.

Hobbes, Thomas. *Leviathan.* New York: Viking Press, 1982.

"The Horns of Plenty." Time.com, June 9, 1997. Available online at http://www.time.com/time/magazine/1997/int/970609/environment.the_horns_of_.html.

Hughes, Robert. *The Shock of the New.* New York: McGraw Hill Higher Education, 1992.

Huizenga, John R. *Cold Fusion: The Scientific Fiasco of the Century*. New York: Oxford University Press, 1994.

Hunter, Richard. *Mr. S Leather & Fetters U.S.A. Catalog*. San Francisco: Mr. S Leather, 2001.

Italie, Hillel. "Barnes & Noble.com Starts Digital Imprint." *The Salina Journal*, January 5, 2001. Available online at http://www.saljournal.com/stories/010501/tec_ap_bAndN.html.

James, Caryn. "Nice Is Not Enough." *New York Times*, September 29, 2000.

Jamison-Estrada, Barbara. "Gambling: The New American Landscape." CNN.com, February 9, 2000. Available online at http://www.cnn.com/2000/HEALTH/02/08/gambling.gal.smd/.

Jenkins, Holman. "What's Worse, Imaginary Violence or Real Sex?" *Wall Street Journal*, September 20, 2000.

Jenkins, Stephan. "Semi-Charmed Life." EM Blackwood Music, Inc. and 3EB Publishing, 1999.

Kahn, Alfred. "The Tyranny of Small Decisions: Market Failures, Imperfections, and the Limits of Economics." *Kyklos* 19 (1966), pp. 25–26.

Kaplan, Robert. *The Nothing That Is: A Natural History of Zero*. New York: Oxford University Press, 2000.

Kelley, Tina. "Sympathy for Migrant Workers After Attack." *New York Times*, September 21, 2000.

Kelling, George, and Catherine Coles. *Fixing Broken Windows*. New York: Simon & Schuster, 1997.

Kellner, Mark. "Making Mailing Easy." *Silicon Alley Reporter*, Issue 26, Vol. 3, no. 6 (2000).

Kendrick, Walter. *The Secret Museum: Pornography in Modern Culture*. Berkeley: University of California Press, 1996.

Kirkpatrick, David. "As Publishers Perish, Libraries Feel the Pain." *New York Times*, November 3, 2000.

———. "Dictionary Publishers Go Digital." *New York Times*, August 21, 2000.

———. "Random House to Establish Exclusively Digital Unit." *New York Times*, July 31, 2000.

———. "With Plot Still Sketchy, Characters Vie for Roles; The Struggles Over E-Books Abound, Though Readership Remains Elusive." *New York Times*, November 27, 2000.

Kleg, Milton. *Hate Prejudice and Racism*. New York: State of New York University Press, 1993.

Krugman, Paul. "Dow Wow, Dow Ow." *New York Times*, February 27, 2000.

———. "Going for Broke." *New York Times*, July 2, 2000.

———. "Unsound Bytes." *New York Times*, October 22, 2000.

———. "What Price Fairness?" *New York Times*, October 4, 2000.

Kurtz, Howard. "Who Blew the Dot-Com Bubble?; The Cautionary Tale of Henry Blodget." *Washington Post*, March 12, 2001.

Kushner, David. "For Hard-Core Gamers, the Lure of the East." *New York Times*, March 22, 2001.

Laker Airways v. Sabena Belgian World Airlines, 731 F.2d 909, 926–27 (D.C. Cir. 1994).

Lakoff, Robin Tolmach. *The Language War*. New York: Public Affairs, 2000.

Lane, Frederick. *Obscene Profits: The Entrepreneurs of Pornography in the Cyber Age*. New York: Routledge, 2001.

Leland, John. "Family's Choices Can Blunt the Effect of Video Violence." *New York Times,* September 25, 2000.

Llop, Cristina. Personal interview, November 1999.

Lohr, Steve. "Code Name: Mainstream." *New York Times*, August 28, 2000.

Luce, R. Duncan, and Howard Raiffa. *Games and Decisions*. New York: John Wiley & Sons, 1957.

"Making the Case for Racial Reparations: A Forum." *Harper's*, November 2000.

Mann, Charles, "A Whole New Vision for Napster," *Yahoo! Internet Life*, June 2001.

———. "Napster-Proof CDs," Inside.com. Available online at http://www.salon.com/tech/inside/2001/03/27/cd_protection/print.html.

Marin, Rick. "Online Journalists Keep Their Eyes on Daily Numbers." *New York Times*, November 11, 1999.

Markoff, John. "Bridging Two Worlds to Make On-Line Digital Music Profitable." *New York Times*, September 13, 1999.

Marriot, Michel. "Let the Game Wars Begin." *New York Times*, April 26, 2001.

Matises, Marvin. "Send Ethnographers into New-SKU Jungle." *Brandweek*, September 25, 2000.

McCabe, Ian Christopher. "Lawmakers, Health Professionals Blast Entertainment Industry for Marketing Adult Material to Children." CNN.com, September 13, 2000.

Montaigne, Michel de. *The Complete Essays*, Book I, Essay 26. New York: Penguin, 1993.

Morgenson, Gretchen. "Day Trading Not Usually Worth Risk." *New York Times*, July 31, 1999.

———. "S.E.C. Says Teenager Had After-School Hobby: Online Stock Fraud." *New York Times,* September 21, 2000.

Morikawa, K., T. Ben-Akiva, and M. Yamada. "Forecasting Intercity Rail Ridership Using Revealed Preference and Stated Preference Data." *Transportation Research Record*, No. 1328.

Muensterberger, Werner. *Collecting: An Unruly Passion*. New York: Harcourt, 1995.

Muto, Sheila. "San Francisco's Dot-Com Meltdown May Worsen." *Wall Street Journal*, March 28, 2001.

"The Napster Deal." *New York Times*, editorial, November 2, 2000.

National Gambling Impact Study Commission Report Recommendations, June 1999.

"Neo-Nazi Web Sites Reported to Flee Germany." *New York Times*, August 21, 2000.

Nietzsche, Friedrich. *The Gay Science*. New York: Vintage, 1974.

1970 Spot News. "Racial Protest at Cornell University." April 20, 1969. From "The Pulitzer Photographs: Capture the Moment," May 23–September 23, 2000, Newseum/NY, New York.

Norris, Floyd. "Palm's Saga: A Tale of Vanishing Profits and Absurd Prices." *New York Times,* April 14, 2000.

Ochoa, Sheana. "The Pros and Cons of E-Books." CNN.com, September 25, 2000.

Paglia, Camille. "The Mouth That Roared." *TV Guide,* October 21, 2000.

Phelps, Edmund S., ed. *Private Wants and Public Needs.* New York: W. W. Norton & Company, 1965.

Platt, Charles. "Steaming Video." *Wired,* November 2000.

"Reality Sets In." *New York Times,* editorial, November 5, 2000.

Reitzes, D. C., and J. Boles, "Exploring the Links between Gambling, Problem Gambling and Self-Esteem." *Deviant Behavior: An Interdisciplinary Journal* 18 (1997).

Report of the Commission on Obscenity, President's Commission on Obscenity, 1970.

Richtel, Matt. "A Video Game Maker Hits Reset; Electronic Arts Bets on Future of Web-Based Interaction." *New York Times,* August 21, 2000.

———. "Bettors Find Online Gambling Hard to Resist." *New York Times,* March 29, 2001.

———. "Canada Arrests 15-Year-Old in Web Attack." *New York Times,* April 20, 2000.

———. "The Casino on the Desktop." *New York Times,* March 29, 2001.

———. "Las Vegas Casinos Shift Stand, Backing Internet Wagering." *New York Times,* May 17, 2001.

Riesman, David, Nathan Glazer, and Reuel Denny. *The Lonely Crowd.* New Haven: Yale University Press, 1950.

Rodriguez, Richard. "Across the Borders of History." *Harper's,* March 1987.

———. *Days of Obligation.* New York: Viking, 1992.

———. "Mixed Blood." *Harper's,* March 1987.

Rosen, Jeffrey. *The Unwanted Gaze: The Destruction of Privacy in America.* New York: Random House, 2000.

Rosenberg, Scott. "The Net Scare." Salon.com, February 20, 2000.

Rousseau, Jean-Jacques. *The Social Contract and the Discourses.* New York: Everyman's Library, 1993.

Rowe, David. *The Limits of Family Influence.* New York: Guilford Publications, 1994.

"Salon.com Relaunches New Sections and Redesign." *The Write News,* May 26, 2000. Available online at http://writenews.com/2000/052600_salon_business.htm.

Saracevic, Alan. "Bricks For the Clicks: Bechtel Understood Long Ago That the Net Would Need Real-World Facilities." *Business 2.0,* June 2000.

Scheer, Robert. "Nowhere to Hide." *Yahoo! Internet Life,* October 2000.

Schelling, Thomas. *Micromotives and Macrobehavior.* New York: W. W. Norton & Company, 1978.

Schiffman, Betsey, and Kathleen Cholewka. "Enron, Blockbuster Partner for Movie Mania." Forbes.com, July 20, 2000.

Schiffrin, Andre. *The Business of Books.* New York: Verso, 2000.

Schneider, Jennifer. "How to Recognize the Signs of Sexual Addiction: Asking the Right Questions May Uncover Serious Problems." National Council on Sexual Addiction and Compulsivity. 1991. Available online at http://www.ncsac.org.

Seelye, Katherine. "The 2000 Campaign: The Vice President's Wife." *New York Times,* May 19, 2000.

Seife, Charles. *Zero: The Biography of a Dangerous Idea.* New York: Penguin, 2000.

Sheehy, Jeff. Personal interview, October 1999.

Shiller, Robert. *Irrational Exuberance.* Princeton, NJ: Princeton University Press, 2000.

Shilts, Randy. *The Mayor of Castro Street.* New York: St. Martin's Press, 1988.

Shirky, Clay. "The Genome's Open-Source Approach." *Business 2.0,* June 13, 2000.

Shorris, Earl. "The Last Word." *Harper's,* August 2000.

Siebel, Thomas M., and Pat House. *Cyber Rules.* New York: Doubleday, 1999.

Soros, George. "The Capitalist Threat." *The Atlantic Monthly,* February 1997.

Steinberg, Jacques. "Parents Say Censoring Films Is Their Job, Not Politicians'." *New York Times,* September 28, 2000.

Stevenson, Richard. "Global Trade Strengthens Economies, Greenspan Says." *New York Times,* November 15, 2000.

"The Stick That Sickens." *Newsweek,* October 6, 1969.

Stoller, Robert. *Pain and Passion: A Psychoanalyst Explores the World of S & M.* New York: Perseus Press, 1991.

———. *Perversion: The Erotic Form of Hatred.* Washington, D.C.: American Psychiatric Press, 1986.

"Stress, Anxiety & Why Gamblers Gamble." *The Wager* 5, no. 27 (July 2000). Available online at http://www.thewager.org.

Surrette, Ray. "The Media as a Cause of Crime." In *Media, Crime, and Criminal Justice.* Pacific Grove, California: Brooks/Cole Publishing, 1992.

Swisher, Kara. "Read All about It: Can Web-Only News Sites Ever Pay Off?" *Wall Street Journal,* July 17, 2000.

Tannen, Deborah. "What's in a Frame? Surface Evidence of Underlying Expectations." In *New Directions in Discourse Processing,* ed. R. O. Freedle. Westport, CT: Greenwood Press, 1979.

Tessler, Joelle. "Where the Web Gets Real: Amazon.com's Huge Nevada Warehouse Turns Virtual Orders into Cardboard Boxes Filled with Merchandise." (San Jose) *Mercury News,* November 20, 1999.

Thompson, W. N., R. Gazel, and D. Rickman. "The Economic Impact of Native American Gambling in Wisconsin." *Wisconsin Policy Research Institute Report* 8, no. 5 (1995).

Thorson, J. A., F. C. Powell, and M. Hilt. "Epidemiology of Gambling and Depression in an Adult Sample." *Psychological Reports* 74 (1994).

Turner, J. C., and R. L. Brown. "Social Status, Cognitive Alternatives and Intergroup Relations." In *Differentiation Between Social Groups: Studies in the Psychology of Intergroup Relations,* ed. H. Tajfel. New York: Academic, 1978.

Turning Point Project. "E-Commerce and the Demise of the Community." *New York Times,* July 24, 2000.

U.S. Attorney General. Youth Violence: A Report of the Surgeon General. Available online at http://www.surgeongeneral.gov/library/youthviolence/sgsummary/summary.htm.

Volberg, R. A., and M. W. Abbott. "Gambling and Problem Gambling Among Indigenous Peoples." *Substance Use & Misuse* 32, no. 11 (1997).

Weber, Thomas. "The X-Files." *Wall Street Journal*, May 20, 1997.

Weitzman, Mark. "Technology and Terror: Extremism on the Internet." *National Council of Jewish Women Journal*, winter 1998/1999.

"What the Internet Cannot Do." *Economist*, August 19, 2000.

Wilcox, Joe. "IBM Appoints Chief Privacy Officer," CNET News.com, November 28, 2000. Available online at http://news.cnet.com/news/0-1003-200-3898890.html.

Wilson, James, and George Kelling. "Broken Windows: The Police and Neighborhood Safety." *Atlantic Monthly*, March 1982.

Wolfe, Tom. *Hooking Up*. New York: Farrar, Straus & Giroux, 2000.

Zimring, Franklin, and Gordon Hawkins. *Crime Is Not the Problem: Lethal Violence in America*. New York: Oxford University Press, 1997.

Zuckerman, Amy, "Continents Clash on Content." *New York Times*, April 18, 2001.

INDEX

About the Author

LOUIS E.V. NEVAER is an economist, entrepreneur, consultant, editor, and formerly a publisher of newsletters for top management in international finance. Among his previous books published by Quorum are *Into—and Out of—the Gap* (2001), *New Business Opportunities in Latin America* (1996), *Strategies for Business in Mexico* (1995), and *The Protectionist Threat to Corporate America* (1989).